High-Performance Cycling

Asker E. Jeukendrup, PhD
Editor

Human Kinetics

Library of Congress Cataloging-in-Publication Data

High-performance cycling / Asker E. Jeukendrup, editor.
p. cm.
Includes bibliographical references and index.
ISBN 0-7360-4021-8
1. Cycling--Training. I. Jeukendrup, Asker E., 1969-
GV1048.H54 2002
796.6'2--dc21
2002022233

ISBN: 0-7360-4021-8

Permission notices for material reprinted in this book from other sources can be found on page x.

Acquisitions Editor: Martin Barnard; **Developmental Editor**: Leigh LaHood; **Assistant Editors**: Kim Thoren and Carla Zych; **Copyeditor**: Jennifer Merrill Thompson; **Proofreader**: Erin Cler; **Indexer**: Betty Frizzéll; **Permission Manager**: Toni Harte; **Graphic Designer**: Robert Reuther; **Graphic Artist**: Sandra Meier; **Photo Manager**: Les Woodrum; **Cover Designer**: Jack W. Davis; **Photographer (cover)**: Cor Vos; **Art Manager**: Carl D. Johnson; **Illustrator**: Accurate Art, Inc.; **Printer**: Bang Printing

Human Kinetics books are available at special discounts for bulk purchase. Special editions or book excerpts can also be created to specification. For details, contact the Special Sales Manager at Human Kinetics.

Printed in the United States of America

10 9 8 7 6 5 4 3 2 1

Human Kinetics
Web site: www.humankinetics.com

United States: Human Kinetics
P.O. Box 5076, Champaign, IL 61825-5076
800-747-4457
e-mail: humank@hkusa.com

Canada: Human Kinetics
475 Devonshire Road Unit 100, Windsor, ON N8Y 2L5
800-465-7301 (in Canada only)
e-mail: orders@hkcanada.com

Europe: Human Kinetics
Units C2/C3 Wira Business Park, West Park Ring Road, Leeds LS16 6EB, United Kingdom
+44 (0) 113 278 1708
e-mail: hk@hkeurope.com

Australia: Human Kinetics
57A Price Avenue, Lower Mitcham, South Australia 5062
08 8277 1555
e-mail: liahka@senet.com.au

New Zealand: Human Kinetics
P.O. Box 105-231, Auckland Central
09-523-3462
e-mail: hkp@ihug.co.nz

To my parents
who motivated me to take up cycling,
and to my wife, Antoinette,
who tolerates my obsession with my profession and sport

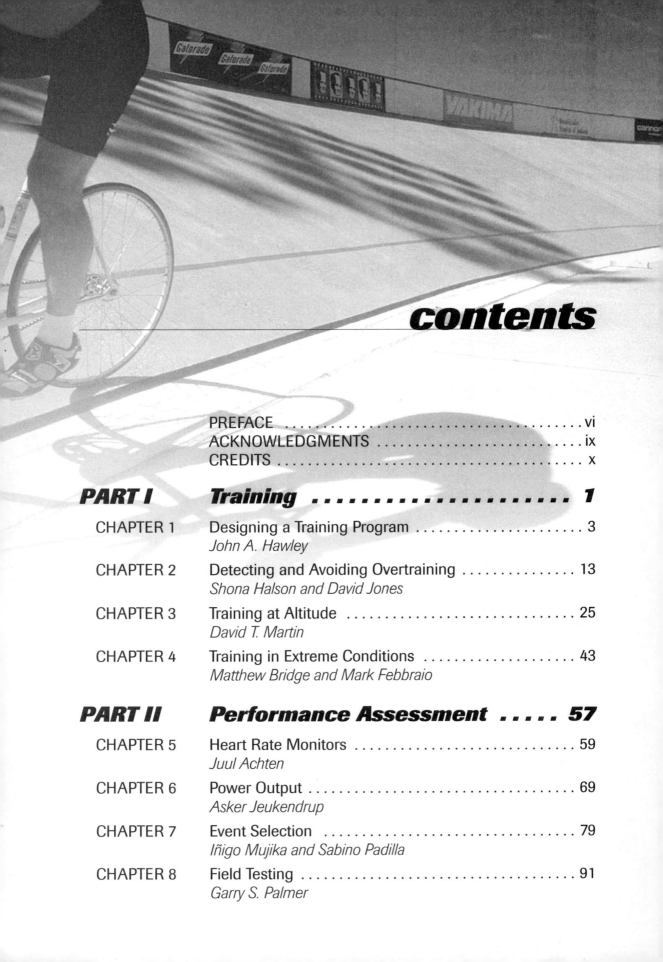

contents

preface

In the past few decades cycling has changed enormously. Not only have we seen new materials such as titanium and carbon fiber used in bicycle design but we have also seen the development of new training principles and training tools that have had a huge effect on the way cyclists race and train throughout the season. Heart rate monitors, for example, were rare only 20 years ago but are almost a standard tool of cyclists these days. Sport science in general has developed in a similar way: Although it was virtually absent in cycling a couple of decades ago, it is impossible to think of cycling now without some aspects of sport science. Many say that it was Greg LeMond who changed cycling by snatching overall victory in the final time trial of the Tour de France by just eight seconds using the then-revolutionary aerobars. Before LeMond, cyclists never thought about using these fancy aerobars, and it was almost taboo to suggest using a scientific approach in a sport that was dominated by men with spirit, determination, and guts. Although the heroism that makes the sport so special will continue to exist even in the presence of sport science, it is impossible to ignore the power of this "new knowledge." Cycling is one of the most difficult sports—with the Tour de France one of the most grueling sporting events in the world. Nevertheless, these races are won or lost by very small margins. Especially at this level, a scientific approach is vital for optimizing performance.

Having worked with cyclists of all abilities, from Tour riders and world champions to amateurs, I realized that there was a need for a book that clearly explains these scientific principles. There are quite a few books on cycling—some of them cover historical aspects, some of them are novels, other books discuss equipment or maintenance of bikes. Few of the cycling books discuss the physiology, biochemistry, biomechanics, and nutritional aspects of cycling, and even fewer of these are based on science.

However, a book with just science would not be very helpful to you, the cyclist. An enormous amount of scientific information is out there, but most of it is in scientific journals that are not easily accessible for everyone. Additionally, if information is available, it is not always clear how to apply it to a daily life situation. Clearly a translation is required from scientific language to the language of the "real world."

The purpose of this book, therefore, is to present guidelines based on the available scientific information.

To get the best possible information in this book, I invited experts from around the world to contribute. The authors have all worked closely with athletes (most with cyclists); many of them are cyclists themselves, and they are all able to communicate a scientific message to the athlete and his coach. This book should be a manual on sport science for cyclists, coaches, and sport scientists. Every chapter provides ideas about how to apply sport science. The book is therefore a performance manual for every serious cyclist.

This book contains five distinct sections. Part I discusses training-related issues. In chapter 1, John A. Hawley describes the most important training principles in detail and discusses how they apply to modern cycling. Chapter 2 discusses the problems of improper training: What are the symptoms of overtraining? How do we recognize overtraining, or, if it is too late, how do we treat it? In chapter 3, Dave Martin of the Australian Institute of Sport discusses the effects of altitude training. Dave is one of the leading scientists in this area. You will learn the latest ideas about altitude training: Should we live high and train low? Can hypobaric tents help? Finally, because cyclists often face different and potentially fatiguing weather conditions, chapter 4 deals with training in extreme conditions.

Part II discusses methods of performance assessment. Chapter 5 reviews the advantages and disadvantages of using a heart rate monitor. Chapter 6 is based on the use of power-measuring devices in training and competition. Chapter 7 discusses laboratory tests that can be performed to determine your best discipline. Chapter 8 describes field tests for those who do not have access to often-expensive laboratory facilities.

Part III, "Body and Machine," deals with the more technical aspects of equipment, aerodynamics, and biomechanics. Chapter 9 discusses the effect of body position on aerodynamics, and chapter 10 covers the effects of equipment on aerodynamics. Chapter 11 deals with some of the most important biomechanical aspects of cycling.

Part IV is about nutrition. Nutrition can be of great importance, especially in long-lasting events—therefore, these chapters discuss optimal strategies for fluid and carbohydrate delivery. Chapter 12 examines the extreme energy needs of cycling along with strategies for losing weight. In chapter 13, Ronald Maughan deals with hydration strategies and the composition of sports drinks. In chapter 14, Mark Hargreaves covers preparation for one-day races, and in chapter 15 recovery is the central topic because this is a crucial part of stage races or repeated days of hard training. In chapter 16, Louise Burke of the Australian Institute of Sport turns the scientific advice of the first few nutrition chapters into practical eating principles that will help you to structure and plan your diet. In chapter 17, Jeffrey C. Little and Stella L. Volpe deal with the ever-popular nutrition supplements: Do they really help?

The last section deals with both conditioning and medical issues. In chapter 18, Adrie van Diemen and Jabik Jan Bastiaans discuss the potential of strength training in the preparation of a cyclist. This topic is controversial, and these authors share some of their experiences with elite cyclists while also discussing innovative studies. Grahame Brown discusses typical cycling injuries and their treatment in chapter 19. A common problem of cyclists involved in strenuous training programs is that they often catch colds and other minor infections that then affect their ability to train and race. In chapter 20, Michael Gleeson discusses the effects of hard training on the immune system and gives advice to help prevent these colds. Chapter 21 concerns erythropoietin (EPO). What is EPO? How does it work? How good and reliable are the detection methods? Unfortunately, the use of EPO in cycling has received a lot of negative publicity. Nowadays, however, tests have been developed to detect EPO in urine or blood. Finally, chapter 22 summarizes all the chapters: How does altitude training compare to getting a better position on the bike? How much can performance theoretically improve?

—Asker Jeukendrup

acknowledgments

I am very grateful to many people who have contributed to this book. First of all to the authors of this book who managed to find the time despite their busy lives, often devoted to cycling. I am also grateful to all scientists and coaches thoughout the world who, through hard work and dedication, helped to develop some of the ideas and concepts presented in this book.

My personal experiences as a cyclist and my work with professional riders were crucial to understanding our sport of cycling better. Therefore I would like to thank all of the cyclists, team leaders, and support staff of the Rabobank cycling teams and in particular Theo de Rooij, Adrie van Houwelingen, Geert Leinders, Piet Hubert, and Jan Raas for giving me the opportunity to be involved in cycling at the highest level.

I would also like to thank my parents who motivated me to start cycling and took me and my bicycle to different countries in Europe. My best cycling experiences include riding long mountain climbs alongside them, and these rides certainly taught me not to give up but to continue until I reach the finish.

I would also like to acknowledge Luke Moseley and Clare Gutch for assisting me in putting this book together and the excellent assistance of Leigh LaHood during the editing of the chapters. Last but certainly not least, I want to thank my wife, Antoinette, who supported me and allowed me to devote excessive amounts of time to my work and allowed me to travel while she stayed behind at home.

credits

Table 2.1: Reprinted, by permission, from Rushall, 1990, "A tool for measuring stress tolerance in elite athletes," *Journal of Applied Sports Psychology* Vol 2, 1: Taylor & Francis, Inc.

Figures 6.2 and 6.3: Reprinted, by permission, from Jeukendrup, Craig, and Hawley, 2000, "The bioenergetics of world class cycling," *Journal of Science and Medicine in Sport* 3(4):414-33.

Table 7.2: Adapted, by permission, from Padilla, Mujika, Orbañanos, and Angulo, 2000, "Exercise intensity during competition time trials in professional road cycling," *Medicine and Science in Sports and Exercise* 32:850-856.

Table 7.3: Adapted, by permission, from Padilla, Mujika, Orbañanos, and Angulo, 1999, "Level ground and uphill cycling ability in professional road cycling," *Medicine and Science in Sports and Exercise,* 31:878-885.

Table 7.4: Adapted, by permission, from Jeukendrup, Craig, and Hawley, 2000, "The bioenergetics of world class cycling," *Journal of Science and Medicine in Sport* 3(4):414-33.

Table 12.1: Adapted, by permission, from Jeukendrup, Saris, and Wagenmakers, 1998, "Fat metabolism during exercise: a review. Part1: fatty acid mobilization and muscle metabolism," *International Journal of Sports Medicine* 19:231-244.

Figure 12.1: Reprinted, by permission, from Saris, van Erp-Baart, Brouns, Westerterp, and ten Hoor, 1989, "Study on food intake and energy expenditure during extreme sustained exercise: The Tour de France," *International Journal of Sports Medicine* 10:S26-S31.

Table 13.2: Reprinted, by permission, from Maughan and Shirreffs, 1998, Fluid and electrolyte loss and replacement in exercise. In *Oxford textbook of sport medicine*, 2nd ed, edited by Harries, Williams, Stanish, and Micheli (New York: Oxford University Press), 97-113.

Table 15.2: Reprinted, by permission, from Hawley and Burke, 1998, Peak performance: training and nutritional strategies for sport. (Allen & Unwin Pty Ltd.)

Tables 16.3 and 16.4: Adapted, by permission, from Hawley and Burke, 1998, Peak performance: training and nutritional strategies for sport. (Allen & Unwin Pty Ltd.)

Sidebar on page 206: Adapted, by permission, from Williams, 1998, *The ergogenics edge*, (Champaign, IL: Human Kinetics), 5-7.

Table 17.2: Reprinted, with permission, from Food and Nutrition Board, Institute of Medicine. Copyright 1997, 1998, 2000, 2001 by the National Academy of Sciences. Courtesy of the National Academy Press. Washington, D.C.

Tables 20.1 and 20.2: From *Basic and applied sciences for sports medicine* by R.J. Maughan. Reprinted by permission of Butterworth-Heinemann.

Figure 20.2: Reprinted, by permission, from Robson, Blannin, Walsh, Castell, and Gleeson, 1999, "Effects of exercise intensity, duration and recovery on in vitro neutrophil function in male athletes," *International Journal of Sports Medicine* 20:128-35.

Table 20.4: Reprinted, by permission, from Blannin, Chatwin, Cave, and Gleeson, 1996, "Effects of submaximal cycling and long term endurance training on neutrophil phagocytic activity in middle aged men," *British Journal of Sports Medicine* 30:125-29.

part I

Training

Training is without a doubt one of the most effective ways to improve performance. Cyclists often spend hours and hours on their bicycles and they cover large distances. Professional cyclists may ride up to 40,000 kilometers per year—far more than most people will drive their cars. Over the past decades, however, we have seen significant changes in the way cyclists train. Generally, there is a noticeable trend for reducing the volume and increasing the intensity of training. Interval training, which has been a common form of training in athletics for many years, has only relatively recently been introduced in cycling. Several training methods have been developed, some of which became popular but then disappeared off the scene again. It seems that training science is a relatively soft science, meaning that there is no one truth. Different methods may work for different people, and different cyclists and coaches will have different opinions and preferences.

Despite years and years of experience and trial-and-error experiments by many cyclists, our understanding of training is fairly limited. In fact, very few scientific studies examine what types of training will result in the optimal effect. Training methods in the past and at present are based on a series of principles that have been formulated on common sense and experience. From a scientific point of view, there is very little information. However, we do have *some* information and this can help us to construct effective training programs.

One of the potential dangers is developing an overtraining syndrome. Inappropriate training, or decreased recovery, may result in a chronic state of fatigue and decreased performance. When performance is decreased, a natural response often is to train harder to obtain the desired training effects. However, sometimes this may result in further reductions in performance or a fatigue state that is not easily reversible. Chapter 2 discusses these issues. What factors increase the risk of developing overtraining and what can we do to prevent overtraining?

Most top cyclists will at least have tried altitude training as a method to boost their performance. However, does altitude training really improve athletic performance? Coaches and athletes have asked this apparently simple question for more than 100 years. There have been important developments in this area, and slowly we are starting to understand the effects of altitude training on the adaptation that might occur. We have seen the development of altitude chambers and tents, some of which are now commercially available. Chapter 3 explains the current thinking about altitude training and discusses specific issues. What if a cyclist is rehabilitating from a lower-body injury that prevents high power outputs? What if a cyclist is attempting to enhance adaptations to early-season, low-intensity training? What can altitude training achieve? Should we live at altitude and train at sea level ("live high, train low"), or should we live and train at altitude? Chapter 3 discusses these and other questions.

Finally, chapter 4 discusses issues related to training in extreme conditions. Cyclists often will have to train in very cold or very hot conditions. This can have a tremendous impact on performance and even health if no precautions are taken. However, there are a few measures that you can take to protect yourself against these conditions and to minimize the detrimental effects on performance. For instance, one of the possibilities is to acclimate before competing in very hot climates. We discuss strategies to combat the heat and the cold as well as the potential effects on cycling performance.

Taken together, part I should give you some idea as to how training can affect performance. You should not expect ready-made training programs in these chapters but they will provide you with the knowledge to design a training program based on scientific principles. Part I also provides you with ideas about how to avoid overtraining, incorporate altitude training, and prepare for training and competition in extreme conditions.

chapter 1

Designing a Training Program

John A. Hawley

Apart from genetic endowment, no factor plays a more important role in determining cycling performance than the physiological adaptations induced by training. Improvements in cycling performance require the application of appropriate training techniques; a systematic, injury-free buildup to competition; a balanced diet; and, on the day of a race, appropriate nutrition and sound tactical strategies. Successful performance is more likely if a cyclist has adhered to a training schedule based on the scientific principles of conditioning than if he has adopted a hit-and-miss, trial-and-error approach to his physical preparation. Training is therefore very different from simply exercising or performing a workout; it is well planned and there is a clearly defined goal. This chapter provides the reader with the necessary information on how to design and structure a training program aimed to improve cycling performance. Where available, such information is based on scientific studies. It should be noted, however, that our present knowledge of the effectiveness of specific cyclist training interventions on selected adaptive responses and their consequences for endurance performance is severely limited.

Scientific Principles of Training

The scientific principles of physical training provide a foundation on which all sport-specific training programs are based. These principles have been outlined in detail in previous publications (Hawley 2000; Hawley and Burke 1998) and are only summarized here.

Progressive Overload

The principle of progressive overload states that once a cyclist has adapted to a specific training stimulus, the training impulse (see page 6) must be increased to attain further adaptations and performance improvements. The degree of adaptation to any training program depends on the interaction between training volume, intensity, and frequency and the ability of a cyclist to continually meet the demands of a greater training impulse.

Recovery

Training adaptations take place in the recovery period after training, and recovery is therefore a crucial element of any training program. A training session is likely to be of the greatest benefit to a cyclist if it forces the body to adapt to the stress of a particular workout. One of the goals of any training program should be to attain the maximal training impulse with the minimum risk of injury or illness (i.e., adequate recovery). A major role of a coach is to recognize the early warning signs of overtraining and ensure that programs are structured to each cyclist's unique needs. (For ways to recognize early symptoms of overtraining, see chapter 2.)

Specificity

Any training-induced adaptation is specific to the type of training undertaken. So the closer the physiological demands of a training session are to the requirements of the cyclist's specialized event, then the better the subsequent performance outcome. Accordingly, the core of any cyclist's training program should reflect the specific demands of his or her event, thereby facilitating the desired training adaptation.

Reversibility

Consistency of training is a key factor of successful endurance cycling programs. However, it is inevitable that at some stage, cyclists will undergo periods during which training is reduced substantially or even ceased altogether because of injury. Reversibility, or detraining, is simply the loss of training-induced adaptations. Our knowledge of the physiological responses to detraining in highly-trained cyclists is limited. Nevertheless the available evidence indicates that most of the central and peripheral physiologic adaptations of training regress rather rapidly toward pretraining levels with the cessation of training. For example, VO_2max has been observed to decrease by 15 to 20 percent after 12 weeks in highly trained endurance athletes (Coyle et al. 1984). Therefore, any time a cyclist is injured and cannot ride he or she should try to take up alternate exercise modes that have similar neuromuscular recruitment patterns to cycling. Such a practice will minimize the loss of cycle training-induced adaptations.

Individuality and the Genetic Ceiling

The scientific principles of physical training are general guidelines that can be applied to cyclists of all abilities. However, the individual response to a particular training session will vary among cyclists, largely because of genetic factors. Indeed, up to 80 percent of the variability in the magnitude of adaptation to a training stimulus and subsequent performance can be attributed to genetic influences (Bouchard et al. 1992). As such, cyclists who wish to perform at a high level should choose their parents wisely!

Core Components of Training

The key components of any training program aimed to enhance cycling performance are volume, intensity, and frequency. The total training load as well as the training effect are dependent on these individual components. By choosing the volume, the intensity, and the frequency of training, the coaches or the cyclists themselves can plan their training to achieve the desired training effect.

Volume

The majority of cycling coaches generally have assumed that improvements in cycling performance are directly related to training volume. In this regard, professional cyclists typically ride 30,000 to 35,000 kilometers per year, a volume of training that clearly differentiates them from less genetically gifted, albeit well-trained cyclists (Jeukendrup et al. 2000). Training volume is determined by the distance covered in a given time period. Although volume traditionally has been expressed as the distance cycled in any seven-day period (i.e., kilometers per week), many coaches now advocate 10- or 14-day training blocks, or microcycles, in which a rider undertakes a prescribed volume of work.

Intensity

There are many different measures of training intensity. These can be objective measures directly related to performance outcomes (i.e., speed, power output, race position); physiological markers normally based on laboratory or field-derived maximal test data (i.e., percentage of maximal heart rate, percentage of maximal oxygen uptake [$\dot{V}O_2max$], or a prescribed blood lactate concentration); or subjective criteria (i.e., ratings of perceived effort). The sensitivity and usefulness of each of these different measures of intensity will depend on a number of factors including the prevailing environmental conditions (e.g., extreme heat and/or altitude may reduce the speed at a given power but increase heart rate and perception of effort) and riding tactics (drafting will increase speed but reduce power output and heart rate). For a comprehensive discussion of the different indicators of training intensity commonly used by cyclists, see Jeukendrup and van Diemen (1998). In this book, chapter 5 discusses the use of heart rate and chapter 6 discusses the use of power.

Frequency

Training frequency simply refers to the number of training sessions a cyclist performs in a given period of time. Over the past two decades there has been a progressive increase in the frequency of training sessions undertaken by endurance riders, a trend aimed at increasing the total training volume. However, it is not known whether increasing the frequency of training sessions while maintaining the same training volume has a positive or negative effect on performance. For example, is it better for performance gains to ride 160 kilometers over two sessions a day, or complete the same volume as one continuous ride?

The Training Impulse

It is important for the cyclist to recognize that different types of training result in different physiological responses (adaptations) but also cause different reactions and stresses to the body (table 1.1). In an attempt to quantify and compare the effects of training sessions of different durations and intensities, Dr. Eric Bannister (1991) proposed a single global index of training called the TRaining IMPulse (TRIMP). The TRIMP of any training session can be estimated by multiplying the training volume by the training intensity according to the following formula:

$$\text{TRIMP} = A \times B \times C$$

where A is the training time in minutes; B is [average training heart rate – resting heart rate]/[maximal heart rate – resting heart rate]; and C is $0.64 \times e^{1.92B}$. The resulting index or score has the dimension of work done or energy consumed in performing the exercise task. A problem with this variable is that training performed at a particular intensity for a particular duration produces the same TRIMP as training performed at twice the intensity for half the duration. Yet training at the higher intensity usually has a disproportionately greater effect on the body. To correct for the inaccuracy arising from using the heart rate response as a single measure of the intensity of training, Bannister et al. (1999) recently proposed that the intensity score be multiplied by an arbitrary factor based on the exponential rise in blood lactate concentration with the fractional elevation in exercise heart rate above rest. This factor supposedly gives more quantitative credit to short, intense training than longer, less intense workouts.

However training is quantified, if the stimulus or impulse is too low, then the cyclist is not obtaining the maximal benefit from a session. Conversely, if the training stimulus or impulse is too high, then the cyclist eventually will become fatigued and unable to sustain the training program. For more information about quantifying the training, see chapters 5 and 6.

Goals and Characteristics of a Training Program

The physiological demands for success in road cycling are unique and have been documented elsewhere (Jeukendrup et al. 2000; Padilla et al. 2000; Palmer et al. 1994). Road races are characterized by a constantly changing work rate and/or speed, which is largely dependent on terrain and tactics. In contrast, during individual time trials a rider sustains the highest average power output possible for the duration of a race. As such, training programs for improving road cycling performance should evoke multiple adaptations that enable a rider to increase energy production from both aerobic and anaerobic pathways and delay the onset of muscular fatigue (Jeukendrup et al. 2000).

TABLE 1.1 Summary of Training Techniques for Endurance Cyclists

Type of workout	Phase of training	Duration	Intensity (percent of HR_{max})	Frequency (sessions/week)	Primary benefits
Prolonged distance	Base training General preparatory phase	1-6 hours	60-75	3-4	Improved $\dot{V}O_2$max and O_2 transport Improved endurance capacity Increased oxidative enzymes Enhanced ability to utilize fat as a fuel and spare endogenous carbohydrate stores (glycogen sparing) Improved economy/efficiency
Aerobic intervals Transition training	Several weeks before competition	8-10 repetitions of 5 minute with 1 minute recovery	85-90	1-2	Improved $\dot{V}O_2$max and ability to maintain a high steady-state speed or power output Increase in speed or power output at the lactate threshold Improved fatigue resistance at race pace Enhanced lactate tolerance and muscle buffering capacity Improved neuromuscular recruitment patterns at race pace
Power/speed training	Several weeks before competition and during taper	8-10 repetitions of up to 1 minute with 5-10 minutes recovery	Maximal	1-2	Enhanced maximal speed/power production Improved capacity of ATP-PC system to produce power Increased glycolytic enzyme activity
Weight/resistance training	Off-season	1 hour	–	1-2	May improve specific muscular weakness Increased strength and muscular endurance Enhanced cycling performance

© David Brownell

In road races, differences in terrain and tactics result in a constantly changing work rate or speed.

Training is a complex procedure because it is performed in a time frame that can range from a few seconds to many years. As such, training can be characterized on a continuum: Workouts may last several minutes to many hours and be either continuous or composed of many discrete work bouts (repetitions) interspersed with rest intervals (recovery). The nature of workouts differs depending on the phase of training, but after some time, a repeated pattern of workouts may emerge, sometimes known as a microcycle. A series of microcycles makes up a mesocycle. Repeated sets of mesocycles make up a macrocycle or training year. Finally, over a period of years, athletes develop a training history.

Structure of a Training Program

A prerequisite for successful cycling performance is the planning or periodization of a training program. Periodization is the organization of a cyclist's training system into distinct phases (mesocycles). Periodization should take into consideration a cyclist's immediate (weeks), medium (months), and long-term (years) competition goals. During each phase of training, primary emphasis is given to the development of one (or more) physiological objective. For the majority of readers, most training cycles normally will fit into a single periodized year.

The phases (or macrocycles) of any training program for cyclists can be classified into four main categories:

1. Conditioning or general preparatory phase
2. Transition or competition preparation phase
3. Taper followed by competition phase
4. Recovery phase

Conditioning or General Preparatory Phase

The conditioning or general preparatory phase (or mesocycle) should last a minimum of six to eight weeks for high school or veteran cyclists and as long as possible (given race commitments) for a state-level or nationally competitive rider. The primary aim of this phase of training is to provide a base of aerobic conditioning before more intense training is undertaken. The primary physiological benefits ascribed to this phase of training have been extensively reviewed elsewhere and are summarized in table 1.1.

An important goal of the general preparatory phase is to condition the cyclist to prolonged, continuous, submaximal riding and increase the working muscles' resistance to fatigue. During this phase of training, the volume of cycling is high (200 to 300 kilometers per week for high school and veteran riders, 300 to 600 kilometers per week for club riders, more than 600 kilometers per week for professionals). It has been suggested that cyclists progressively increase the volume of training until such time that performance over their specialized distance fails to improve (Hawley and Burke 1998). Although such a recommendation is attractive, it has not been scientifically tested. Nevertheless, it does make intuitive sense and provides a definitive end point at which the cyclist should begin to perform more event-specific training (i.e., the transition or competition phase).

The intensity of training in the general preparatory phase should range from 60 to 80 percent of maximal heart rate (55 to 75 percent of $\dot{V}O_2max$), and depending on the ability of the cyclist, the frequency of training should be a minimum of 5 to 10 rides per week. The majority of these workouts should be ridden in low gears, "spinning" at cadences of 95 to 105 revolutions per minute to develop an effective technique and reduce the risk of injury. Cyclists should include uphill and downhill rides with attention to bike-handling skills. The magnitude of adaptation in the general preparatory phase is likely to be greatest when the cyclists' weekly training impulse is marginally below the threshold that would, if continued over a period of several months, eventually overextend them and lead to overtraining. Although weight training, circuit training, and stretching routines sometimes are added to the normal on-road sessions, there is limited scientific evidence to suggest that such practices enhance endurance performance above and beyond the gains made by just riding (see chapter 18).

Transition or Competition Preparation Phase

The transition phase should last three to six weeks, depending on the length of the subsequent competition phase. The primary aim of this phase of training is to expose the body to sustained, intense cycling at power outputs that approximate planned race pace. The shift from general conditioning to the transition or competition preparation phase also is facilitated by the introduction of time trials over a variety of intermediate race distances that help to develop a cyclist's pace judgment and further improve bike-handling skills at speed. There is a slight decrease in the total volume of training, although several studies have shown that cyclists should merely aim to replace a portion of their base training (about 15 to 20 percent) with transition training (Hawley et al. 1997; Lindsay et al. 1996; Stepto et al. 1999). Transition training should be undertaken no more than twice a week. Although training prescription during this phase of training can be based on blood lactate concentrations, there is little scientific evidence to support that this method is any better than other methods. More to the point, such monitoring is highly impractical and usually very imprecise. However, continuous training at individually prescribed power outputs or heart rates might be a useful adjunct for monitoring the intensity of workouts.

An example of a transition session would be the following: Warm up with 20 to 30 minutes of low-gear spinning, then do 8 to 12 five-minute repetitions at approximately 90 percent of maximal heart rate (85 percent of $\dot{V}O_2max$, or 80 percent of peak aerobic power output if undertaking this session on an ergometer), with 60-second spinning recovery between each bout, followed by a 20-minute warm-down. Cyclists should start transition training with four to six repetitions and, over the course of two to three weeks, build up to 10 to 12 repetitions. If riders have no objective way to monitor the intensity (such as a heart rate monitor or power-measuring device), then they should aim to ride the work bouts at their *current* best 40-kilometer race pace, which for most cyclists will be the highest speed or power output sustainable for about one hour.

Several studies have shown that two sessions per week of transition training for just three weeks lead to an increase in $\dot{V}O_2max$ of 3 to 4 percent and improve 40-kilometer time-trial performance by 2 to 3 percent (Hawley et al. 1997; Lindsay et al. 1996; Stepto et al. 1999). Of interest is the finding that after transition training a cyclist can sustain both a higher *absolute* and *relative* power output or speed for 40 kilometers (Westgarth-Taylor et al. 1997).

Taper Followed by Competition Phase

The primary aim of the taper followed by competition phase of training is to prepare the cyclist for several major competitive peaks within the season. There is a marked decrease in the total volume of training (up to 50 percent before a major competition) to facilitate adequate recovery between training sessions and races. However, the reduction in training volume necessary for an effective taper should not be achieved at the expense of a big drop-off in the number of training sessions undertaken; the cyclist should not reduce training *frequency* by more than 30 percent than is normal for this phase of training. The results of scientific studies show that a taper can improve performance by up to 3 percent (e.g., see Shepley et al. 1992).

The principal emphasis of the taper is to undertake training sessions at power outputs or speeds that are substantially faster than planned race pace. Figure 1.1 displays the results of a training study in which competitive cyclists replaced 15 to 20 percent of their training volume with workouts of different intensities and durations (Stepto et al. 1999). The results of that study revealed that the most effective workouts for enhancing 40-kilometer time-trial performance were the shortest, most intense sessions (12 repetitions × 30 seconds at maximal power output or speed with 4- to 5-minute recovery) and the more event-specific workouts conducted at near race pace (8 repetitions of 4 minutes at 92 percent of maximal heart rate [or 85 percent of peak aerobic power output] with 4-minute recovery). It is likely that the short, more intense workout would be advantageous for cyclists competing in mass-start road races where a rider often has to "chase down" a group of riders or perform high-intensity work for short periods in breakaways.

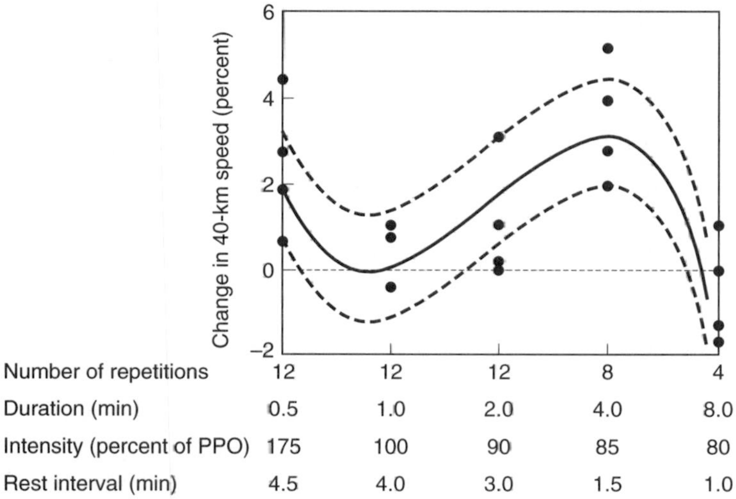

Figure 1.1 Percentage change in 40-kilometer time-trial speed after five interval training programs of different intensities and durations.

Recovery Phase

The recovery phase should last between six and eight weeks depending on the periodization of the cyclist's year and ability level. Nowadays, most top riders will only take a limited time off the bike and usually undertake some form of alternate training to maintain some degree of cardiorespiratory fitness. The primary aim of this phase is to allow the cyclist a period of recuperation, both physical and mental, from the preceding season. This phase should address the presence of any chronic injury and its complete rehabilitation. The presence of any chronic injury and its complete rehabilitation should be addressed in this stage. If bike position is to be changed, riders should make such adjustments before they embark on their next general conditioning phase. For both the coach and rider, the recovery phase allows for an objective appraisal of the previous season's training and, if necessary, the revision of future goals based on the cyclist's progress (or lack thereof) to that point.

Summary

When planning a training program for cyclists, the rider's specialist event should be identified and appropriate training techniques employed to improve those factors that are the most critical determinants of successful performance. The core components of a training program can be divided into four main phases:

1. General preparatory or base phase
2. Transition phase
3. Taper and competition phase
4. Recovery phase

Successful performance is more likely if a cyclist has maintained a training program based on scientific principles rather than adopting a trial-and-error approach. Finally, the outcome of any training program is a rider's performance on race day. Fortunately, cycling lends itself to objective scientific analysis because performance measures (speed, power output, race position) are easily observed and quantified. As such, each rider is strongly recommended to continually evaluate his performance outcomes and, if possible, determine how they relate to the preceding training cycle.

chapter 2

Detecting and Avoiding Overtraining

Shona Halson
David Jones

In a bid to improve their performance, cyclists spend a great deal of time on their bicycles training hard and long to increase their fitness levels. Though there appears to be a positive link between increasing training load and improving performance, most athletes recognize that getting the balance wrong between training and recovery can lead to reduced performance. Overtraining is often thought of as an imbalance between anabolic (building-up) and catabolic (breaking-down) processes. Achieving the right balance seems to be one of the keys to peak performance, yet the pressures to extend the training just a little bit further are very strong. It is vital that athletes and coaches be aware of the true benefits and risks of intensive training.

The end product of too much training and too little recovery is often termed *overtraining*. There are several different terms to describe overtraining in the literature, including *staleness, burnout, overreaching, overwork, overstrain,* and the *unexplained underperformance syndrome* (Kreider et al. 1998; Budgett et al. 2000). This chapter uses the following definitions:

- *Overreaching:* An accumulation of training or other stresses resulting in a short-term decrement in performance, from which recovery may take several days, or possibly a week or two.
- *Overtraining:* An accumulation of training or other stresses leading to a long-term decrement in performance, from which recovery may take several weeks or months.

Essentially, these two conditions are defined by the time for which the loss of performance persists and takes to recover.

Causes of Overtraining

Before we can begin to identify ways to prevent and treat overtraining, it is important to understand the mechanisms involved. The body is very adaptable. Faced with a new stress it will normally adapt to cope with the situation, but if the stress is too great or comes too frequently, the end result may be damage. A useful analogy might be one of the current theories about the way muscle responds to weight training. If a very large weight is lifted, the high forces generated in the muscles may cause small areas of damage. These small areas of damage then stimulate the muscle to repair and grow in size and strength so that the next time the same weight is lifted it is within the capability of the muscle and no new damage is caused. If, however, the muscle is repeatedly stressed with little time for repair, the damage may turn to scar tissue and the strength may be permanently impaired.

The body's responses to endurance training are complex, involving changes in the muscles' ability to use oxygen and different fuels; changes in the heart, blood vessels, and capillaries; and changes in the hormonal systems controlling the use of carbohydrates and fats. All can respond and adapt positively to increased use but excessive stimulation can cause problems, especially with the hormonal balance of the body.

Figure 2.1 represents theoretical changes in performance that may occur with increases in training loads, and there is a critical point where performance gains are maximized. At training loads below this point, *undertraining* occurs and athletes do

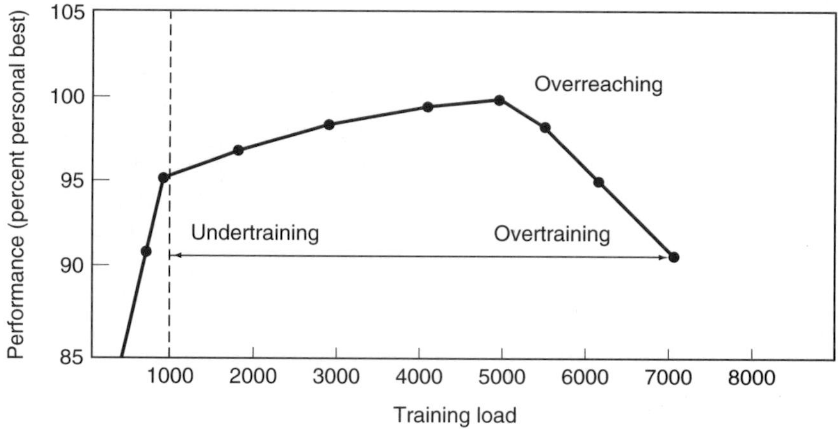

Figure 2.1 Performance graph illustrating the changes in performance that occur with increases in training load. The units used are arbitrary.

not perform at maximal levels. It is important to note that initially large increases in performance occur in response to small increases in training load. However, as performance improves, large loads are required to cause relatively small improvements in performance.

After the critical point is reached, increases in training load will result in a decline in performance. Initially this is evident in the form of overreaching, and, if appropriate rest is provided, supercompensation can occur and further improvements in performance are possible. If adequate recovery does not occur or high training loads are continued, a state of overtraining may ensue.

Although excessive exercise and insufficient recovery are usually the main causes of overtraining, other factors can make the situation worse (Kuipers and Keizer 1988; O'Toole 1998):

- Monotony of training with the same routine day after day, week after week
- Frequent competition, especially that requiring high-intensity and high-quality performances
- Medical problems such as colds or allergies
- Inadequate nutrition, especially in the form of poor fluid and carbohydrate intake
- Psychological stress from work, school, family, and so forth
- Environmental stress in the form of extreme temperature, humidity, and altitude

Some of the more specific causes of overtraining in endurance cyclists are related to the nature of cycling training and competition, and in particular stage races. Elite cyclists have high training volumes, up to 1,200 kilometers per week. Often exercise is monotonous with most of the training exercise occurring at 65 to 70 percent of maximum heart rate. During stage races these effects are compounded as racing occurs on consecutive days and there is little recovery time. In addition, many professional cyclists have 90 to 110 race days per year, which results in high levels of both exercise and psychological stress. Finally, cyclists often combine high training loads with a negative energy balance to decrease body weight, especially at the beginning of the competitive season. Negative energy balance, a low carbohydrate intake, and an unbalanced diet are predisposing factors to the development of overtraining.

Because the specific underlying mechanisms of overtraining remain largely unknown, most studies have simply tried to identify diagnostic markers. Jeukendrup et al. (1992) reported lower submaximal and maximal lactate concentrations in cyclists who were overreached and speculated that this might be due to difficulty activating the breakdown of glycogen or a low muscle glycogen content. However, it seems that low muscle glycogen is not the cause. In an experiment by Snyder et al. (1995), subjects completed 15 days of intensified training and consumed 160 grams of liquid carbohydrate in the two hours following each exercise bout. On completion of this period, all subjects were considered overreached yet they had maintained normal muscle glycogen levels.

Several investigations into changes in hormonal responses to overreaching have been performed. However, because of methodological difficulties, individual differences, and standardization techniques, results of such studies are contradictory. Some studies also fail to report performance changes and thus it is difficult to determine whether overreaching or overtraining has occurred.

The hormones that play an important role in anabolic and catabolic processes are testosterone and cortisol, respectively, and the ratio of these two has been suggested as an indicator of overtraining. However, the evidence is not conclusive. Total and free testosterone concentrations have been shown to decrease as well as to remain unchanged (Urhausen et al. 1998a). Similarly, cortisol concentrations after overtraining or overreaching have been reported to be increased, decreased, and unchanged (Fry et al. 1992; Hooper et al. 1993).

Raised levels of adrenaline (epinephrine) and noradrenaline (norepinephrine) are indicators of both physical and mental stress but, once again, the results of investigations into catecholamine production and overtraining are contradictory (Lehmann et al. 1997; Urhausen et al. 1998a).

An area at the base of the brain, the hypothalamus, is responsible for maintaining many body functions such as temperature and regulating hormone levels, and several investigations have supported the hypothesis that problems in this area may be involved in causing overtraining. Low adrenocorticotrophic hormone (ACTH; one of the hormones regulated by the hypothalamus) responses to exercise as well as lower resting levels have been identified in those who overtrain (Urhausen et al. 1998a). Barron et al. (1985) reported a decreased ACTH and cortisol response to low blood sugar caused by administering insulin. One of the problems associated with this type of investigation is that the lower hormonal responses may simply reflect shorter exercise durations as a result of fatigue from overtraining.

Nevertheless, there is continued interest in possible changes in the hypothalamus related to overtraining (Keizer 1998). Serotonin in the brain is a neurotransmitter that plays several roles and is involved in the pathways that control mood, appetite, and arousal. Drugs that alter serotonergic function, such as Prozac, have major effects on mood, and increases in serotonergic activity have been linked with the sensations of fatigue as a result of prolonged exercise. Chronic fatigue syndrome is a disorder that may arise as a result of viral infections such as glandular fever. It often causes a crippling sensation of fatigue quite unrelated to any physical activity and is similar, in some respects, to overtraining. With the use of a drug that mimics the action of serotonin, these patients have been shown to have serotonergic pathways in the brain that are more sensitive than normal matched controls (Bakheit et al. 1992).

The critical question is whether similar changes are seen in overtraining or overreaching. We recently induced a state of overreaching in cyclists and performed the same challenge test before training, at the end of intensified training, and after two weeks of recovery. The test involves giving the drug buspirone and measuring the release of the stress hormone prolactin from the pituitary gland which is, in turn, controlled by the hypothalamus. Hormone release was found to be doubled in response to the same dose of drug during the recovery period. This increased response to a drug challenge was reflected in an increased release of prolactin during exercise, and it all suggests that overreaching is associated with overactivity of the central serotonergic pathways—but how this comes about remains unknown.

Signs and Symptoms of Overtraining

Despite the great scientific interest in overtraining, there is no simple test and the problem can only be diagnosed by a combination of symptoms. The main symptom is a prolonged and unexplained decline in performance. *Unexplained* means that it is not explained by obvious injury, change in equipment, or disruption of training.

This loss of performance can be seen in a number of experimental studies. Jeukendrup et al. (1992) investigated the effects of 14 days of intensive training on cycling performance and found a 5 percent slower time-trial performance in endurance-trained road cyclists as they became overtrained. We also have shown a 9 percent decline in simulated time-trial performance after a 50 percent increase in training volume, most of which was in the form of increased intensity (Halson et al. in press). Urhausen et al. (1998b) asked subjects to cycle at 110 percent of their anaerobic threshold until exhaustion. Before a period of intensified training, these subjects could cycle for nearly 23 minutes, whereas after the training stress they could only keep going for just over 16 minutes. Other investigations in sports such as swimming and running have reported similar declines in performance (Hooper et al. 1993; Fry et al. 1992).

Other measures that have been examined in controlled research investigations are maximal heart rates and lactate concentrations. Often one of the first signs of overreaching is that cyclists complain they cannot get their heart rates up to the desired levels. When recorded in races, average heart rates are usually lower, and in training, cyclists have problems reaching the target heart rate zones. Jeukendrup et al. (1992) reported significant declines in maximal heart rate. In a recent investigation we reported a decline in maximal heart rate during a simulated time trial from 179 to 168 beats per minute. Additionally, it appears that peak blood lactate concentrations also may be reduced, although the results are somewhat contradictory (Jeukendrup et al. 1992).

Athletes who are overtrained may show signs of emotional stress. Excessive fatigue, lack of concentration, depression, and anxiety are just some of the symptoms associated with changes in mood related to overtraining. Following is a list of some of the more common signs and symptoms that may be used when trying to recognize the development or existence of overtraining:

- Unexplained underperformance
- Prolonged recovery
- Reduced maximal heart rate
- Reduced maximal blood lactate concentration
- Increased sleeping heart rate
- Excessive fatigue
- "Heavy" muscles
- Upper respiratory tract infections or other frequently recurring infections, such as colds
- Increased susceptibility to illnesses and allergies
- Sleep disturbances
- Changes in appetite
- Depression
- Loss of competitive drive
- Increased anxiety and irritation
- Decreased ability to narrow concentration

Prevention of Overtraining

Overtraining can be prevented through careful monitoring of the athlete and an understanding of the causes, signs, and symptoms associated with underperformance. Following are seven steps that can be easily implemented and integrated into an athlete's training program to aid in the prevention of overtraining.

Seven-Step Plan for Avoiding Overtraining

STEP 1: Monitor performance regularly.
STEP 2: Periodize and individualize your training program.
STEP 3: Monitor your psychological state.
STEP 4: Keep a training diary.
STEP 5: Practice good nutrition.
STEP 6: Screen for and manage infection.
STEP 7: Educate yourself.

STEP 1: Monitor Performance Regularly

It is imperative that an athlete's performance is regularly monitored to detect early signs of underperformance. This is best achieved by completing a high-intensity performance test under standardized conditions every two to three weeks. For example, a cyclist with access to laboratory testing equipment could complete a simulated time trial of a fixed amount of work and identify any changes in time taken to complete the test. In the absence of such equipment, athletes may choose a set route or circuit and complete this distance in the shortest time possible. Any changes in performance can be noted, and if there are no reasonable explanations for the reduced performance such as weather conditions, a period of rest should be prescribed.

This method of regular performance monitoring also can be beneficial in monitoring improvements as a result of training. If this is to be useful, however, the starting reference values need to be reliable (i.e., not taken when carrying an injury or even possibly overtrained). Also, the macro and micro training cycles must be taken into account. If testing outdoors, the influence of the environmental conditions, rain, and temperature should be kept in mind. Performance monitoring should occur at standardized times. For example, similar activities should be performed on the day before the test, and testing should occur at the same time of the day.

Changes in physiological variables such as heart rate, lactate, or oxygen consumption should be viewed in conjunction with changes in performance to determine if such physiological changes are the result of positive or negative adaptation to training. For example, reduced submaximal lactate production usually indicates a positive adaptation to training (i.e., less lactate is produced at a given workload and hence is indicative of fatigue resistance). However, if this lowered submaximal lactate production coincides with a decline in performance, this may suggest a failure to activate glycogen breakdown and the occurrence of overreaching. The heart rate should be monitored during the tests and any changes in maximal and average heart rate noted. If a reduced heart rate is noted in conjunction with an impaired performance, increased recovery should be provided.

© Greg Crisp/SportsChrome USA

Without access to laboratory equipment, performance testing can be done using a set route and with recognition of environmental conditions such as heat.

STEP 2: Periodize and Individualize Your Training Program

An athlete's training program should be structured to ensure that it provides the appropriate amount of training stress and recovery. This structuring of the training program is known as periodization; it includes increases in training stress and quantified periods of reduced or no training. Periodization of training ensures that appropriate recovery is integrated into the training program and thus significantly minimizes the risk of developing overtraining.

A method of monitoring training to prevent overtraining is to record the *training load* (Foster 1998). This is achieved by using training impulse (TRIMP, as described in chapter 1) or rating the intensity of the entire training session on a scale of 1 to 10 and multiplying this by the duration of the training session. This will result in a numerical value for the magnitude of the session. This can allow athletes to quantify and monitor the training load over time. *Training monotony* should be monitored to ensure that the same training routine is not carried out day after day. A weekly training load that has a high degree of monotony is more likely to result in overreaching or overtraining.

Athletes and coaches should understand the individual nature of tolerance and responses to stress. Some athletes will tolerate physical or psychological stress better than others, and for this reason all assessments should be tailored to the individual and training programs should be directed at and designed for individual athletes.

STEP 3: Monitor Your Psychological State

Because overtraining commonly results in mood disturbances, monitoring your psychological state can provide early warning signs of overtraining. One of the most common and easy ways is to use a questionnaire such as the Profile of Mood States (POMS). The 65-item questionnaire yields a global measure of mood as well as subscales of tension, depression, anger, vigor, fatigue, and confusion. An increase in all subscale scores, with the exception of vigor, is associated with overtraining. The POMS questionnaire can be completed on a weekly basis and changes in psychological state monitored. However, there has been some criticism of the POMS for its inability to discriminate between the fatigue associated with usual training and the fatigue associated with either overreaching or overtraining.

Another method of monitoring the stress associated with training and overtraining is using the Daily Analysis of Life Demands in Athletes (DALDA) questionnaire, shown in table 2.1 (Rushall 1990).

This questionnaire is divided into Part A, the sources of stress, and Part B, the symptoms or manifestation of this stress. The total "a" scores, or "worse than normal"

TABLE 2.1 DALDA Questionnaire

Part A

1.	a	b	c	Diet
2.	a	b	c	Home life
3.	a	b	c	School/college/work
4.	a	b	c	Friends
5.	a	b	c	Sport training
6.	a	b	c	Climate
7.	a	b	c	Sleep
8.	a	b	c	Recreation
9.	a	b	c	Health

Part B

1.	a	b	c	Muscle pains	**14.**	a	b	c	Enough sleep
2.	a	b	c	Techniques	**15.**	a	b	c	Between-session recovery
3.	a	b	c	Tiredness	**16.**	a	b	c	General weakness
4.	a	b	c	Need for a rest	**17.**	a	b	c	Interest
5.	a	b	c	Supplementary work	**18.**	a	b	c	Arguments
6.	a	b	c	Boredom	**19.**	a	b	c	Skin rashes
7.	a	b	c	Recovery time	**20.**	a	b	c	Congestion
8.	a	b	c	Irritability	**21.**	a	b	c	Training effort
9.	a	b	c	Weight	**22.**	a	b	c	Temper
10.	a	b	c	Throat	**23.**	a	b	c	Swellings
11.	a	b	c	Internal	**24.**	a	b	c	Likability
12.	a	b	c	Unexplained aches	**25.**	a	b	c	Runny nose
13.	a	b	c	Technique strength					

a = worse than normal

b = normal

c = better than normal

Reprinted from Rushall 1990.

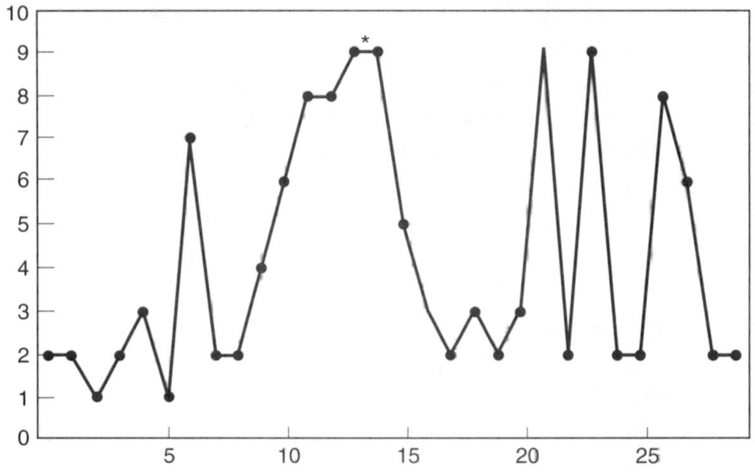

Figure 2.2 Illustration of changes in "a" scores for DALDA, Part B. An asterisk (*) indicates abnormal fatigue.

responses, are summed and graphed. Figure 2.2 illustrates changes in total "a" scores over a 30-day period. The total "a" scores for each day then can be graphed and an indication of fatigue levels determined. A period of baseline assessment should occur, with the recognition that scores may oscillate because of fatigue from single training sessions. However, if scores remain elevated for more than four consecutive days, a period of rest should be advised. For example, figure 2.2 shows that high fatigue scores (more than five "a" scores) can be generated as a result of normal training processes (days 1 to 8). Given appropriate recovery, this fatigue is reduced and on the following day levels of fatigue are once again within normal ranges (fewer than five). However, the high scores on days 9 to 15 indicate that inadequate recovery and/or increased exposure to stress has occurred. The asterisk indicates that fatigue scores have been above five for a period of four days or longer. This suggests that recovery and/or a reduction in training/nontraining stressors is needed. Additionally, if an athlete is experiencing high levels of nontraining stress from sources such as the workplace or home, he should address these issues and minimize the stress from these elements. Figure 2.2 also illustrates that given a period of recovery that results in lowered fatigue levels (days 16 to 20), normal patterns of fatigue are evident.

Therefore, the questionnaire can be used to identify high levels of fatigue that are persistently above what is normal for the individual. If fatigue scores are consistently high, recovery should be provided. It is important to recognize that high levels of fatigue often occur as a result of training; however, this should decline after appropriate periods of rest. The DALDA can be completed daily and should be done at the same time each day. The questionnaire results always should be viewed on an individual basis because what might constitute fatigue for one athlete may not for another.

STEP 4: Keep a Training Diary

It is important that the athlete keep a diary or training log. Not only should this diary contain information on training performed, but it should also contain the results of performance tests, maximum heart rate, sleeping heart rate, psychological questionnaire results, and any minor illnesses experienced. An accurate and comprehensive diary can be one of the best tools to aid the early identification of overtraining. Keeping a detailed and accurate measure of performance allows the athlete and coach to determine whether the athlete's performance is improving (correct training) or declining (incorrect training). If a decline in performance is evident alongside reductions in maximal heart rate and changes in mood state, time for recovery should be provided.

STEP 5: Practice Good Nutrition

Adequate energy intake in combination with proper fluid intake is essential for optimal endurance performance. Although overtraining may occur in the presence of sufficient carbohydrate intake (Snyder et al. 1995), insufficient energy intake makes the athlete much more vulnerable. A negative energy balance, carbohydrate depletion, and dehydration may increase the body's stress response to exercise and alter hormonal response to exercise (Jeukendrup 1999). Athletes should consume adequate carbohydrate and fluids before, during, and after training and competition. Chapters 12 and 13 provide guidelines for determining and assessing appropriate energy intake and fluid ingestion, respectively.

STEP 6: Screen for and Manage Infection

Regular medical assessments are important in the early identification of illness that may underlie the symptoms of fatigue. It is also extremely important to minimize the risk of infection by taking the following precautions:

- Develop an awareness of the increased risk of infection after competition and training.
- Avoid ill athletes.
- Use good personal hygiene.
- Avoid using other athletes' water bottles.
- Consider vaccination against influenza.
- Recognize that exercising with an infection may increase the duration and severity of illness.
- Do not train with a fever.
- Do not return to training at the same level after an illness.

For additional information, see chapter 20.

STEP 7: Educate Yourself

It is essential that athletes and coaches educate themselves about the causes of overtraining as well as have the means to identify its occurrence. Early detection of signs and symptoms and periods of appropriate recovery are both integral aspects in the prevention of overtraining. In essence, athletes and coaches should be in constant communication about training and recovery status and have a solid knowledge of ways to prevent and detect overtraining.

Treatment of Overtraining

Scientific information on the treatment of overreaching and overtraining is limited. However, the treatment regime appears obvious: Reduce, but don't completely halt, the training schedule. Compliance with the treatment may be a serious issue and some other form of exercise or distraction may be needed to stop the athlete from experiencing withdrawal symptoms.

In the case of overreaching, reduced training alone may be effective in restoring performance. A reduction in training volume and intensity, in conjunction with at least two to three complete rest days, may be sufficient for recovery. In the case of overtraining, rest and a break from training are required. However, total inactivity may be a serious source of stress for the athlete, and allowing two to three days per week of minimal intensity and duration exercise may enhance recovery. Initially, aerobic activity at a heart rate of 120 to 140 beats per minute for short periods (up to 20 minutes) can be prescribed. Progression to longer sessions can occur gradually over a 6- to 12-week period (Budgett 1998).

If the athlete is allowed to perform small amounts of exercise and understands that complete recovery may not be instantaneous, the process of recovery and a return to previous levels may be enhanced. Proper medical attention for any illnesses that may have arisen from the training period should be immediately addressed. Similarly, if the athlete is experiencing depression, professional treatment should be recommended.

Summary

It is paradoxical that the need for increases in training loads to enhance performance can ultimately be the cause of fatigue and a serious decline in performance. It is this delicate balance between training and overtraining that athletes, coaches, and scientists strive to realize.

Given appropriate knowledge of the causes and symptoms, overtraining can be avoided. Training programs that include periods of regeneration and recovery from exercise and appropriate progression in load are essential in reducing the risk of overtraining. Athletes and coaches also should monitor performance and psychological state to discover any early indications of fatigue and underperformance. Finally, if overtraining does occur, rest and medical attention may be required.

chapter 3

Training at Altitude

David T. Martin

Does altitude training improve athletic performance? Coaches and athletes have asked this apparently simple question for more than 100 years. Similarly, for more than a century, scientists have been interested in how altitude affects human physiology. It was 1878 when Swiss physiologist Paul Bert suggested that the oxygen-carrying capacity of the blood (i.e., hemoglobin concentration) would be higher in individuals living at altitude. For those aware that the oxygen-carrying capacity of the blood contributes to endurance performance, the potential benefits of altitude training were an intuitive extension of Bert's original hypothesis.

Research in Altitude Training

Altitude training is one of the most studied and widely written-about topics in sport science. To say that other scientists have addressed the topic of altitude training is a gross understatement. A number of highly respected physiologists have taken the time to read the literature, conduct experiments, and develop their own interpretations of the data. Summaries of altitude training research are published in many comprehensive and insightful reviews. European scientists have performed much of the early applied research conducted with elite athletes. In addition to it remaining a popular research topic in Europe, Australian and American researchers have performed recent studies examining the effects of altitude training on athletic performance. Of particular interest to competitive cyclists and coaches is the comprehensive and insightful scientific review of altitude training published by Australia's altitude experts, Allan Hahn and Chris Gore (2001). Two other review papers recently published include Wilber's examination (2001) of the many altitude training techniques currently used by athletes and Baker and Hopkins' applied evaluation (1998) of the live-high, train-low approach. In addition to these scientific reviews, numerous journalists and coaches have published articles in popular sporting magazines commenting on results of scientific studies and discussing their own opinions regarding altitude.

However, despite all the research and published reports, it continues to be a difficult task for a coach to determine how to use altitude training most effectively. It is not the purpose of this chapter to reiterate what has been said so well in previous scientific reviews examining altitude training but to focus on training issues in light of the many altitude training options that are available.

Learning From Altitude Research

What have we learned from the extensive amount of scientific attention devoted to altitude training? To begin with, the majority of the acute physiological responses to exercise at altitude have been established and documented. Adaptations to prolonged altitude exposure also have been described. Further, we now know that the performance response to altitude training is dependent on many different variables—for example, genetics, fitness, fatigue, altitude exposure, and iron status (Dick 1992). Interestingly, some physiological adaptations to altitude (i.e., changes in maximal aerobic capacity) do not always coincide with improvements in performance (Hahn and Gore 2001), whereas in some cases altitude-induced adaptations of improved oxygen transport capacity appear to give the athlete a performance advantage (Stray-Gundersen et al. 2001).

Despite an abundance of research, experts do not currently agree on the primary physiological mechanisms responsible for improved performance following moderate altitude exposure (Hahn et al. 2001). Thus, experienced exercise physiologists up to date with the scientific literature generally answer the question of whether altitude training can improve athletic performance by stating, "It depends."

Understanding the Altitude Stimulus

At sea level, the barometric pressure is approximately 760 millimeters mercury and the fractional concentration of oxygen is typically 20.93 percent. The partial pressure of oxygen in the inspired air is calculated by multiplying the total barometric pressure by the fractional concentration of a particular gas (e.g., oxygen, nitrogen, carbon dioxide). The partial pressure of oxygen at sea level is 159 millimeters mercury (760 millimeters mercury times 20.93 percent oxygen). Partial pressure is important to understand, as it establishes a diffusion gradient that heavily influences the transfer of oxygen from the environment to active skeletal muscle. As an athlete ascends to higher and higher altitudes, the barometric pressure decreases whereas the fractional concentration of oxygen remains at 20.93 percent. Thus, the partial pressure of oxygen at natural altitude decreases in proportion to the reduction in barometric pressure.

It is possible in semi-enclosed environments to enrich the air with nitrogen, an inert gas that typically makes up 79 percent of air. As a result, the fractional concentration of oxygen is reduced. Although barometric pressure remains at sea-level values (i.e., normobaric), the partial pressure of oxygen in this environment is reduced to values that are normally encountered at altitude. Research published as early as 1920 indicated that the physiological response to altitude is predominately dependent on the partial pressure of inspired oxygen. Additionally, early research established that ventilatory and hematological responses to simulated altitude were similar regardless of whether the partial pressure was reduced via a decrease in pressure or a decrease in the fractional concentration of oxygen.

Establishing reductions in barometric pressure at sea level can be accomplished, but these manipulations require a substantially greater effort than decreasing partial pressure via reductions in the fractional concentration of oxygen—a technique that can be achieved by either rebreathing expired air or using air with an artificially high concentration of nitrogen. *Hypobaric hypoxia* is used to describe a low partial pressure of oxygen produced by decreasing total pressure, whereas *normobaric hypoxia* is used to describe a low partial pressure of oxygen resulting from a low fractional concentration of oxygen without a change in barometric pressure. Another manipulation that has received some scientific attention involves breathing enriched oxygen while at altitude (*hypobaric hyperoxia*). This technique simulates the partial pressure of oxygen encountered at sea level.

Historical Overview

Early altitude research was designed to monitor physiological responses to acute altitude exposure. Altitude research in the early 1900s also examined the physiological differences between altitude natives and similar populations living at sea level. Throughout the later part of the 1900s, sport scientists monitored athletes training and competing at altitude, documenting the effects of altitude on athletic performance. Much of this research was motivated by the 1968 Olympics in Mexico City, a competition that raised the international awareness of the effects of moderate altitude on elite performance (Dick 1992). Some coaches began using altitude training to prepare endurance athletes for sea-level competition under the assumption that altitude-induced increases in red blood cell mass would improve oxygen delivery to working muscles and thus improve performance (Dick 1992). Others adopted a more traditional approach and used altitude training camps and simulated altitude to prepare for competition at altitude.

Unique techniques for simulating altitude have become popular over the past 20 years (Wilber 2001). The two most popular approaches of simulating altitude require either hypobaric chambers, in which atmospheric pressure can be decreased to replicate altitude conditions, or nitrogen houses and tents, in which nitrogen enrichment is used to decrease the concentration of oxygen. These technical advancements have emerged in conjunction with a new approach to altitude training termed "live high, train low" (Levine and Stray-Gundersen 1992). Proponents of this technique believe that athletes living and sleeping at altitude but training at sea level will enjoy the benefits of living at altitude without a risk of acute altitude sickness or experiencing altitude-induced reductions in training intensity.

Another unique modification of the live-high, train-low approach involves living and training at moderate altitude but breathing air with high concentrations of oxygen during high-intensity intervals to minimize any altitude-associated reductions in training intensity (Morris et al. 2000). Yet another approach used by some endurance athletes involves living and training at sea level but breathing hypoxic gases to simulate altitude during training sessions (Vogt et al. 2001). Athletes training at altitude also can sleep in an environment with elevated oxygen concentrations in attempts to minimize any sleep disruptions and maximize recovery. Like other unique approaches to altitude training, this particular approach has not been carefully studied. See table 3.1 for the options regarding this approach.

Finally, there are some who advocate breathing hypoxic gases at rest for a period of one to three hours based on research documenting that even brief periods of hypoxic exposure can stimulate the body to produce erythropoietin (EPO), a hormone primarily responsible for stimulating red blood cell production. This technique has become popular despite any evidence indicating that the subtle transient elevations in EPO due to breathing a low oxygen-content gas are responsible for increasing red blood cell mass.

Thus, many techniques are available for the cyclist interested in manipulating the oxygen availability in the inspired air. With all these options, what is the altitude training technique that is best for particular training and competition goals?

Ethical Issues

Before discussing different altitude training approaches, we should consider some ethical issues, as some coaches, athletes, scientists, and sport administrators consider the use of simulated altitude environments by athletes as "artificial" and "potentially dangerous," and therefore a form of cheating (Wilber 2001). However, those supporting the use of simulated oxygen environments point out that there are no published reports documenting that the use of simulated altitude results in health problems to any greater extent than natural altitude training (Hahn and Gore 2001). Additionally, elite competitors in many sports have adopted the use of high-technology products for both training and competition as they attempt to improve performance. For example, it is popular for elite athletes to use heat chambers (an artificially hot environment) to induce heat acclimation before important competition in warm conditions. Additionally, athletes now benefit from indoor running tracks, swimming pools, and even winter sport venues that make snow.

Thus, the argument that simulated altitude environments are unethical because they are "artificial" does not have merit. In today's elite sport culture, we could say that coaches and support staff who do not encourage the use of artificial altitude environments to supplement training are unethical for withholding a potentially valuable training technique. Currently, neither the International Olympic Committee nor the Union Cyclist Internationale specifically bans the use of simulated altitude facilities or the use of high or low oxygen mixtures while training. Additionally, the Norwegian Olympic Committee has determined that the use of simulated altitude houses and tents is similar in concept to other training practices that elite athletes engage in normally (Wilber 2001). Despite the many interesting ethical debates that focus on simulated altitude, most coaches and athletes evaluate new training products

TABLE 3.1 **Three Basic Altitude Training Options**

LIVING		TRAINING: High	TRAINING: Low
		High	**Low**
LIVING	High	Live at natural altitude Train at natural altitude	Live at natural altitude Travel to low altitude to train
	High	Live in simulated altitude Train in simulated altitude	Live at natural altitude Travel to low altitude for high-intensity training
	High		Live at natural altitude Use enriched oxygen gas to simulate training at sea level
	High		Live at sea level Train at sea level Sleep at altitude using a nitrogen house or tent
	High		Live at sea level Train at sea level Sleep at altitude using a hypobaric hypoxic room
	High		Live at sea level Train at sea level Passive exposure to simulated altitude for one to three hours a day
	Low	Live at sea level Train at altitude	Live at sea level Train at sea level
	Low	Live at altitude Train at altitude Sleep in an oxygen-enriched room	
	Low	Live at sea level Train at altitude using hypoxic gases	
	Low	Live at sea level Train at altitude using hypobaric chambers	

and techniques in light of whether they are safe, legal, and potentially effective in enhancing performance. At this time, simulated altitude environments satisfy all three criteria.

Issues and Options for Cyclists in Altitude Training

The remainder of this chapter focuses on training issues encountered by competitive cyclists. After describing each issue, we present a series of altitude training options with a brief discussion of why a particular approach may be worthwhile. It is important to point out that altitude training is not a magical treatment that produces outstanding performances for all athletes. Like other forms of training, altitude training does not work for everyone and this approach may not be effective when an athlete is exceptionally tired or ill. Unfortunately, it is possible for inexperienced coaches and athletes to fixate on the unique and exciting aspects of altitude and forget about fundamental training issues (i.e., progressive overload, variability, specificity, recovery; see chapter 1). The astute coach and athlete attempt to recognize those periods throughout the year in which altitude training may enhance the training process. It is probably too simplistic to view altitude training camps as either "good" or "bad." Instead, we should think of altitude exposure as a stimulus that needs to be modified based on training responses. An applied review of altitude training makes a reference to a former Russian coach who believed that everyone could benefit from altitude (Dick 1992). Of course, the difficult task is to make sure that the application of the altitude training is appropriate for each individual.

Physical training for athletes is designed to stimulate adaptations that ultimately lead to improved performances. Altitude training techniques have been developed and refined to facilitate gains in fitness by either (a) providing additional stress during training or recovery, or (b) reducing the stress associated with training and recovery. At certain times of the year a cyclist will want to experience an additional overload to promote more extreme or unique adaptations. In contrast, there are other times in the year when recovery is more important.

ISSUE: A cyclist is attempting to enhance adaptations to early-season low-intensity training

Option 1—Live high, train high. A fairly traditional approach to altitude training adopted by some national running, swimming, rowing, and cycling programs involves an early-season altitude training camp lasting for two to three weeks (Dick 1992). This camp represents the first of three camps held throughout the year leading up to the most important competition of the year. The first altitude camp of the year is held after one to two months of training and is conducted at altitudes between 1,600 and 2,700 meters. Training volume is moderate to high but training intensity is reduced.

> 1 kilometer = 0.62 miles
>
> 1 meter = 3.3 feet

At altitude, a given absolute training intensity (i.e., power output) will result in a greater cardiovascular stress (i.e., heart rate, ventilation, cardiac output). However, it is possible that cyclists merely decrease their absolute intensity at altitude resulting in a similar cardiovascular load (i.e., time at a given heart rate) for a reduced absolute power output (Brosnan et al. 2000). Some national team coaches generally believe that an early-season altitude camp is beneficial because it somehow primes the athlete to adapt faster and to a greater extent upon subsequent altitude exposure. Despite the popularity of early-season training camps, little if any data are available to document that these camps are superior to similar training performed at sea level. Interestingly, recent data collected from relatively untrained subjects demonstrate that adaptations in aerobic enzymes are superior when six weeks of low-intensity training is performed at a simulated altitude of 3,850 meters compared with similar training performed at sea level (Vogt et al. 2001). Whether similar adaptations occur at lower altitudes is currently not known.

Option 2—Live low, train high. The advent of different devices that decrease the partial pressure of inspired oxygen while athletes are training at sea level allows them to live low but train high. Similar to real altitude training, cyclists are able to experience the additional cardiovascular overload associated with a low oxygen partial pressure environment during training. Although research is available indicating that training under hypoxic conditions promotes unique physiological responses and adaptations (Vogt et al. 2001), it is questionable whether there are any long-term advantages associated with this approach when encountered early in the year. One advantage of this technique compared to natural altitude is that the cyclist is able to sleep and recover in an oxygen-enriched environment (Vogt et al. 2001). Additionally, for many athletes, live-low, train-high programs can be both logistically and economically superior to other altitude methods.

Another technique for obtaining a similar stimulus can be achieved in geographic locations where the athlete can travel to high altitude for specific training sessions. For instance, cyclists living in Salt Lake City, Utah, can drive for one to two hours up to moderate altitude (2,700 meters) for training sessions and then return to Salt Lake City (1,250 meters) to recover and sleep (Stray-Gundersen et al. 2001).

ISSUE: A cyclist is rehabilitating from a lower body injury that prevents high power outputs

Option 1—Live high, train high. For injured athletes who are forced to work at low power outputs, an advantage of training at altitude is that the cardiovascular response is higher for any given power output (Dick 1992). At higher altitudes this response is even more exaggerated. The cyclist who is unable to achieve high power outputs can therefore train at relatively high heart rates despite low power. As the injury heals, the cyclist can progressively train at lower altitudes until he reestablishes his typical heart rate–power output relationship. One of the disadvantages of living and training at natural altitude is the difficulty in modifying the magnitude of the altitude stimulus and the possible deleterious effects of prolonged exposure to altitude on healing and general recovery.

Option 2—Live low, train high. The use of simulated altitude during training sessions can enable the injured cyclist to overcome some of the potential limitations associated with living and training at altitude. As indicated in option 1, both heart rate and ventilation are noticeably elevated for a given power output while a cyclist is training at altitude. By carefully decreasing the percentage of oxygen in the inspired air, the cyclist can effectively increase the cardiovascular response for a given power output.

ISSUE: A cyclist is fit and requires a novel overload

Many competitive cyclists, especially those at the highest level, train year-round. Lucia et al. (2001) have commented that professional road cyclists typically ride their bikes more than 30,000 to 35,000 kilometers per year and race 80 to 100 times per season. Racing for some professional cyclists may start as early as March and the World Championships are typically held in October, which makes for a long season (Lucia et al. 2001). For some national and professional teams, overall fitness appears to improve rapidly over a period of two to three months and then many laboratory indicators of fitness plateau. Some competitive cyclists do not know what kind of training they should do after they complete three to six weeks of resistance training, three to six weeks of base training, and two to three weeks of high-intensity training and racing.

Option 1—Live high, train high. An athlete can use an altitude training camp for two to four weeks at 1,500 to 2,700 meters after initial training to promote a novel overload. Previous training sessions that the cyclist adapted to well will again become challenging at altitude (Dick 1992). Unlike altitude training used to prepare for important competition, early-season altitude training camps can be far more rigorous (Gore et al. 1998). Brosnan and colleagues (2000) were particularly interested in the increased stress associated with training at altitude and examined many physiological parameters in a group of Australian National Team female road cyclists training at a simulated altitude of 2,100 meters (normobaric, hypoxic). Cyclists reduced power output during threshold intervals and high-intensity intervals by approximately 6 percent compared with training intensity adopted during the low-altitude condition. Interestingly, cyclists achieved the same training heart rate, blood lactate, and perception of effort in both low- and high-altitude training sets. Unfortunately, researchers were unable to evaluate the prolonged effects of training at altitude to determine whether sea-level power output in training sets could be reestablished. Although this adaptation may seem unlikely, there are anecdotal reports of swimmers and cyclists achieving absolute training intensities (lap times, power outputs) at the end of an altitude training camp that are similar to the intensity achieved earlier in the year at sea level. It is now apparent that altitude training camps at moderate altitude can be useful for providing a novel overload promoting unique physiological adaptations that an athlete may not achieve as easily at sea level (Vogt et al. 2001).

Another interesting aspect to an altitude training camp held early in the season is the approach with regard to training volume and intensity. In many cases, national team coaches in rowing, swimming, and cycling adopt very aggressive training programs for these early-season altitude camps, achieving some of the biggest volumes of training encountered throughout the year. One early-season training camp that has been viewed as particularly beneficial for the Australian track cycling team is notorious for adopting incredibly high weekly training distances with ample amounts of high-intensity work (Gore et al. 1998).

Option 2—Live low, train high. Researchers established early on that the physiological response to breathing a gas with a low percentage of oxygen is very similar to the physiological response to natural altitude. Similar to the philosophy outlined in option 1, it is possible for cyclists to achieve an additional overload by simulating altitude conditions during typical training sessions (Vogt et al. 2001). Once a cyclist has achieved the majority of the adaptations that can be attributed to a standard training program, it is possible to use altitude to provide an additional training load. Cyclists can attempt to achieve power outputs during standard interval training programs at altitude that they previously achieved at sea level. Some research in this area has documented that this type of exposure can produce unique adaptations in skeletal muscle that potentially could have a performance-enhancing effect (Vogt et al. 2001). As suggested in option 1, when athletes adopt living-low, training-high programs early in the season, training loads can be 90 to 100 percent of those experienced at sea level.

Option 3—Live high, train low. A unique technique for acquiring the live-high, train-low stimulus involves living at altitude but breathing a gas with a high concentration of oxygen during high-intensity intervals (Wilber 2001). Breathing a gas with enriched oxygen has been shown to increase the training intensity at altitude (Wilber 2001). Morris et al. (2000) also reported that breathing oxygen-enriched air increased power output during high-intensity training at altitude. Furthermore, these researchers observed an improved ability to engage in high-intensity exercise at altitude after three weeks of training with enriched oxygen. The higher training intensity at altitude appears to provide the stimulus for additional adaptation. Thus, a cyclist looking for an additional overload can live and sleep at altitude without compromising training intensity. It is possible that living high and training low for a week or two serves as great preparation for a camp in which athletes will be living and training at altitude.

ISSUE: A cyclist is sick or fatigued during the first week of altitude camp

Option 1—Live low, train high. Cyclists experience the stress of moderate altitude during both exercise and rest (Hahn and Gore 2001). Heart rate and ventilation, which are primarily controlled by the autonomic nervous system, are elevated at moderate altitude and this response also is observed during sleep. It is possible, though not well documented, that a fatigued athlete or a sick athlete will not benefit from the additional stress of altitude. One way to alleviate the overall stress experienced by an athlete is to avoid altitude all together. However, often a training camp is scheduled for a particular time and location and it becomes difficult for a cyclist to completely remove himself or herself from the group. The standard approach to altitude training with a sick or fatigued cyclist is to allow the cyclist to back off high-intensity training and to "see how it goes." Another more aggressive approach would involve driving the cyclist to lower elevations each night to sleep (i.e., an enriched oxygen environment).

Interestingly, in some high-altitude venues, workers are allowed to sleep in special rooms that are filled with oxygen-enriched air. This approach has been shown to produce promising results in regard to the overall well-being of the workers (West

2001). The overall objective in this situation is to alleviate the stress of altitude for the sick or fatigued athlete so that the recovery process is not impaired. Unfortunately, little relevant data are available to support this approach with athletes.

Option 2—Live high, train easy high, train hard low. A different approach to dealing with the sick or fatigued athlete at altitude is to provide supplemental oxygen during high-intensity training sessions (Morris et al. 2000). This intervention would allow the athlete to achieve target power outputs without any excessive metabolic strain due to altitude. The key to this option is to control the power output during the high-intensity training so that training intensity is of high quality but not maximal. The purpose of the supplemental oxygen is to alleviate stress, not to facilitate a supramaximal effort that may ultimately result in excessive fatigue (Morris et al. 2000). Supplemental oxygen can be delivered from canisters containing compressed air to the cyclist via a mouthpiece or a mask.

ISSUE: A cyclist is preparing for competition at moderate altitude

Many cycling competitions are now held at altitudes ranging from 600 to 2,700 meters. Although 600 meters may appear to be trivial in regard to requiring specific preparation, research has demonstrated that simulated pursuit performance can be reduced even at this seemingly low altitude (Gore et al. 1997). The scientific literature well supports two concepts: (a) Power output at moderate altitude is typically reduced below sea-level values, and (b) altitude acclimatization generally produces a performance advantage (Dick 1992). Another issue that is rarely discussed is the ability to appropriately pace an all-out effort under the new oxygen constraints associated with altitude. How long an athlete needs to acclimate and familiarize himself with optimal pacing strategies is difficult to establish, but most experts agree that one to three weeks of time living and training at moderate altitude can be beneficial. Another issue for the competitive cyclist is the prolonged climbs that attain significant elevations (greater than 1,500 meters) (Lucia et al. 2001). Specific preparation for these climbs at altitude will likely aid performance.

Option 1—Live high, train high. Numerous cycle races (both track and road) around the world are conducted at altitude (Hahn and Gore 2001). Additionally, many stage races involve climbs that attain altitudes greater than 1,000 meters (Lucia et al. 2001). How long is required at altitude before a cyclist is fully acclimated? Competitive cyclists have asked this question for many years. Unfortunately, there is not an abundance of research available in this area and the research that does exist does not always pertain to the competitive cyclist. In coaching circles it is common to hear about two strategies: (a) Arrive just a day prior to competition (no acclimatization), or (b) spend as long as possible training and living at the competition venue (Dick 1992). However, it may be the case that many of the desired adaptations to altitude occur within the first week of exposure (Hahn and Gore 2001). These adaptations would include a rapid hemoconcentration, improved sleep quality, and improved pacing strategies based on high-intensity training sessions (Hahn and Gore 2001).

For those looking to benefit from an increase in red blood cell mass, it may take a minimum of three to four weeks at an altitude of 2,500 meters (Levine and Stray-Gundersen 1992). Whether a competitive road cyclist can use altitude to improve red blood cell mass is not known, and although some scientists think this adaptation is

Training at altitude is an option that can help cyclists acclimatize their bodies to the differences for competition at higher altitudes than they are used to.

possible, there are others who doubt this mechanism is responsible for improved performance in elite cyclists (Hahn et al. 2001).

Option 2—Live high, train high, sleep low. A fairly novel approach to preparing for altitude competition involves promoting physiological adaptations by performing training at the competitive altitude while at the same time using enriched oxygen environments to recover from the novel stress. This approach assumes that the altitude exposure during sleep is not critical for complete altitude acclimatization. No published research is available specifically evaluating this technique for enhancing cycling performance at altitude.

Option 3—Live high, train low. A number of studies have documented the physiological adaptations to live-high, train-low camps (Hahn and Gore 2001; Hahn et al. 2001). However, little, if any, data have explored the effectiveness of this approach on performance at altitude. The rationale behind this approach centers on the observation that live-high, train-low camps can possibly produce increased muscle-buffering capacity, cycling economy, red blood cell mass, and maximal oxygen uptake (Baker and Hopkins 1998; Hahn and Gore 2001; Hahn et al. 2001). Further research examining live-high, train-low approaches and their effects on performance at altitude is warranted.

Option 4—Train high, live higher. If living at altitude before competition is good, then wouldn't living higher be more advantageous? Some cross-country skiers may use this approach before the 2002 Winter Olympic Games in Park City, Utah. Although some countries may have unpublished data supporting this novel approach, there are currently no published studies available to establish whether this technique is advantageous. Sleep disturbances and possible altitude sickness would be of particular concern when athletes are sleeping at altitudes greater than 3,000 meters because both are known to occur with increased prevalence at progressively higher altitudes (Dick 1992).

ISSUE: A cyclist is preparing for competition at sea level

Training at altitude to enhance sea-level performance may be one of the most controversial areas of altitude training (Hahn and Gore 2001; Hahn et al. 2001). Although there are many anecdotal reports of athletes who have trained at altitude for two to four weeks before performing well at an important sea-level competition (Dick 1992), the scientific literature does not clearly support this practice. However, promising data have emerged that support the concept of living high but training low (Hahn and Gore 2001; Stray-Gundersen et al. 2001). Scientists currently are debating the precise mechanisms explaining why live-high, train-low camps are advantageous (Baker and Hopkins 1998; Hahn et al. 2001; Stray-Gundersen et al. 2001). It is possible that improved performances after living high, training low occur because athletes can engage in high-intensity, competition-specific training and at the same time experience some of the adaptations associated with living and sleeping at altitude (Levine and Stray-Gundersen 1992).

Other novel altitude training techniques include intermittent hypoxic exposure (IHE) and intermittent hypoxic training (IHT) (Wilber 2001). Whereas IHE typically involves exposure to high altitude one to three hours daily during rest, IHT techniques involve breathing air with a reduced partial pressure of oxygen during training sessions. Only preliminary scientific data are available for assessing the advantages of IHE or IHT (Wilber 2001).

Option 1—Live high, train high. Many stories have been told about a great cyclist or a great cycling program that has successfully used altitude training before an important competition. For instance, the successful German and Australian track cycling programs were big advocates of altitude training through the 1980s and 1990s, and some champion road cyclists have used altitude training to prepare for important events such as the Tour de France and the one-hour record (Burke 1995). However, as mentioned earlier, the available scientific data do not suggest that training at altitude noticeably improves sea-level performance (Hahn and Gore 2001). In two comprehensive reviews of scientific studies in this area, researchers have concluded that any positive effects of altitude on sea-level performance either do not exist or are so small that they cannot be clearly identified (Baker and Hopkins 1998; Hahn and Gore 2001).

Researchers have pointed out that living and training at moderate altitude carries risks. These risks include

- A decreased ability to train at high absolute intensities,
- a decreased ability to recover,
- a decreased ability to sleep,
- an increased risk of illness, and

- difficulty adopting ideal pacing strategies (Baker and Hopkins 1998; Hahn and Gore 2001).

Individual susceptibility to these risks may mask any performance effect. Those in favor of altitude training camps before sea-level competition like to point out that just like an interval-training program, altitude training only works when the training component of the altitude camp is appropriate (Dick 1992). Additionally, it may be the case that to enjoy maximum benefits of altitude training, cyclists must eat an adequate diet rich in carbohydrates, increase fluid intake, and ensure sufficient iron stores (Baker and Hopkins 1998). Unfortunately, there is no agreed-on formula for determining the elevation and duration of an altitude camp. Additionally, there is no evidence-based rationale describing how long after an altitude camp peak performance will occur (Gore et al. 1998). For these reasons, coaches of high-performance programs tend to replicate altitude training approaches that worked well for them in the past or that have been adopted by other successful coaches.

When altitude training is used for the final preparation of cyclists who are competing at sea level, camps typically are held at altitudes between 1,800 and 2,500 meters, for two to four weeks, and the camp ends two to three weeks before competition (Dick 1992). Training at altitude generally will involve an “easy” introduction, then a high-volume, high-intensity block, followed by an “easy” final two to three days before the athlete returns to sea level (Dick 1992). While at altitude some coaches will adjust training zones in an attempt to compensate for the elevated heart rates and lactates associated with a given power output (Burke 1995). However, this approach is probably not necessary, as it has been shown that athletes naturally compensate power output in threshold and high-intensity intervals so that heart rate and blood lactate are similar to values obtained at sea level (Brosnan et al. 2000).

The duration of the taper after the altitude training program probably depends on how fatigued the athlete becomes during the altitude training camp. For severe fatigue it may take two to three weeks before a cyclist is able to demonstrate peak form, but for an athlete who has coped well with the altitude training camp, peak form may occur within the first week of arriving at sea level.

In summary, elite cyclists who have had exceptional sea-level performances after an altitude camp demonstrate that certain types of altitude training can be permitted. Data do not prove, however, that altitude training is superior to sea-level training for enhancing performance at sea level. Scientific data suggest that in many cases the problems associated with altitude training may outweigh any potential benefits. Some coaches who frequently use altitude training camps believe that altitude training to enhance sea-level performance only works if you know what you are doing (Dick 1992). Perhaps future studies will begin to evaluate types of training programs at altitude that are most likely to produce improved performances at sea level instead of evaluating the type of altitude exposure that works best with a generic training program.

Option 2—Live high, train low. Although Finnish researchers were among the first to formally evaluate the effectiveness of the live-high, train-low approach in the early 1990s, it is fair to say that American researchers Levine and Stray-Gundersen (1992) are responsible for the majority of the published research in this area. More recently, Australian sport scientists have taken a strong interest in this popular altitude training technique (Hahn et al. 2001).

Thus far, this strategy has been shown to be effective with 400-meter runners, collegiate middle-distance runners, elite middle-distance runners, elite rowers, and elite female road cyclists (Hahn and Gore 2001). All these studies used a group of fitness-matched control athletes (i.e., with no altitude exposure) to ensure that changes in performance were not merely due to training. The magnitude of the performance advantage associated with the live-high, train-low approach is approximately 1 to 2 percent (Hahn and Gore 2001), a magnitude of improvement that may not seem like much, but as it is widely known, at world-class competition the top places are sometimes separated by less than 1 percent. Live-high, train-low camps can be achieved using natural altitude (i.e., driving to lower elevations for intense training sessions) (Levine and Stray-Gundersen 1992) or using artificial devices such as hypobaric hypoxic rooms and normobaric hypoxic rooms or tents (Hahn et al. 2001).

Cyclists using simulated altitude environments have the luxury of remaining at sea level but sleeping at high altitude. Levine and Stray-Gundersen have adopted a live-high, train-low approach of sleeping at 2,500 meters and performing high-intensity training at 1,250 meters for a period of three to four weeks using natural altitude (Stray-Gundersen et al. 2001). These researchers have performed studies indicating that the live-high, train-low approach is equally effective if athletes perform low-moderate intensity training sessions at altitude (Stray-Gundersen et al. 2001). The key to success seems to rely on high-intensity training performed at lower elevations where the greater oxygen availability increases the absolute intensity. Within a week of completing a live-high, train-low program, elite distance runners showed a sea-level performance improvement of 1.1 percent (Stray-Gundersen et al. 2001).

Because the live-high, train-low approach also increases the hormone EPO, hemoglogin concentration, and maximal oxygen uptake, Levine and Stray-Gundersen frequently conclude that improvements in performance are primarily due to altitude-induced increases in red blood cell mass (Stray-Gundersen et al. 2001). However, Australian researchers also have documented improvement in performances after live-high, train-low camps (two to three weeks at 2,700 meters) without an increase in red blood cell mass or maximal oxygen uptake (Hahn et al. 2001). Australian sport scientists attribute gains in performance

Elite female road cyclists comprise one group that has benefited from the live-high, train-low approach for sea-level competition.

to an altitude-induced increase in oxygen-independent (anaerobic), energy-yielding systems. In their comprehensive review of the literature, Hahn and Gore point out that, although not universal, others have observed an increase in muscle-buffering capacity following altitude training (Hahn et al. 2001).

Critics of the live-high, train-low approach point out that a proper placebo-controlled design has yet to be conducted and therefore it is possible that the gains in performance after living high, training low are primarily due to the athlete's belief in the treatment (i.e., the placebo effect). Regardless of why performance after living high, training low works, strategies that tend to have the most consistent benefits involve sleeping at either natural or simulated altitude around 2,500 to 2,700 meters for two to four weeks. Training during this period is of moderate to high volume and approximately 20 percent of training is spent at threshold-training intensity or higher. Like all training programs, training variability and adequate recovery are important. Research conducted thus far suggests that sleeping at high altitude up to 3,000 meters does not noticeably interfere with low-altitude training.

Option 3—Live high, train low with supplemental oxygen. Some altitude training venues do not allow athletes to conveniently access sea level for high-intensity training sessions. Sport scientists have demonstrated that by breathing oxygen-enriched air, cyclists living at altitude can substantially improve their power output when performing high-intensity interval exercise (Morris et al. 2000). Thus, similar to the traditional live-high, train-low approach, this technique allows athletes to live at altitude while training at sea level (Wilber 2001). One published study has evaluated the effectiveness of breathing enriched oxygen during interval training sessions while living at altitude and examined the effects of this training program on sea-level performance (Morris et al. 2000). Results from this study suggest that like other live-high, train-low approaches, there is a slight advantage to living at altitude but training in environments where oxygen availability is enhanced. In the study by Morris et al. (2000), cyclists lived and trained at 1,860 meters and during high-intensity interval training (five times five minutes, three days per week) breathed a gas containing approximately 26 percent oxygen. Whether it is more effective to breathe a gas with a higher oxygen concentration at a higher altitude is not known, but theoretically this treatment would enhance both the hypoxic stress at rest and the power output during training.

Option 4—Live low, with intermittent exposure to hypoxia, train low. Brief exposures to simulated altitude are thought by some to stimulate an increase in EPO and, consequently, red blood cell mass and maximal oxygen uptake (Wilber 2001). Protocols in this area vary considerably from intermittently breathing a gas with 9 to 10 percent oxygen (6,400 meters) for 60 minutes twice a day to passive exposure to hypobaric hypoxia (4,000 to 5,500 meters) three times a week. Those who have studied the effects of intermittent hypoxic exposure generally look at a treatment duration between two and four weeks (Wilber 2001). Although it is true that brief exposure to extreme altitude can stimulate increases in EPO (Wilber 2001), it has not been clearly established that these changes are responsible for any substantial increase in red blood cell mass, maximal oxygen uptake, or performance in well-trained athletes. Unfortunately, very little research has been published in this area, and in those studies that are available, proper control groups have not been included.

For those selling devices that allow the athlete to experience IHE, much anecdotal information is cited. It may be tempting to believe that changes in resting hematocrit, hemoglobin, and performance after a period of IHE substantiate the effectiveness of this technique. However, rapid changes in plasma volume (hemoconcentration) known to occur after exposure to altitude can explain elevations in hematocrit and hemoglobin without a true increase in red cell mass. Additionally, a placebo effect or a training effect generally can explain improvements in performance. Thus, available evidence does not strongly support the use of IHE.

Option 5—Live low, train high. Exercise at altitude produces many novel physiological responses compared with the same training at sea level. Coaches and athletes have long realized that absolute training intensity (running speed, cycling power, boat speed) tends to be reduced at altitude. Brosnan et al. (2000) specifically documented that self-selected power output during threshold and high-intensity sprint training was reduced by approximately 6 percent at a simulated altitude of 2,100 meters. Interestingly, in Brosnan's study, training heart rate, blood lactate, and perception of effort at both simulated altitude and sea level were similar (Brosnan et al. 2000). Whether the novel stress of training at altitude is detrimental because of the reduced power output or whether the novel altitude stress induces unique adaptations that can ultimately be used to enhance sea-level performance is a pertinent question. Studies have documented that living low but training high can produce a number of peripheral adaptations in skeletal muscle (e.g., mitochondrial volume, capillary density, and myoglobin concentration) that either don't occur or occur to a lesser extent with a similar amount of sea-level training (Vogt et al. 2001).

But even more important to the competitive cyclist is the observation that living low but training high can increase maximal oxygen uptake and endurance performance at sea level (Terrados et al. 1988). Terrados and colleagues monitored eight competitive road cyclists before and after three to four weeks of training. Four cyclists completed all their training at sea level whereas the other four cyclists trained in a hypobaric chamber simulating 2,300 meters. The group living low but training high had a slightly greater increase in sea-level performance than the group living and training at sea level (Terrados et al. 1988).

More recently, Vogt and coworkers (2001) performed a similar study using noncompetitive cyclists. In this study, one group lived and trained at sea level for six weeks whereas another group lived at sea level but performed high-intensity training at a simulated altitude of 3,850 meters. Although power output during high-intensity training was noticeably reduced in the altitude training group, sea-level performance during a laboratory incremental exercise test was improved to a greater extent than the group that trained at sea level. Researchers also observed that mitochondrial density in skeletal muscle increased to a greater extent in the group living low but training high (Vogt et al. 2001). Although not collected from competitive cyclists, these data support the concept that, despite a reduced power output, training at altitude can promote a unique remodeling of skeletal muscle that ultimately improves endurance performance at sea level. An additional advantage of training high but living low compared with traditional altitude training is that the cyclist is able to recover in an oxygen-enriched environment. Whether the elite cyclist is better off living low and training high or living high and training low before important sea-level competition is currently unknown.

Summary

Altitude training techniques basically fit into three major categories: living high, training high; living high, training low; and living low, training high. Research suggests that the competitive cyclist may benefit from all three approaches depending on the time of year and the specific training goals. More specifically, living and training at altitude can be beneficial as a unique early-season overload and also when preparing for competition at altitude; living high but training low is specifically used to enhance sea-level performance; and living low but training high may be useful for enhancing both sea-level and altitude performance. Studies have not specifically compared living-low, training-high and living-high, training-low strategies to determine which one is best for improving sea-level performance. Passive exposure to altitude and its effects on sea-level or altitude performance have rarely been studied, although commercially available products currently are advertised as "proven effective."

Unfortunately, much of the altitude training research is very context specific. In other words, data are difficult to extrapolate across sports or to different fitness levels. Thus, those cyclists interested in altitude training need to make informed guesses and try out protocols that have theoretical merit at times of the year when performances are not critically important. In this way the best altitude training programs can be refined on an individual basis. Although current research is attempting to determine what type of altitude approach works best for a generic training program, some coaches are trying to identify the best type of training to interface with different types of altitude exposure. Although some coaches and scientists currently believe the use of simulated altitude environments by competitive athletes is unethical, others consider this training development as a training innovation synonymous with the use of heat chambers before competition in hot environments. As with many novel training techniques, it is probably the case that altitude-induced improvements in performance occur when altitude training supplements a well-designed and appropriately administered training program.

Acknowledgments

The ideas that this chapter presents are the direct result of the many stimulating altitude training discussions with Australian national cycling coaches James Victor, Brian Stephens, Damian Grundy, Shayne Bannan, and Heiko Salzwedel. Special thanks to Drs. Allan Hahn and Chris Gore, who not only have taken the time to examine the intricacies of altitude training from a very applied perspective but also have taken the time to teach coaches and other sport scientists about their findings. Dr. Gore has provided many helpful edits and suggestions that have improved this chapter considerably. Finally, thanks to those sport scientists who have documented their experiences working with elite athletes training at altitude. These observations are important for those currently working with competitive athletes as they enable altitude training techniques to be productively refined.

Training in Extreme Conditions

Matthew Bridge
Mark Febbraio

The range of temperatures that a human can experience on Earth is vast—from the freezing conditions of the snow-covered poles to the extreme heat of the deserts. The lowest-ever recorded temperature was at the Russian Antarctic station in 1958 with an air temperature of −87.4 degrees Celsius (−125 degrees Fahrenheit), whereas temperatures in the region of 50 degrees Celsius (122 degrees Fahrenheit) often are experienced in the world's deserts. Obviously very few humans actually experience these sorts of temperatures, with the majority of the world's populations being concentrated in temperate climates. However, cyclists can experience sizable changes in temperatures during just one race. In races such as the Tour de France, the temperature is often more than 30 degrees Celsius (86 degrees Fahrenheit). When this is compared to the 5 to 10 degrees Celsius (41 to 50 degrees Fahrenheit) on top of the high mountains such as the Col d'Aubisque and the Col du Galibier, it is easy to see why cyclists must be able to cope with markedly different temperatures.

This chapter examines how the body copes with large temperature variations and assesses the consequences of any failure to adapt to the climate. Finally, it discusses how we can help our body maintain thermal equilibrium while we exercise in different conditions.

Performing at Different Environmental Temperatures

Changes in the environment can have profound effects on performance. Studies have shown that even relatively small changes in temperature can affect performance. A study by Galloway and Maughan (1997) looked at exercise capacity (time to volitional fatigue) at four different environmental temperatures: 4, 11, 21, and 31 degrees Celsius (39, 52, 70, and 88 degrees Fahrenheit, respectively). The authors found that exercise capacity was greatest at 11 degrees Celsius (94 ± 16 vs. 81 ± 27 vs. 81 ± 16 vs. 51.6 ± 11 minutes, respectively). In a similar study (Parkin et al. 1999), exercise capacity was greater at 3 degrees Celsius than at 20 and 40 degrees Celsius (68 and 104 degrees Fahrenheit, respectively; 85 ± 8 vs. 60 ± 11 vs. 30 ± 3 minutes, respectively). In a recent study looking at the effects of heat and humidity on the Australian National Road Cycling Squad, performance during a 30-minute time trial was reduced at 32 degrees Celsius (90 degrees Fahrenheit) compared to 23 degrees Celsius (73 degrees Fahrenheit) (Tatterson et al. 2000). Average power output throughout the trial at 32 degrees Celsius (323 ± 8 watts) was reduced by 6.5 percent from the values in the 23 degrees Celsius (345 ± 9 watts) trial, whereas heart rate and perceived exertion were increased. It is not entirely clear which temperature is optimal for prolonged cycling exercise. It is clear, however, that endurance performance is dramatically reduced in hot conditions. Note, though, that in all these trials the investigators did not allow for the effects of the wind chill experienced while cycling outdoors and they therefore can give us only a guide to temperature's effects on cycling. The following sections discuss the effects of temperature on exercise performance in more detail.

Internal and External Heat

The human body is working constantly to maintain various balances, or equilibriums, within its internal systems. One of the most important of these is the maintenance of body temperature. The body must react to different temperature stresses placed on it by both internal and external factors to maintain a core body temperature of about 37 degrees Celsius (98.6 degrees Fahrenheit). The body is placed at risk when core temperature either exceeds or falls below this level. A rise of just a few degrees may result in denaturation of proteins within the body, whereas a fall in temperature results in symptoms of hypothermia. Both of these conditions eventually will result in death.

The human body is approximately 20 percent efficient when cycling (maximum is about 25 percent; see chapter 11). This means that for all the energy we use while cycling, only about 20 percent of it is used for propelling the bike forward. Most of the other 80 percent is "wasted" through heat production. Let us consider an example:

When climbing a mountain, a professional cyclist may produce more than 400 watts of power for an hour or more. If that cyclist is 20 percent efficient, a total of 2,000 watts has to be generated, of which 1,600 watts are wasted as heat.

If we consider this in terms of energy expenditure over one hour,

1 watt = 1 joule per second (0.24 calories per second)

400 watts (useful) + 1,600 watts (waste) = 2,000 watts (total)

1,600 watts of heat production for one hour equals 1,600 joules per second × 3,600 seconds = 5,760 kilojoules (1,371 kilocalories)

Thus, 5,760 kilojoules (1,371 kilocalories) are "wasted," and as we have discussed, the majority of this waste is in the form of heat production. In addition to producing internal heat, the rider can gain heat from the environment.

Environmental Heat and Cooling

Cycling is an outdoor sport, and therefore a rider may gain additional heat from the environment in the form of

- solar radiation directly from the sun or reflected off the surface of the road,
- sky thermal radiation (the heat radiation of the air), or
- ground thermal radiation (the heat radiation of the ground).

There are various measures of the environmental heat stress; one widely used measure is the Wet-Bulb Globe Temperature index. This is a single temperature that takes into account air temperature, humidity, radiated heat, and wind velocity and thus provides an indication of the impact of the environment on exercising athletes.

© David Brownell

Cyclists can be affected by heat through radiation directly from the sun or reflected off the road.

Although it is possible to gain heat from the environment, it is also possible to lose heat to the environment, as any cyclist will know when riding downhill fast after being soaked by a rainstorm. Most of this heat loss is due to the air speeding past the rider and its cooling effect. As we will see later, the movement of air past a rider is very important in dissipating heat from the body. However, when riders are working hard climbing a mountain and producing a lot of heat, speeds are low and cooling in this way is less effective.

Temperature Regulation

A change in body temperature is sensed by temperature-sensitive nerves around the body that send information about these changes back to the brain as well as local temperature regulatory systems. The main controller of temperature regulation is located in an area of the brain, the hypothalamus. The hypothalamus is our temperature control center, and information from various sources around the body is integrated here. Appropriate messages are sent out to the body to maintain temperature equilibrium via changes in the cardiovascular system and heat loss and retention mechanisms.

Losing Body Heat

In our earlier example, if the cyclist kept climbing at that rate (400 watts) for some time, his body temperature soon would increase to dangerous levels, especially if it was a warm summer day. To ensure that the cyclist does not overheat, the body's temperature control systems respond by sending neural signals to the cardiovascular system to vasodilate the blood vessels in the skin and to redirect blood flow from the core to the skin. As a result, more warm blood is directed to the skin where there are several mechanisms through which the heat can be dissipated to the environment. These mechanisms (conduction, convection, radiation, and evaporation) coupled with the cardiovascular changes discussed earlier are the body's primary way to respond to overheating. This section looks at each of these in turn and considers their effectiveness in cycling.

- **Conduction** Conduction is the heat loss through the direct transfer of heat from one molecule of a solid, liquid, or gas to another. The rate of heat loss depends on the temperature gradient between the skin and the surrounding environment. At environmental temperatures that are above skin temperature, no heat loss is possible through conduction. In most situations, conduction accounts for less than 2 percent of total body heat loss, and heat even can be gained if the environmental temperature is sufficiently high.
- **Convection** Convection is heat exchange between a solid medium and one that moves (i.e., air movement while cycling); this movement is known as a convective current. During cycling, heat loss through this mechanism depends on how fast the warm air next to the body is removed and replaced by cooler air.
- **Radiation** Radiation is the transmission of energy waves that are emitted by one system and absorbed by another. We are usually warmer than the environment, and as a result, heat is normally transferred from our body to the environment. If the environmental temperature is higher than that of the body, this cannot occur.

• **Evaporation** Heat dissipation also can occur through the evaporation of fluid, which during exercise means sweat or water on the skin. The amount of sweat secretion depends on the density of sweat glands in the skin and the amount of sweat secreted per gland. The human body has roughly 2 to 4 million sweat glands, of which the most active are concentrated on the chest and back with lower sweating rates on the legs and arms.

Evaporation occurs when a liquid changes to a gas. As the liquid (sweat) is evaporated off the skin, the skin's surface is cooled. You can demonstrate this effect by placing a small amount of a strong alcoholic spirit on the skin on a warm day; the skin instantly feels cold because the alcohol evaporates very quickly compared to water.

High environmental temperatures and prolonged strenuous exercise may result in sweat rates as high as 3.0 liters per hour in trained athletes. Indeed, the highest ever reported sweat rate for an athlete was 3.7 liters per hour during the marathon at the 1984 Summer Olympic Games.

Heat loss through sweat evaporation is influenced by the amount of moisture in the air (relative humidity). Air that is hot and dry readily receives evaporated sweat because there is little moisture in the air already. On the other hand, air that is hot and wet is already saturated with water; therefore, it is very difficult to add any more through the evaporation of sweat. Relative humidity provides a measurement of the amount of water in the air relative to completely saturated air (100 percent relative humidity). As the relative humidity climbs over 50 to 70 percent, evaporation is increasingly more difficult and more body heat is stored instead of dissipated. Therefore, in a very humid environment the body relies more and more on nonevaporative dry heat loss mechanisms (i.e., convection and radiation).

Conserving Body Heat

In response to the cold the body will try to conserve heat by reducing heat loss, increasing heat production, and mobilizing metabolic fuels. This section discusses these factors in more detail.

• **Reducing Heat Loss** The first response to cold is the constriction of peripheral skin blood vessels, which keeps the warm blood in the core of the body and preserves the heat that would otherwise be lost to the environment. The effectiveness of skin vasoconstriction in maintaining body temperature is influenced by the amount of fat under the skin (subcutaneous) in the body. A larger amount of subcutaneous fat results in better conservation of heat, as fat is an excellent insulating material.

• **Producing Heat** The next phase of conserving body heat is shivering. Heat production by shivering is stimulated when heat loss causes skin temperature to fall rapidly to a "shivering threshold." These contractions produce very little work and therefore result in most of the energy used being converted to heat.

• **Mobilizing Fuels** The final phase of heat conservation is the release of the hormones adrenaline and noradrenaline into the bloodstream. These hormones in turn stimulate the release of fuels into the bloodstream. In addition, the overall metabolic rate is increased by the release of thyroid hormone from the thyroid gland.

Performing in Cold Environments

Cold conditions have a detrimental effect on both high-intensity and endurance exercise performance. In this section we discuss these effects and describe the measures that can be taken to counteract them.

High-Intensity Exercise

High-intensity exercise is the ability of the muscles to make repeated near-maximal contractions. When a slight cooling of muscle occurs there are benefits to muscular endurance (Crowley et al. 1991), though maximal power output is reduced; therefore, a lower maximal power output is achieved but it can be sustained for longer. This is likely to be the result of a decreased metabolic rate in the muscle reducing the drain on anaerobic energy systems. If muscle temperature continues to drop and falls below 27 degrees Celsius (81 degrees Fahrenheit), muscular endurance has been found to decrease (Haymes and Wells 1986). This is likely to be due to a reduction in muscle-shortening velocity, in nerve conduction, and possibly in muscle-fiber activation. Both maximal muscle strength and maximal power have been shown to be reduced at low muscle temperatures (Crowley et al. 1991). It is likely that the fall in temperature increases the time taken for muscle fibers to reach maximum tension; in addition to this, there is a slowing of chemical reactions within the muscle and possible increases in muscle viscosity.

Aerobic Endurance and Capacity

As mentioned earlier, cold environmental temperatures can reduce exercise capacity. Interestingly, this is not due to a fall in core temperature. There may, therefore, be another reason that exercise capacity is reduced. In a study mentioned earlier, Galloway and Maughan (1997) examined the oxygen uptake ($\dot{V}O_2$) and minute ventilation (V_E) of cycling at different temperatures. $\dot{V}O_2$ and V_E increased the most during exercise at 4 degrees Celsius. Other studies also have found ventilation to be increased in the cold. These increases in $\dot{V}O_2$ and V_E are most likely due to increased muscle tone before shivering starts or are due to shivering itself. The increased ventilation indicates that there may be an increased demand on the respiratory system during exercise in the cold; this may result in cold-induced asthma, especially in individuals already suffering from asthma.

$\dot{V}O_2$max and maximal heart rate are reduced at cold temperatures. The reduction in $\dot{V}O_2$max is caused by a fall in the amount of oxygen delivered to the exercising muscles. This fall occurs because of two factors, a fall in maximum heart rate and a tighter binding of oxygen to hemoglobin in the blood. A lower maximum heart rate will result in a reduced maximal cardiac output. The cardiac output determines how much blood is delivered to the working muscles during exercise, so a fall in cardiac output results in less blood and therefore less oxygen being delivered to the muscles and lower maximum work rates being attainable. Additionally, when blood temperature falls below 37 degrees Celsius (98.6 degrees Fahrenheit), less oxygen is delivered to the muscles from the blood as hemoglobin binds oxygen molecules more tightly.

During exercise in the cold, when core temperature falls there is an increased reliance on anaerobic metabolism, resulting in increased blood and muscle lactate levels (Rennie et al. 1980). This may occur as a result of the reduced oxygen delivery to muscles. Shivering will put additional strain on aerobic metabolism and cause additional rises in blood lactate levels. Under these conditions the source of the energy to support shivering is primarily from muscle glycogen stores and blood glucose (Vallerand and Jacobs 1992). During races and training an athlete is particularly dependent on these sources; therefore, any additional drain on these energy reserves leaves him susceptible to premature fatigue.

Hypothermia

Two of the main factors in the lowering of body temperature during exercise are the unanticipated wetting of clothing and prolonged exposure to the cold. Hypothermia is a particular problem for cyclists for a number of reasons. First, the rate of energy production will fall as fatigue sets in, resulting in a fall in the body's heat production. This can occur while the clothing is wet through sweat or rain. With additional factors such as long downhills (causing large heat losses due to windchill), it is easy to see how dangerous temperature drops can occur. Following are symptoms of hypothermia:

- Uncontrollable shivering
- Grayish skin color
- Slow, slurred speech
- Memory lapses
- Irritability
- Loss of finger mobility
- Stumbling or staggering
- Drowsiness and wanting to sleep
- Exhaustion
- Inability to move after rest

The initial goal in the treatment of hypothermia is to increase core body temperature to a normal level. The easiest way to do this outside of a hospital is through warming the body's surface. The following treatments have been recommended as immediate measures:

- Inhaling warm, dry air
- Drying the cyclist and keeping him or her out of the wind
- Insulating the cyclist
- Insulating hot water bottles and placing them in the underarm and groin areas
- Huddling with the cyclist to ensure close body-to-body contact
- Using radiant heat
- Drinking fluids, but only if the cyclist is alert and able to swallow

Protection Through Clothing Choice

The most common method to combat the cold is to wear more clothing. If this clothing is bulky, however, it will result in increased work being done to overcome any restrictions that the clothing may impose on movement. Additionally for the cyclist, increased clothing may increase drag on the bike, making riding less aerodynamic. Sweating still occurs during exercise in the cold, and the body temperature for the onset of sweating in the cold is lower than in exercise in a thermoneutral environment. This sweating will lead to increased heat loss at a time when the body wants to conserve heat. There is also the possibility that the sweat may freeze on any clothing being worn or lead to an increased windchill. Either of these events could result in a drastic drop in body temperature possibly leading to hypothermia.

Perhaps the most valuable source of information on exposure to a cold environment is a windchill chart. This chart shows the effective temperature once any wind is taken into account. This is particularly important for cyclists, who are effectively creating a wind around themselves. When looking at a windchill cart, remember that clothing will affect the equivalent temperatures shown in the chart.

Different amounts of clothing are required to maintain body temperature at different work rates. A standard measurement unit, the "clo," is defined as the clothing insulation necessary to maintain the comfort of a seated adult in a room at 21 degrees Celsius (70 degrees Fahrenheit), 50 percent relative humidity, and an airspeed of 6 meters per minute.

To avoid becoming chilled or overheated and sweating too much, cyclists should wear multiple layers of garments that are light and insulating. It is also necessary that these garments be "breathable" (i.e., they allow the removal of excess moisture away from the skin). Polypropylene fabrics that wick moisture away from the skin are more effective in this respect than cotton or wool that retains moisture. An outer layer that is waterproof and windproof is important—much of the effect of a cold wind can be reduced with a good outer jacket. Again, breathable fabrics such as Goretex or Sympatex are best; these allow sweat to escape and prevent chilling from wet clothes. On a cold day it is always better to be able to take layers off than to not have enough clothing. You should also pay attention to clothing on the cessation of exercise, especially if clothing is wet with sweat, as there is a risk of rapid cooling.

Wet feet greatly increase the risk of cold injury; therefore, a good pair of waterproof and windproof overshoes is essential in cold conditions. The same can be said of gloves because they are the control contact point on the bike and any reduction in dexterity of the fingers will adversely affect control performance.

Hydration

Hydration is also important in the cold because dehydration will lead to increased fatigue, and sweating and respiratory water losses still occur in cold conditions. Therefore, it is important to maintain your fluid intake during rides in the cold. Fluids stored in insulated water bottles are best as they will be more tempting to the chilled rider; if this is not possible, filling your bottles three-quarters full with warm or hot water at the beginning of a ride will help. Maintaining a source of carbohydrate is also important, because any shivering experienced will deplete carbohydrate energy stores.

Warm-Up

Raising the temperature of the legs and core before exposure to cold will result in a longer period before temperature falls to performance-limiting levels. Scientists have investigated the effects of different warm-up strategies before exercise in a cold environment (10 degrees Celsius, 50 degrees Fahrenheit) (Takahashi et al. 1992). These studies showed that the optimal preparation was 30 minutes at 50 percent $\dot{V}O_2max$. It therefore seems that a prolonged moderate-intensity warm-up is best on a cold day.

Performing in Hot Environments

As mentioned earlier, rises in body temperature activate the heat loss mechanisms of the body and warm blood is moved away from the central organs and to the periphery to enable heat to be lost through the skin. The brain regulates the redistribution of blood flow, optimizing blood flow to the skin as well as to the exercising muscles to match oxygen delivery with consumption. To do this, heart rate must increase to cope with this change in cardiac output. This heart rate increase is compounded by dehydration and a loss of plasma volume, which can lead to heat illnesses.

Performance Limitations in the Heat

Many scientific studies have shown a premature fatigue or reduction in performance in the heat—whether this is a reduced time-to-fatigue or an increased time to complete a time trial. Exercise in the heat may result in increased core temperature, dehydration, and heat illness.

Hyperthermia

Hyperthermia is an increase in body temperature above normal values. Several studies have suggested that the overall limiting factor to exercise capacity in the heat is core temperature (Nielsen et al. 1997). This is supported by studies that have shown that although there is an increased rate of carbohydrate oxidation in the heat at the point of fatigue, there is a higher muscle glycogen concentration than at cooler temperatures (Galloway and Maughan 1997; Parkin et al. 1999). It seems, therefore, that when the body reaches a certain temperature—around 39.5 degrees Celsius (103 degrees Fahrenheit) for most people—the motivational drive to exercise is so reduced that we stop. A study by Nielsen and colleagues supports this notion (Nielsen et al. 1993). These authors had subjects exercise to exhaustion in a hot environment for 10 consecutive days. Although exercise to exhaustion increased from approximately 40 minutes on day 1 to 70 minutes on day 10, body core temperature at fatigue was identical each day—indicating an upper limit to core temperature that is sensed by the body. This hypothesis also has been supported by studies that have manipulated core body temperature before exercise and seen changes in times to fatigue (Gonzalez-Alonso et al. 1999).

There are three ways in which hyperthermia reduces exercise performance:

1. There is an increased perception of fatigue that may be related to either increased cardiovascular strain and heart rate or increases in body temperature, or possibly both.
2. Endurance exercise capacity (time-to-fatigue) is reduced. There is, however, very little change in maximal strength and power (Sargeant 1987).

3. Metabolism is shifted from aerobic mechanisms toward anaerobic, resulting in an increased rate of depletion of muscle and liver glycogen stores and blood glucose levels (Sawka and Wenger 1988). This is of primary importance in prolonged endurance events such as cycling that rely on these stores.

Dehydration

One of the body's primary defense mechanisms to increases in body temperature is sweating, as mentioned earlier in this chapter. Sweat rates vary from person to person but typical levels in trained athletes are around 2 to 2.5 liters per hour during intense exercise. If we consider that the maximum rate of emptying fluids from the stomach is 0.8 to 1.2 liters per hour, it is easy to see that there will be a net fluid imbalance resulting in lost body weight and blood volume. This is not a good situation for an athlete to be in because only a small loss in body weight, 1 to 2 percent, has been shown to have dramatic effects on endurance and $\dot{V}O_2$max exercise performance (Gonzalez-Alonso 1998). Maximal strength is not so drastically affected below body weight losses of 5 percent, but short-term, repeated contractions that last 30 seconds or more are greatly affected with body weight losses of 6 percent (Horswill 1991). This is probably the result of reduced muscle blood flow, waste removal, and heat dissipation. Hypohydration, chronic dehydration over four or more hours, has great effects on endurance and aerobic capacity even in cool and mild environments. Chapter 13 discusses, in greater detail, dehydration and strategies to prevent it.

Heat Illnesses

Athletes run the risk of developing heat illness if they do not prepare adequately before exercise in the heat and use correct strategies during exercise. Table 4.1 gives the various heat illnesses with their most common symptoms, treatment, and possible complications.

Combating Hyperthermia and Dehydration

Although cyclists cannot alter the conditions in which they have to ride, there are several strategies to combat the heat and delay hyperthermia and dehydration. These strategies include heat acclimation or acclimatization, fluid replacement, precooling, and the choice of clothing. This section discusses these in more detail.

Heat Acclimation/Acclimatization

Heat acclimation or acclimatization is the most important preventive measure before exercise in a hot environment. It is a process in which an athlete is exposed gradually to exercise heat stress on several days before competition in the heat. The athlete may carry this out either in an artificial environment such as a sauna or heat chamber in an exercise physiology laboratory (acclimation) or by moving to the hot environment several days before competition (acclimatization). This exposure stimulates adaptive responses to the heat that improve heat tolerance and exercise performance. These adaptations include the following:

- Lowering resting body temperature
- Reduced perceived exertion
- Reduced heart rate during exercise
- Reductions in perceived effort

TABLE 4.1 Heat Illnesses

Illness	Symptoms	Treatment	Complications
Heat exhaustion: This is the most common form of heat illness. It occurs when intensity and duration of exercise are great or when a large dehydration exists. The cardiovascular system cannot meet the demand of supplying both the muscles and skin with blood. Acclimatization reduces risk.	High rectal temperature greater than 39 degrees Celsius (102 degrees Fahrenheit) Profuse sweating Impaired mental function	Rest and cooling Oral fluid replacement Allow 24 to 48 hours for recovery	No serious complications unless hyperthermia is prolonged
Exertional heatstroke: This is a life-threatening condition. It is caused by thermoregulatory overload or failure, with core temperatures in excess of 40 degrees Celsius (104 degrees Fahrenheit).	Vomiting, diarrhea Coma, convulsions Impaired mental function Cessation of sweating Onset may be rapid in people exercising Life-threatening condition	Hospitalization Cold water immersion	Mortality rate of 10 to 80 percent dependent upon the duration and intensity of the hyperthermia and the speed and effectiveness of the cooling
Heat cramps: This form of heat illness is mostly seen in unacclimatized individuals. It results from a whole-body salt deficiency.	Cramping in the abdominal and large muscles of the extremities Cramp is very localized and may move around the muscle (different from exertional cramps)	Oral rehydration .1 percent saline solution—about 1/3 teaspoon table salt in 1 liter water	No lasting complications
Heat syncope: Brief fainting spell that occurs during exercise in the heat before large increases in body core temperature	Pale skin Weakness Vertigo Nausea Tunnel vision	Lay the sufferer in the shade with legs elevated above head. Replace fluid and salt losses and avoid sudden or prolonged standing.	

- Increases in blood plasma volume
- Increased sweating rates (in some individuals)
- Decreased salt losses in sweat

These adaptations result in (a) improved heat transfer from the body core to the periphery and the loss of this heat to the environment, and (b) reduced cardiovascular strain and the improved ability to cope with dehydration and reduced blood volume.

Individuals adapt to this heat stress at different rates. Fitter athletes tend to adapt quicker and may reach a fully adapted state after only 5 days of heat exposure, whereas other athletes may take up to 14 days of heat exposure to reach a fully adapted state. Following are some recommendations on heat exposure with a view to adapting to exercise in the heat:

- The aim of the heat-exercise exposure should be to attain a high skin and core body temperature without putting the athlete at risk. Ideally, heat-exercise exposure will last 90 to 100 minutes in an environment matched to that of competition, at an exercise intensity at or around 50 percent $\dot{V}O_2max$. The buildup to this duration and intensity should be gradual. An ambient temperature of 45 degrees Celsius (113 degrees Fahrenheit) is most commonly used in physiological research with the relative humidity adjusted to that of the competition environment.
- Exercise should be with a partner or supervised during the heat acclimation to ensure safety.
- Monitoring rectal temperature during or immediately after training is a good guide to how hard you can push yourself and also helps to maintain athlete safety. Your rectal temperature should remain below 39 degrees Celsius as a safety guide.
- Exercise heat exposure does not have to be continuous and repeated every day. It has been found that heat exposure every third day for 30 days bestows the same benefits as 10 days of back-to-back heat exposure.
- Acclimating in a hot and dry environment does not adequately prepare you for exercise in a hot and wet environment.

Fluid Replacement

The majority of fluid losses at rest in a temperate environment are through urine production, but respiratory water loss and diffusion of water through the skin also contribute to a loss of about 2.5 liters per day. When you live and exercise in a hot environment, these fluid losses may increase to as much as 10 to 12 liters per day. It is important for athletes living in such environments to drink enough fluids to match this loss. Chapter 13 gives a full explanation of the importance of hydration.

Precooling

Several studies have found that precooling the body before exercise in the heat improves endurance capacity and performance (Gonzalez-Alonso et al. 1999; Kay et al. 1999). Gonzalez-Alonso and colleagues (1999) have shown increases in endurance capacity in the range of 11 to 23 minutes. One area in which the use of a cooling jacket could be of benefit is during warm-up before a time trial. Wearing a cooling jacket packed with ice, an athlete is able to increase muscle temperature and fully optimize the body for the time trial while not producing a significant core body hyperthermia that would be detrimental to the subsequent performance. This is all the more significant when we consider that professional cyclists often warm up for an hour or more before time trials and that this warm-up is the same in hot environments.

There are also several studies that report beneficial effects of head cooling on exercise capacity and perceived exertion in hot environments (Marvin et al. 1998).

On a hot day, a marathon runner cools his head by pouring a cup of water over his head rather than into his mouth. There is no doubt that this relieves the runner.

Choice of Clothing

When thinking about exercising in the heat, you should pay attention to your choice of clothing. It not only has to help you keep cool but also should offer some protection from the sun. In this respect, loose-fitting clothing would be most appropriate, though this is obviously detrimental to drag and therefore not suitable to the cycling environment. Therefore, we must pay attention to the fabrics from which the clothing is constructed. The fabric should be porous to allow skin cooling via evaporation of sweat, radiation, and convection.

Helmet choice is another important area. Up to 50 percent of heat loss is through the head, which has lots of small blood vessels close to the skin allowing good heat transfer. Therefore, a helmet with lots of ventilation is the best choice. The best-ventilated helmets now cool the head to the same degree as if no helmet were worn (Ellis 2001). In choosing a helmet, you should pay attention to the number of vents at the front of the helmet, because most air enters helmets through these vents and under the rim. When you are climbing at slower speeds, very little air will enter the helmet, and here it is important to have several vents to allow evaporative cooling of the head (Ellis 2001). The obvious problem that arises in choosing a well-ventilated helmet is during time trials, when the aerodynamic advantages of unvented helmets are important to the overall performance but they do not allow cooling of the head and the subsequent improvements in heat loss. This is an area that has not been fully investigated yet, and perhaps there is the potential for some form of local cooling within the helmet during the time trial.

Summary

Cycling performance is reduced in cold and hot environments, though full study of cycling in the cold has not yet been carried out. In the cold, there are reductions in contraction speed and power production, although there might be slight benefits through a reduced usage of carbohydrate stores. Special attention should be paid to choosing the correct clothing for the conditions, be it waterproof, windproof, or both. It is wise to have a long duration of warm-up of at least 30 minutes before competition to adequately prepare the body.

Exercise capacity and performance in the heat are clearly reduced from levels in cooler conditions. It is important to maintain hydration and to keep the body cool. The best preparation before competing in the heat is to acclimatize by training for 10 to 14 days in the expected competition climate before competing. There are benefits to precooling the body before exercise in the heat, especially when a prolonged warm-up is used, and every effort should be made to keep the body cool during competition through suitable choices of helmet and clothing.

part II

Performance Assessment

In modern cycling there is an increased need to monitor and measure performances. This is certainly an area that has developed enormously in the past decade. We now have speedometers, heart rate monitors, and even power-measuring devices. This will help athletes to spend their often limited time as efficiently as possible, but it also may prevent them from doing too much, too fast. In addition, these tools will provide feedback that can be used for later analysis.

Cyclists can use such performance assessments as guidance in training and competition, and more and more of them are using these tools. However, athletes, coaches, and even sport scientists often struggle with questions about how to use these tools: How do I use a heart rate monitor? Should I train at a certain heart rate? Should I train in a certain heart rate zone, and if so, how do I determine these heart rate zones? How do I use power in my training? Should I train at a certain power output? How do I know if I am training enough? How do I know if I am training too much or too intensely?

Part II offers answers to these questions. It discusses the advantages as well as the disadvantages of the available tools and formulates guidelines.

We also can assess performance in standardized conditions so that it is not dependent on weather conditions, race tactics, or other external factors. This can give valuable information about someone's condition, it can help to prevent overtraining, and it can be important in defining training goals. For instance, chapter 7 discusses how these laboratory tests can help you determine your strengths and weaknesses. Training may aim at improving the strengths even further or reducing the weaknesses. Unfortunately, these laboratories may not be accessible for everyone, and therefore chapter 8 discusses alternatives—tests that can be performed in field conditions, requiring no fancy equipment or expensive techniques.

Heart Rate Monitors

Juul Achten

Heart rate monitors have become a common training tool in endurance sports in recent years. Most cyclists have at least tried heart rate monitors and many use them consistently to monitor their training and to help them train at the planned exercise intensity. Heart rate monitors have developed rapidly from large instruments suitable only for laboratory use around 1900 to the size of a watch in recent years. There have also been developments in the accuracy of the measurement, the storage capacity of the heart rate monitors has increased, and new functions have been added. There are various ways in which heart rate monitors can be used, and this chapter discusses the possible applications of the heart rate monitor.

In addition to the applications mentioned here, heart rate monitoring also has various limitations and it is important to know the limitations if you want to interpret the collected information appropriately. The relationship between heart rate and other physiological parameters often is determined in an exercise laboratory. Some factors have been identified that can potentially influence this relationship. This chapter discusses the most important factors.

Applications of Heart Rate Monitor

Heart rate monitors often are used to control and monitor the intensity of training sessions. Especially in cycling in which other indicators of intensity, such as speed, are not very accurate, heart rate can be useful in monitoring the exercise intensity. Heart rate measurements may become more powerful and accurate indicators of exercise intensity when related to other physiological parameters. Besides monitoring the intensity of training sessions, more recently heart rate monitors are being used to determine the intensity of cycling races. This information can be useful for cycling coaches and trainers and for researchers who want to learn more about the physiological demands of cycling. A less frequently used application of heart rate monitors, which has received more attention recently, is for the detection of early markers of overtraining.

Numerous cyclists already use a heart rate monitor and others are planning to use this tool. However, many questions exist among cyclists about how to use the heart rate data. This section discusses the most important applications of the heart rate monitor for cyclists in training and overtraining.

Monitoring Exercise Intensity

The training process often is broken down into three important components: frequency, duration, and intensity. Frequency and duration are relatively easy to monitor; however, it is much more difficult to accurately measure the intensity of a training session. Exercise intensity can be defined as the amount of energy expended every minute to perform a certain task. The energy needed for muscle contraction is derived from the breakdown of adenosine triphosphate (ATP). Therefore, the best way to measure energy expenditure is to determine how much ATP is broken down. Unfortunately, it is very difficult to measure how much ATP is converted into mechanical energy. Another way to measure energy expenditure is to measure oxygen consumption. Although this is easily done in a laboratory using indirect calorimetry, it is difficult to measure it when cycling on the road or track. We therefore need a more indirect measure to determine exercise intensity.

Some of the most obvious measures of exercise intensity in cycling are not very accurate (Jeukendrup and van Diemen 1998) (see chapter 6). Some riders prefer to determine the intensity by feeling. Although this may not always be accurate, experienced riders are often very good at predicting the intensity of their training. However, for most riders it is preferable to get a more objective measure of exercise intensity. Two practical measures of exercise intensity in a nonlaboratory situation are power output and heart rate. Chapter 6 discusses the newest developments in the measurement of power output, whereas this chapter focuses on using heart rate as an indicator of exercise intensity.

Although measuring heart rate is easy with the currently available tools, the interpretation of this heart rate is more difficult. Imagine two cyclists riding next to each other on a flat road. They are both riding at a heart rate of 140 beats per minute. While one of them is cycling with great ease, the other one may be struggling to keep up. This indicates that there is a lot of individual variation in heart-rate responses in cyclists. Therefore, heart rate is often expressed as a percentage of maximum heart rate or heart rate reserve (which is maximal heart rate minus resting heart rate). But even with these methods, there is considerable individual variation. To determine the "individual" intensity of an exercise bout, heart rate can be related to other parameters, such as blood lactate concentrations, measured in the same cyclist during exercise.

A frequently-used method to divide a training load into different intensity categories is by associating it with lactate production. During a graded exercise test to exhaustion, in which exercise is started at a low workload that is gradually increased during the test, heart rate and blood lactate accumulation can be measured simultaneously.

Once lactic acid accumulation has been related to heart rate, the question now is, what is the best way to use this information? It has been shown that below a certain intensity, exercise can be sustained for a prolonged period with no accumulation of lactic acid in the blood and little perception of effort. Above this intensity, lactic acid begins to build up and the exercise feels much more difficult. If this critical intensity is high, the athlete will be able to exercise at a high power output for a long time, which will benefit his performance. There are numerous methods to determine this critical intensity (or "lactate threshold"). Some researchers have used set values, such as 2 and 4 millimoles (mmol) of lactate per liter of blood. Although the exercise intensity at 2 mmol per liter of lactate or 4 mmol per liter of lactate can be determined relatively objectively, it does not take into account individual variation. Others have therefore attempted to develop a more individual approach. One of these approaches is to draw a baseline through and determine the intensity where lactate is 1 mmol per liter above this baseline. Another method is the so-called Dmax method. The intensity is marked that has the maximum distance (D) from the lactate curve to a line connecting the first and last point of the graph. The various available methods can give very different results, even though they are all generally referred to as *lactate thresholds.* So far, none of the methods has been identified as the gold standard, and different laboratories and coaches are using different methods.

As mentioned earlier, a high lactate threshold is associated with the ability to exercise for a long period at a high intensity. In addition, it has been shown that training increases the intensity at which lactate starts to accumulate. Two commonly observed changes in the lactate curve after training are (1) lower lactate levels at baseline, and (2) the accumulation of lactate commencing at a higher workload. Once these points on the lactate curve have been determined, they can be linked to heart rate.

In summary, for the determination and monitoring of the intensity of an exercise bout, a heart rate monitor can be a useful tool. Heart rate monitoring can be more individualized and more accurate when it is related to other parameters such as oxygen uptake or blood lactate concentration, which can be determined in a laboratory.

Evaluating Races

Many athletes also use heart rate monitors to monitor exercise intensity during races. Scientists have used these data to study the intensity of racing in cyclists with different levels of ability. Palmer et al. (1994) studied seven riders during a four-stage cycle race. The riders completed two road races of 105 and 110 kilometers, a 16-kilometer time trial, and a short hill climb. Both in the hill climb and time trial, the cyclists spent more than 95 percent of the racing time at heart rates above 80 percent of their maximal heart rate (HRmax). During the two road races, heart rate was lower but still more than 80 percent of the racing time (more than two hours) was spent at heart rates greater than 70 percent HRmax.

Lucia et al. (1999) investigated the heart-rate responses during different stages of the Tour de France. During the flat stages, 85 percent of racing times were spent at heart rates below 75 percent HRmax. On the contrary, during a stage with numerous mountain passes, this percentage dropped to 63 percent. During these stages, the riders had heart rates above 90 percent of their maximum during 10 percent of the time. Since these races normally last between five and seven hours, this means that these riders have near maximal heart rates for 30 to 45 minutes. Padilla et al. (2000) investigated in more detail the intensity of time trials in another study. Eighteen international-level professional road cyclists were followed during the time trials of nine different stage races from 1993 to 1995. The time trials were divided into five categories according to their distance, terrain, and racing format. It was shown that the prologue time trial elicited higher mean heart rate and mean percent HRmax than all other time-trial categories. Furthermore, during the prologue time trials, which on average were 7.3 ± 1.1 kilometers and were completed in 594 ± 99 seconds, the cyclists spent a significantly higher percentage (92 ± 7 percent) of their racing time above lactate threshold (in this study defined as 4 mmol per liter) than in any of the other time trials. However, in absolute values, the longest cycling times above lactate threshold were in the team time trial (42.2 ± 25.8 minutes).

Exercise intensity varies with the type and stage of the race as well as the level and condition of the athlete. High-level athletes exhibit relatively low average heart rates during the flat stages of a race.

Padilla and colleagues (2001) also studied some top-level athletes during mass-start stages of stage races. The average heart rate during flat, semi-mountainous, and high-mountain stages was approximately 51, 58, and 61 percent HRmax, respectively. The athletes spent 32, 58, and 93 minutes above lactate threshold (in this study defined as 4 mmol per liter) during the three different types of stages.

To summarize, there are reports of exercise intensities during races in cyclists of all levels, including professional cyclists. During races like the Tour de France, the highest heart rate is reached during time trials. Amateur cyclists spend large percentages of the total race time at intensities above 80 percent of the maximum heart rate. Professional cyclists spend less time at high heart rates, but during decisive moments in the race heart rates can be very high (near maximal) and can be sustained for relatively long periods.

Detecting and Preventing Overtraining Syndrome

Chapter 2 discusses the main causes and symptoms of overtraining and overreaching. It has become clear that overtraining can be a significant problem for many riders. Overtraining is characterized by a number of hormonal or neuronal changes, which are likely to affect heart rate. Therefore, heart rate measurements while sleeping, at rest, and during exercise have been suggested as markers to detect overtraining at an early stage. This section discusses changes in heart rate and heart rate variability at rest and during exercise that occur with overtraining.

Heart-Rate Changes

To detect changes in heart rate, a baseline measure of heart rate must be obtained when the cyclist is rested and in good shape. Regular measurements of resting and exercise heart rate hereafter will provide an immediate indication of physical condition. Endurance training has been shown to affect both resting heart rate and the heart-rate response to an exercise stimulus. Heart rate will decrease at rest and at the same absolute exercise intensity after several weeks of training.

During early stages of the overtraining syndrome, often referred to as overreaching or sympathetic overtraining, the sympathetic nervous system dominates and resting heart rate is usually elevated. Although resting heart rate (morning pulse) is often used as an indicator of early overtraining, it may not be the most sensitive indicator. Average heart rate measured during sleep seems to track the decreases in performance much more accurately with increases in training volume and more intensity (Jeukendrup et al. 1992; Stray-Gundersen et al. 1986). So, during periods when training load is increased more than normal, it is advisable to check sleeping heart rate every four to five days and compare this to sleeping heart rate when fully rested.

The responses of heart rate during exercise can be divided into changes that occur at submaximal and at maximal heart rates. In a recent study by Billat et al. (1999), it was shown that heart rate was decreased from 155 to 150 beats per minute at 14 kilometers per hour in overtrained runners. More recently, Hedelin et al. (2000a) also found significantly decreased heart rates (approximately five beats per minute lower) at five different submaximal intensities. Others found similar submaximal decreases in heart rates in their subjects after a period of intensified training. On the contrary, Urhausen et al. (1998) reported that the overtrained subjects in their study had similar submaximal heart rates compared to normal conditions.

Heart rate during maximal exercise has been shown to decrease when subjects are overtrained. In 1988, Costill et al. showed that after 10 days of intensified training, the average maximal heart rate in 12 male swimmers significantly decreased from 175 ± 3 to 169 ± 3 beats per minute. Jeukendrup et al. (1992) showed that after 14 days of intensified training, maximal heart rate of cyclists declined significantly from 175 ± 3 to 169 ± 3 beats per minute. Similar results were found in other studies.

Overall, there is a tendency for the sleeping (and resting) heart rate to be higher and heart rates during submaximal and maximal exercise to be lower in people who are overreached or overtrained. Sleeping heart rate (average heart rate during the night) seems to be a more sensitive indicator of overtraining than resting heart rate (heart rate measured upon waking). Apart from checking sleeping heart rate regularly, you should keep a training log in which you register average heart rates during a standard training ride, preferably a time trial on a standardized circuit. This makes it easy to monitor changes in your heart-rate response to exercise and changes in performance over time. Because decreases in submaximal heart rate associated with overtraining also are seen when athletes become more trained, the heart-rate responses should be interpreted with caution and they should be used in conjunction with other indicators of overtraining, as mentioned in chapter 2.

Heart Rate Variability Changes

The beat-to-beat variability of the heart (heart rate variability, or HRV) is also affected by changes in the autonomic nervous system and could potentially be used for revealing changes due to overtraining (Pichot et al. 2000; Uusitalo et al. 2000). The normal variability in heart rate is due to the combined action of the sympathetic and parasympathetic nervous systems. In a healthy person, the heart rate at any given time represents the combined effect of the parasympathetic nervous system, which slows heart rate, and the sympathetic nervous system, which accelerates it.

To determine HRV, the time between beats needs to be determined for a set period. Figure 5.1 displays an electrocardiogram (ECG) in which the QRS complex of each beat is marked. The time between two R peaks can be measured on the ECG. The more variety there is in the time between consecutive R peaks, the greater the variability. To get an indication of the variability in your heart rate, you can calculate the mean and standard deviation of the consecutive R-R intervals.

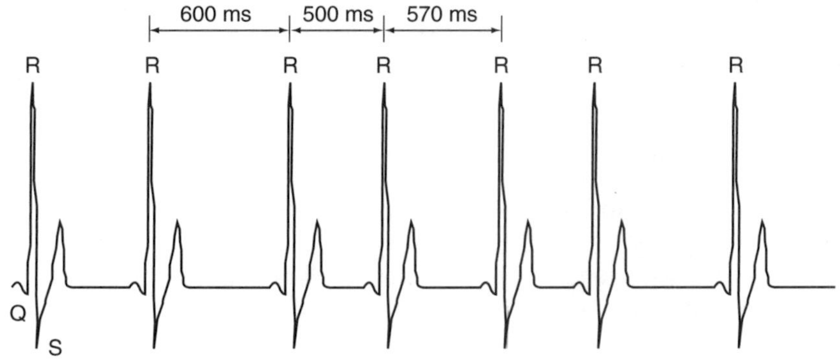

Figure 5.1 Electrocardiogram showing beat-to-beat differences.

Several studies have been performed comparing the HRV of athletes and untrained individuals (Goldsmith et al. 1997; Shin et al. 1997), and it seems that heart rate variability is positively associated with aerobic fitness. Unfortunately, there are few studies that have investigated the effects of overtraining on HRV and the results from these studies are far from conclusive (Hedelin et al. 2000a; Hedelin et al. 2000b; Uusitalo et al. 2000).

Despite this, it has been suggested that heart rate and HRV can be used to indicate whether an athlete has recovered from a previous training or race. One suggested method for measuring recovery after a training session is via an orthostatic test. For this test, you simply lie quietly for 10 minutes at the same time every day while monitoring your heart rate, which should stay constant during the 10-minute period. You then stand up and check your heart rate exactly 15 seconds after standing, and then again during the period 90 to 120 seconds after standing. A heart rate monitor works best for this, although you also could manually count your heartbeats for 15 seconds after standing up and again between 90 and 120 seconds after standing—and then multiply the number of counted beats by 4 to obtain the respective pulse rates.

In healthy individuals, the resting, 15-second, and 120-second heart rate will be remarkably constant from day to day. For example, an athlete's heart rate might be 60 beats per minute at rest but climb to 95 beats per minute 15 seconds after standing up and then drop to 80 beats per minute two minutes after standing up. Normally when a person stands up, gravity causes blood to pool in the large vessels of the legs and lower trunk and the blood pressure in the neck drops. The reduced blood pressure is detected by pressure receptors and results in stimulation on the sympathetic autonomic nervous system, causing a rise in heart rate and constriction of the blood vessels (diameter decreased).

It has been suggested that during overtraining, standing heart rates are elevated. Usually these changes are observed 90 to 120 seconds after standing up. In a study performed with Finnish cross-country skiers, the heart rates in this period increased by more than 10 beats per minute in many of the Finnish athletes who subsequently overtrained.

Both heart rate and HRV should be determined at rest and during an orthostatic test when training intensities and volumes are relatively low and the athlete is feeling rested. This allows baseline data to be collected, which can be compared to data collected during periods of hard training.

Factors Influencing Heart Rate During Cycling

As described earlier, the relationship between heart rate and other parameters (oxygen uptake and lactate) can be used to monitor exercise intensity. Often these relationships are determined in an environment in which the temperature and humidity of the ambient air are controlled. Furthermore, people will attempt to enter a test under the best possible circumstances, having had enough sleep, carbohydrates, and fluids the day(s) before. In the field, however, these factors cannot always be controlled and can influence the relationship between heart rate and oxygen uptake or lactate. This section discusses some of these factors and gives a summary of the most influential factors.

Day-to-Day Variability

Even with the best equipment available, heart-rate measurements can only be used to monitor exercise intensity when the *intra*-individual differences are small. The day-to-day variability in the heart-rate response to a certain exercise stimulus has been investigated on several occasions. From these studies it has become clear that this day-to-day variation is relatively small. Differences between two and six beats per minute are seen when subjects cycle at the same workload on separate days. It is therefore recommended to train in a heart-rate zone of 15 to 20 beats per minute and not at one set heart rate.

Cardiac Drift

After prolonged moderate-intensity exercise in a neutral or warm environment, a continuous time-dependent increase in heart rate usually is observed. After 60 minutes of exercise, the heart rate can even increase by up to 20 beats per minute compared to the beginning of exercise. This drift is caused mainly by the increase in core temperature during exercise. In this case, the increase in heart rate does not reflect an actual increase in exercise intensity. This is illustrated by the following example: When cyclists are asked in a laboratory to cycle for two hours at a steady heart rate, the only possible way for them to do this is by decreasing the work rate toward the end. Therefore, when training in a thermoneutral or hot environment, a cyclist should aim for the lower border of the training zone in the starting stages of training. As training progresses, the cyclist will reach the required heart rate because of the cardiac drift.

Temperature

Exercise tests performed in a laboratory are normally performed at an ambient temperature between 15 and 18 degrees Celsius. As soon as exercise is performed at different temperatures, the relationship between oxygen uptake and heart rate changes. Under these conditions, heart rate does not accurately reflect the intensity of exercise measured in the laboratory.

Cycling in the cold can result in an increased oxygen uptake with heart rates similar to those in normal conditions. So, during cycling in cold conditions, heart rate may underestimate the exercise intensity.

It has been shown that heart rate will increase gradually with increased core temperature (Gonzalez-Alonso et al. 2000). Core temperature increases not only with increases in ambient temperature but also when exercise in moderately hot conditions is performed for a long period. Increases between 10 and 30 beats per minute for the same work rate have been reported when cyclists exercised in hot compared to cool or thermoneutral conditions (Gonzalez-Alonso et al. 1999). As a result, heart rate is not an accurate indicator of exercise intensity in a hot environment, because it will overestimate the "real" workload. However, heart rate can be used to assess whole-body stress (Jeukendrup and van Diemen 1998). Even though the intensity of a work bout in the heat is not as high as in cool weather, the amount of stress the body is under may be increased.

Dehydration

Related to exercise in the heat are the effects of dehydration (water loss) on heart rate. The body's most important method of losing heat in a hot environment is through evaporation (see chapter 4).

The rate of water loss through perspiration can reach values of greater than 1 liter per hour during severe work. So, during hard exercise in a hot environment, dehydration will occur and plasma volume will drop. A reduced blood volume will result in an increased heart rate in order to maintain cardiac output. Dehydration alone can cause an increase in heart rate of approximately 5 percent, and when dehydration is accompanied by hyperthermia, increases of approximately 9 percent have been reported (Gonzalez-Alonso et al. 1997). As in hot conditions, heart rate is a better indicator of whole-body stress than of exercise intensity.

Position on the Bike

Recently, much attention has been paid to the importance of aerodynamics in cycling and the different ways that it can be improved (see chapter 9). One of the major changes that all cyclists are familiar with is changing body position by using aerobars. Several scientific studies have shown that both oxygen uptake and heart rate are higher during cycling in the aero position, compared with hands positioned on the brake hoods or drops (Gnehm et al. 1997; Heil et al. 1995; Sheel et al. 1996). These increases are attributed to the increased contribution of the shoulder muscles and a less efficient hip angle. Overall, however, the effects on metabolic cost are usually negligible compared with the beneficial effects of cycling in a more aerodynamic position.

The relationship between exercise intensity and heart rate as determined in a laboratory can be affected by numerous factors when an athlete is cycling in the field. Table 5.1 gives a summation of the main influential factors on heart rate for exercise in a non-laboratory-based condition, and it gives an indication of the magnitude of the influence. In addition, the table presents ways to reduce the distortion between heart rate and $\dot{V}O_2$ (energy expenditure).

TABLE 5.1 Factors Influencing Heart Rate (HR) During Cycling

Factors	Effect on HR	Difference	Remedy
Day-to-day variability	Differences between days	2-6 bpm	Training zones, not set values
Cardiac drift	Increase HR over time	5-25 bpm	Start at the low border of your training zone
Cool	Lower HR	10-30 bpm	Train at the low border of your training zone
Heat	Higher HR	10-30 bpm	Train at normal HR; use HR as indicator of whole-body stress
Dehydration	Higher HR	2-7%	Remain hydrated; use HR as indicator of whole-body stress
Position on bike	Higher HR on aerobars	2-5 bpm	–

bpm = beats per minute

Summary

Over the past few decades, heart rate monitors have become a regular part of the cyclist's outfit. This is not surprising because technology has made it possible to not only obtain your heart rate when you are cycling, but also to retrieve the information after your ride and analyze your training in more detail.

The most important application of the heart rate monitor is the determination of the intensity of the exercise. This application is mainly used during training, but it is used during races as well. Heart rate may be a better indicator of the exercise intensity when the heart rate is related to other parameters such as oxygen uptake or lactate concentration. In many laboratories you will be able to perform a test in which all these parameters are measured simultaneously. You then can use the results of the tests to relate a heart rate (zone) during a training session to, for instance, a lactate concentration.

The heart rate monitor can also be used for the early detection of overtraining. Heart rate, or more accurately, changes in heart rate, can be used as one of the markers for overtraining. Changes in resting and sleeping heart rate and decreases in maximal heart rates of up to 10 beats per minute often are seen in individuals who become overreached. Baseline measures collected during a normal training week, when the cyclist is feeling well and rested, are important. It is advised to record sleeping heart rate during one or two nights every month and resting heart rate every morning. It is then wise to repeat these measurements regularly, especially during weeks of very hard training. By keeping a training log it is easy to detect any changes due to training and possibly overtraining.

There are several factors, such as environmental temperature, that influence the relationship between heart rate and oxygen uptake or lactate. It is important to consider these factors when interpreting the heart rate data. When interpreted correctly, heart rate monitoring can be a very useful tool.

chapter 6

Power Output

Asker Jeukendrup

One of the most exciting developments in the science of cycling has been the recent introduction of devices to measure power output during cycling. As chapter 1 discusses, there are three core components of training: duration, intensity, and frequency. Of these, intensity is the most difficult component to control and monitor. Chapter 2 also mentions that, to avoid overtraining, one must monitor training and keep a record of the training load. For this purpose it is also necessary to accurately monitor the exercise intensity. Finally, monitoring exercise intensity can be helpful in evaluating races and even in developing racing strategies in some conditions. The tools to measure and monitor exercise intensity are limited. Chapter 5 discusses the advantages and disadvantages of heart-rate monitoring as a tool. In this chapter we discuss a relatively new tool to measure and monitor exercise intensity: power output.

Until recently, it was only possible to obtain power measurements in an exercise laboratory. However, recent technological developments have made it possible to measure power on the athlete's normal bike and to record power output over time. In this chapter we discuss how you can use these power-measuring devices in both training and competition. Subsequently, we present examples of power output profiles during track races and races such as the Tour de France. However, we first discuss what the term *power* means and how it can be measured.

What Is Power?

Power is the amount of energy generated per unit of time. In cycling it is the amount of energy that is transferred onto the pedals every second. This is not the same amount of energy as is generated by the body. Unfortunately, humans are only about 20 to 25 percent efficient when cycling. That means that 75 to 80 percent of all energy generated by the muscles does not result in external power on the pedals but is mostly lost as heat.

Power often is expressed in joules per second or in watts. We also can use similar units when we talk about the power of a car engine. Usually we express this power in horse power (HP), where 1 HP = 600 watts. Most cyclists can reach peaks up to 600 to 1,200 watts in a single sprint and top track sprinters can generate up to 2,300 watts in a single sprint. A normal Sunday morning ride is typically between 100 and 200 watts, although riders hardly ever average those figures. As soon as you stop pedaling, power output is zero and average power output will be reduced. Also, drafting behind one or more riders may save 25 to 40 percent of the energy needed for forward movement at a speed of 40 kilometers per hour (McCole et al. 1990). This chapter later discusses examples of drafting and the effects on power.

A measure that often is used to evaluate a cyclist's performance is maximal power output (Wmax). This usually is obtained by a graded exercise test to exhaustion. After a warm-up, the workload is increased every one to five minutes until the cyclist cannot continue. The workload during the final stage is called Wmax. Wmax is a good indicator of aerobic power and predicts 40-kilometer time-trial performance very well (Hawley and Noakes 1992). Chapter 7 discusses such stress in more detail.

How to Measure Power

In the laboratory, power can be measured by using a cycle ergometer. There are various types of cycle ergometers available; the difference among them is mainly the source of the resistance. Some are based on mechanical friction, some on electrical resistance, and some on air resistance or hydraulic fluid resistance.

With mechanically braked cycle ergometers, a belt encompassing a flywheel is tightened or loosened to adjust the resistance against which you pedal. The faster you pedal, the greater the power output. If a constant power output is required, it is important to maintain a constant cadence. With electrical or electromagnetically braked devices, resistance is provided by an electrical conductor that moves through a magnetic field. The strength of the magnetic field determines the resistance. An advantage of this type of ergometer is that it can be controlled so that the resistance is constant regardless of cadence. Air-braked cycle ergometers are often used as training devices and power output is cadence dependent.

The recent availability of a reliable and valid bicycle crank dynamometer (SRM, Schoberer Rad Messtechnik, Weldorf, Germany) has made it possible to accurately determine power output during a variety of track and road cycling events (Broker et al. 1999; Jeukendrup and van Diemen 1998; Martin et al. 1998). Strain gauge strips are attached to the cranks, and they measure the stretch of this metal as force is applied to the pedals throughout the pedal stroke. These stretch recordings then are converted to power measurements, proportional to the pedaling force. Power then is measured from the sum of tangential forces on the pedals and of the angular velocity (speed of rotation). Martin et al. (1998) attached the SRM to a mechanically braked cycle ergometer (Monark 818) to calibrate the SRM system. The small differences between the Monark and the SRM system were attributed to power loss in the chain drive system of the ergometer, and it was concluded that the SRM system was a valid and accurate device to measure power. Scientific literature lacks data on other power-measuring systems.

Power Versus Speed

Most cyclists have small computers that display their speed, and they often use this as an indicator of exercise intensity. However, speed is a very poor indicator of the exercise intensity (Jeukendrup and van Diemen 1998). This becomes clear when comparing speed measurements with power output measurements. There is often no relationship between speed and power output and, under some circumstances, there may even be a negative correlation. This is not surprising if you consider that the highest power outputs are often obtained when cyclists ride uphill or accelerate after a corner. In those situations, the speed is relatively low but power output is very high. In contrast, during downhills when power output is minimal, the obtained speed can be very high. Speed is, therefore, a very poor indicator of exercise intensity and can probably only be used in conditions with flat roads, no wind, and no drafting.

Power Versus Heart Rate

As mentioned earlier, power is a direct reflection of the exercise intensity, whereas heart rate responds to changes in power. Power, therefore, will change rapidly and a power curve will show considerable variation. Heart rate, on the other hand, is relatively stable because it takes a while to adapt heart rate to the changing demands (increased or decreased power output).

In chapter 5 we discuss that heart rate changes with temperature, altitude, and so forth, and therefore the relationship between heart rate and power output will change. In hot conditions, for instance, power will be lower at a given heart rate compared to cool conditions. Figure 6.1 gives an example. This is a heart rate and power recording

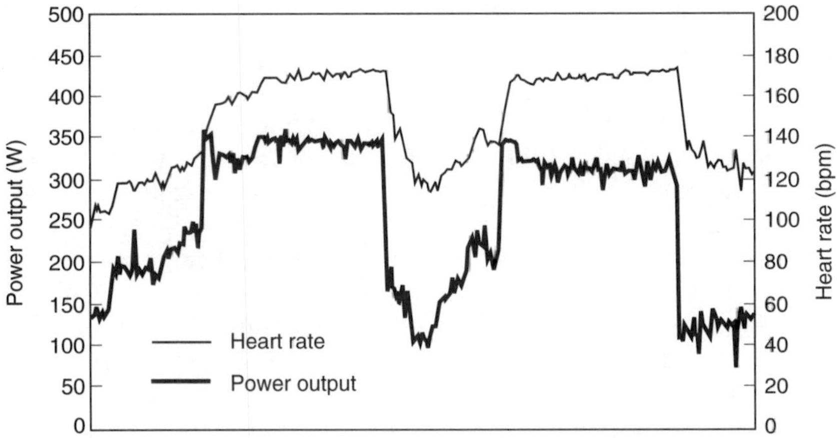

Figure 6.1 Power output and heart rate during an indoor training session. This rider maintained a constant heart rate, but in the second 20-minute block of hard exercise, a drop in power output becomes apparent.

from a professional cyclist's indoor training session (turbo trainer). The rider tried to maintain a constant heart rate around 170 for two bouts of 20 minutes with a 5-minute recovery between the bouts. Figure 6.1 shows that the rider was fairly successful in doing so. However, you also can see a clear drop in the power to achieve this heart rate. This phenomenon is caused by the cardiovascular drift discussed in chapter 5. We discuss earlier that heart rate is probably a better indicator of physiological stress, whereas power is a better indicator of true exercise intensity and performance (Jeukendrup and van Diemen 1998). The two measures therefore give different information and the information obtained is additive.

How to Use Power in Training

Training can be guided by power measurements rather than heart rate. The most obvious reason for doing this is that power is what really matters. Cyclists win time trials because of high power, not because of high heart rates. You can estimate what power output you need to achieve to ride a personal best or to win a race. This power output could be the target of a training session. With heart rate this would not be possible, because heart rate depends on various environmental factors (as chapter 5 discusses in detail). So if you want to ride a time trial at a speed of 40 kilometers per hour (with average aerodynamics) this would require approximately 275 watts (see chapters 9 and 10 for more details about modeling and the effects of position and equipment on aerodynamics). You could focus your training on maintaining 275 watts for duration close to an hour or slightly higher workloads for a shorter period.

Feedback about power output also can help you maintain a constant power output that is likely to influence time-trial performance. Pacing studies suggest that maintaining a constant power output results in the best performance (although this has never been systematically studied in cyclists). Anecdotal information from professional cyclists also shows that the best time trialists are those who can ride a consistent, even pace.

Drafting

Early studies have reported that drafting behind another rider or riders reduces the oxygen cost of cycling by 25 to 40 percent (Kyle 1979; McCole et al. 1990). The largest effect of drafting can be observed at high speeds when a cyclist is surrounded by other riders. Power output can decrease dramatically in those conditions and drafting skills are therefore important in road racing. Following is an excellent example of this drafting skill during a road race. A world-class cyclist participated in the Tour de France, and though the average speed in the six-hour level stage was 40 kilometers per hour, this cyclist with excellent drafting skills managed to reduce his average power output to just 98 watts. In optimal conditions with no wind and level roads, and with a good aerodynamic position, riding at that speed would require approximately 275 watts (Martin et al. 1998). Drafting in a team time trial, however, does not result in the same drafting effect that a rider might obtain in the peloton. Drafting allows for some recovery, however, as can be seen in the heart-rate trace in figure 6.2 (see page 74). In a 4,000-meter pursuit on the track, power output of riders has been reported to be 64 to 71 percent lower than the power produced by the lead cyclist.

© Bob Yellen

Drafting usually has the most notable effect at high speeds in large groups of cyclists.

Examples of Power Measurements

To demonstrate the value of measuring power and to get a better feel for the numbers obtained, it is often useful to study some examples. Therefore, we will discuss some examples from the literature describing power measurements in elite cyclists on the track and on the road.

Track Cycling

Broker et al. (1999) were the first to report SRM power output profiles on elite track cyclists during *simulated* competition. They collected data on seven members of the U.S. 4,000-meter pursuit team during a 2,000-meter ridden at a speed (60 kilometers per hour) that would place a team in first position at most international competitions. When cycling at this speed, the riders in first, second, third, and fourth position generated average power outputs of 607 ± 45, 430 ± 39, 389 ± 32, and 389 ± 33 watts, respectively. In relative terms, riders in second, third, and fourth positions only needed to generate 71, 64, and 64 percent of the power output sustained by the lead cyclist. When the data were averaged over all four riding positions, they ranged from 70 to 75 percent (425 to 455 watts) of the power of the lead rider (Broker et al. 1999). These data concur with those collected by Neil Craig on elite Australian team pursuit cyclists during the 1998 World Cup (Jeukendrup et al. 2000).

Broker et al. (1999) reported an average power output of 607 watts for the lead rider. This is higher than the 581-watt value found for Australian riders under competition conditions. Such a discrepancy can probably be explained by the differences in riding speed. The data of Broker et al. were collected at a speed of 60 kilometers per hour, whereas the actual speed during the World Cup competition was 56 to 58 kilometers per hour. In addition, riding skill and technique, riding position, body mass and frontal surface area, equipment design, and environmental and track conditions would all be expected to affect riding speed and the power output necessary to sustain that speed. Although the *average* power output data provide useful information about minimum requirements of a 4,000-meter team pursuit, the individual rider profile highlights the variable demands of this event. Figure 6.2 presents the power profile, cadence, speed, and heart-rate response of a rider during a 4,000-meter team pursuit in World Cup competition.

Instantaneous power output was approximately 1,250 watts at the start and only dropped to less than 1,000 watts after the first 8 to 10 seconds of the race. Thereafter, depending on the rider's position in the team, power output fluctuated between 600 and 650 watts in the lead position and between 350 and 400 watts when a cyclist was riding behind other team members. This clearly illustrates the variable power demands of team pursuit racing and highlights the need for rapid response times to accelerate and decelerate into team formation, depending on the rider's position within the race.

In contrast with the oscillating power requirements of the 4,000-meter team pursuit (figure 6.2), the power profiles for riders competing in individual 4,000-meter pursuit races are generally much more even. Figure 6.3 displays the power output profiles for an elite male riding a 4,000-meter race and an elite female riding a 3,000-meter race during a World Cup event.

Compared with the profile for the 4,000-meter team pursuit (figure 6.2), there is a much narrower range of power outputs required to ride competitively at this level. Power output during the first 5 to 10 seconds of both races is remarkably similar (approximately 1,000 watts for male and female riders). However, despite the shorter

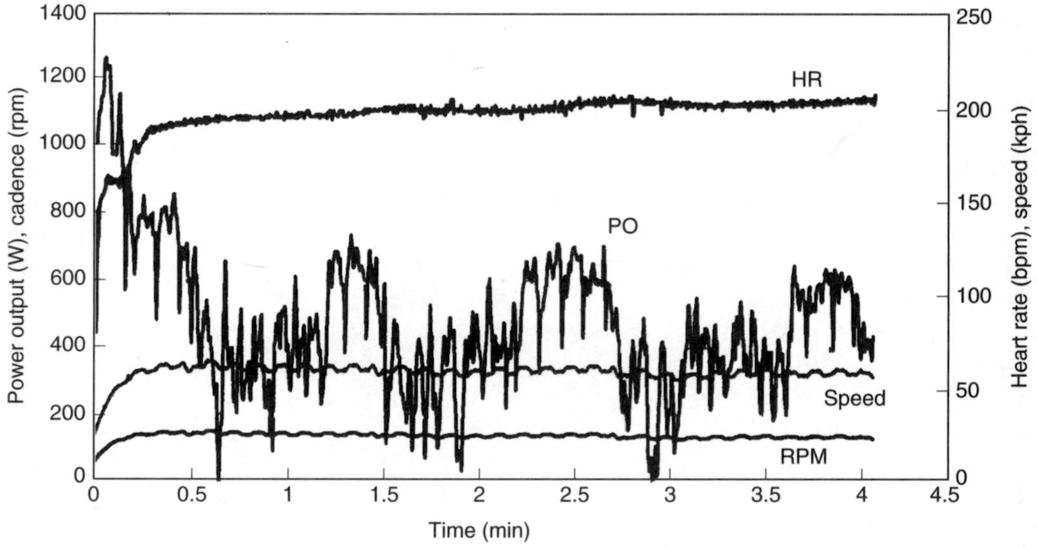

Figure 6.2 Power output (PO), heart rate (HR), cadence (RPM), and speed profile for a cyclist riding a 4,000-meter team pursuit race during a World Cup competition.

Reprinted from Jeukendrup, Craig, and Hawley 2000.

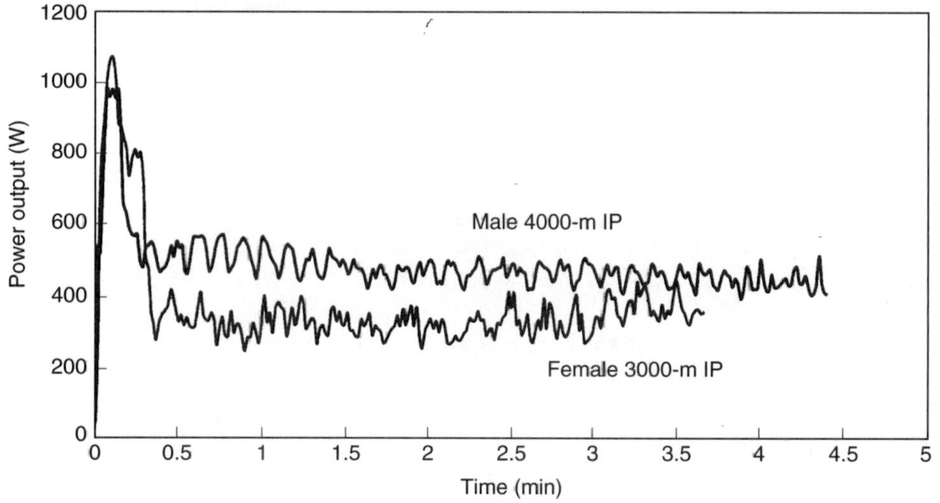

Figure 6.3 Power output profile for a male cyclist riding a 4,000-meter individual pursuit and a female cyclist riding a 3,000-meter individual pursuit race during World Cup competition.

Reprinted from Jeukendrup, Craig, and Hawley 2000.

race distance, the power output for the female rider (363 to 381 watts) is considerably lower for the remainder of the race compared to the male rider (475 to 500 watts). Interestingly, the female rider demonstrates superior fatigue resistance (i.e., has less of a decline in relative power output) over the race duration than the male rider, whose power drop-off is marked, especially during the last 45 to 60 seconds of the event. In a mathematical model of the power requirements of the 4,000-meter individual pursuit, Broker et al. (1999) estimated that a rider with a mass of approximately 79 kilograms (174 pounds) who was 1.82 meters tall would need an average power output of 479 watts for a race time of 4 minutes, 31 seconds. This estimate agrees well with average power output data collected for Australian riders competing in international events and riding comparable times (N.P. Craig, unpublished observations).

Measurements of power can be used on the track to improve bend-riding skills. Riders often will reduce speed in the bends (especially on short tracks), and maintaining a constant power in the bends will prevent this.

Road Cycling

With the use of power-measuring devices, data have been collected during time trials in major international races. The heart rates measured during these time trials concur with data from previous studies (Lucia et al. 1999; Padilla et al. 2000b). Because power output data are highly individual and dependent on a cyclist's mass and anthropometric profile, equipment, and position on the bicycle, these data are presented as a case study.

The average power output during one 30-kilometer time trial in a recent Tour de France was 381 watts for an average speed of 30 kilometers per hour. This corresponded to over 85 percent Wmax for this rider. Whereas most time trials on a flat course will be characterized by a relatively constant power profile, this uphill time trial displays a highly intermittent profile with power outputs varying from 260 to 460 watts, heart rates ranging from 135 to 165 beats per minute, and speeds as low as 17 up to 62 kilometers per hour.

Another example of an uphill time trial involves a 38-kilometer time trial that was predominantly uphill but included a downhill section. Average power output was 320 watts and average speed 33.1 kilometers per hour—illustrating the dissociation between speed and power output. As noted previously, speed is often a poor indicator of the exercise intensity during cycling, especially when the cyclist is riding on hilly terrain. In the mountains, speed and exercise intensity seem almost inversely related: The highest speed is recorded at the lowest power output in a downhill section of the race.

Studies have shown that the power output recorded with power-measuring devices corresponds to the power outputs calculated from heart rate and a predetermined relationship between power output and heart rate in a laboratory (Grazzi et al. 1999; Padilla et al. 2000b). Padilla et al. (2000b) estimated that the power output of professional cyclists during uphill time trials was 331 to 376 watts, representing 75 to 83 percent of Wmax. There are also case reports of world hour record holders that indicate the extreme physiological demands of time trials. For example, it has been estimated that Christopher Boardman had to produce an average power output of 442 watts for 60 minutes to ride at an average speed of 56.375 kilometers per hour (Keen 1997). This equates to an average oxygen uptake of 5.6 liters per minute or 81 milliliters per kilogram per minute. Although such a sustainable power output is extreme, Miguel Indurain with a much larger drag coefficient set a previous one-hour world record of 53.040 kilometers by producing an estimated average power output of 510 watts (Padilla et al. 2000a). It can be estimated that the oxygen uptake during this ride must have been around 6.25 liters per minute or close to 80 milliliters per kilogram per minute. This rider had a Wmax of 572 watts and so was able to sustain close to 90 percent of Wmax for the duration!

Professional cyclists produce exceptional power outputs (greater than 320 to 450 watts) during time trials ranging in distance from 5 to 70 kilometers. The absolute power output depends on the duration of the time trial, the course profile, and the role of a cyclist within the team.

SRM to Measure Aerodynamics

With the help of power-recording devices, it is possible to minimize drag on the bicycle and to find the most aerodynamic position. To perform such a test, it is important to have stable environmental conditions. There should be no wind, a smooth road surface, no gradients, constant atmospheric pressure, and so on. The best way to perform these tests is on an indoor cycling track or on an outdoor cycling track with a constant wind condition.

The test is based on the premise that the power required to ride at a constant speed should decrease when the aerodynamic drag is reduced. You should start with a standard position, standard clothing, and standard equipment. Ride at a constant speed (preferably close to racing speed) and record your power. Make sure that you obtain sufficient measurements (at least 15 to 20 minutes) so that you can average these measurements and get more reliable results. Once you have obtained these baseline measurements, you can make an adjustment to position and bike and ride at the same speed again. The recordings of power will reflect the changes in aerodynamic drag. Because power may vary, this method may require quite a few repetitions before you can obtain a good estimate of the aerodynamic changes.

Summary

Power is the amount of energy transferred onto the pedals per unit of time. Power can vary from 0 (no pedaling) to about 2,300 watts in elite track sprinters. Power-measuring devices are relatively new and useful tools for monitoring training and evaluating performance. Power monitoring has advantages and disadvantages compared with heart-rate monitoring. Power measurements are more directly related to performance and are less dependent on environmental conditions. On the other hand, power is much more variable and it is more difficult to use power as guidance of the training intensity. Power-measuring devices can be used in a variety of ways—for example, to estimate aerodynamics, to develop pacing strategies in time trials, to evaluate races or training sessions, to obtain measures of energy expenditure during cycling, and to develop or improve drafting skills.

Power also has been used to evaluate races of elite cyclists, and when these data are analyzed it becomes clear that power demands can vary considerably, especially at the elite level. In one road race it is possible to record a very low average power for one cyclist (below 100 watts) and a very high average power for another (200 to 250 watts). As more and more manufacturers are starting to produce power-measuring devices and prices are likely to drop, power may be the cyclist's training tool of the future.

chapter 7

Event Selection

Iñigo Mujika
Sabino Padilla

Professional road cycling is characterized by the range of events that riders participate in. These events differ in their duration, their type (individual time trial or mass start), and the terrain over which the race is run (see table 7.1). The duration of the events ranges from 6 to 15 minutes for a prologue time trial to 90 to 100 hours for a three-week stage race. Obviously, the physiological demands for these events are very different. As a result, different people with different physical characteristics will excel in different events. Selecting the event you are most suited to is an important part of fulfilling your potential.

In individual time trials a cyclist will try to cover a certain distance as fast as possible. The time will determine who the winner is. These time trials can range from a very short 3 kilometers to very long time trials of over 100 kilometers. A similar event is the team time trial. In these races a team of two to nine cyclists will attempt to cover a certain distance as fast as possible. Because of the effects of drafting, these events are usually fast, and group riding and drafting skills are an important factor.

There are also mass-start races in which time is less important but the winner is the first rider who crosses the finish line. These races are usually between 60 and 300 kilometers. When such a race is performed on a local circuit of 3 to 7 kilometers, it often is referred to as a *criterium. Classics* are races with a long tradition and history and often these will be 250 kilometers or more.

Stage races are a combination of time trials, team time trials, and road races and may last 2 to 21 days. Some races such as the Tour de France may cover over 3,500 kilometers. The overall winner is the rider with the overall fastest time. The

TABLE 7.1 Union Cycliste Internationale Competition Calendar

Competition modality	Duration	Examples	Racing format	Duration (min.)
Major tour races	21-22 days	Tour de France	Mass start	~300-350
		Giro d'Italia	Individual time trial	~10-75
		Vuelta a España	Team time trial**	~75
Stage races	4-10 days	Paris-Nice	Mass start	~300-350
		Tirreno-Adriatico	Individual time trial	~10-75
		Vuelta al País Vasco	Team time trial**	~75
World Cup classics	1 day	Paris-Roubaix	Mass start	~300-350
		Milano-San Remo		
		Clásica San Sebastián		
World Championships	2 days*		Mass start*	~300-350
			Individual time trial*	~50-75
Olympic Games	2 days*		Mass start*	~300-350
			Individual time trial*	~50-75
Other 1-day races	1 day	Subidaa	Mass start	~300-350
		Montjuic		

* The mass-start race and the time trial are independent of each other.

** The team time trial is not necessarily included in these races.

largest time differences are made in mountain stages or time trials, and an important factor in these races is, of course, the day-to-day recovery of the cyclist. Most stage races will start with a short time trial (3 to 6 kilometers), called a *prologue*.

Recently, Padilla et al. (2000b) investigated the importance of various physical characteristics in relation to time-trial and road-race (mass-start) performance. The aim of this chapter is to help the racing cyclist identify his potential and match that potential to the event that most suits him. First, we discuss some of the available information about physical characteristics in relation to cycling performance. Then we discuss various laboratory tests that can be done to evaluate a cyclist. Finally, we estimate a cyclist's performance potential and discuss whether you need an optimum body shape (morphotype) for professional road cycling.

Demands of Road Cycling

Knowing the demands of competition (i.e., exercise intensity and workload) is the first step to ascertain the potential performance ability of individual cyclists. An indication of the exercise intensity can be obtained from measurements of heart rate during competition (see chapter 5; Jeukendrup and van Diemen 1998; Lucía et al. 1999, 2000; Padilla et al. 2000b, 2001; Palmer et al. 1994). These values then can be compared to individual reference values such as maximal heart rate (HRmax), heart rate at the lactate threshold (HR_{LT}), or heart rate at the onset of blood lactate accumulation (HR_{OBLA}) (see following). The training impulse, or TRIMP (see chapter 1), has been proposed as this integrative marker of the exercise load undertaken by the athlete during training and competition (Banister 1991). TRIMP integrates exercise volume (time) and intensity (heart rate) and was recently used to characterize professional road-cycling competition and to model the load of a typical three-week stage race (Padilla et al. 2000b, 2001).

Table 7.2 reports exercise intensity and workload during competition time trial. It can be seen that the highest TRIMP score is for the team time trial, indicating it is the hardest time trial. In addition, it has been suggested that HR_{LT} and HR_{OBLA} (see following) could be valuable indexes for determining appropriate competition pace for time-trial events lasting respectively longer and shorter than 30 minutes (Padilla et al. 2000b). Table 7.2 also shows competition intensity and load during the mass-start races. The TRIMP scores reflect that high-mountain stages are the hardest of all, followed by the semi-mountainous and the flat stages. The overall win in a several-day cycling race is mainly dependent on a high aerobic capacity, because high submaximal aerobic requirements and a specific work distribution are present in all competition formats (Lucía et al. 2000; Padilla et al. 2000b, 2001). However, in one-day races or mass-start stage wins, other factors such as delaying the onset of fatigue or anaerobic power and capacity can determine the outcome of competition (Craig et al. 2000).

Laboratory Performance Tests for Road Cyclists

From a metabolic perspective, road cycling is an endurance sport that places extremely high aerobic demands on the athlete. This is reflected by the high oxygen uptake and power output values displayed by professional cyclists both at maximal and submaximal exercise intensities. The evaluation of a road cyclist's performance potential should include the determination of physiological and mechanical variables such as maximal oxygen uptake ($\dot{V}O_2max$), lactate threshold (LT), onset of blood lactate accumulation (OBLA), maximal power output, and mechanical efficiency. This can be done either on a cycling ergometer in a laboratory or on a bicycle in a velodrome (see chapter 8). Even though professional athletes often express their preference for sport-specific field tests performed with equipment with which they are most familiar, laboratory testing on cycle ergometers has been shown to be a valid means to evaluate a cyclist's physiological and performance potential (see chapter 8).

While absolute performance-related measures of an athlete (maximal power output, $\dot{V}O_2max$, etc.) can give us an indication of the cyclist's potential, an elite cyclist's performance level can be more accurately predicted when physiological values obtained under laboratory conditions are expressed relative to his anthropometric characteristics (body weight, height, composition, surface area). This is due to the influence of these variables on road-cycling performance. The following sections present some of the most important determinants of cycling performance that should be assessed in the laboratory.

TABLE 7.2 Characteristics of Male Professional Road Cycling Competition

Characteristic	STAGE TYPE							
	Prologue TT (n = 12)	Short TT (n = 18)	Long TT (n = 19)	Uphill TT (n = 8)	Team TT (n = 7)	FLAT (n = 125)	SEMO (n = 99)	HIMO (n = 86)
Distance (km)	7.3 ± 1.1	$28.0 \pm 8.6^{*}$	$49.2 \pm 8.0^{*\#}$	$40.6 \pm 4.8^{*\#\dagger}$	$67.0 \pm 0.5^{*\#\dagger\pounds}$	210 ± 35	$197 \pm 32^{\$}$	$190 \pm 29^{\$}$
Time (min.)	10 ± 2	$39 \pm 11^{*}$	$66 \pm 12^{*\#}$	$75 \pm 8^{*\#}$	$75 \pm 3^{*\#}$	312 ± 60	302 ± 57	$355 \pm 67^{\$@}$
Speed (km/h)	46.3 ± 2.8	$43.1 \pm 3.0^{*}$	44.7 ± 2.0	$32.5 \pm 2.0^{*\#\dagger}$	$53.4 \pm 1.8^{*\#\dagger\pounds}$	40.7 ± 3.1	$39.5 \pm 3.1^{\$}$	$32.7 \pm 3.7^{\$@}$
Heart rate (bpm)	177 ± 5	$172 \pm 9^{*}$	$162 \pm 6^{*\#}$	$158 \pm 7^{*\#}$	$165 \pm 5^{*\#}$	119 ± 10	$130 \pm 9^{\$}$	$135 \pm 9^{\$@}$
% HRmax	89 ± 3	$85 \pm 5^{*}$	$80 \pm 5^{*\#}$	$78 \pm 3^{*\#}$	$82 \pm 2^{*}$	51 ± 7	$58 \pm 6^{\$}$	$61 \pm 5\$^{@}$
% HR_{LT}	114 ± 8	$108 \pm 9^{*}$	$103 \pm 8^{*}$	$101 \pm 5^{*\#}$	$105 \pm 11^{*}$	65 ± 10	$74 \pm 11^{\$}$	$79 \pm 9^{\$@}$
% HR_{OBLA}	100 ± 3	$95 \pm 7^{*}$	$89 \pm 5^{*\#}$	$87 \pm 2^{*\#}$	$92 \pm 4^{*}$	57 ± 8	$65 \pm 7^{\$}$	$69 \pm 6^{\$@}$
Watts	380 ± 62	362 ± 59	347 ± 46	342 ± 32	353 ± 42	192 ± 45	$234 \pm 43^{\$}$	$246 \pm 44^{\$}$
TRIMP	21 ± 3	$77 \pm 23^{*}$	$122 \pm 27^{*\#}$	$129 \pm 14^{*\#}$	$146 \pm 6^{*\#\dagger\pounds}$	156 ± 31	$172 \pm 31^{\$}$	$215 \pm 38^{\$@}$

Note: TT, time trial; FLAT, flat mass-start stage; SEMO, semi-mountainous mass-start stage; HIMO, high-mountain mass-start stage; HRmax, maximal heart rate; LT, lactate threshold; OBLA, onset of blood lactate accumulation; LT ZONE, $HR_{LT} \pm 3$ beats/min; OBLA ZONE, $HR_{OBLA} \pm 3$ beats/min; TRIMP, training impulse (Banister 1991).

* Significantly different from prologue TT; $^{\#}$ significantly different from short TT; † significantly different from long TT; $^{\pounds}$ significantly different from uphill TT; $^{\$}$ significantly different from FLAT; $^{@}$ significantly different from SEMO. To compare power output values with those measured on electromagnetically braked ergometers, 9 percent should be added to values in table due to the friction in the transmission system of Monark ergometers (Åstrand 1970). Values are mean ±SD.

Adapted from Padilla, Mujika, Orbañanos, and Angulo 2000.

Measuring the Body

It is important to have information about a cyclist's body size and shape. Most of these anthropometric variables are easy to measure and for most of the measurements no expensive equipment is required.

Body surface area (BSA, in meters squared) can be estimated easily from each cyclist's body mass (BM) and height (H), using the equation described by Du Bois and Du Bois (1916):

$$BSA = 0.007184 \times BM^{0.425} \times H^{0.725}$$

where BM is in kilograms and H is in centimeters.

The frontal area (FA, in meters squared) of the cyclist and the bicycle can either be estimated or be more precisely measured. For the approximate estimation, it is assumed that FA can be considered proportional to BSA (Di Prampero et al. 1979), and based on previously measured values (Swain et al. 1987), the value of FA is considered to be 18.5 percent of BSA. The FA also can be estimated by taking photographs of the cyclist in the riding position and of a reference rectangle of a known area. The contour of the ensemble cyclist-bicycle and that of the rectangle then are cut out and weighed. The subject's FA is estimated by comparing the masses of the pictures of the ensemble cyclist-bicycle and that of the reference area (Swain et al. 1987).

Testing Protocol

Different exercise scientists use different testing protocols in different laboratories around the world. Some protocols are intended to evaluate aerobic capacity while others are designed to assess a cyclist's anaerobic capacity. For information on anaerobic testing (of interest to sprinters and track cyclists), see Craig et al. (2000). The protocol that follows is the aerobic capacity test consistently used by the authors for professional road cyclists, with satisfactory results. It consists of an incremental maximal laboratory test on a mechanically or electromagnetically braked cycle ergometer adapted with a racing saddle, drop handlebars, and clip-in pedals. Initial resistance is set at 110 watts and it is increased by 35 watts every four minutes, with one-minute passive recovery intervals between workloads. Pedal rate is maintained constant at 75 revolutions per minute throughout the test. Subjects keep cadence with a metronome. Testing continues until the subjects are no longer able to maintain the required pedal rate. Blood samples are obtained immediately after completion of each workload for blood lactate (BL) concentration determination. BL values attained during the last workload maintained for at least two full minutes are considered as maximal. Heart rate is recorded throughout the test. On mechanically-braked cycle ergometers cadence should be kept constant, for example, by using a metronome.

Maximal Power Output

Maximal power output (Wmax) is the highest workload a cyclist can maintain for a complete four-minute period. When the last workload is not maintained for four full minutes, Wmax is calculated as follows (Kuipers et al. 1985):

$$Wmax = W_f + (t/240) \times 35$$

where W_f is the value of the last complete workload (in watts), t is the time the last workload is maintained (in seconds), and 35 is the power output difference between the last two workloads. It should be noted that if power output values obtained on mechanically braked cycle ergometers (such as Monark) are to be compared with those measured on electromagnetically braked ergometers, 9 percent should be added to the former because of the friction in the transmission system (Åstrand 1970).

Maximal Oxygen Uptake

You can determine $\dot{V}O_2max$ directly, or when this equipment is not available or if you want to avoid any possible interference of gas-analyzing equipment with the subject's cycling performance, you can estimate $\dot{V}O_2max$ (in liters per minute) from Wmax, using the regression equation proposed by Hawley and Noakes (1992):

$$\dot{V}O_2max = 0.01141 \times Wmax + 0.435$$

Blood Lactate

Capillary blood samples (25 microliters) often are taken from a previously hyperemized earlobe during the first recovery seconds after each workload. Measurements of lactate in these small blood samples usually can be performed rapidly. When lactate concentrations are plotted against the exercise intensity, specific points on the lactate curve can be identified. The LT is identified on each subject's BL concentration–power output plot as the exercise intensity that elicits a one mmol per liter increase in BL concentration above average baseline lactate values measured during exercise at 40 to 60 percent of $\dot{V}O_2max$ (Hagberg and Coyle 1983). The exercise intensity corresponding to the OBLA is identified on the BL concentration–power output curve by straight-line interpolation between the two closest points as the exercise intensity eliciting a BL concentration of 4 mmol per liter (Sjödin and Jacobs 1981) (see also chapter 5).

Wind-Tunnel Testing

An increasing number of cycling teams are including wind-tunnel testing in their testing routines. The aim is to determine the cyclist's drag coefficient (also known as aerodynamic efficiency coefficient, or C_x). Indeed, a drag coefficient has been proposed as a measure of aerodynamic efficiency. See chapters 9 and 10 for more information about wind tunnel testing and aerodynamics.

Characteristics of Professional Road Cyclists

As mentioned earlier, one of the most outstanding characteristics of all professional road cyclists is their high aerobic power and capacity. This is true at both maximal and submaximal exercise intensities (see table 7.3). Quite impressive Wmax and $\dot{V}O_2max$ values have been consistently reported in the literature (Lucía et al. 1998, 1999; Padilla et al. 1999, 2000a,b). Testing a group of world-class professional road cyclists using the protocol described in the preceding section, Padilla et al. (1999, 2000a,b) recently reported Wmax values ranging between 349 and 525 watts (5.7 and 6.8 watts per kilogram). This indicates that when the 9 percent accounting for the friction in the transmission system of the ergometer is added, one of the athletes attained a Wmax of 572 watts! The same subjects presented with $\dot{V}O_2max$ values of 4.4 to 6.4 liters per minute (69.7 to 84.8 milliliters per kilogram per minute), HRmax of 187 to 204 beats per minute, and peak BL concentration at the end of the previously mentioned incremental testing protocol of 6.9 to 13.7 mmol per liter (table 7.3).

As table 7.3 shows, typical physiological characteristics of professional road cyclists at LT include having a power output of 334 watts (76 percent Wmax), an oxygen uptake of 4.0 liters per minute (77 percent $\dot{V}O_2max$), and a heart rate of 163 beats per minute (84 percent HRmax). Typical values corresponding to the OBLA are 386 watts (87 percent Wmax), 4.5 liters per minute (86 percent $\dot{V}O_2max$), and 178 beats per minute (92 percent HRmax). A recent study on a five-time winner of the Tour de France, however, reported a power output at OBLA of 505 watts (after addition of the previously mentioned 9 percent correction) and an oxygen uptake at this intensity of 5.65 liters per minute (Padilla et al. 2000a). Professional road cyclists also present with a mean mechanical efficiency, averaged through the entire range of submaximal and maximal cycling intensities, of 23 percent (range 21.5 to 24.5) (unpublished observations).

In cycling, physical work is determined to a great extent by aerodynamic resistance (which mainly depends on FA, air density, and speed of motion) and rolling resistance

TABLE 7.3 Maximal and Submaximal Physiological Characteristics of Male Professional Road Cyclists (n = 24)

		RANGE	
Characteristic Max.	**Mean**	**Min.**	
Wmax (W)	439	349	525
Wmax (W/kg)	6.4	5.7	6.8
$\dot{V}O_2max$ (l/min)	5.4	4.4	6.4
$\dot{V}O_2max$ (ml/kg/min)	78.8	69.7	84.8
HRmax (bpm)	194	187	204
[La]peak (mmol/l)	9.9	6.9	13.7
W_{LT} (W)	334	202	417
W_{LT} (% Wmax)	76	58	83
$\dot{V}O_2LT$ (% $\dot{V}O_2max$)	77	74	83
HR_{LT} (bpm)	163	146	174
W_{OBLA} (W)	386	275	478
W_{OBLA} (% Wmax)	87	76	94
$\dot{V}O_2OBLA$ (% $\dot{V}O_2max$)	86	81	91
HR_{OBLA} (bpm)	178	168	191

Note: Wmax, maximal power output; $\dot{V}O_2max$, maximal oxygen uptake; HRmax, maximal heart rate; [La]peak, peak blood lactate concentration; LT, lactate threshold; OBLA, onset of blood lactate accumulation. To compare power output values with those measured on electromagnetically braked ergometers, 9 percent should be added to the values in the table due to the friction in the transmission system of Monark ergometers (Åstrand, 1970).

Adapted from Padilla, Mujika, Orbañanos, and Angulo 1999.

(dependent on BM, the pressure in the tires, and the characteristics of the road surface and tires). The factors that are physiologically important, therefore, are the physical characteristics of a cyclist (i.e., his or her morphotype). In the laboratory, the ergometer allows us to measure work, but not the interaction between the cyclist and the environment. To more accurately predict the athlete's performance potential under field conditions, it is necessary to assess his or her physiological capacity relative to anthropometric characteristics (i.e., BM, FA, and BSA). This procedure is called *scaling*. Scaling of maximal and submaximal power output and oxygen uptake values can be performed by relating these values to individual anthropometric characteristics, including BSA, FA, BM, $BM^{0.79}$, and $BM^{0.32}$. It has been suggested that oxygen uptake and power output values relative to BM and $BM^{0.79}$ are the best predictors of uphill cycling ability, whereas $BM^{0.32}$ would be the best index to ascertain cycling potential on flat terrain (Padilla et al. 1996, 1999).

Thus the laboratory represents a noncompetitive situation that gives us information on the physiological potential of a cyclist. This potential is just one of several variables that determine performance in road cycling competition, but it is helpful in the diagnosis of a rider's strengths and weaknesses. Reference values for different cycling events and performance levels can be found elsewhere (Jeukendrup et al. 2000) and are summarized in table 7.4.

However, it should be kept in mind that the performance-predicting potential of laboratory testing is not without limitations. Indeed, three-week stage races usually are won or lost by time gaps of 200 to 400 seconds, representing 0.07 to 0.13 percent of the overall time. Moreover, differences among top riders usually are attained in

TABLE 7.4 Criteria for Classification of Trained, Well-Trained, Elite, and World-Class Road Cyclists

Category	Trained	Well-trained	Elite	World-class
Training and race status				
Training frequency	2-3 times a week	3-7 times a week	5-8 times a week	5-8 times a week
Training duration	30-60 min.	60-240 min.	60-360 min.	60-360 min.
Training background	1 year	3-5 years	5-15 years	5-30 years
Race days per year	0-10	0-20	50-100	90-110
UCI ranking	--	--	first 2,000	first 200
Physiological variables				
Wmax (W)	250-400	300-450	350-500	400-600
Wmax/kg (W/kg)	4.0-5.0	5.0-6.0	6.0-7.0	6.5-8.0
$\dot{V}O_2max$ (l/min)	4.5-5.0	5.0-5.3	5.2-6.0	5.4-7.0
$\dot{V}O_2max$/kg (ml/kg/min)	64-70	70-75	72-80	75-90
Economy (W/l/min)	72-74	74-75	76-77	>78

Adapted from Jeukendrup et al. 2000.

time trial and mountain stages. If we estimate the average duration for a time trial or climbing a mountain pass to be 60 minutes, even a 60-second difference between two riders would represent only 1.7 percent. Laboratory measurements are unlikely to pick up such small differences!

Optimum Morphotype for Road Cycling

Professional road cyclists are required to perform on level, uphill, and downhill roads, both individually and drafting behind other cyclists. In any of these situations, a cyclist's performance is determined partially by his anthropometric characteristics. For example, BM determines gravity-dependent resistance and has a major influence on uphill cycling performance, whereas FA has a major influence on aerodynamic resistance and affects performance when the rider is cycling individually on level roads (Swain et al. 1987). Differences in morphological characteristics of professional road cyclists have contributed to the appearance of morphotype-dependent specialists, with clearly differentiated roles during the different phases of a race. These include flat-terrain riders whose main role is to control the race on level roads; uphill riders who perform their work mainly in the hills; all-terrain riders, who are able to perform fairly well on all types of terrain; time-trial specialists, who excel in these individually raced events; and sprinters, who come to the front for the final few kilometers of a race.

While Padilla et al. (1999) have documented the characteristics of flat-terrain riders, hill climbers, time-trial specialists, and all-terrain riders, no specific data on the characteristics of sprinters are available in the literature. Within these four groups of riders, quite considerable differences have been observed in absolute Wmax, W_{LT}, W_{OBLA}, and $\dot{V}O_2max$ values. Flat-terrain riders and time-trial specialists presented with the highest values of all. This was also true when values were reported relative to $BM^{0.32}$ (a measure of flat cycling ability, mentioned earlier). These results are indicative of the superior performance ability of these riders on level roads and in individual time-trial events. However, scaling of these values relative to BM and $BM^{0.79}$ (a measure of hill-climbing ability, as mentioned) modified the differences among groups in the expected sense. Interestingly, when Wmax, W_{LT}, and W_{OBLA} were reported relative to BM and $BM^{0.79}$, the highest values were shown by uphill riders and time-trial specialists. This observation indicates that these two groups have a similar aptitude in uphill cycling, which is in agreement with actual competition results of mountain stages, in which small, light uphill specialists often share top positions with bigger, heavier time-trial specialists.

These results suggest that time-trial specialists show an overall performance advantage over the other groups because they display similar power outputs as flat-terrain riders in absolute terms and they are as powerful as uphill specialists in relation to their BM. An additional conclusion from the previously mentioned study (Padilla et al. 1999) is that there is no optimum morphotype to be a professional road cyclist but that individual morphotype will determine specific roles in competition and event selection.

In addition to the results showing that time-trial specialists have a performance advantage over other groups, history suggests that the results of three-week stage races (Tour de France, Giro d'Italia, Vuelta a España) are largely determined by performances in the time trial. The overall standings of these competitions indicate an optimum compromise between the cyclist's anthropometric characteristics on the one hand (which determine to a great extent the resistance he must overcome, therefore the total workload) and his physiological attributes on the other (through which he will overcome such resistances and perform such work). Table 7.5 shows the time differences of the top three competitors over three such races. It can be seen that the majority of the time gained by the winner (a time-trial specialist) over the competition was in the time trial. Therefore, not only do time-trial specialists have a performance advantage, but in recent years races have been structured so that time trials have a major influence on the outcome of the race. However, it must not be forgotten that performance also depends on other variables, such as thermoregulatory, recovery, and psychological capacities; health condition; and race strategy.

A final reflection based on our data and experience is that cyclists are seldom "pure" hill climbers or "pure" time-trial specialists. Indeed, each model, or type, of road cyclist is defined by external characteristics such as BM and body dimensions, and internal characteristics such as aerobic and anaerobic capacities. It is our view that the most important performance-determining characteristics are the internal ones because cyclists with quite different external characteristics have been shown to have similar performance levels in competition. Therefore, rather than "optimum" morphotypes for climbing or time trial, we believe that there are times, circumstances, and training states in which a cyclist can perform as an optimum climber, an optimum time-trial specialist, or both. This would be the case, for instance, when a cyclist is able to perform at high steady-state power outputs at OBLA in relation to his or her

TABLE 7.5 Impact of Time Trials (TT) and Mountain Climbs on the Final Overall Standings of Some Three-Week Stage Races

Race and final standings	Final time difference (s)	TT distance (km)	TT time difference (s)	Uphill distance (km)	Uphill time difference (s)
Tour de France 1991		135.4		351	
1. Indurain	–		–		–
2. Bugno	216		122		93
3. Chiapucci	356		352		48
Tour de France 1992		137		349	
1. Indurain	–		–		105
2. Chiapucci	275		495		–
3. Bugno	649		273		418
Giro d'Italia 1992		112		328.3	
1. Indurain	–		–		–
2. Chiapucci	312		273		28
3. Chioccioli	436		392		223

Indurain was the fastest rider in the TT of all three races and the mountain climbs of the Tour de France 1991 and the Giro d'Italia 1992; Chiapucci was the fastest rider in the mountain climbs of the Tour de France 1992.

Cyclists' body shapes vary considerably and this in part determines the event that will suit them best.

BM, $BM^{0.79}$, and $BM^{0.32}$ and presents with high Wmax values both in absolute terms and relative to the cyclist's body dimensions.

Terminology

So when are you a "trained" cyclist? What values do you need to achieve to be classified as an elite or even a world-class cyclist? Unfortunately, there is no consensus in the scientific literature as to what constitutes an elite, world-class, trained, well-trained, or untrained cyclist. Subjects in several published studies have been classified as *elite* cyclists, whereas subjects with similar physiological characteristics have been termed *moderately trained* in other investigations. The scientific literature is polluted by investigations that purport their subjects to be elite cyclists but who are clearly not elite and would stand no chance of success in races against real elite cyclists.

Because of the confusion that currently exists, Jeukendrup et al. (2000) proposed a unifying classification and terminology (see table 7.4 on page 86). Note that a classification of untrained, trained, or well-trained is separate from a classification of novice, elite, or world-class cyclist. The first classification refers to the amount of training undertaken and is independent of any (maximal or submaximal) physiological characteristics. For example, a world-class cyclist with a very high $\dot{V}O_2max$ can be classified as untrained if he does not perform any training for a long period. In table 7.4 we have combined the two classifications and set criteria for each of the performance ability categories. The distinction between trained and well-trained cyclists should not be applied to individuals but only to groups of cyclists or subjects. This is because certain individuals can be classified as highly trained but still lack the genetic endowment necessary for superior performance. On the other hand, those cyclists with excellent genetic endowment may achieve very high physiological ratings without (much) training. The data presented in this chapter are derived from a very small and elite group of professional road cyclists who can be defined as world class.

Summary

We can measure a number of variables in a laboratory situation that give us an indication of someone's abilities. The data from professional cyclists presented in this chapter show that there are strong correlations between a cyclist's body size and shape and a cyclist's maximal aerobic power and the ability to perform in different disciplines.

For example, good climbers will have a high power-to-weight ratio but also have to be able to perform well in flat road races where a large absolute power output is required. Time-trial performance is influenced by the aerodynamic drag, and therefore the cyclist's position and body surface area must be taken into account.

Regular assessments in a laboratory can be helpful to evaluate performance and detect early overtraining. It also can help to define weaknesses on which you need to work. Important measurements include body weight, body surface area, Wmax, $\dot{V}O_2max$, OBLA, and LT.

Field Testing

Garry S. Palmer

Unlike sports such as swimming and distance running, the highly variable nature of cycling (because of different race tactics, courses, environmental conditions, and drafting) means that it is difficult for cyclists and their coaches to accurately use competitive performance to monitor changes in physiology, training status, fitness, or nutritional state. This can mean that weaknesses in fitness can remain undetected and the athlete will continually fail to achieve optimal performance. As a result, some method of assessing physical conditioning, or fitness, must be used.

Reasons for Testing

There are two main reasons for undertaking fitness testing or, more specifically, physiological assessment of an athlete. The first is to systematically monitor changes in the athlete's physiology over time and relate such changes to the effectiveness of the current training regimen. In this case you would expect the changes in various types of training to influence different aspects of physiology. For example, for a novice rider, an improvement in muscular efficiency would be expected after endurance training, whereas an increase in anaerobic power would be expected when a rider had focused on high-intensity sprint training. Additionally, if testing is undertaken on a regular basis, it may be possible for the coach to use the results to evaluate early warning signs of overtraining (see chapter 2).

The second main reason for undertaking testing is to identify the specific strengths and weaknesses of an athlete's physiology that may influence the achievement of a particular goal (e.g., a cyclist who has an impressive anaerobic power may be a good sprinter and is, therefore, likely to achieve success in track cycling events). This topic is addressed in chapter 7.

Once you have analyzed the demands of a particular discipline (e.g., road racing and mountain biking have differing requirements) or single event (some riders have been known to evaluate world championship courses two years in advance), you can compare the results of the physiological evaluation with what may be considered optimal. By making this comparison, any areas in which performance is lacking will be highlighted, and you can design appropriate training programs to overcome these weaknesses.

It must be noted, however, that although two riders may show similar outcomes in physiological evaluation, their performance in actual competition may vary considerably. This is because there are many other aspects that can affect competitive performance. Therefore, the real value of fitness testing is to systematically monitor changes in physiology over time. Any changes in physiological performance then can be used when reviewing the next training program. Chapter 7 discusses laboratory based methods of physiological assessment and how they can be used to determine specific strengths or weakness of a cyclist. Here we will discuss physiological assessment in the light of monitoring training progress. In addition, chapter 7 focused on laboratory based measurements, which unfortunately are not always readily accessible or affordable for everyone. Therefore, we will also discuss alternative methods that can be used outside the laboratory environment.

What and How to Test

The importance of exercise testing is well understood by athletes in many sports including cycling. However, the question arises as to what is the most appropriate method of testing physiological characteristics. To answer this, three factors must be considered. The first is to ensure sport specificity of the testing method, the second is to assess validity of the tests chosen, and the third is to examine the reliability of the tests.

Before undertaking any test procedure, cyclists and their coaches must ensure that any testing protocols administered accurately reflect the energy requirements of their particular event (these are outlined in this chapter and in chapter 7). More important, you also should undertake the testing in conditions similar to those met during your competition. For example, a test cannot be truly deemed sport-specific if a cyclist is made to ride a laboratory ergometer in which the position or the gearing differs significantly from his usual training/competition bicycle. Additionally, if a cyclist is accustomed to riding outdoors (at an average speed of approximately 30 to 40 kilometers per hour) with a "normal" ambient temperature of approximately 15 degrees Celsius, it is likely that riding indoors in approximately 20 degrees Celsius with no wind cooling effect will yield differing physiological responses (especially in heart rate and sweat rate). Therefore, a sport-specific test should stress the energy systems that would be important to competitive outcome under conditions in which his riding position and environment are as close to "normal" as possible.

It is important that the test measures what it claims to measure (i.e., the test should be valid), and if it were repeated it should provide the same results (i.e., be reliable). Although this sounds obvious, if a testing procedure does not accurately measure what it is designed to do, the interpretation of results may prove difficult at best and, at worst, impossible. Consider an athlete wishing to relate maximal oxygen consumption with performance. Unfortunately, because of ability, the test chosen by this athlete lasted less than five minutes. As a result, as much as 30 percent of the power produced may have been generated by anaerobic (non-oxygen-using) sources. Therefore, changes in power output observed in subsequent tests would be difficult to put down to changes in aerobic ability, anaerobic ability, or both.

To further ensure the reliability of the testing so that ongoing comparisons in test results can be made, some amount of pretest control should be assumed. This should include some athlete and environmental controls. Essentially, before testing, a cyclist should do the following:

- Be fully fit—that is, illness and injury free.
- Be in a rested condition—that is, able to perform maximally. Ideally, the cyclist should be in the same physical condition as would be expected for an important competition. A minimum rest period of 24 to 48 hours from previous heavy training or competition is often recommended.
- Be fully hydrated and carbohydrate repleted. Nutritional preparation for a test could be similar to preparation before a race. For guidelines for optimal preparation, see chapter 14.
- Have a standardized (or quantified) warm-up that will allow maximal performance without the risk of injury.
- Use his or her usual training or competition equipment, including bike, shoes, and clothing. Where the use of the cyclist's own bicycle is not possible, the cyclist should take great care to exactly replicate his or her normal position before commencing the testing.
- Undertake the tests when he or she is used to competing and training.
- List training, diet, environmental conditions, and any other stressors that may influence performance in the days preceding the testing.

The cyclist who wishes to fully maximize the potential benefits of cycle testing should therefore consider undertaking physiological assessment under carefully controlled conditions so that ongoing changes in physiology and strengths and weaknesses can be carefully monitored. The actual methods of testing used often depend on the physiological stresses of the particular event but usually employ some manner of testing submaximal (endurance) exercise, maximal aerobic performance, and sprinting ability.

Physiological Determinants of Cycling Performance

The physiological characteristics of trained cyclists have been provided in great detail both in this book (see chapter 7) and in other scientific journals (Coyle et al. 1988, 1991; Faria et al. 1989; Martin et al. 2001; Hawley and Stepto 2001). In general, these sources suggest that having a high maximal oxygen uptake and peak aerobic power output may prove beneficial to endurance performance. In conjunction with this is the ability of a well-trained athlete to sustain a high economy of motion. This means that the athlete will use the least amount of oxygen possible to produce the highest

Most cycling involves both endurance and sprint abilities, which require anaerobic power and capacity.

work by the muscle. Most cycle racing, however (with possibly the exception of time trials), requires both endurance and sprint abilities, and therefore anaerobic power and capacity also must be viewed as important.

Laboratory Measures of Physiological Characteristics

From an overview of the number of texts (Australian Sports Commission 2000; Maud and Foster 1995; MacDougall et al. 1991) and journal articles (e.g., Hopkins et al. 2001) pertaining to laboratory-based methods of measurement, it is clear that there is no definitive laboratory-based test that can be used to determine the physiological characteristics of an athlete. The chosen method of testing often is a reflection of the preferences of the sport scientist or a result of the particular needs of the athlete. However, for cycling several basic areas should be considered, which include the following.

Maximal Characteristics

Maximal oxygen uptake ($\dot{V}O_2$max) is one of the most frequently used measures of athletic endurance ability. Simply stated, $\dot{V}O_2$max is the ability of an individual to extract oxygen from the atmosphere, deliver it to the working muscle, and use it to combust fuel. The more oxygen that can be used for oxidation, the greater power the muscle can produce. A cyclist would hope to have the highest ability to consume oxygen to deliver as much power as possible. Hence, at the same time point as measuring $\dot{V}O_2$max, a measure of peak aerobic power (Wmax) often is taken (see chapters 6 and 7).

Additionally, oxygen uptake can be considered in absolute (total oxygen consumed per minute) and relative (oxygen consumed per kilogram of body weight per minute) terms. A rider who hopes to achieve a high power output for a short duration would hope to have a high absolute $\dot{V}O_2$max, whereas an endurance rider (who would require a low body weight to assist in climbing) would hope to have a high relative $\dot{V}O_2$max. Likewise, a cyclist with a high power-to-body-mass ratio (Wmax/BM) is expected to climb well and to have a good ability to accelerate (chapter 7). Thus, changes in body mass also may have a bearing on changes in specific measures and performance outcome.

Finally, measuring heart rate at the same time point as $\dot{V}O_2$max allows for the use of heart rate as an indicator of aerobic training intensity. It is important to note that heart rate also will be affected by psychological stress, dehydration, thermal stress, poor nutrition, and fatigue, and so standardization of testing methods and evaluation of maximal heart rate at a known point (maximal aerobic power) is important (see chapter 5).

Although there may be many variations on a theme, $\dot{V}O_2$max is best measured by the athlete undertaking a continuous incremental test to exhaustion. For the non-elite rider, this is best achieved when the workload chosen is increased at a rate in which the athlete fatigues between 8 and 12 minutes. This time is optimal because if the test were shorter, anaerobic metabolism would be a major influencing factor, and if the test were much longer, the result might be affected by fatigue. However, many sport scientists like to use stages of up to 5 minutes when working with elite or extremely well-trained cyclists. In those cases the test can last as long as 50 minutes (Australian Sports Commission 2000). The advantage of the longer stages is that submaximal measures can be obtained in the same test.

Submaximal Economy

Submaximal economy is most easily defined as the oxygen cost to work at a given (known) intensity. As a rider becomes more biomechanically efficient, the oxygen cost to work at a given intensity will fall. In addition to this, as the athlete's endurance training status increases, the delivery mechanisms (i.e., transport of oxygen in blood to working muscle) will become more effective and again economy will increase. Both of these factors will help the athlete produce a larger amount of work for a given oxygen cost (or a lower oxygen cost for the same workload), thereby increasing his or her endurance capabilities. In addition, such changes also may indirectly increase an athlete's $\dot{V}O_2$max by both improving the delivery system and enhancing muscular contraction.

To test submaximal economy, an athlete usually would undergo several (two to three) periods of exercise for five to six minutes at a fixed intensity, usually at a range of intensities up to 40-kilometer time-trial race pace. During this period, both heart rate and $\dot{V}O_2$ could be assessed. Oxygen cost for a given power then would be used to evaluate economy (Coyle 1995).

Blood Lactate Threshold

Blood lactate threshold is another method for determining submaximal economy. Lactate is produced when the body is unable to supply all of its energy needs aerobically (using oxygen). Through the taking of blood samples (usually from a finger prick) over a range of workloads, a blood lactate profile can be determined. The point where lactate begins to rise faster than workload indicates a transitory threshold that may prove valuable for training prescription.

Although lactate testing can be undertaken at the same time as a measure of submaximal economy, its true value has not been clarified. There are difficulties in accurately assessing the threshold point, because there appears to be day-to-day variation of lactate responses (see chapter 5). Additionally, problems arise in the mathematical method of accurately determining the exact threshold. Therefore, the determination of lactate threshold and its use in training may not be beneficial to all athletes.

Time-Trial Ability

A further method of measuring the submaximal capabilities of a cyclist is by undertaking laboratory-based time trials. These normally would be over a time period approximating to a distance of about 20 kilometers and are a reflection of the actual demands of cycling competition. They are, however, reliant on the athletes' ability to pace themselves effectively (and an assumption that an athlete is well motivated). Although a time-trial test can be a good indicator of sustained power production and average heart rate for an effort of this type, which relates well to actual time-trial performance in the field (Palmer et al. 1996), it is difficult to accurately determine any other physiological response because of the self-paced and, hence, non-steady-state nature of the effort.

Anaerobic Power and Capacity

Although an athlete may rely on good endurance capabilities to successfully complete a race, a large proportion of success in road cycling and mountain biking depends on anaerobic capabilities. Many laboratories use the standard Wingate protocol (Australian Sports Commission 2000) to test anaerobic ability. This requires the athlete to complete as much work as possible in a 30-second sprint test. Peak power and average power in the 30 seconds are given to equate to anaerobic power (the maximal power generated by the muscle) and anaerobic capacity (the total power that the muscle can produce using anaerobic sources). These are thought to equate to an athlete's ability to sprint.

Testing on a Velodrome

Tests can be performed under fairly standardized conditions on a track. A similar progressive test as used in a laboratory (see chapter 7) has been applied on a velodrome, with road cyclists as subjects and with satisfactory results. In this test, the cyclist performs fixed-distance stages at a progressively increasing speed. Initial speed is set at 28 kilometers per hour, and it is increased by 1.5 kilometers per hour until exhaustion, with one-minute passive recovery intervals (Padilla et al. 1996). The power output developed by a cyclist at a given velodrome speed is estimated as follows (Di Prampero et al. 1979):

$$W = (0.045 \times P \times v) + [0.041 \times BSA \times (P_b/T) \times v^3]$$

where 0.045 is rolling resistance, P is the mass of the cyclist and his bicycle (in kilograms), v is speed (in meters per second), 0.041 is air resistance, P_b is atmospheric pressure (millimeters of mercury), and T is air temperature (Kelvin). If we assume an efficiency of 25 percent, $\dot{V}O_2$ is estimated as follows (Di Prampero et al. 1979):

$$\dot{V}O_2 = [R_1 \times P \times v + R_2 \times BSA \times (P_b/T) \times v^3] + MB$$

where $R_1 = 8.6 \times 10^{-3}$, $R_2 = 7.8 \times 10^{-3}$, and MB is the basal metabolism, considered to be equal to 3.6 milliliters $O_2 \times$ kilograms per liter per minute.

As chapter 6 discusses, the velodrome also can be used to obtain measurements of aerodynamics. Ideally, these tests at constant speed are carried out using a power-measuring device. After several laps at constant speed, the power is averaged. After a change in position, the same test is performed again at the same speed. Improved aerodynamics should result in decreased power output at a given speed. If no power-measuring device is available, a heart rate monitor could be used to identify changes in aerodynamic drag. It must be noted, however, that heart rate will not be sensitive enough to pick up small differences that might be expected if the position on the bicycle is already near optimal.

Field-Based Testing

Although laboratory-based fitness tests may be deemed the gold standard for performance monitoring, they are likely to prove costly and may be difficult for all riders to access. However, as the results of frequent testing will benefit all riders, cyclists must consider undertaking similar tests either on the road or on an indoor cycle. The main difficulty in such field testing is the reliability of the results gained, and therefore the rider should ensure the test conditions are standardized wherever possible (as previously highlighted for laboratory testing). Ideally, the cyclist should undertake testing on an indoor home trainer under controlled conditions or on a short road circuit free from traffic, tight bends, and hazardous junctions. If you are doing the test on an indoor trainer, ensure that both the contact force between wheel and roller and the tire pressure are constant between tests to ensure the same rolling resistance for each test. This can be simply checked: Accelerate to a certain speed (e.g., 40 kilometers per hour), stop pedaling, and measure the time it takes for the wheel to reach a stop. If the rolling resistance is constant, this time should be constant each time a test is undertaken. A lower rolling resistance will cause the wheel to turn longer.

An additional problem with field testing is that currently there are no scientific studies linking performance in field-based tests, done outside the velodrome, to those undertaken in controlled laboratory conditions—and as a result both the athlete and coach need to be aware that some physiological responses (e.g., $\dot{V}O_2$max, economy, blood lactate) cannot be estimated from field-based testing. However, this does not detract from the value of the assessments that the athlete can undertake.

Cyclists can use virtually any protocol because the critical factor for any method of testing is that the test be easily repeatable, giving accurate, reliable results. However, for the test to be valid (i.e., similar to the physiological responses measured during competition), some degree of sport specificity is advised. Hence, we would advise the following protocol (shown in figure 8.1) for determining submaximal aerobic, maximal, and sprint capabilities.

Submaximal Test

Figure 8.1 portrays an example of a test protocol that any rider could easily use. The first 15 minutes of the test act as a standardized warm-up and with repeat testing

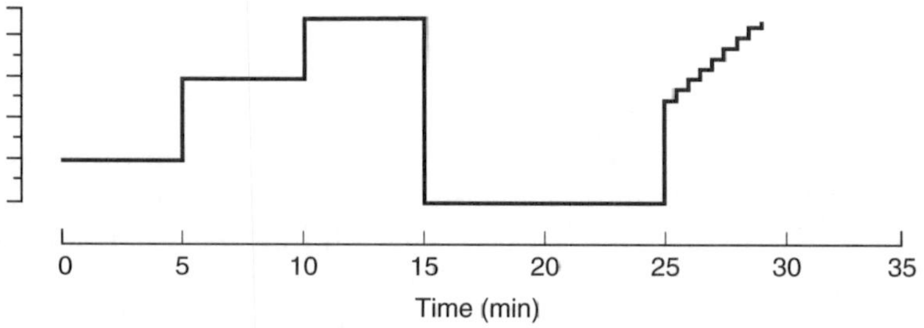

Figure 8.1 Proposed testing protocol.

would give an indication of changes in submaximal physiology. This is followed by a five-minute recuperation period before commencing a period of incremental effort to exhaustion.

During the submaximal bout, the final speed should equate to current 40-kilometer (approximately 25-mile) time-trial pace, the second speed should equal current endurance training pace (the average riding speed for a two- to three-hour training ride), and the first effort should match warm-up intensity. Each of these workloads should be maintained for five minutes before any increase in pace. Ideally, heart rate should be measured each 30 seconds of the 15-minute effort; however, a simple recording of heart rate during the last 10 seconds of each bout would be sufficient if advanced heart-rate monitoring apparatus was not available.

Unless you observe large changes in your performance ability (e.g., five minutes over 40 kilometers), future tests should be performed at the same intensity and using the same gearing. Ideally, with improvements in fitness, you should observe a fall in heart rate for each work stage. Additionally, if funding and facilities are available (e.g., by a local cycling club), it also may be beneficial to record lactate at the end of each stage (this should show a fall with endurance training) and power output for the last 60 seconds of each work stage (to monitor there were no differences in effort between tests).

Maximal Test

During the maximal test, you would be required to increase your speed every 30 seconds by one kilometer per hour until exhaustion (figure 8.1). For most riders, a starting speed of between 25 and 35 kilometers per hour would be appropriate; however, several attempts may initially be required for you to be happy with the regular pace changes, and to find the correct starting workload. Because of the increases in speed, you should change gears as and when you feel comfortable. Additionally, if you feel the need to be "out of the saddle," this would be reasonable for short periods. If you do the test on an indoor trainer, use a fan to reduce heat stress.

Although a rider and coach can neither measure nor predict oxygen uptake from this test, they can assess improvements in physiological function by the maximal speed that could be attained. Additionally, observing heart rate during the last 30 seconds before fatigue would give a true indicator of maximal aerobic heart rate and could be used for training purposes (see chapter 5).

As with the submaximal efforts, using a relatively low-cost power-measuring system (see chapter 6) would give a more accurate indication of changes in performance capabilities. Additionally, a rider could use an accurate measure of power to determine maximal power-to-weight ratio, which is a good indicator of climbing and sprinting (acceleration) ability.

Sprint Test

Rarely does a rider perform a single sprint, and some reflection of this could easily be made in a testing protocol. Therefore, after a recovery period of 45 to 60 minutes (remember to keep this the same for future tests), you should undertake a series of three hill sprints. Optimally, you should use a hill that has a constant gradient for approximately one kilometer. From a standing start (assistance may be required for this), you would try to cover as much distance as possible in 30 seconds. A note of this distance should be made. This process should be repeated two more times with a three-minute recovery of easy riding between each effort. To make comparisons between future tests, maintain the selected gearing throughout the three efforts and record it for future reference.

Although this assessment again will not provide any immediate indicators of strengths and weaknesses, you can, as with the other tests, use it to evaluate the efficacy of a training regimen. Endurance training would be expected to have little bearing on the distance covered in the initial sprint but may influence performance in the second and third sprints via improved recovery. When you undertake speed and power training, the distance in the initial sprint would be expected to increase, and there also may be a slightly smaller drop-off in the performance of the second and third sprints.

When to Test

Each person must decide the most appropriate time to undertake physiological assessment. The optimal solution is to undertake testing as frequently as possible (essentially every four to eight weeks). However, this may cause problems because each athlete should have a full rest day before testing and may be unable to train satisfactorily on the day of the test. Therefore, we propose that the athlete undertake some form of physiological assessment between two and six times a year.

Ideally, riders should undertake a test before and after each different training phase and either shortly before or after their major competitions to get an ongoing view of the year. Cyclists or their coaches should continually use testing as a method of monitoring changes in physiology as a result of training and, where appropriate, change the training as necessary.

Summary

Physiological assessment for any sport can give an athlete and coach useful feedback on both the efficacy of a training regimen and the strengths and weaknesses of the individual athlete. However, the testing methods must be both valid and reliable. Additionally, cyclists should plan to test maximal, submaximal, and anaerobic (sprint) capacities to consider the full physiological profile required for success. Although standardizing external factors in a laboratory setting is easier, field-based testing may be valuable in some conditions. Finally, athletes should undertake assessment on a frequent basis with strict standardization before and during the test to make meaningful comparisons.

part III

Body and Machine

The first bicycles were built in the 19th century. As bicycle technology in the late 19th century continued to advance, riders soon saw beyond the practicalities of this two-wheeled invention, and bicycle racing was born. The first record of an organized race took place outside of Paris in 1868. The event was a hit, and soon more races were scheduled. Bicycle racing continued to grow in popularity, both in Europe and in the United States. In 1891, Henri Desgrange—later the organizer of the first Tour de France—set the first World Hour record at a speed of just over 35 kilometers per hour.

The first bicycles were made of wood and later steel and weighed between 15 and 25 kilograms (33 to 55 pounds). Nowadays, top bicycles are made of aluminum or carbon fiber and weigh between 7 and 9 kilograms (15 to 20 pounds). Whereas the first bicycles did not have gears, today road bicycles have between 18 and 20 gears. The shape of bicycles has changed considerably as well, with aerodynamic tubing becoming more and more common.

Clearly technology has advanced enormously and this also is reflected in the World Hour record. Sharp improvements were noticeable from the moment aerodynamics became an important issue. On the other hand, now that the Union Cycliste Internationale has changed regulations and there are severe limitations on a rider's body position and the construction and shape of the bicycle, the distance covered in one hour is reduced again. These examples illustrate the importance of body shape and position and the design and material of the bicycle. Biomechanics also has received a lot of attention, and part III's chapters about body and machine discuss all these factors.

Body Position and Aerodynamics

Jim Martin
John Cobb

The recent Union Cycliste Internationale (UCI) rule changes regarding bicycle design and the large number of aero products on the market highlight the performance-enhancing potential of aerodynamic bikes. It is certainly possible to gain "free" speed with the use of such equipment: to go faster for no increase in effort or fitness. However, improvements in the aerodynamics of the machine must be viewed within the context of the bicycle and rider combination. Here is a simple exercise to illustrate the point: Stand in front of a mirror with your bicycle. Which is larger, your bike or your body? Clearly, the frontal area of your body is much larger than that of your bicycle. This simple observation is important to cycling because aerodynamic drag is a function of frontal area. Consequently, your body is much more of a determinant of your aerodynamic drag than your bicycle is.

Even though your body has a large frontal area, the frontal area you present during cycling can be modified by changing your body position. Another simple exercise will illustrate how dramatic those changes can be: Set your bicycle up on a trainer in front of a mirror and observe your frontal area with your hands on the tops of the handlebars, the brake hoods, and the drops, and with your elbows on the aerobars. You will observe a dramatic range in frontal area as you change from one position to the next. Indeed, within each of those hand positions, you can substantially affect your frontal area by flexing or extending your arms. Each of those observed changes will significantly alter your cycling velocity. This chapter uses a mathematical model to explore the way in which changes in body position influence cycling velocity.

Cycling Model

$$P_{TOT} = [V_a^2 V_G \tfrac{1}{2}\rho (C_D A + F_w) + V_G C_{RR} m_T g \cos(\tan^{-1}(G_R)) + V_G(91 + 8.7V_G)10^{-3}$$
$$+ V_G m_T g \sin(\tan^{-1}(G_R) + \tfrac{1}{2}(m_T + I/r^2)(v_f^2 - v_i^2)/(t_i - t_f)]/E_C$$

where

- V_a is the air velocity of the bicycle tangent to the direction of travel of the bike and rider (which depends on wind velocity and the ground velocity of the bicycle)
- V_G is the ground velocity of the bicycle
- ρ is air density
- C_D is the coefficient of drag of the bicycle and rider
- A is the frontal area of the bicycle and rider
- F_w is an expression equivalent to the drag area (C_DA) of the spokes
- C_{RR} is the coefficient of rolling resistance
- m_T is the total mass of the bicycle and rider
- g is the acceleration due to gravity
- G_R is the gradient of the road surface
- $V_G(91 + 8.7V_G)10^{-3}$ is an expression for wheel-bearing friction
- I is the combined moment of inertia of two wheels
- r is the radius of the bicycle wheel
- subscripts i and f represent initial and final conditions of measurement interval
- E_C is the efficiency of the chain-drive system

The velocity of the bike and rider is the result of the balance between the propulsive force applied to the pedals and the sum of all the resistive forces acting on the bike. These resistive forces include some obvious (wind resistance or drag and rolling resistance) and some less obvious (inertia of the wheels and efficiency of the chain system) forms of resistance. Martin et al. (1998) proposed an equation to model the power required to maintain any velocity (see sidebar).

The model was validated by comparing predicted power with power measured during outdoor road cycling (Martin et al. 1998). In this study, the modeled power agreed with the measured power (modeled power = 1.00 × measured power; R^2 = 0.97, SEE = 2.7 watts). Thus the equation enables us to examine the effects of different body positions on cycling velocity under various conditions.

Baseline Values for Drag Area

Over the past decade, many wind-tunnel tests of cyclists have been conducted at the Texas A&M University Aerodynamics Laboratory, the General Motors Aerodynamics Laboratory, and the Dutch National Aerospace Laboratory. Data were collected on more than 100 athletes ranging from world-champion cyclists to novice triathletes. Drawing on those data, the researchers compiled drag-area (i.e., the product of frontal area and coefficient of drag; C_DA) values for several common cycling positions (see table 9.1). These data are representative of the specified body position for a 70-kilogram (154-pound) rider and a standard bicycle and wheels (i.e., non-airfoil-shaped tubing, rims, and spokes; chapter 10 addresses the effects of aerodynamic equipment).

TABLE 9.1 Drag Area of Typical 70-kg (154-lb) Cyclist in Several Common Riding Positions

	Hand position	Arm position	Drag area (cm^2)
Standing	Brake hoods		4,080
Seated	Top of handlebar	Straight arms	4,010
Seated	Brake hoods	Bent arms	3,240
Seated	Handlebar drops	Bent arms	3,070
Seated	Aerobars	Typical	2,914
Seated	Aerobars	Optimized	2,680

Body Position, Power, and Velocity on Flat Terrain

The relative importance of the various resistive forces varies with velocity, terrain, environmental conditions, road surface, and mechanical specifics of the bicycle. For cycling over relatively level terrain, however, the principal resistive force is usually aerodynamic drag. That is, most of the power you deliver to your pedals acts to push you and your bicycle through the air.

To demonstrate the effects of body position, the reference drag-area data were used in the model to predict the velocity that would result if a rider produced 100 to 400 watts in each of the referenced positions. In this modeled scenario, it was assumed that the road was level and there was no wind. Figure 9.1 shows the absolute velocities predicted for each power and position. For each body position, the power-velocity relationship was curvilinear and velocity at 400 watts was approximately 66 percent greater than at 100 watts. The observation that a threefold (300 percent) increase in power only increased velocity by about 66 percent serves to highlight the fact that power, for flat terrain and calm conditions, is mainly a function of velocity cubed.

To illustrate just how important a good position can be, we use the example of a good club-level cyclist who is able to produce an average of 300 watts for a 40-kilometer

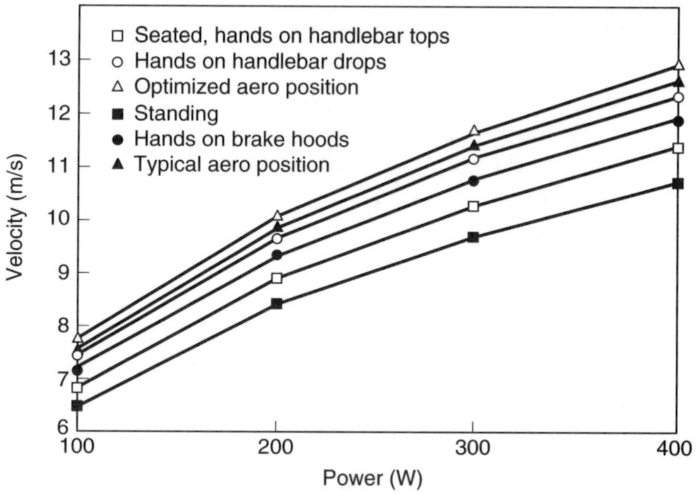

Figure 9.1 Power-velocity relationships for level road cycling with six body positions. Positions with a lower drag area allow higher velocity for any specific power output, and velocity varied by approximately 20 percent for the positions modeled. Velocity increased approximately 66 percent when power increased from 100 to 400 watts.

time trial. Figure 9.1 shows that the difference in velocity resulting from the drag of being seated with hands on the tops and being in a typical aero position is 1.1 meters per second (4 kilometers per hour).

This equates to a huge 6-minute, 14-second difference (64 minutes, 43 seconds compared to 58 minutes, 29 seconds) over a flat 40-kilometer time trial. Possibly more important is the change that optimizing your aero position can have—reducing your drag by 8 percent increases your speed by 0.3 meter per second (1.1 kilometers per hour) for the same power output, leading to a decrease in time of approximately 1 minute, 30 seconds (58 minutes, 29 seconds compared to 56 minutes, 57 seconds).

Another way to exhibit the effect of drag area on velocity is to group the data from figure 9.1 by power output and plot the data with drag-area values on the x-axis (see figure 9.2). In this way, it is clear that, for any specific power output, velocity increases with reduced drag area. When velocity for each power is expressed as a percentage of the velocity for the standing position (see figure 9.3), it is clear that relative differences in velocity are nearly independent of power (19.4 percent for 100 watts and 20.4 percent for 400 watts).

The observation that changes in position produced proportionately similar changes in velocity for all the power outputs evaluated may seem surprising. Indeed, a comment often heard from cyclists is that they believe aerodynamics are not critical until they ride above some certain velocity. That is, they seem to believe that improvements in aerodynamic drag will not affect their performance unless they ride at or above some critical velocity. Our data do not support the notion of such a critical velocity. Rather, our model predicts that, for flat terrain and calm conditions, any decrease in drag area will increase cycling velocity by a similar proportion regardless of the initial velocity or power.

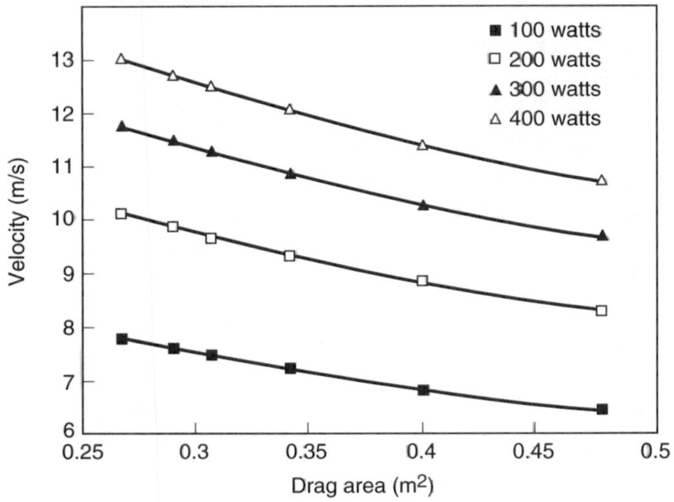

Figure 9.2 Velocity versus drag area for level road cycling with four power outputs. For each power output, velocity decreased curvilinearly with an increasing drag area.

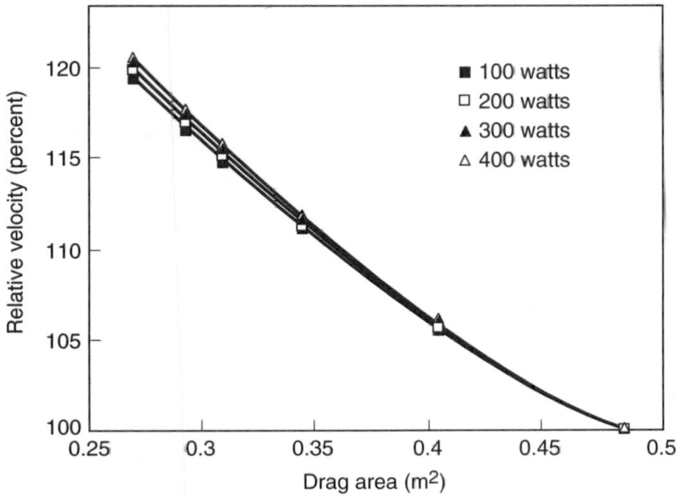

Figure 9.3 Relative velocity versus drag area for level road cycling with four power outputs. Relative velocity is the ratio of velocity for each position to the velocity for the standing position. For each power output, velocity varied by approximately 20 percent from standing to the optimized aero position. The relationships were nearly independent of power.

Body Position, Power, and Velocity During Climbing

During uphill cycling, a portion of cycling power is required to overcome gravity. As road grade becomes increasingly steep, the portion of total power required to overcome gravity increases. Additionally, cycling velocity typically is reduced when climbing and power associated with aerodynamic drag (absolute and as a proportion of total power) also is reduced. Consequently, it may seem that the aerodynamic effects of body position are not applicable, or at least not important, when climbing. That perception is supported by the observation that many excellent climbers climb, and attack on climbs, while standing (i.e., in a high drag-area position). However, other elite climbers are known to remain seated even on steep climbs. It seems, therefore, that the importance of aerodynamics during climbing is unclear. To determine the extent to which drag area affects uphill cycling, we used the mathematical model to determine the velocity that would result from producing 100 to 400 watts on road grades of 5, 10, and 15 percent in three of the referenced positions: standing, seated with hands on the brake hoods and arms bent, and the optimized aerobar position.

We found that for climbing at higher powers and less steep gradients, aerodynamics are still important (see figure 9.4). For example, compared with the seated position, cycling in an optimized aerobar position up a 5 percent incline increased velocity by 0.6 percent at 100 watts and 3.7 percent at 400 watts compared to riding on the tops of the handlebars (as most cyclists do). If you compare this to a 15 percent climb in which the same change in position produces improvements of only 0.1 percent at 100 watts and 0.7 percent at 400 watts, you can see that as the gradient increases and speed falls the importance of aerodynamics is reduced.

The model predictions for uphill cycling velocity serve to emphasize the interactive effects of cycling power, body position, and road grade on cycling velocity. Even though the relationship is complex and interactive, our results allow for certain broad generalizations regarding climbing and body position. First, the effects of changes in body position were smallest for the 100-watt condition and increased with each increase in power. Therefore, those who climb with high power or climb moderate grades will realize improvements in velocity if they climb in a seated position compared with a standing position.

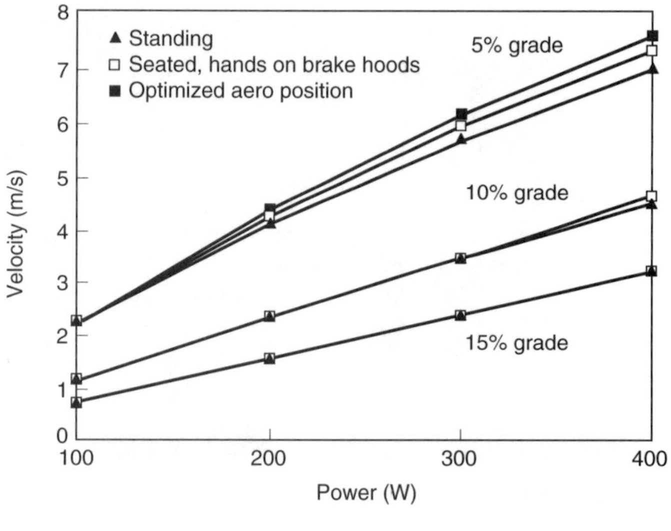

Figure 9.4 Power versus velocity relationships for three body positions and three road grades. Velocity decreased with increasing road grade. Additionally, the effects of body position on velocity were reduced with increasing road grade.

At lower power outputs and steeper grades, our model indicated that position had little effect on cycling velocity when power was equal in the seated and standing positions. However, when a cyclist is standing up to pedal, additional metabolic energy is required to support body weight. Ryschon and Stray-Gundersen (1991) reported that oxygen uptake was 3.4 milliliters per kilogram per minute greater for a standing position compared with a seated position during submaximal cycling. That increase in energy expenditure suggests that maximal sustained power would be reduced by approximately 17 watts when a rider is cycling in the standing position. Consequently, it is more appropriate to compare seated and standing climbing by changing both drag area and power output. If this reduced power (i.e., 83, 183, 283, and 383 watts) was used in our model and a grade of 15 percent was assumed, then the velocity was reduced by 17 percent compared to 100 watts and 4 percent compared to 400 watts.

Thus, even on the steepest road grades, it may be essential for the cyclist to remain seated for reasons related to metabolic cost and aerodynamic drag. Riders with lower power output will particularly benefit by climbing in a seated position because the 17-watt "cost of standing" represents a large portion of their total power, and elite cyclists also will benefit significantly because of the combined effects of power and aerodynamic benefits. Training should therefore concentrate on seated climbing even though there may be many competition scenarios in which standing climbing is unavoidable. All cyclists know that for maximum force production, only standing up will do, and sometimes to break away or respond to an attack you have to sacrifice efficiency for short-term power.

© Newsport Photography

A cyclist can lose up to 17 watts of power output while standing, so seated climbing is a good option, especially for cyclists with lower power outputs.

Important Elements of Position

Throughout this chapter, we have used a set of reference values for aerodynamic drag area. Although these values represent good approximations to the drag area of a 70-kilogram (154-pound) rider in each position, those values are not fixed. Rather, a cyclist can influence his drag area in several ways. Riding with knees close to the centerline of the bicycle frame can reduce drag area by approximately 8 percent compared with riding with knees wide apart. This knee position will affect drag similarly whether the rider uses conventional racing handlebars or aerobars.

For riding with standard handlebars, arm position, including elbow bend and forearm alignment, can even more dramatically influence drag area. Bending the elbows allows the rider to lower his torso and thus reduce frontal area. Indeed, carefully positioned arms with the forearms horizontal and parallel to the bicycle can reduce drag area by up to 12 percent compared with widely positioned arms or straightened elbows. A wide-elbow position may result from poor technique, but it also may be due to poor bike fit and thus may not be within the control of the rider. Specifically, if the saddle-to-handlebar distance is too short, the rider may be forced to widen the arms so that they do not contact the legs. Consequently, drag area may be substantially increased because of a poorly fitted frame-stem-handlebar combination.

Optimal Time-Trial Position

Riders often ask, "How do I optimize my time-trial position?" The simple answer is, "Go to a wind tunnel and have your aerodynamic drag measured in various positions." But, of course, not every cyclist has the opportunity to take part in wind-tunnel optimization. As an alternative, we offer several suggestions that will help riders position themselves using only a trainer and a mirror or video camera. We recommend the following procedures to establish a preliminary position before wind-tunnel testing, and this often will result in a position that is within a few percentages of the optimal drag area.

Over the past 10 years, two very different approaches for optimizing aerodynamic position have been used. During the early 1990s, it was recommended that riders use a dedicated time-trial bicycle with a steep seat-tube angle (78 to 84 degrees). With bicycles like this, a low drag-area position could be achieved with a relatively formulaic procedure. Those positions are, at the present time, allowed for triathlons and by some national cycling federations. However, UCI rules currently prohibit forward seat positions. Within the current UCI rules, low drag-area positions can be achieved but the procedure is less formulaic and depends on individual morphological characteristics.

To achieve a low drag position with a forward seat position, start with your current road position. You achieve the aero position by "rolling" that position forward until the torso is horizontal. Specifically, the elbow pads should be lowered and the seat should be moved forward (and slightly up) so that the body rotates about the bottom bracket and the joint angles at the hip and knee are maintained. You can use a mirror or a video camera to assure yourself that your torso is horizontal and that your relative hip, knee, and ankle angles are maintained during this procedure. This procedure usually results in seat positions that require a bicycle seat-tube angle of 78 to 84 degrees depending on body type. Taller or more slender riders tend to require less steep seat-tube angles, whereas shorter or more muscular riders require greater seat-tube angles to achieve a horizontal torso. You can achieve a similar position using a standard frame with a forward-angled seat post and a long stem. However, that configuration may result in a bicycle that may not handle well. If you are to use a forward position, we recommend that the frame be specifically designed for proper handling with that position.

Once you have achieved the horizontal torso position, it has been our experience that details regarding positioning of the arms are less critical. Changing elbow-pad width (center to center) from 11 to 14 centimeters has almost no effect on total drag area, but wider positions (greater than 20 centimeters) can increase drag area by 0 to 3 percent. Similarly, arm angles (measured from horizontal) of 5 to 40 degrees have very little influence (0 to 3 percent) on drag area. The small effect of these changes on drag area suggests that, once a horizontal torso position is established, differences in arm position only affect the location of the arm's frontal area but do not significantly affect coefficient of drag or total drag area.

Cyclists must accomplish aerodynamic positioning for bicycles with conventional seat-tube angles with more subtlety. Initially, riders must learn to roll their hips over as described by Lemond and Gordis (1987). This posture can be difficult to adopt, but it is an essential element of a low drag-area position with a standard bicycle. The level to which the elbow pads can be lowered will be limited by contact between thigh and torso (which will occur at acute hip angles). Because the elbow pads cannot be radically lowered, frontal area cannot be dramatically reduced for a conventional seat-tube-angle bicycle. Rather, reductions in drag area must be accomplished with careful positioning of the hands, arms, and shoulders to reduce the coefficient of drag. Specifically, the width of the hands and elbows and the angle of the forearms are critical elements that, in an optimal configuration, act to channel airflow around the rider's torso. Additionally, the contour of the rider's shoulders can influence the point at which airflow separates. Rounding the shoulders and rolling them forward (i.e., protraction and downward rotation of the shoulder joint) can allow airflow to stay attached further around the rider's body and thereby reduce pressure drag. The combined effects of redirecting (arm and hand position) and smoothing (shoulder contour) airflow around the body can reduce drag area by 10 to 20 percent.

Comfort and Power

Optimized aerodynamic positions can be uncomfortable in two ways. First, by rotating the hips forward, the cyclist places pressure directly on highly sensitive areas. Additional seat padding may help to distribute that pressure but probably will not completely eliminate the discomfort. Some riders try to alleviate this problem by tilting the nose of the saddle down, but that approach will result in a tendency for the rider to slide forward, off of the saddle. That sliding force must be restrained with forces produced at the shoulders and arms that can become fatigued very quickly. Second, riders may experience muscle soreness or strain in the muscles that extend the neck. This discomfort will be reduced with training and can be ameliorated with stretching and massage.

Riders often express concern that changes in position may compromise their power or efficiency. Heil et al. (1995) investigated the effects of seat-tube angle on metabolic efficiency and reported that efficiency was significantly greater with 83- and 90-degree seat-tube angles than with a 69-degree seat-tube angle. Similarly, Price and Donne (1997) reported that efficiency with an 80-degree seat-tube angle was higher than that with 68 or 74 degrees. Thus, steep seat-tube-angle bicycles should not decrease metabolic efficiency and, indeed, may improve efficiency. Conversely, Heil et al. (1997) reported that reductions in mean hip angle increased cardiovascular stress for a given power output. Such decreases in hip angle often occur when riders attempt to reduce their frontal area by lowering their elbows excessively. Therefore, you must exercise caution when adjusting your position to avoid excessive hip flexion.

Summary

This exploration has produced several useful findings for the cyclist. Typical cycling positions exhibit drag-area values that range from 0.48 to 0.27 meter squared, which can mean up to a 20 percent difference in velocity for a given power output. Surprisingly, the proportional difference in velocity is nearly independent of power, suggesting that novice and elite cyclists will realize similar benefits from improved aerodynamic positioning. When a rider is cycling uphill, differences in cycling velocity related to drag area are markedly reduced but are still substantial for less steep grades and for high power outputs. Even though the effect of drag area is reduced during uphill cycling, adopting a standing position is not recommended because of increases in metabolic energy expenditure. Finally, for any given cycling position, drag area can be affected by the position of the knees, elbows, arms, and shoulders.

chapter 10

Bicycle Frame, Wheels, and Tires

Jim Martin
John Cobb

Differences in aerodynamic drag area between a standard bicycle and a fully aerodynamic bicycle can produce significant gains in cycling velocity that can be realized simply by changing components. Chapter 9 discusses the effects of changes in body position on aerodynamics and performance. This chapter presents aerodynamic drag-area data for a variety of wheel, fork, handlebar, and frame configurations as well as drag-area and rolling-resistance data for tires. As in the previous chapter, we use the mathematical model presented by Martin et al. (1998) to predict the cycling velocity that should result for each bicycle configuration and a variety of power outputs. To best illustrate the effects of changes in aerodynamic drag area, the modeled conditions are a horizontal road surface and no wind. Additionally, the effects of bicycle mass and aerodynamic drag area on cycling velocity are modeled for several road grades. The baseline configuration for our modeling is a bicycle with standard-sized round tubing, oval-legged fork, standard wheels (box section rims and round wire spokes), and standard racing handlebars with clip-on aerobars (see figure 10.1)—a configuration that should yield a drag area of approximately 2,914 centimeters squared (cm^2) when the bike is ridden by a 70-kilogram (154-pound) cyclist in a typical aerodynamic position.

Figure 10.1 Standard bicycle.

Used with permission of Cervélo.

Bicycle components are available from several manufacturers and often in several models. In this chapter we present a range of values of drag area for each general configuration but do not specify the make or model. We have chosen this approach because models often change from year to year and thus it is impossible for us to predict what the best brand or model will be when you read this. Instead, by describing the factors that affect performance in general terms, we hope to give you the ability to make informed decisions now and in the future.

We present aerodynamic drag-area data for a range of yaw angles. Yaw angle is the angle at which air flows over the wheel and is a function of the speed and direction of both the wind and the cyclist (i.e., the angle of the component relative to the net air velocity). A unique aspect of the modeling presented in this chapter is the use of drag-area values that are averaged over several yaw angles. As you will see, this is an important factor because the drag area of wheels, forks, and frames is differentially affected by yaw angle. The drag area of standard components tends to increase with increasing yaw angle, whereas the drag area of streamlined components tends to decrease with increasing yaw angle. Consequently, crosswind conditions (i.e., higher yaw angles) will increase differences between standard and well-designed aerodynamic components. Our use of data, averaged over yaw angles of 0 to 15 degrees, is intended to simulate real-world conditions with variable wind conditions, and it predicts a greater benefit for aerodynamic equipment than that reported in previous modeling (Jeukendrup and Martin 2000).

Wheels

For the purposes of this chapter, bicycle wheels are divided into four general categories:

1. standard box-section rim with round wire spokes (see figure 10.2a);
2. aero rim with oval or bladed wire spokes (see figure 10.2b);

Figure 10.2 *(a)* Standard wheel; *(b)* aero rim with wire spokes; *(c)* aero wheel with composite spokes; *(d)* disc wheel.

Photos *b*, *c*, and *d* used with permission of Hed Cycling Products.

3. composite spoke wheel (see figure 10.2c); and
4. disk wheel (see figure 10.2d).

Greenwell et al. (1995) have reported aerodynamic drag-area values of several wheels in each category, and table 10.1 summarizes these. To account for the fact that the rear wheel is partially shielded by the bicycle frame, we assume that the difference in drag area (for a bicycle and rider) associated with a rear wheel is half of that associated with the wheel itself.

Standard wheels exhibit the highest average drag area (212 cm^2), and drag area increases with increasing yaw angle (see table 10.1). These wheels may be reliable for training and economical to repair; however, their high drag area, particularly in crosswind conditions, makes them less suitable for racing. Wheels with aero rims exhibit lower average drag-area values (124 to 163 cm^2; table 10.1). The best wheels

TABLE 10.1 Wheel Drag Area for Four Categories of Wheels (cm^2)

Wheel type	0° Yaw angle	7.5° Yaw angle	15° Yaw angle	Average
Standard	181	219	235	212
Aero rim	135 to 142	108 to 181	131 to 166	124 to 163
Composite	139 to 139	100 to 146	108 to 131	123 to 131
Disk/composite	139 to 139	77 to 89	-15 to 50	67 to 92

Adapted from Greenwell et al. 1995.

TABLE 10.2 40-km Time-Trial Performance and Time Saved Compared With Standard Wheels

Wheel type	40-km time for 100 watts	40-km time for 200 watts	40-km time for 300 watts	40-km time for 400 watts
Standard	87:50	67:43	58:29	52:48
Aero rim	86:37	66:46	57:39	52:02
Composite	86:36	66:44	57:37	52:01
Disk rear and composite front	86:20	66:32	57:26	51:51

of this configuration can reduce the drag area of a bicycle and rider by approximately 4.5 percent and should increase cycling velocity by 1.5 percent—a time savings of approximately 46 to 73 seconds for a 40-kilometer time trial (see table 10.2).

Composite wheels also exhibit low average drag area (123 to 131 cm^2), and drag area tends to decrease with increasing yaw angles. This reduced drag, or "sail effect," means that these wheels perform much better than standard wheels in crosswind conditions. However, the larger surface area of these wheels can produce an unwelcome side effect: when used as a front wheel, they can be difficult to control in crosswind conditions, particularly when the wind is gusty or the cyclist is passed by motor vehicles. Some riders do not find this problematic, but others have told us that they feel very uncomfortable riding a deep-section front wheel in windy conditions. Wheels of this configuration will reduce the drag area of a bicycle and rider by approximately 4.6 percent compared with standard wheels and increase cycling velocity by approximately 1.5 percent, which should yield a time savings of 47 to 74 seconds over 40 kilometers (see table 10.2).

Disk wheels exhibit the lowest average drag-area values (67 to 92 cm^2), and drag area decreases with increasing yaw angles (see table 10.1). The large surface area of disc wheels makes them unsuitable for use as a front wheel except for in perfectly calm conditions such as indoor track cycling. Consequently, for our modeling purposes, we assume that a disc wheel is used as a rear wheel in combination with the best composite spoke front wheel. Compared with conventional wheels, that combination will reduce the drag area of a bicycle and rider by approximately 5.5 percent and thus increase cycling velocity by 1.8 percent or decrease 40-kilometer time by 57 to 90 seconds (see table 10.2).

In general, cyclists can realize significant gains in performance when using any of the good aerodynamic wheels in comparison to standard wheels. Differences in aerodynamic drag area among the well-designed deep-section and composite wheels are relatively small and, consequently, cycling velocity is similar for those configurations.

Tires

Tires affect cycling velocity by their rolling resistance and by their aerodynamic drag area. Our baseline modeling condition has used a coefficient of rolling resistance (C_{RR}) value of 0.0032, which is representative of an average racing clincher tire (Martin et al. 1998). Kyle (1986) has reported the C_{RR} for high-performance road-racing tubular and clincher tires to be 16 percent lower (0.0027) when measured on an asphalt surface. Some road-racing tubular tires, however, exhibit C_{RR} values as high as 0.0059 (Kyle 1986). These values for C_{RR} can significantly affect cycling velocity and 40-kilometer time-trial performance, as shown in table 10.3. Compared with an average racing clincher tire, a high-performance racing tubular or clincher tire (C_{RR} = 0.0027) can increase velocity by 0.4 to 1.2 percent (depending on power output) for a time savings of 12 to 62 seconds over a 40-kilometer time trial. Conversely, a high-rolling-resistance tubular tire can decrease velocity by 2.4 to 6.3 percent (an increase of 78 seconds to almost six minutes for 40 kilometers). Note that rolling resistance dramatically affects the performance of cyclists who produce 100 watts because, at that power output, a high proportion of total power is dissipated to rolling resistance.

TABLE 10.3 Effect of Rolling Resistance and Aerodynamic Drag Area of Tires on 40-km Time-Trial Performance

Tire	40-km time for 100 watts	40-km time for 200 watts	40-km time for 300 watts	40-km time for 400 watts
Average racing clincher $C_{RR} = 0.0032$	87:50	67:43	58:29	52:48
High-performance tubular or clincher $C_{RR} = 0.0027$	86:12	66:57	57:59	52:25
High-resistance tire $C_{RR} = 0.0059$	95:24	71:13	60:44	54:27
Clincher tire with sharp transition from tread to casing $C_{RR} = 0.0032$, drag area increased by 60 cm^2	88:22	68:09	58:52	53:08

Some tires are manufactured with a sharp transition at the edge of the tread section; the outside radius of the treaded portion can be one to two millimeters larger than the radius of the sidewall. We investigated the effects of tire configuration on the aerodynamic drag area of the tire-wheel combination by mounting a variety of tires on the same set of wheels. The size of all tires (and hence the frontal area) was the same but drag area was found to differ, suggesting that the tread configuration had a substantial effect on coefficient of drag, probably because the abrupt transition in radius caused flow over the tire to separate.

Those data indicate that tire configuration can change the drag area of the tire-wheel combination by up to 40 cm^2 (we assume an increase of 60 cm^2 for two tires on a bicycle) compared with tires that have a smooth transition from tread to sidewall. Interestingly, this effect is most pronounced with shallow section rims and is reduced with deeper section rims, and essentially eliminated with disc wheels, suggesting that airflow can become reattached to the deeper section rims. A 60-cm^2 increase in drag area will reduce velocity by approximately 0.6 percent and increase 40-kilometer time by 20 to 32 seconds (see table 10.3).

Forks

The bicycle fork (along with the head tube, the front wheel, and the handlebars) represents one of the leading edges of the bicycle, and thus it is among the most important components (see table 10.4). Forks with airfoil-shaped legs (see figure 10.3) reduce the average drag area of a bicycle and rider by approximately 2.5 percent compared with standard oval-shaped legs and increase cycling velocity by approximately 1 percent—a time savings of 25 to 41 seconds over 40 kilometers (see table 10.5). Conversely, the greater drag area of oversized round-legged forks will *increase* the drag area of the bike and rider by approximately 2.3 percent and decrease velocity by approximately 1 percent—a time *cost* of 23 to 35 seconds over 40 kilometers.

TABLE 10.4 Effect of Fork Configuration on Aerodynamic Drag

Fork configuration	Drag area at 0° yaw angle (cm^2)	Drag area at 5° yaw angle (cm^2)	Drag area at 10° yaw angle (cm^2)	Drag area at 15° yaw angle (cm^2)	Average drag area (cm^2)
Oval legs	146	167	164	118	149
Airfoil-shaped legs	88 to 131	82 to 140	82 to 150	22 to 99	76 to 130
Oversized round legs	208	227	226	198	215

Figure 10.3 Aero fork.

Used with permission of Profile Design, LLC.

TABLE 10.5 **Effect of Aerodynamic Drag Area of Different Forks on 40-km Time-Trial Performance**

Fork configuration	40-km time for 100 watts	40-km time for 200 watts	40-km time for 300 watts	40-km time for 400 watts
Oval legs	87:50	67:43	58:29	52:48
Airfoil-shaped legs	87:10	67:11	58:01	52:22
Oversized round legs	88:26	68:12	58:54	53:10

Handlebars

Several configurations of aerodynamic handlebars are available to the racing cyclist, ranging from a standard racing handlebar with a clip-on aerobar (see figure 10.4b) to fully integrated aerodynamic handlebars with streamlined tubing (see figure 10.4a), and even including single-purpose aerobars with no alternative hand positions (i.e.,

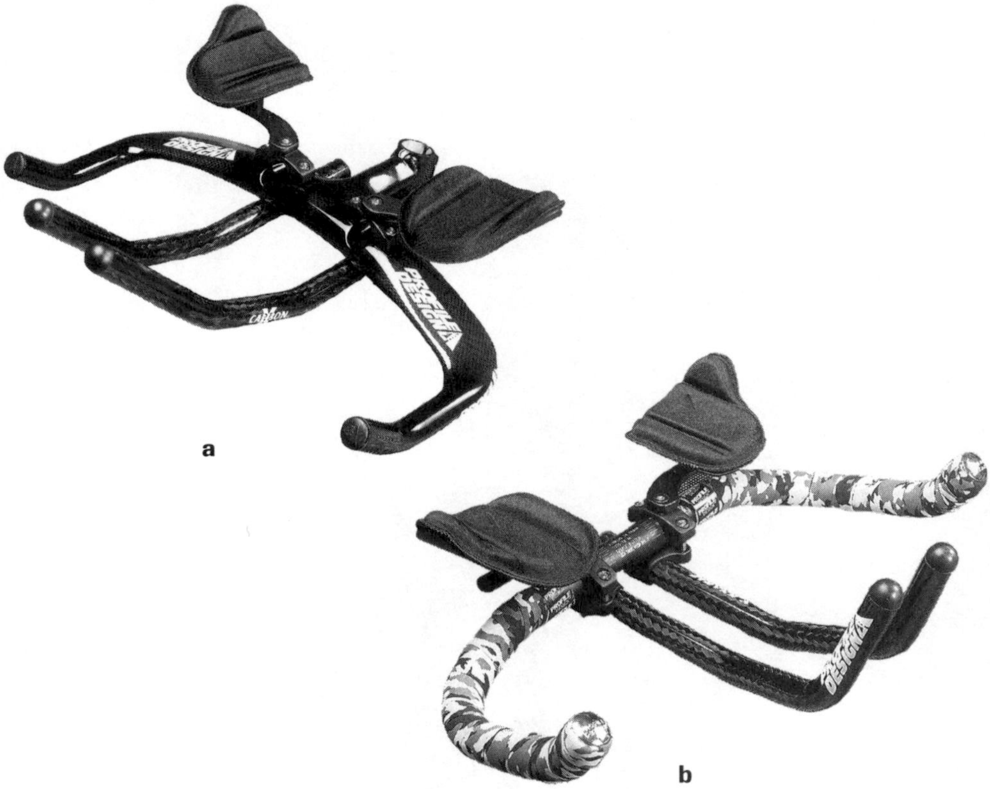

Figure 10.4 *(a)* Integrated aerobar with airfoil-shaped tubing; *(b)* standard handlebar with clip-on aerobar.

Used with permission of Profile Design, LLC.

only the elbow-support position). Drag-area data for bare bicycles and for bicycles with a rider indicated that the drag area of standard racing handlebars with a clip-on aerobar was similar to that of cow-horn bars with a clip-on aerobar. Compared with those combinations, integrated aerodynamic handlebars that use airfoil-shaped tubing for the extension from the stem to the hand grip can reduce aerodynamic drag area by approximately 126 cm^2 (see table 10.6) and therefore decrease the drag area of the bike and rider by approximately 4.3 percent—a time savings of 45 to 70 seconds over 40 kilometers. The drag area at various yaw angles was not available for these handlebar configurations. The use of single-purpose aerobars without alternative hand positions should reduce drag area by approximately 181 cm^2 (see table 10.6) and therefore decrease the drag area of the bike and rider by approximately 6.2 percent—a time savings of 64 to 101 seconds over 40 kilometers.

Frames

Bicycle frames are available in a wide variety of configurations, but many contemporary frames can be grouped into one of three general categories:

TABLE 10.6 Drag Area and Cycling Velocity for Three Handlebar Categories

Handlebar configuration	Drag area (cm²)	40-km time for 100 watts	40-km time for 200 watts	40-km time for 300 watts	40-km time for 400 watts
Standard or cow-horn bars with clip-on aerobars	Reference	87:50	67:43	58:29	52:48
Integrated airfoil-shaped bars	-126	86:40	66:48	57:40	52:03
Single-purpose bars	-181	86:09	66:23	57:19	51:44

- *Standard:* a "double-diamond" configuration constructed with standard-sized round tubing (see figure 10.1, page 114)
- *Semi-aero:* a double-diamond configuration with some airfoil-shaped tubes, typically the down tube (see figure 10.5a)
- *Full-aero:* those with all airfoil-shaped frame tubes and/or alternative frame configurations (see figure 10.5b and c).

It should be noted that we tested frames with the fork supplied by the manufacturer. In many cases, the supplied fork was built of airfoil-shaped tubing, which can reduce drag substantially. The drag-area values reported in table 10.7 have been adjusted to account for differences in fork configuration. Additionally, the measured drag area of a bicycle frame is highly dependent on the configuration in which it was tested (e.g., seat or no seat, pedals or no pedals, bars or no bars, whether or not the drag of the mounting fixture was accounted for). The data we present here were recorded in the Oran W. Nicks Low Speed Wind Tunnel at Texas A&M University in College Station. Each bicycle was identically configured with matched seat heights, no handlebars, and cranks and pedals horizontally aligned.

TABLE 10.7 Aerodynamic Drag of Different Frames

Frame	Drag area at 0° yaw angle (cm²)	Drag area at 5° yaw angle (cm²)	Drag area at 10° yaw angle (cm²)	Drag area at 15° yaw angle (cm²)	Average drag area (cm²)
Standard	799	863	980	1012	913
Semi-aero	767 to 847	779 to 855	807 to 923	807 to 875	809 to 870
Full-aero	654 to 771	658 to 695	626 to 646	594 to 610	637 to 676

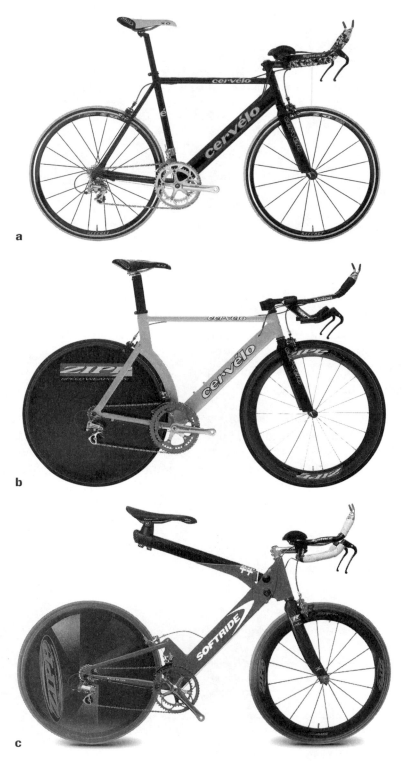

Figure 10.5 *(a)* Semi-aero frame; *(b)* full-aero frame (Cervélo); *(c)* full-aero frame (Softride).

Photos *a* and *b* used with permission of Cervélo; photo *c* used with permission of Softride, Inc.

The average drag area of semi-aero frames is 43 to 104 cm^2 lower than that of a standard frame (see table 10.7). The lower drag area of these frames will reduce the drag of the bicycle and rider by approximately 3.6 percent compared with a standard frame. That reduction should increase cycling velocity by approximately 1.2 percent and reduce 40-kilometer time by 37 to 58 seconds (see table 10.8). Full-aero frames exhibit even lower drag-area values: 238 to 276 cm^2 less than that of standard frames. These values for drag reduction are much greater than those previously reported because they represent the average for a variety of yaw angles intended to simulate real-world conditions that include crosswinds (if just the zero yaw-angle condition were considered, the expected reduction in drag would be only 145 cm^2). The best full-aero frames should reduce the drag area of a bicycle and rider by a surprisingly large 9.5 percent compared with a standard frame. That decrease in drag area should increase cycling velocity by 3.2 percent or decrease 40-kilometer time by 99 to 156 seconds (see table 10.8).

TABLE 10.8 Effect of Aerodynamic Drag Area of Different Frames on 40-km Time-Trial Performance

Frame configuration	40-km time for 100 watts	40-km time for 200 watts	40-km time for 300 watts	40-km time for 400 watts
Standard	87:50	67:43	58:29	52:48
Semi-aero	86:52	66:57	57:49	52:11
Full-aero	85:14	65:39	56:40	51:09

A typical question cyclists ask when selecting an aerodynamic bicycle frame is, "What are the key elements of a low aerodynamic-drag frame?" Low drag area can be achieved in two general ways: by decreasing the drag area of each frame member and/or by reducing the number of elements encountered by the airstream. The drag area of each frame member typically is reduced by using thin, airfoil-shaped tubing. Indeed, frames made entirely of thin airfoil-section tubes exhibit some of the lowest drag-area values. Cyclists can reduce the number of elements encountered by the airstream by eliminating frame members (see figure 10.5c) or by integrating the rear wheel into the frame (see figure 10.6, a close-up of a Cervélo seat tube). That second method is effective when the design allows the airflow around the seat tube to remain attached to the wheel, thus the only leading edge encountered by the airstream is that of the seat tube.

Figure 10.6 Rear wheel integrated into frame.

Used with permission of Cervélo.

Combined Effects of Aerodynamic Equipment and Body Positioning

Thus far we have separately considered the effects of wheels, forks, handlebars, tires, and frames and compared them to a standard-configuration bicycle; however, it is unlikely that many cyclists would choose to make only one aerodynamic modification to their bicycle. Rather, cyclists often attempt to optimize every aspect of their bike. Therefore, the question arises, "What is the maximum benefit that can be derived from aerodynamic equipment?" If we assume that the effects of the individual components are independent and additive (an assumption that has not been systematically tested), and all the best components are selected, then it should be possible to reduce drag area to approximately 2,223 cm^2—a reduction of 23.7 percent compared with the total drag area of a standard bicycle and rider. That reduction in drag area should elicit an increase in velocity of 8.9 percent, resulting in a decrease in 40-kilometer time-trial time of 3.6 to 5.6 minutes (see table 10.9). Thus, changes in equipment alone can reduce drag area and improve performance dramatically.

TABLE 10.9 Drag Area and Cycling Velocity for Fully Aerodynamic Bicycle and Optimized Body Position

Configuration	Drag area (cm^2)	40-km time for 100 watts	40-km time for 200 watts	40-km time for 300 watts	40-km time for 400 watts
Standard	2,914	87:50	67:43	58:29	52:47
Aero equipment	2,223	80:58	62:15	53:42	48:27
Aero equipment and optimized body position	1,993	78:23	60:11	51:53	46:48

In addition to selecting optimal equipment, cyclists also may choose to optimize their body position. Chapter 9 presents data indicating that optimal body positioning could reduce aerodynamic drag area by approximately 230 cm^2 compared with a typical time-trial body position. Thus, the combined use of aerodynamic equipment and optimal body position (see chapter 9) could reduce total aerodynamic drag area to 1,993 cm^2. Indeed, this is almost exactly the drag area we have observed in a few world-class cyclists. Such a low drag area would increase cycling velocity by 12.6 percent compared with a standard bicycle and typical position—a time savings of 6.0 to 9.5 minutes with no increase in power demand.

Weight Versus Drag Area

To clearly illustrate the effects of differences related to aerodynamic drag area, we only modeled cycling over flat roads in previous sections. However, bicycle races are rarely conducted on flat terrain and, consequently, cyclists occasionally select equipment to optimize cycling velocity while climbing. During uphill cycling, some portion of the cyclist's power is used to lift the weight of the bike up the grade, and velocity usually is substantially reduced. Thus, it may seem that weight is a more important factor than aerodynamic drag. Indeed, many cyclists have told us that they believe weight is a critical issue and much more important than aerodynamic drag when they are climbing. However, the relationship of cycling velocity to power, mass, and road grade is quite complex; thus the concomitant effects of those variables may not be obvious.

To determine the relative importance of weight and aerodynamics on uphill cycling velocity, we have modeled four bicycle configurations that might represent typical options available to racing cyclists. In each case it was assumed that a 70-kilogram rider adopted a typical climbing position with hands on the brake hoods and elbows bent, which should produce a drag area of approximately 3,420 cm^2 with a standard frame and wheels. The modeled configurations were as follows:

1 kilogram = 2.2 pounds

1. *Standard:* a bicycle with a mass of 9 kilograms, standard-sized round tubing, and standard wheels
2. *Low-mass standard*: a bicycle with an identical configuration to the "standard" but with a mass of only 6.8 kilograms (i.e., Union Cycliste Internationale rule 1.3.019—low-mass limit)
3. *Low-mass aero wheel*: a bicycle with a standard frame configuration but with low drag-area wheels (mass, 7.3 kilograms; drag area, 3,244 cm^2)
4. *Full-aero*: a bicycle with an optimized aerodynamic frame, fork, and wheels (drag area of 2,910 cm^2), and a mass of 9 kilograms

We present modeling results for those configurations as time saved per kilometer compared with the standard configuration (see table 10.10). As expected, when two bicycles are identical in aerodynamic drag, the low-mass bicycle allows for significant time savings when climbing: 1 to 6 seconds per kilometer when climbing a moderate (3 percent) grade, and 6 to 27 seconds per kilometer when climbing a very steep (12 percent) grade. Similarly, when two bicycles with similar mass but different drag area are compared, the low drag-area configuration will save up to 4 seconds per kilometer depending on road grade and power output.

When we compare configurations that differ in mass and aerodynamic drag area, the complex relationship of cycling velocity with power, mass, and road grade begins to emerge. Both the low-mass aero wheel and full-aero configurations will provide faster climbing than the low-mass standard configuration for some conditions but not for others. The low-mass standard configuration saves time for riders who produce 100 watts under all modeled climbing conditions. Riders with power outputs of 200 to 400 watts will benefit by using either of the aerodynamic configurations when climbing 3 percent grades, and the most powerful riders will even benefit when climbing grades of up to 6 percent.

Benefits of using a full-aero configuration also depend on road grade and power output. The low-mass standard will provide superior climbing performance for the

TABLE 10.10 Effects of Mass and Aerodynamics at Different Road Grades

Mass, aerodynamics, and road grade	Time saved at 100 watts (sec./km)	Time saved at 200 watts (sec./km)	Time saved at 300 watts (sec./km)	Time saved at 400 watts (sec./km)
Low-mass bicycle (6.8 kg)				
0% grade	0.3	0.1	0.1	0.1
3% grade	6.2	2.5	1.5	1.0
6% grade	13.5	6.3	3.8	2.6
12% grade	27.1	13.4	8.7	6.4
Low-mass bicycle with aero wheels (7.3 kg)				
0% grade	2.2	1.7	1.5	1.3
3% grade	5.8	3.2	2.4	1.9
6% grade	10.8	5.5	3.7	2.9
12% grade	21.1	10.5	7.0	5.3
Aero frame, fork, and wheels (9 kg)				
0% grade	6.6	5.3	4.6	4.2
3% grade	3.2	3.9	3.9	3.8
6% grade	1.2	2.0	2.5	2.7
12% grade	0.3	0.6	0.9	1.2

cyclist who produces 100 watts. The full-aero configuration, on the other hand, provides time savings for cyclists who produce 200 to 300 watts when climbing 3 percent grades. Elite cyclists who produce 400 watts will benefit from a full-aero configuration at grades up to 6 percent. The possible scenarios become even more complex when one considers that most courses will include some combination of road grades, from flat to steep, and include descents as well as climbs. The modeling shown in table 10.10 presents only a few combinations of power, mass, drag area, and road grades but serves to illustrate the complex interaction of cycling power, bicycle mass, aerodynamic drag area, road grade, and velocity during uphill cycling.

Summary

Aerodynamic and lightweight components can dramatically affect cycling velocity. For cycling over flat terrain, reductions in aerodynamic drag area will produce proportionately similar increases in cycling velocity (up to 8.9 percent) for all riders regardless of their power output. The absolute decrease in time for any given distance (e.g., 40 kilometers) will be greater for those who produce less power simply because the total time required to complete that distance is greater. Differences in cycling velocity related to aerodynamic wheels, forks, and frames reported in this chapter are somewhat greater than those previously reported because our modeling used drag-area values averaged over yaw angles of 0 to 15 degrees. For riders who produce less power and cycle at lower velocity, differences in bicycle mass (during uphill cycling) and rolling resistance will produce proportionately greater improvements in cycling velocity. For uphill cycling, equipment selection must balance aerodynamic drag area and weight. Riders who produce less power will perform better with lightweight equipment, whereas riders who produce more power will perform better with aerodynamic equipment. For all riders, whether novice or elite, power is limited and speed precious. Therefore, minimizing aerodynamic drag area, rolling resistance, and mass is critical for optimal performance at all levels.

chapter 11

Biomechanics

Jos de Koning
Knoek van Soest

In cycling competition there are two types of races: road races, in which the competitors cycle all together and strive to pass the finish line first; and time trials, in which individuals or teams try to cover a certain distance in the shortest time possible. In both situations tactics are important and success depends on choices made by the cyclist and coach about issues such as leading or following, team strategy, and pacing. Regardless of the chosen tactics, in both types of races the factor governing the ultimate success or failure is the energy-producing capacity of the athlete harnessed through the bike. Other chapters in this book examine how cyclists can use the latest research to optimize their performance through training, diet, and technology. However, any performance improvement is ultimately due to an improvement in the relationship between power produced and energy lost. So that you fully understand the basis of such changes, this chapter deals with the fundamental principles of cycling, the factors that affect the amount of power produced by a cyclist, and the relationship between this muscular power and cycling speed.

The Body As a Power Plant

Among cyclists, terms such as *strength, endurance,* and *"souplesse"* are often used to qualify one's abilities. From a mechanical point of view, it is the mechanical power generated by the cyclist that is most directly related to speed. Factors such as strength and endurance only contribute to this mechanical power in some way.

The mechanical power delivered by a cyclist is a measure of the amount of mechanical energy produced per second. A component of time is important in the calculation of power because there is a continuous loss of energy to air and surface friction. Put simply, we continuously collide with air molecules during cycling and the energy that we transfer onto these molecules needs to be replenished. Furthermore, additional mechanical energy is needed to climb mountains (to overcome gravity), and finally, power is needed to accelerate.

Why is it that we express the performance level of cyclists in terms of mechanical power output, not in terms of the more familiar variable "force"? There is nothing wrong with the statement that, to travel at a constant velocity, the cyclist has to generate a propulsive force that compensates for the frictional forces. However, a description in terms of forces gives a less complete image than when using the term *power* because it is not only the capacity to generate force but in particular the capacity to generate this force while moving at a high speed that determines performance. The advantage of an analysis in terms of mechanical power is that the concept of power captures the combination of force and velocity in one quantity.

As an example, consider air friction. The air-friction force depends on the velocity with which the air flows around the cyclist. Consider the following two situations:

1. The cyclist is standing still in a strong head wind of 10 meters per second.
2. The cyclist moves at a speed of 10 meters per second while there is no wind.

Clearly, the air flows past the cyclist at the same speed in both cases. Thus, the air-friction force will be the same. However, it is clear that the cyclist in situation 1 does not have to exert himself (all he has to do is pull on his brakes to prevent being blown backward), whereas the cyclist in situation 2 will be exercising severely. Note that an analysis in terms of forces that act on the system would show no differences. An analysis in terms of power does show a difference because, as stated earlier, power depends on the combination of force and velocity. In fact, the power generated (or dissipated) by a force equals the product of force and velocity of its point of application: power = force × velocity. Power is formally expressed in watts or kilowatts; one kilowatt equals 1,000 watts. Thus, in the first situation, in which the velocity of the cyclist is zero, the power that the air-friction force dissipates from the cyclist is zero, whereas this power equals air-friction force multiplied by cycling velocity in the second situation.

In cycling, the frictional forces due to air resistance are in fact not very large (20 to 25 Newtons at 10 meters per second). However, in combination with a speed of the cyclist, a considerable mechanical power (200 to 250 watts) has to be generated by the cyclist to compensate for the power lost to these frictional forces at that speed. In conclusion, the power dissipated by frictional forces depends on speed. If the cyclist wants to travel at a constant speed, he must replenish this power.

If this is the case, then what happens when there is a difference between power production by the cyclist and power dissipation by the frictional forces? To understand this, we have to introduce another concept: the *kinetic energy* of a cyclist. Every object that is moving (has velocity) is able to change the environment in some way, and the magnitude of this change is based on that velocity (the capacity to change the environment or "perform work" is called energy in mechanics). Thus, a cyclist is still able to overcome frictional forces for a while even when he has stopped pushing on the pedals. But his velocity diminishes as a result. The study of mechanics teaches us that at every point in time during this process, the power lost to these frictional forces is exactly equal to the decrease in kinetic energy per second of the cyclist. This also holds true in reverse: When a cyclist increases his speed, he will have to generate an extra amount of power that is equal to the rate of increase in his kinetic energy. In the case that a cyclist is cycling at a constant speed, the change in kinetic energy is zero, thus the generated power equals the power losses to friction. With this knowledge we can constitute an equation in which the relationship between the terms of power is stated—the so-called mechanical power balance of cycling:

power generated = frictional losses + rate of change in kinetic energy

A lot of research has focused on understanding and describing these terms as accurately as possible and subsequently using equations like this to determine the relationship between the mechanical power of cyclists on the one hand and their velocities on the other. This power equation also enables us to predict the influence of many factors that affect friction and thus performance, such as air pressure, road condition, altitude above sea level, and cycling posture.

Source of Mechanical Power

Until now, we have not considered the question of where and how the cyclist actually generates mechanical power. The "where" is easily answered: Mechanical power is produced by the muscles the cyclist employs. The "how" is the topic of the following paragraphs. When it is stated that a competitive cyclist needs to possess a good fitness level, we can think of several meanings of this concept of fitness—that is, great endurance capacity, good mental preparation ability, high oxygen consumption, and so forth. Here also, it is important to reserve a few terms for well-defined factors. *Physical fitness* and *endurance* are terms that generally are used in the study of training to indicate the ability of an athlete to liberate energy. To understand this, we need to briefly touch on the field of exercise physiology.

As stated in answer to the "where" question, the engines that are at a human being's disposal and that are used to generate the necessary power are the muscles. Muscles are able to exert force while shortening. Mechanically speaking, this exertion of force over a certain distance of shortening means that muscles are able to perform work (work = force × distance = power × time). The force that can be produced by a muscle depends on its velocity of shortening. Furthermore, muscle force depends on muscle length; there is a limited range of muscle lengths in which a muscle can generate active force. This chapter later discusses the effect of these relationships on cycling performance. At this point, we want to discuss the sources of the mechanical work done by a muscle.

Athletes can perform muscular work only because energy that has been obtained from the diet is available to the muscle cells. By liberating a certain amount of this energy per unit of time by means of muscle contractions, the athlete can generate mechanical power. Up to a certain extent this process can be compared with a gasoline engine. Here also, mechanical power is obtained from the energy that is stored in gasoline molecules. This energy is liberated by burning (oxidizing) the gasoline in the presence of oxygen (combustion). It is a pity that not all energy that is stored in gasoline can be converted into useful power. With a gasoline engine we are pleased

© Nigel Farrow

As Tyler Hamilton and Lance Armstrong use their muscles to produce pedal power, the muscles shorten and exert force.

when 40 percent of the energy in gasoline can be applied usefully. The remainder inevitably disappears as heat. This percentage of energy that is applied usefully is called the *efficiency* of an engine.

Humans as well are only able to use a certain percentage (maximally about 25 percent) of the available chemical energy in their nutrients as useful mechanical power. The remainder is liberated as heat. For this fraction we use the term *mechanical efficiency.* In cycling, mechanical efficiency is approximately 22 percent. The value of efficiency depends on the position on the bicycle and the revolutions per minute at which the rider cycles. Together with the efficiency, the total amount of available useful power is determined by the maximal amount of chemical energy (usually called metabolic energy) that cyclists can liberate in their muscles per unit of time.

Just like in a gasoline engine, chemical energy in humans is liberated by oxidizing nutrients. However, this process is more complicated than the one in a gasoline engine. An engine's maximal power is independent of the total distance that needs to be covered. Therefore, the maximal speed of a car will be more or less similar, whether one makes a short ride or needs to cover a large distance. This is completely different in human beings. Over a short distance (so in a short period of time) humans can generate much higher powers than over longer distances. During a short sprint, the power that an athlete generates can average more than 1,000 watts. This, however, cannot be sustained for long. Over longer distances, even elite cyclists will not generate powers above 400 watts.

Muscle-Fuel Replenishment

The dependence of metabolic power output on duration is caused by the oxidation mechanism within the muscle fibers and by the supply of fuel. The fundamental fuel for muscles is the so-called energy-rich phosphates. This fuel is available inside the muscle fibers, but to a limited extent. It must be replenished right after the start of exercise. Without replenishment, the supply of energy-rich substances would run out within seconds. This replenishment takes time and it is the rate of replenishment that partly limits exercise intensity. The quickest replenishment occurs under the influence of a process that is independent of oxygen supply. This process, called anaerobic metabolism, can generate powers of up to 400 to 800 watts during cycling.

This level of power, however, can only be sustained for 20 to 30 seconds, after which time one is forced to switch to a supply system that is slower: aerobic oxidation. This type of oxidation happens under the influence of oxygen that needs to be transported from the open air to the muscles through the lungs, heart, and blood vessels. Exercises that last longer than approximately 30 seconds are predominantly dependent on this supply system. The degree to which someone is able to liberate energy aerobically is relatively simple to determine in a laboratory by means of an exercise test. During this test, one can measure the maximal amount of oxygen that an athlete can consume. This is the subject of other chapters in this book.

In competitive cycling, both anaerobic and aerobic processes are of great importance, and although there are obvious differences in energy expenditure between cycling specific sprint distances on the track and cycling a 250-kilometer stage in the Tour de France, total endurance is determined by both processes. Therefore, we distinguish two types of endurance: aerobic endurance (aerobic power output) and anaerobic endurance (anaerobic power output).

The previous discussion has shown that the power that a cyclist can generate is closely related to his or her endurance capacity. This does not mean, however, that someone with great endurance is automatically able to cycle fast. What we can say is that great endurance is an important prerequisite for a competitive cyclist.

The Body–Bicycle System

The previous section introduced the power equation for the "bicycle + cyclist" system. In this section, we use the power equation for the cyclist alone to discuss how the following factors affect performance:

- (The direction of) the pedal force
- The timing of muscle activation
- The gear selection
- The saddle height

The structure of the power equation for the cyclist alone is identical to that for the "cyclist + bicycle" system, but the terms involved are different:

Concentric muscle power + eccentric muscle power = pedal power + change in leg energy

In this equation, concentric muscle power refers to the power produced by muscles during shortening (concentric contraction); eccentric muscle power refers to the power dissipated by muscles during lengthening (eccentric contraction); pedal power refers to the power delivered to the pedal by the pedal force; and change in leg energy refers to the sum of the changes in translational and rotational kinetic energy and the changes in potential energy of feet, lower legs, and upper legs.

Pedal Power

The mechanical power produced by the cyclist flows to the bicycle at the pedals. We refer to this power as pedal power. We mentioned earlier that mechanical power equals the product of force and velocity. In the context of power flow at the pedal, we have to be more precise, because here, the direction of both pedal force and pedal velocity also plays a role. The pedal force can be broken down into two components: one acting in the direction of the crank and one acting perpendicular to this. Intuitively, it is clear that the pedal-force component that is directed along the crank does not contribute to propulsion. Generally, this force component is referred to as F_{rad}, because it acts along the radius of the circular pedal path. No power is associated with F_{rad}. Indeed, it is only the component of the pedal force that is directed perpendicular to the crank that propels the system. As this force component is tangential to the circular pedal path, it usually is referred to as the tangential force, F_{tan}. The pedal power associated with F_{tan} equals the product of the pedal velocity and F_{tan}. The pedal velocity is found by multiplying the crank angular velocity by the crank length. The pedal power can be negative—for instance, when a downward pedal force is applied during the upstroke.

Direction of the Pedal Force

The fact that the radial component of the pedal force does not contribute to pedal power has led some to suggest that cyclists should consciously attempt to direct the pedal force tangentially. This suggestion clearly makes sense if it is assumed that, through a change in coordination, the pedal-force direction can be improved while maintaining its magnitude; a pedal force of a given magnitude can best be directed tangentially. Training studies have been carried out to test this idea. In these studies, feedback was given to cyclists about pedal-force direction and they were trained to "improve" the pedal-force direction—that is, to make the radial component of the pedal force zero. Even though cyclists were successful in doing so, the results in terms of power output were disappointing: Power output decreased rather than increased.

In fact, logical reasoning is all that is needed to understand these results. From the preceding discussion it follows that maximization of pedal power at a given cadence and thus at a given pedal velocity is the same as maximization of F_{tan}, *irrespective* of the accompanying F_{rad}. So if we compare instructions to a cyclist—(1) "maximize F_{tan}" versus (2) "maximize F_{tan} but keep F_{rad} close to zero at the same time"—it is obvious that instruction 2 can never result in a higher pedal power than instruction 1. In fact, it is almost certain to result in a lower pedal power: Complying with the constraint imposed on F_{rad} in the case of instruction 2 will almost certainly negatively affect F_{tan}.

Another way to think about this is to analyze how the cyclist actually generates the pedal force. This is a complex mechanical question. Without going into the details, we can say that F_{tan} and F_{rad} depend on (a) leg and crank position, (b) leg and crank velocity, and (c) muscle forces. So, for any given position and velocity of leg and crank, the only way to affect the pedal force is through the muscle forces. Each muscle that produces force contributes to the pedal force. Interestingly, these contributions are independent of each other and can simply be summed to find the total contribution of muscle forces to the pedal force.

Another interesting fact is that the *direction* of a muscle's instantaneous contribution to the pedal force is fully determined by the position of leg and crank. As an illustration, in figure 11.1 the contribution of a muscle force of 1,000 Newtons to the pedal force is plotted for the vasti (knee extensors) and for the soleus (ankle extensor) for a horizontal crank orientation. We can see that the direction of contribution of each of these muscles to the pedal force is such that they generate both a tangential and a radial force on the pedal. This is the normal situation: At most crank angles, the force by any muscle considered results in a mix of tangential and radial pedal force.

What is the consequence of this situation, when the total F_{rad} is required to be zero? Clearly, it means that muscle forces must be interrelated in such a way that the sum of their contributions to F_{rad} yields the desired value of the total F_{rad} (i.e., zero). It is extremely unlikely that maximal activation of all active muscles will result in the desired F_{rad}. In other words, some muscles will have to be submaximally active, and as a result the power produced by these muscles also will be submaximal, and performance will be degraded.

Figure 11.1 The direction of the contribution of a muscle force to the pedal force depends only on the position of leg and crank. Here, this direction is shown for the vasti (knee extensors) and for the soleus (ankle plantarflexor), for the position of the leg as shown.

In conclusion, logical argumentation and an analysis of the way in which muscles contribute to the total pedal force show that requiring F_{rad} to be zero (requiring an "effective" direction of F_{pedal}) is bound to have a negative effect on performance. In other words, it is not a good idea, from a mechanical point of view, to attempt to direct the pedal force tangentially. From a mechanical point of view, all that matters is F_{tan}; the magnitude of F_{rad} is irrelevant to performance.

Muscle Timing

We can conveniently describe intermuscular coordination in cycling in terms of muscle activation as a function of crank angle. In these terms, the question to be answered for every muscle group is, in what part of the crank cycle should it be activated by the cyclist? Based on the previous discussion, one would be tempted to think that a muscle should be activated in the part of the crank cycle where it generates positive pedal power. Inspection of the power equation for the cyclist, introduced earlier and repeated here for convenience, shows that the situation may be a little more complex:

Concentric muscle power + eccentric muscle power =
pedal power + rate of change in leg energy

From this equation we can see that muscle power at any point in time can contribute not only to pedal power (which is what the cyclist would like best) but also may be used to change the translational and rotational kinetic energy of the leg segments. This happens, for example, during the first part of both the downstroke and the upstroke, during which the angular velocity of the leg segments increases. The question now becomes, is this power "lost," or does it contribute to propulsion at some later time? Part of the answer to this question follows from the fact that the change of the leg's energy over a full crank revolution must be zero during constant velocity cycling. It follows that the power "injected" in the leg segments at one stage must either flow to the pedal (which is what a cyclist would prefer) or be absorbed by the muscles at some stage during the crank revolution. Power absorption by muscles occurs when the muscles are active and thus produce force while lengthening—a situation referred to as eccentric muscle contraction.

From an energy point of view, this is an unfortunate occurrence because power that is absorbed by muscles during eccentric contraction is converted into heat. In other words, this power is dissipated without contributing in any way to propulsion. In a task like walking, eccentric muscle contractions are essential because the swing leg must be decelerated just before heel strike. In cycling, however, the deceleration of the leg is not necessarily brought about by eccentric muscle contraction; the pushing force of the pedal against the foot can cause the deceleration, and in the process the kinetic energy that was present in the leg will flow to the pedal. In conclusion, if the cyclist succeeds in avoiding eccentric contractions, all positive muscle power must flow to the pedal at some point during the crank cycle.

Now let us return to the question of where in the crank cycle a muscle must be activated. By now, the answer stands out clearly: To maximize the average pedal power, muscles should be maximally active while shortening so that positive muscle power is as high as possible. Furthermore, muscles should not produce any resistive force while lengthening, so as to avoid power being dissipated during eccentric contractions.

Actually, cyclists do not entirely comply with the mentioned recommendation; from detailed measurements, we know that they start to activate muscles just before they start shortening. This is easily understood as it takes a little time for muscles to build up their force after they are activated; by muscles becoming activated just before they start shortening, muscle force is already high when the shortening phase starts. Similarly, by muscles becoming deactivated just before they start lengthening, force already has dropped to a low value when the eccentric phase actually starts.

Cadence Selection

In running, there is a direct relationship between speed of progression and the angular velocity of the leg segments. This has two consequences. First, the higher the running speed, the larger the negative muscle work that must be done to decelerate the leg segments (see previous discussion). Second, the higher the angular velocity of the leg segments, the higher the shortening velocity of the muscles, and since concentric muscle power decreases with increased shortening velocity, concentric muscle power is reduced when the speed of progression is increased to high values. Together, these consequences limit the running speed that an athlete can achieve. The presence of a gearing system in bicycles de-couples the velocity of the cyclist's leg from his speed of progression. This is why sustainable speeds in cycling are much higher than they are in running.

Given the presence of a gearing system, the question then is what pedaling rate should a cyclist select? What factors affect this optimal rate? In answering these questions, we have to differentiate between sprinting and steady-state cycling because task requirements are different for these. For sprint cycling, in which the aim is to maximize power output over a short period, our understanding can be summarized as follows: Pedaling rate affects mechanical power output in two ways. First, it determines the importance of the force buildup time (see preceding discussion). At a higher cadence the crank rotates through a larger angle during force buildup, and as a result, the change in muscle length that occurs during force buildup is larger. Consequently, the higher the pedal rate, the lower the average force over the period of shortening, and thus the lower the muscle work per contraction. In other words, from the perspective of the force-buildup phenomenon, a low pedaling rate would be best.

However, there is another important factor to be considered. As mentioned earlier, concentric muscle power depends on muscle shortening velocity, just as power production in a car depends on the number of revolutions per minute. The shortening velocity at which power output is maximal is referred to as the optimal shortening velocity. To allow most muscles to shorten at their optimal velocity, the pedal rate should be well over 150 revolutions per minute.

Our current understanding of sprint cycling is that the optimal cadence of 120 to 130 revolutions per minute can be understood as the optimal compromise between these two factors. From this it can be concluded that for sprint performance, both fast force-velocity and fast activation dynamics are important; training activities that tend to induce changes in muscle that make either of these slower are likely to be detrimental to sprinting performance.

What about steady-state cycling? Here, metabolic factors play a role, in addition to the factors mentioned earlier. From experimental studies it is well known that sustainable power output is maximal for cadences in the order of 90 to 100 revolutions per minute. Surprisingly, it has been consistently found that efficiency is not optimal at this rate; at a fixed external power output, oxygen uptake has been reported to be minimal at a pedaling rate as low as 50 to 60 revolutions per minute. Even though our understanding of this paradox is currently far from complete, the experimental finding does indicate beyond a doubt that in cycling, central physiological processes mediated by the cardiovascular system are not the sole performance-limiting factors. Local physiological processes, such as the input of nutrients and removal of waste products, both related to local perfusion, must be important factors in submaximal steady-state cycling. The exact importance of mechanical and metabolic factors in determining the optimal cadence in steady state cycling is still unclear.

Saddle Height

A final factor that affects the power-producing capacity of the human leg is saddle height. Clearly, saddle height affects the range of joint angles that occurs during cycling. As a result, it also will affect the contact forces in the joints, which is likely to be related to the risk of injury. This issue, however, is beyond the scope of this chapter. Therefore, this section focuses on the relationship between saddle height and power production by muscles. With a lower saddle, the knee will be in a more flexed position throughout the pedal cycle. As a result of this difference in joint angle, muscle length also will be different; the lower saddle leads to a more flexed knee, which leads to a larger length of the knee extensor muscles.

How does this affect muscle power? Remember that muscle power depends on muscle force; now, muscle force is known to depend on muscle length. In other words, by the appropriate choice of saddle height, muscles can be allowed to contract through a range of lengths at which the force they can produce is near maximal. It is generally accepted that for the average cyclist, a saddle height of 98 percent of leg length optimizes the range of lengths traversed for the important power-producing muscles.

Summary

We can conclude several facts from this chapter. The velocity of the cyclist depends on the amount of mechanical power produced by the energy systems and the amount of mechanical power lost to air and surface friction. The amount of mechanical power depends on the rate at which the aerobic and anaerobic energy production systems are working and the mechanical efficiency of the body-bicycle system. The performance of the body-bicycle system is affected by (the direction of) the pedal force, the timing of muscle activation, gear selection, and saddle height.

part IV

Nutrition

Sports nutrition has received considerable attention in the past few years, and this field will continue to develop because it is recognized that nutrition can play an important and sometimes even crucial role in a cyclist's performance. In the 1960s it was common practice to eat large amounts of red meat the day before and sometimes even the morning of an important race. During the race the riders would eat chicken wings while their only bottle would contain tea with sugar. Clearly these practices have changed; now pasta, rice, and bread are important components of the diet, and special sports drinks and energy bars have been developed for use during exercise. However, for many cyclists, sports nutrition is synonymous with "nutritional supplements," but clearly it involves much more than that. In fact, the claims on many nutritional supplements are not always based on scientific findings.

Part IV discusses the energy requirements of cycling; the importance of maintaining energy balance; the roles of carbohydrate, fat, protein, and water intake; the importance of vitamin and mineral intake; and the effects of special diets. How should a cyclist prepare for an important one-day event? What should a rider eat and drink during stage races to optimize recovery? In these chapters, we discuss the effects of food and fluid intake in the preparation for competition, during competition and training, and during recovery. In addition, we outline the effects of several food supplements and potential ergogenic aids, such as creatine, caffeine, and carnitine. We then package these recommendations in a practical format so that you can take the information with you and make some changes to your diet or nutritional practices.

Reading part IV does not require a deep understanding of biochemistry, biology, chemistry, or physiology, but you need to be familiar with some of the main concepts. The first chapter in this part describes these briefly.

chapter 12

Energy Needs for Training and Racing

Asker Jeukendrup

Cyclists can expend large amounts of energy during training and competition. They often spend hours on their bicycles, and sustained power outputs can be relatively high. As a result, the muscle needs to be supplied continuously with energy. While a car engine runs on only one fuel (gasoline), skeletal muscle can obtain energy from as many as three different sources (fat, carbohydrate, and protein). When the gas is not regularly filled up in a car, there is a chance of running out of fuel, and this is also the case in human skeletal muscle. The likelihood of running out of fuel is higher in situations in which there is little time for refueling, such as in stage races or in frequent intensive-training sessions. The purpose of this chapter is to discuss these issues in more detail. For example, how much energy do we expend when we are cycling? Can we replenish the fuels utilized? What are the practical problems in stage races and how can these be overcome? Before we move on to these questions, however, it is important to first study energy metabolism in more detail. What are the most important energy sources and where are the fuels stored? This chapter also may serve as background reading for many of the following chapters.

Energy Metabolism

Energy is the potential for performing work or producing force. The development of force by muscles requires a source of chemical energy in the form of adenosine triphosphate (ATP). In fact, the breakdown of ATP provides the energy for all biological work. Because the amount of ATP stored is very small and is only sufficient to fuel two seconds of maximal work, ATP has to be constantly resynthesized from other sources of energy. There are three different mechanisms involved in the resynthesis of ATP for muscle-force generation:

1. Phosphocreatine (PCr) breakdown
2. Glycolysis, the anaerobic breakdown of glucose or glycogen resulting in ATP synthesis through a process called substrate-level phosphorylation
3. Oxidative phosphorylation, in which the products of carbohydrate, fat, protein, and alcohol metabolism enter the tricarboxylic acid cycle in the mitochondria and are oxidized to carbon dioxide and water

These processes differ in the amount of oxygen required and also in the rates at which they can generate energy for ATP resynthesis.

Phosphocreatine System

The muscle contains a small amount of energy in the form of PCr. The breakdown of PCr can generate energy very rapidly, and this is the main energy source during maximal exercise lasting approximately 8 to 15 seconds (sprints). PCr received a lot of attention in the media in the past few years because it appeared that its stores could be increased simply by the eating of creatine. Although creatine is normally present in our diet (especially in meat and fish), the daily intake of creatine is usually fairly low. Research studies have shown that with creatine supplements (20 grams per day), total creatine concentrations and PCr concentrations in the muscle can be increased substantially. This would mean that there is a larger amount of directly available energy in the muscle, but it also could help the resynthesis of PCr in the working muscle and thus enhance recovery in between intensive bouts of exercise. Indeed, studies confirmed that creatine supplementation can improve performance especially in repeated sprints. This indicates the importance of PCr as a fuel during high-intensity exercise. The effects of creatine supplementation on endurance cycling performance are less clear, and creatine is likely to have little or no effect during longer cycling races. You can find more detailed information about creatine in chapter 17.

Anaerobic Glycolysis

Anaerobic glycolysis refers to the breakdown of glucose-6-phosphate (a product of glycogen or bloodborne glucose) to pyruvate (or lactic acid). PCr breakdown and glycolysis are anaerobic mechanisms (i.e., they do not use oxygen). The formation of lactic acid occurs even in resting conditions. However, at rest and during light to moderate exercise, lactate removal from the muscle and the bloodstream usually equals its production rate, and therefore there is no accumulation of lactate in the muscles.

The breakdown of muscle glycogen and blood-derived glucose is especially important in maximal exercise of several second to several minutes. During high-intensity exercise, lactic acid production is very rapid and will exceed the rate of removal from the muscle and blood. This accumulation of lactic acid often is associated with a burning sensation in the muscle. Lactic acid breaks down to lactate and a hydrogen ion—and contrary to popular belief, it is the accumulation of the hydrogen ions and not lactate that results in fatigue!

Oxidation of Carbohydrate and Fat

For events lasting longer than several minutes, the most important energy sources are carbohydrate, fat, and, to a lesser degree, protein. These fuels are broken down in various biochemical pathways and this ultimately results in the production of ATP.

The oxidation of carbohydrate can provide energy at a relatively fast rate compared to the oxidation of fat. Carbohydrate is therefore the preferred fuel at relatively high exercise intensities (greater than 80 percent of maximal heart rate, or HRmax) when large amounts of energy have to be generated for longer periods of time. In almost all conditions, carbohydrate and fat are oxidized simultaneously but the relative proportions of these fuels are determined by factors such as the exercise intensity. Other factors that influence fuel selection are the duration of exercise (the longer the exercise, the greater the role of fat); diet (the more carbohydrate in your diet, the less fat you will oxidize); and whether you have eaten before exercise (carbohydrate feeding suppresses fat oxidation).

Both carbohydrate and fat are stored in the body. Carbohydrates are stored as glycogen in the muscle and liver. Muscle glycogen can be used directly to fuel contractile processes of the muscle while glucose from liver glycogen first has to be transported by the blood and taken up by the muscle before it can be oxidized. It is important to note that total carbohydrate stores are small. The total amount of muscle glycogen of a 70-kilogram cyclist is about 400 grams (see table 12.1), although trained individuals may have larger glycogen stores, while the liver can store approximately 80 to 100 grams of glycogen. There is also a small amount of glucose in the blood (20 grams). Expressed in terms of energy, the body carbohydrate stores represent approximately 8,000 kilojoules (2,000 kilocalories). In comparison with this, fat stores are very large and theoretically could provide energy for days, whereas the glycogen stores can become depleted within 60 to 90 minutes.

It has been estimated that a cyclist (with average efficiency and aerodynamics) requires about 83 kilojoules per minute (21 kilocalories per minute) to ride at 40 kilometers per hour. We therefore can calculate that the 500 grams of glycogen stored in the body can fuel about 95 minutes of cycling at this speed. The amount of energy stored as fat for a 70-kilogram male and a 55-kilogram female cyclist (average body composition) would provide 400,000 kilojoules (100,000 kilocalories) and 500,000 kilojoules (125,000 kilocalories), respectively. In other words, if only fat or only carbohydrates could be utilized as a fuel, the carbohydrate stores from exercising muscles would deliver energy for no more than 90 minutes of cycling at 40 kilometers per hour, while energy derived from fat stores would theoretically be satisfactory for 110 hours of riding at this pace.

1 kilogram = 2.2 pounds

TABLE 12.1 Energy Stores of 70-kg Man

Substrate	Amount (g)	Energy (kJ)	Energy (kcal)
Carbohydrate			
Plasma glucose	20	320	80
Liver glycogen	100	1,600	400
Muscle glycogen	400	6,400	1,600
Total	**520**	**8,320**	**2,080**
Fat			
Plasma FFA	0.4	14	3.6
Plasma TG	4	140	36
Adipose tissue	12,000	450,000	108,000
IMTG	300	11,000	2,700
Total	**520**	**461,154**	**135,040**

Note: FFA = free fatty acids; TG = triglycerides; IMTG = intramuscular triglycerides.
Adapted from Jeukendrup, Saris, and Wagenmakers 1998.

Of course, adipose tissue contains the largest quantity of fat, and most of the fat in humans is stored in subcutaneous and deep visceral adipose tissue. The storage of fat is dynamic, which means that in the case of a negative energy balance (see later in this chapter), the size of the individual fat cells will decrease, whereas with a positive balance, the excess of fatty acids will be converted into triglycerides and the growth of fat cells will result. Although adipose tissue is by far the most important site of storage, fat also is stored within the muscle. The total amount of fat stored in all muscle cells has been estimated to be approximately 300 grams. These intramuscular triglycerides (IMTG) also play an important role in energy provision, and interestingly, trained cyclists seem to have more IMTG than untrained cyclists.

Energy Expenditure

Cycling is among the sports with the highest-reported daily energy expenditures. The levels of energy expenditure have been measured and estimated with various techniques. One of the methods often used is the doubly labeled water method, an accurate technique that allows measurements of energy expenditure over longer periods (days). This method has been used in races such as the Tour de France to measure the amount of energy the riders expend each day. During the three weeks of the Tour de France, the riders expended an average of about 25 megajoules (6,500 kilocalories) per day with extremes up to 36 megajoules (9,000 kilocalories). The latter is almost four times as much as someone with similar weight and an average daily activity pattern. Such extreme energy expenditures usually are only seen in the long stages, and, although these measurements have never been performed, energy expenditure in some of the long spring classics such as the Tour of Flanders may even exceed 36 megajoules (9,000 kilocalories).

Nowadays, we can easily obtain estimates of energy expenditure from power-measuring devices (see chapter 6) or heart rate (see chapter 5). However, power output gives the most accurate estimate as it is more directly related to energy expenditure. The power output is a certain percentage of the energy expenditure, usually 15 to 25 percent. In other words, only 15 to 25 percent of the energy we generate is used for cycling movement, with the remainder of the energy lost as heat. The energy cost of cycling also depends on aerodynamics. Someone with a very good position on the bike will expend less energy at a given speed. Table 12.2 gives an estimation of energy expenditure of cycling at different speeds, varying terrains, and varying wind conditions. This table can help cyclists get an idea about the energy they are expending.

Eating Enough

Cyclists are usually good eaters. This is not surprising because they have to eat to match their high energy expenditures. There are various reports in the literature of food intake by cyclists, especially during competition. Table 12.3 lists the energy intakes reported by cyclists competing in a variety of events.

During the Tour de France, when energy expenditures may amount up to 36 megajoules (9,000 kilocalories), one can imagine the difficulties of maintaining energy balance. In a study, Saris et al. (1989) compared the energy expenditures and intakes (see figure 12.1), and one can see that the cyclists maintain energy balance fairly well. On some of the very hard days with energy expenditures of more than 24 megajoules (6,000 kilocalories), it is difficult to match the energy expenditures, and often the riders are in slight 500- to 1,500-kilocalorie negative energy balance. On rest days

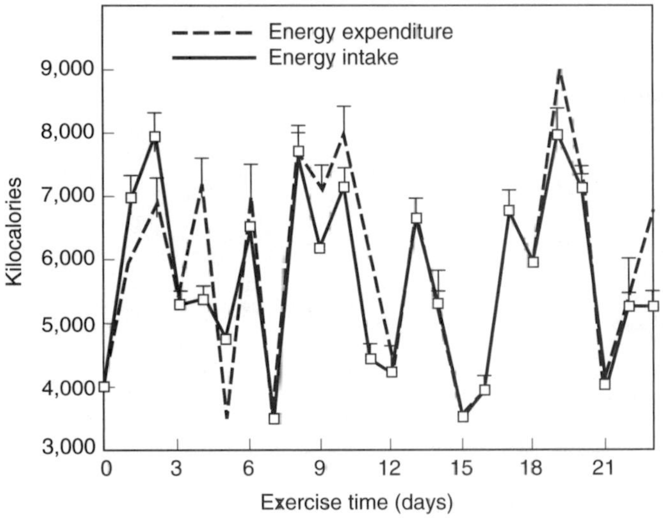

Figure 12.1 Energy intake versus energy expenditure during the Tour de France.

Reprinted from Saris et al. 1989.

TABLE 12.2 **Energy Expenditure at Different Speeds**

	Standing (kcal/min)	Seated, hands on brakes (kcal/min)	Aero position (kcal/min)	Standing (kcal/hr)	Seated, hands on brakes (kcal/hr)	Aero position (kcal/hr)
Flat road, no wind						
Riding at 20 km/h	4.7	3.5	3.3	283	212	198
Riding at 25 km/h	8.5	6.1	5.7	508	369	341
Riding at 30 km/h	13.9	9.9	9.1	836	595	548
Riding at 35 km/h	21.5	15.1	13.8	1,288	905	829
Riding at 40 km/h	31.4	21.8	20.0	1,883	1,311	1,199
Riding at 45 km/h	44.0	30.5	27.8	2,642	1,828	1,669
Riding at 50 km/h	59.8	41.2	37.5	3,587	2,470	2,251
Flat road, 11 m/s head wind						
Riding at 20 km/h	33.3	22.7	20.7	1,999	1,365	1,239
Riding at 25 km/h	48.7	33.2	30.1	2,922	1,990	1,807
Riding at 30 km/h	67.6	46.0	41.7	4,056	2,758	2,503
Riding at 35 km/h	90.4	61.3	55.7	5,421	3,681	3,340
5% gradient uphill						
Riding at 20 km/h	20.5	19.3	19.1	1,232	1,161	1,147
Riding at 25 km/h	28.2	25.9	25.5	1,695	1,555	1,528
Riding at 30 km/h	37.7	33.6	32.9	2,260	2,019	1,971
Riding at 35 km/h	49.1	42.8	41.5	2,948	2,565	2,490
10% gradient uphill						
Riding at 20 km/h	36.4	35.2	34.9	2,181	2,110	2,096
Riding at 25 km/h	48.0	45.7	45.2	2,881	2,741	2,714
Riding at 30 km/h	61.4	57.4	56.6	3,683	3,442	3,395

TABLE 12.3 Food Intake of Cyclists During Competition

Cycling population	Energy intake (MJ/day)	CHO intake (g/day)	CHO intake (g/kg/day)	Protein intake (g/day)	Fat intake (g/day)	Reference
Training						
Irish Olympic team	16.3	523	7.3	136	143	Johnson et al. 1985
Dutch amateur international level	18.3	663	9.2	115	148	van Erp-Baart et al. 1989
US collegiate level	17.4	609	8.8	147	125	Jensen et al. 1992
Spanish professional team	22.4	770	11.3	176	178	Garcia-Roves et al. 2000
Competition						
US collegiate level	18.7	698	10.1	149	127	Jensen et al. 1992
Amateur cyclists in the Tour de l'Avenir	23.3	873	11.8	207	151	van Erp-Baart et al. 1989
Professional cyclists in the Tour de France	24.3	849	12.3	217	147	Saris et al. 1989
Professional cyclists in the Tour of Spain	23.5	841	12.6	201	159	Garcia-Roves et al. 2000

CHO = carbohydrate

Adapted from Burke et al. 2001.

they seem to compensate for this, and over the course of three weeks they seem to maintain body weight fairly well (Jeukendrup et al. 2000).

However, weight losses have been reported very often during the Tour de France and similar stage races, and this indicates the difficulties of maintaining energy balance. To illustrate this problem we could express the energy intake in a different unit that most people are familiar with: cheeseburgers. When we express daily energy intake in terms of cheeseburgers, cyclists would have to eat 27 cheeseburgers on some days to balance their expenditure. With a normal feeding schedule (breakfast, lunch, and dinner), this would mean at least 5 burgers for breakfast, 5 for lunch, and 5 for dinner, leaving 12 burgers for snacks in between those meals. The problem immediately becomes apparent when we express it this way. But the situation is even more complicated because these cyclists do not have a normal feeding schedule. They may spend up to seven hours on their bicycles, and although they can drink and eat on the bike, there is no time or possibility to consume large meals. This means that the cyclists must consume most of the energy during breakfast and dinner. In reality, dinner especially becomes very large and is often equivalent to 12 cheeseburgers.

To further complicate the problem, hunger feelings often are suppressed for several hours after strenuous exercise. This makes it even more difficult to eat the large amounts. During the second and third week of the Tour de France, riders may suffer from gastrointestinal problems and they may not be able to tolerate the large amounts of food. After hot stages when dehydration may be considerable, the occurrence of gastrointestinal problems is more frequent and in those cases it is important to rehydrate first to reestablish normal gut function.

Energy Balance

When energy intake equals energy expenditure, riders are in energy balance. When the riders eat less than they burn, it is called negative energy balance. When they eat more than they expend, it is called positive energy balance—and in this case they will gain weight.

Cyclists engaged in long-term, high-intensity training or racing must consume carbohydrate drinks in order to maintain their energy balance.

Although it is often difficult to eat large amounts during a race, energy intake in the form of carbohydrate drinks has been shown to be crucial. When cyclists undertook two days of high-intensity cycling with an energy expenditure of approximately 24 megajoules (6,000 kilocalories), they were not able to maintain energy balance without consuming energy drinks (Brouns et al. 1989). When the cyclists were given as much carbohydrate solution during exercise as they could drink, energy balance was maintained.

Energy intake during exercise is therefore extremely important during stage races because it may make up a large percentage of the daily energy intake. Garcia-Roves et al. (1997) recorded food intake during the three major stage races of the Vuelta Ciclista a España and found that cyclists ingested, on average, 13 percent of their daily energy intake while cycling. Most of this was in the form of sports drinks (carbohydrate solutions). However, in this particular study, the fluid intake during the race was extremely low and it is likely that fluid and carbohydrate intake has been underestimated. In the study by Garcia-Roves et al., carbohydrate intake during the race averaged 25 grams per hour, substantially lower than the recommended 60 to 70 grams per hour (see chapter 14). To increase daily energy intake in the form of carbohydrate, maltodextrins can be added to various foods and meals. These carbohydrates have the advantage of not having a strong flavor and as such can be added as invisible calories.

Chapters 14, 15, and 16 discuss several other strategies that can help a rider to maintain energy balance on very long training rides or races. For example, chapter 14 addresses how much carbohydrate should be ingested before and during exercise and what would be the best sources of carbohydrate. Chapter 15 deals with ways to improve recovery and to rapidly restore energy balance after exhaustive exercise. Finally, in chapter 16, we discuss specific eating plans that will help the cyclist put this advice into practice.

Determining Energy Balance

How does a cyclist determine his energy balance? This question is not easy to answer. You can measure or at least estimate both the energy expenditure and the energy intake, and by doing this, you can obtain some idea of energy balance. This can be helpful in situations as discussed earlier, in which large amounts of energy have to be consumed to avoid weight loss, but it also can be helpful in situations in which weight loss is the goal. Following, we list some of the available methods to measure or estimate energy expenditure and energy intake, and we discuss the pros and cons of these methods as well as the practicalities.

Measuring Energy Expenditure

There are various ways to estimate or to measure energy expenditure. You can obtain a rough indication from table 12.2 (on page 146) and get an idea of the energy expenditure of a typical training session. Of course, this will only be a rough estimate since the intensity will change many times during a training session and also the conditions will vary. Therefore, it may be useful to measure energy expenditure a bit more accurately. A useful tool could be a heart rate monitor, especially now that some will provide you with an estimated value for energy expenditure based on heart rate. If you use a power-measuring device, you may obtain a more accurate figure of energy expenditure during a training session (see chapter 6). All these methods have limitations, and the only way to get more accurate information about energy expenditure is in a laboratory situation or by using the very expensive doubly labeled water technique.

Measuring Energy Intake

The energy intake is the other part of the energy-balance equation. There are a multitude of methods to estimate energy and nutrient intake. To choose the most appropriate method, you need to determine what kind of information you need to obtain. Do you want information about energy intake only, or also about nutrient intake? Do you want to know macronutrient and micronutrient intake, and is it important to know the type of carbohydrates, the type of fatty acids, and the quality of the proteins ingested? All techniques will have advantages and disadvantages and sometimes techniques have to be combined to get the best result. The most important methods include a 24-hour recall, a three-day dietary record (or food record), and a seven-day dietary record. Following, we look at the advantages and disadvantages of these methods.

24-Hour Recall

The most common technique of assessing food intake is the 24-hour recall method. A trained interviewer asks the cyclist on one or more occasions to describe the food, drinks, and dietary supplements that he has consumed during the previous 24 hours. The advantages of this technique are that it is easy to administer, time efficient, and inexpensive. The technique also has disadvantages: underreporting is common, even when the person is interviewed by a skilled dietitian. This technique generally underestimates energy and nutrient intake by about 20 percent! Cyclists who are above their ideal weight tend to underestimate their portions, whereas those below their desired weight tend to overreport portions.

Three-Day Dietary Survey

The three-day dietary survey is a relatively simple and reasonably accurate method to determine the total daily energy intake and the quality of food. The daily log of food intake for three days should represent a normal eating pattern. It often is recommended to include two weekdays and one day during a weekend. Experiments have shown that calculations of energy intake made from records of daily food consumption are usually within 10 percent of the actual energy intake.

You may weigh food or estimate the portion sizes. To obtain an accurate measure of food, you can use simple tools such as

- a plastic ruler,
- a standard measuring cup,
- measuring spoons, or
- a balance.

Record all foods consumed, including all beverages. It is recommended that you keep your food diary with you at all times and that you record the food intake immediately when you are consuming the food. When the food diary is completed, the energy intake and nutrient intakes can be calculated using a software package or a food table. This is preferably done by a skilled dietitian, but you also could do it yourself using one of the many online nutrition databases (e.g., **www.dietsure.co.uk** or **www.dietsite.com**).

Seven-Day Dietary Survey

The seven-day dietary survey is almost identical to the three-day food diary. The only difference is the duration of the recording period. The advantage of the extended recording time is that the food recorded may be more representative of the person's normal diet. It includes all weekdays and the two days of the weekend and should give an accurate reflection of someone's nutritional habits. The disadvantage of this method is that with such a relatively long period of recording, people may become tired of recording and tend to forget to write down foods consumed, resulting in a less accurate nutritional assessment. Besides the three- and seven-day dietary surveys, other alternatives have been used with four, five, or six days of recording.

Errors With Food Surveys

Errors in food surveys occur mainly because of memory failures. In general, the stereotypical intakes are recorded accurately but the uncommon foods are sometimes poorly registered. Most errors are made in reporting the frequency of consumption. Errors in estimating the portion size are very common as well. When food is not weighed, the mass of various foods may be underestimated or overestimated considerably. Errors as large as 50 percent for foods and 20 percent for nutrients can be made. Training and instructing the person who is registering food intake can reduce some of these errors. Errors also may occur when individuals don't report their food intake accurately enough, which makes coding of the specific food type very difficult. For example, writing "four potatoes" is not very informative. Were these large baked potatoes or small new potatoes? How were they prepared—cooked, boiled, baked, or fried? Were the skins removed or not? Sometimes food records may be illegible, introducing more coding errors. It is therefore extremely important that individuals are instructed carefully and provide as much detail as possible.

Analysis of Nutrient Intake

Once the information about an individual's diet is obtained, this can be compared to the recommendations. A simple but not very accurate way is to compare the nutrient intake to a guide for diet planning, such as the food guide pyramid (see chapter 17, figure 17.2 on page 210). However, when a three- to seven-day dietary survey is completed, the intake can be analyzed in more detail. To calculate the intake of specific nutrients, you can use the food labels or one of many food-composition databases. In the United States the major source of information is the USDA nutrient database, which is available online (**www.nal.usda.gov/fnic/foodcomp/**). There are various software packages and even some programs online that use this database or databases to calculate food intake. In all cases, you need to enter the exact amount and kind of food into the computer program. If a food is not included in the database, you should choose an appropriate substitute. Most computer programs also allow the user to add new products to the database. With the information on the food label, you can introduce new products. The software usually will produce an average intake over 24 hours of all macronutrients and micronutrients. You then can compare these values to the recommended amounts.

Losing Weight

There is a tendency, especially at the elite level, to reduce body weight and body fat mass. There is a strong belief among cyclists that body weight influences cycling performance, especially in the mountains. Percentages of body fat in elite and world-class cyclists are generally between 5 and 8 percent (Jeukendrup et al. 2000). Chapter 9 discusses how changes in body weight can influence performance in various terrains.

Cyclists often achieve weight loss by reducing energy intake but they also can achieve it by increasing energy expenditure. To lose weight, the cyclist has to be in negative energy balance.

The definition of the classic energy-balance equation states that if energy intake equals energy expenditure, then weight is maintained. However, even if weight is maintained, changes in body composition may occur (e.g., an increase in muscle and a decrease in fat). More recently, a slightly different method has been proposed that states that energy balance is achieved when the individual substrate balances are equal. For example, being in fat balance means that you are oxidizing a similar amount of fat per day as you are ingesting. So dietary intakes of carbohydrate, fat, and protein must equal their oxidation rates to be in energy balance. If body fat is to be lost, energy expenditure must exceed energy intake and fat oxidation must exceed fat intake.

When a cyclist is in negative energy balance, the carbohydrate intake often is insufficient to replenish glycogen stores and fatigue occurs after several days. It is very difficult to train hard and lose weight at the same time. Cyclists at the beginning of the season often increase their training volume while at the same time try to get rid of some of their "winter reserves" of body fat. If no special attention is paid to carbohydrate intake, this may result in glycogen depletion. It will be more difficult to complete training sessions, and when persisted over several weeks, overtraining is likely to develop (see chapter 2). It is therefore important to set realistic goals; the cyclist should try not to lose too much weight at once and should make sure that carbohydrate intake is adequate (see chapters 14, 15, and 16).

For weight loss to be maintained, changes in diet and exercise habits need to become part of a cyclist's lifestyle, and this is usually the difficult part. Athletes often have no problem losing weight but find it much harder to maintain this weight loss for very long. Studies have shown that the people who have the most success at losing weight and maintaining weight loss are those who modify their diet, reduce fat intake, train regularly and often, record their body weight regularly, and receive a high level of social support from their friends and family. The first step is identifying the specific eating habits that have to be changed, followed by setting specific goals to change this behavior. Professional advice from a dietitian often can be very helpful in achieving these goals.

Here are some guidelines:

- Set realistic goals.
- Make your weight loss gradual (0.5 kilogram per week).
- Reduce fat intake (but remember that this will only result in weight loss if you also reduce energy intake).
- Eat more whole grains, cereals, fruits, and vegetables and get adequate fiber (25 grams a day).
- Reduce or eliminate late-night eating.
- Plan ahead and carry healthy snacks with you so that when you get hungry you will not be tempted to eat high-fat snacks.
- Avoid food items high in fat (e.g., butter, oil, high-fat cakes, high-fat meat).
- Always eat some high-carbohydrate food directly after a training session.
- Keep track of your weight; measure it regularly.

- Do long endurance rides at 65 to 75 percent HRmax—these may be the best training sessions to oxidize fat (Achten et al. 2001). Keep in mind, however, that the duration of those rides is probably even more important than the exact exercise intensity.

Summary

Twenty-four-hour energy expenditures of cyclists are the among the highest ever reported. In extreme situations such as the Tour de France, cyclists may expend up to 36 megajoules (9,000 kilocalories) per day. With such high energy expenditures, it is often difficult to maintain energy balance, especially since hunger feelings can be depressed after hard exercise. Carbohydrate solutions become even more important in such conditions.

If you want to know whether you are in energy balance, you can obtain measures of energy expenditure and energy intake. You can obtain simple estimates of energy expenditure by using a heart rate monitor, although other (and more accurate) techniques are also available. A common method to measure energy intake is the three-day dietary record.

If weight loss (body-fat loss) is the goal of a training program, it is important to maintain a negative energy balance while at the same time also maintaining a negative fat balance. Carbohydrate intake should not be compromised too much, so that training can still be maintained at similar levels. If carbohydrate intake is insufficient and training is continued, it is possible that a state of overtraining will develop. We also advise that if you want to lose body weight, do it gradually, and be in negative energy balance by no more than two megajoules (500 kilocalories) per day.

chapter 13

Fluid Balance

Ronald Maughan

Water is the largest single component of the cyclist's body, accounting for about 60 percent of total body mass in typical males and—because of their generally higher body fat content—about 55 percent in women. Typical values for total body water content are therefore about 30 to 50 liters. Despite the fact that daily water intake and loss can vary from less than 1 liter up to 15 liters or even more, total body water content seldom varies by more than about 1 percent from day to day. We maintain water balance at this relatively constant level on a daily basis by balancing intake from food and fluid with losses that occur as urine and sweat. The rate of fluid loss mainly depends on two factors: the ambient environmental conditions (temperature, humidity) and the exercise intensity. Exercise duration and the frequency of exercise sessions also will affect the total sweat loss. Fluid intake usually is dependent on thirst feelings, but thirst (or the lack of thirst) can be overridden by conscious control.

This tight regulation of water balance is achieved by regulation of both intake and output, and it is important in avoiding the adverse effects of a body water deficit, which can include impairments of physical and mental function and an increased risk of heat illness. The detrimental effects of dehydration during exercise are well recognized. Performance will suffer if a fluid deficit is allowed to develop. Sweat loss results in a loss of minerals (electrolytes), as well as water, with sodium being the principal ion lost in sweat. Replacing electrolyte losses is necessary to maintain fluid balance, but it may be more important after exercise than during exercise. A possible exception to this occurs in very prolonged exercise in which sweat losses are high and fluid intake is correspondingly high. In this situation, there may be a requirement for sodium replacement during exercise.

As the previous chapter outlines, carbohydrate is the key energy substrate in hard effort and ingesting carbohydrate-containing drinks is an effective way to provide additional fuel for the working muscles. Commercial sports drinks are formulated to provide a pleasant-tasting drink that can meet the needs for both carbohydrate and fluid during exercise, and the manufacturers recognize that taste is an important factor in stimulating intake. Although ingesting carbohydrate and fluids can improve performance, the requirements will not be the same for all individuals in all situations. The choice of food and fluids will be influenced by a variety of factors, including the nature and duration of the event, the climatic conditions, the pre-event nutritional status, and the physiological and biochemical characteristics of the individual. The circumstances of each rider and the different requirements of training and competition must therefore be considered when making recommendations.

Rehydration after exercise is a key part of the recovery process, and cyclists must ingest sufficient fluid to replace sweat losses and also to account for ongoing urine and other water losses. Additionally, replacement of electrolytes, especially sodium, is crucial for postexercise recovery. Because individual needs for fluid replacement vary greatly among individuals and are also very much affected by environmental conditions, it is difficult to formulate general guidelines that are helpful for each person. Rather, the individual rider must take responsibility for assessing fluid losses and for ensuring that intake is sufficient to meet the requirements.

Basal Water Requirements

The minimum daily water intake necessary to maintain health in adults with a sedentary lifestyle is usually said to be about 1.5 liters. Body size is clearly a factor that has a large bearing on water turnover. It is expected, therefore, that there will be differences between men and women and between adults and children. Unless otherwise specified, the values given here will relate to the average 70-kilogram (154-pound) male with a moderate body-fat content. The extent of the daily water loss and intake will vary from person to person, but a general example for a sedentary person is outlined in table 13.1.

Environmental conditions will affect an individual's water requirements by altering the losses that occur through the various routes. Water requirements for sedentary people living in the heat may be twofold or threefold higher than the requirement for

TABLE 13.1 Daily Body Water Input and Output

	Daily water loss (ml)		Daily water intake (ml)
Kidneys	1,500	Fluid	1,300
Respiratory tract	400	Food	1,000
Gastrointestinal tract	200	Cellular oxidation	300
Skin	500		
Total	**2,600**	**Total**	**2,600**

living in a temperate climate, even when this is not accompanied by pronounced sweating. Losses through the skin and from the lungs will be markedly influenced by the humidity of the ambient air, and this may be a more important factor than the ambient temperature. Respiratory water losses are incurred because of the humidification of the inspired air when it comes in contact with the wet surfaces of the respiratory tract. These losses are relatively small in the resting individual in a warm, moist environment (amounting to about 200 milliliters per day), but they will be increased approximately twofold in regions of low humidity and may be as high as 1,500 milliliters per day during periods of hard work in cold, dry air at altitude. To these losses must be added insensible loss through the skin (about 500 milliliters per day) and urine loss, which usually will not be less than about 800 milliliters per day.

Variations in the amount and type of food eaten will affect water intake because of differences in the water content among foods, but this also will have some effect on water requirements because of the resulting demand for excretion of excess electrolytes and the products of metabolism. An intake of electrolytes in excess of the amounts lost (primarily in sweat and feces) must be corrected by excretion in the urine, with a resulting increase in the volume and osmolality of urine formed. The daily intake of electrolytes is subject to wide variation among individuals, with strong trends for differences among different geographical regions. A high-protein diet requires a greater urine output to allow the excretion of water-soluble nitrogenous waste. This effect is relatively small compared with other losses, but it becomes meaningful when water availability is limited. The water content of food ingested will be influenced greatly by the nature of the diet, and water associated with food may make a major contribution to the total fluid intake. Some water is obtained from the oxidation of nutrients, and this will depend on the total metabolic rate, but it also will be influenced by the nature of the substrate being oxidized.

Fluid intake is driven largely by the thirst mechanism, and although this is relatively insensitive to small fluid deficits, the long-term stability of the body water content indicates that it is effective in ensuring an intake that is sufficient to meet requirements (Shirreffs and Maughan 2000). The kidney ensures that excess fluid is excreted and can act to conserve fluid by reducing urinary losses, but it is not effective if intake is insufficient to meet needs.

Temperature Regulation and Fluid Balance During Exercise

At rest, the energy demand is low and the rate of heat production by the body is correspondingly low, typically about 50 to 70 watts. Body temperature is maintained at a constant level mainly by behavioral mechanisms. We adjust the amount of clothing to a level that is appropriate for the environment. During exercise, heat production increases, normally leading to an increase in body temperature. To prevent body temperature from rising to dangerously high levels during hard exercise, the rate of heat loss must be increased and a number of physiological adjustments are invoked to promote this. When a cyclist is riding outdoors in a cool environment, hyperthermia—an elevated body temperature—is not a problem and keeping warm is often more of a challenge. Because of the relatively high speeds involved in cycling—excluding, of course, the situation in steep climbs—convection is an effective means of heat loss, and the movement of cool air over the skin can remove heat at high rates. In long downhill sections, where the speeds are high and the work rate is low, rates of heat loss will exceed the rate of heat production, leading to a fall in body temperature.

In uphill cycling, two factors change dramatically. The rate of heat production is greatly increased and the reduced speed means that the potential for heat loss by convection is greatly decreased. Metabolic heat production for top riders during a sustained climb may exceed 2,000 watts (two kilowatts). If heat is not lost from the body, this would be sufficient to cause body temperature to rise rapidly, and intolerable levels would be reached within a few minutes if an effective heat loss mechanism is not in operation. In track racing, even higher rates of heat production are achieved, and the temperature of the active muscles will reach exceptionally high levels, even though the exercise duration is short (Craig and Norton 2001).

At low ambient temperatures, there is still a rapid rate of heat loss from the skin surface by physical heat loss to the environment (radiation). The challenge in this situation—when the muscles are working hard and demand a high supply of blood—is to maintain a high rate of blood flow to the skin to maintain skin temperature and thus heat loss (Gonzalez-Alonso et al. 1998). However, in a hot environment, when the ambient temperature is higher than skin temperature, radiation is no longer effective and the only mechanism by which heat can be lost from the body is in evaporation of water from the skin and the respiratory tract.

Complete evaporation of one liter of water from the skin will remove 2.4 megajoules (580 kilocalories) of heat from the body. Provided the humidity of the air surrounding the skin is low, the evaporation of sweat is effective in limiting the rise in body temperature that would otherwise occur. Again, however, at slow speeds, the effectiveness of evaporation is reduced as a hot, humid microclimate develops in the clothing layers over the skin. Total sweat losses in a race or training session are determined primarily by the intensity and duration of exercise and by the ambient temperature and humidity. However, sweat rates vary greatly among individuals, even in the same environmental conditions and when the metabolic rate is apparently similar (Maughan 1985). High rates of sweat secretion can occur during hard exercise even in cool environments and, if the rate of evaporation is high, there may be no sweat visible on the skin surface.

The water that is lost in sweat is derived in varying proportions from the plasma water, the interstitial water (the water that occupies the spaces between the cells), and the intracellular water compartment (the water inside the cells). The effect on plasma volume has attracted much attention, as any decrease in plasma volume is likely to adversely affect both exercise capacity and the ability to regulate body temperature.

As has been mentioned, when the work rate is high, blood flow to the muscles must be maintained at a high level to supply oxygen and substrates at the rates required to sustain aerobic metabolism, but a high blood flow to the skin is also necessary for convecting heat to the body surface where it can be dissipated. When the ambient temperature is high and blood volume has been decreased by sweat loss during prolonged exercise, there may be difficulty in meeting both these requirements. In this situation, skin blood flow is likely to be compromised, allowing body temperature to rise but preventing a dangerous fall in blood pressure. Muscle blood flow is also reduced when cardiac output is reduced, but there is a compensatory increase in the amount of oxygen that the muscle extracts from the blood, allowing oxidative energy metabolism to be maintained at a high rate.

It has been shown that increases in core temperature and heart rate are directly linked to the level of dehydration (Montain and Coyle 1992b). It also has been shown, however, that ingesting fluid during exercise increases skin blood flow and therefore thermoregulatory capacity, independent of increases in the circulating blood volume (Montain and Coyle 1992a). Plasma volume expansion using dextran-saline infusion was less effective in preventing a rise in core temperature than was the ingestion of sufficient volumes of a carbohydrate-electrolyte drink to maintain plasma volume at a similar level. This indicates strong advantages to ingesting fluids during exercise.

Although there is no debate over the fact that any athlete who allows a fluid deficit to develop will fail to perform optimally, there is as much debate over the magnitude of these effects as there is over the mechanisms involved. It often is reported—without any reference to experimental evidence—that exercise performance is impaired when a person is dehydrated by as little as 2 percent of body weight and that losses in excess of 5 percent of body weight can decrease the capacity for work by about 30 percent.

Many riders will be dehydrated to this level in the later stages of a race and yet are able to perform quite well, so it may be that trained individuals are less affected. It has been shown, however, that very small fluid deficits do impair performance, but the methods used are not sufficiently sensitive to detect small changes. A fluid deficit of as little as 1 percent of body mass—only about 700 milliliters for the average rider—is enough to impair time-trial performance. It is equally clear that dehydration can compromise performance in high-intensity exercise as well as endurance activities. Although sweat losses during brief exercise are small, the failure to ensure adequate hydration levels on the starting line of sprint events is likely to have a negative effect on performance. Nielsen et al. (1982) showed that prolonged exercise that resulted in a loss of fluid corresponding to 2.5 percent of body weight resulted in a 45 percent fall in the capacity to perform high-intensity exercise.

The mechanisms responsible for the reduction in exercise performance that occurs in the heat are not entirely clear, but Nielsen et al. (1993) have proposed that the high-core temperature itself is a key factor. This proposition was based on the observation that a period of acclimatization was successful in delaying the point of fatigue, but the fatigue always occurred at the same core temperature. The primary effects of acclimatization were to lower the resting core temperature and to increase the effectiveness of heat-loss mechanisms so that it took longer to reach the critical temperature. This observation is further supported by numerous studies that show that manipulation of the body heat content before exercise can alter exercise capacity: Performance is extended by prior cooling and is reduced by raising body temperature before exercise. There is a clear message here for athletes with regard to their warm-up activities before competition: If the ambient conditions are hot, warm up in the shade, use cooling jackets if available, and generally attempt to exercise the legs while keeping the core cool (see chapter 4).

Leiper et al. (1996) investigated the water intake and water losses in a group of cyclists and a group of sedentary people. The cyclists covered an average daily distance of 50 kilometers in training for competition. The median water turnover rate was higher ($P < 0.001$) in the active group (3.38 [2.88 to 4.89] liters per day) than in the sedentary individuals (2.22 [2.06 to 3.40] liters per day). There was no difference between the groups in the daily urine output (cyclists, 1.96 [1.78 to 2.36] liters; controls, 1.90 [1.78 to 1.96] liters), but the nonrenal losses (primarily sweat) were greater ($P < 0.001$) in the cyclists (1.46 [1.06 to 3.04] liters per day) than in the sedentary group (0.53 [0.15 to 1.72] liters per day). It was rather cool during the measurement period, with average maximum daily temperatures of 10 degrees Celsius and a range from 4 to 18 degrees Celsius, which might account for the rather low sweat rates in spite of the high physical activity level of these cyclists.

Electrolyte Balance

Secretion of sweat onto the skin surface is necessary to limit the rise in body temperature that would otherwise occur, but in prolonged exercise this leads to a loss of electrolytes and water from the body. Although the volume loss can be estimated easily from changes in body mass (after appropriate corrections are applied for substrate oxidation and respiratory water loss), electrolyte loss is rather more difficult to quantify. The extent of these losses has been the subject of much debate largely because of the use of a variety of different but unreliable methods to assess sweat electrolyte content. The values for sweat electrolyte content in table 13.2 give some indication of the great inter-individual variability in the concentration of the major electrolytes.

Sodium is the most abundant positively charged element in the extracellular space, and it is also the major electrolyte lost in sweat. Chloride, which also is mainly located in the extracellular space, is the major negatively charged element. This ensures that the greatest fraction of fluid loss as sweat is derived from the extracellular space, including the plasma. Although the composition of sweat is highly variable, sweat is always hypotonic with regard to body fluids, and the net effect of sweat loss is an increase in plasma osmolality, which closely follows the change in plasma sodium concentration. The fact that the plasma concentrations of sodium and potassium generally increase during exercise suggests that replacement of these electrolytes during exercise may not be necessary.

TABLE 13.2 Concentration of Major Electrolytes in Sweat, Plasma, and Intracellular (Muscle) Water

Electrolyte	Plasma (mmol/l)	Sweat (mmol/l)	Intracellular (mmol/l)
Sodium	137-144	20-80	10
Potassium	3.5-4.9	4-8	148
Calcium	4.4-5.2	3-4	0-2
Magnesium	1.5-2.1	1-4	30-40
Chloride	100-108	30-70	2

Note: The values are collated from a variety of literature sources (Maughan and Shirreffs 1998).

Reprinted by permission from Maughan and Shirreffs 1998.

When the exercise duration is very prolonged and when cyclists take excessively large volumes of low-sodium drinks (such as plain water or cola drinks) during exercise, hyponatraemia (a fall in the plasma sodium concentration) has been reported to occur, with consequent adverse effects. Hyperthermia and hyponatraemia associated with dehydration often are encountered in athletes requiring medical attention at the end of long-distance races, and the symptoms usually resolve on treatments with oral rehydration. Intravenous rehydration with saline, and sometimes with added glucose, is commonly used at some marathon medical facilities, but there is little evidence that this is generally more effective than the oral route.

It has become clear, however, that a small number of individuals at the end of very prolonged events may have hyponatraemia in conjunction with either hyperhydration or dehydration. The cases of hyponatraemia reported in the literature have mostly been associated with ultramarathon or prolonged triathlon events, and there have only been a few cases reported in cyclists, perhaps because no one has looked for this condition. Most of the cases have occurred in events lasting in excess of eight hours, and there are few reports of hyponatraemia in which the exercise duration is less than four hours. These reports indicate that some supplementation with sodium salts may be required in extremely prolonged events in which large sweat losses can be expected and when it is possible to consume large volumes of fluid. They also suggest that medical staff should be alert to the possibility of hyponatraemia occurring in the later stages of long races, but this should not divert attention from the fact that most competitors will be hypohydrated and hypernatraemic.

Drinking Before Exercise

It is important to begin each training session or competition well hydrated to maximize performance and to minimize the risk of heat-related problems. A myth that has been circulating in cycling for many years is that you can adapt to *not* drinking, and coaches have often advised their cyclists to take only one bottle on their long endurance rides. The idea that the body can adapt to exercise in the dehydrated state by deliberately restricting fluid intake is mistaken. If an athlete attempts this, the quality of the training session is reduced. This is one situation in which just because it feels harder to train does not mean that it is doing more good. Attempts to train while dehydrated will greatly increase the risk of heat exhaustion and of life-threatening heatstroke. Every effort should be made to take fluids before training, and the best fluid to take at this time is probably one of the commercially available sports drinks. The major difference between these drinks is taste, and athletes should experiment with different drinks and with different flavors of each brand. It is important to find a product with a taste that is appealing. When the fluid requirement is as much as 8 to 10 liters of fluid per day, several different drinks or different flavors of the same drink may help to encourage consumption by providing some variety.

Monitoring of fluid status is important and riders should learn to recognize the symptoms of dehydration. These include infrequent urination and the passing of small volumes of dark-colored urine. Urine color charts may be helpful in encouraging riders to ensure adequate fluid intake by providing an objective measure of hypohydration, and they may be just as reliable as more sophisticated measurements (Armstrong et al. 1994). Many of the symptoms of jet lag are similar to those of mild dehydration—these include fatigue, headache, and insomnia—and when these symptoms are present it may be wise to increase fluid intake.

Riders who are trying to control or reduce body weight need to be careful with their drinking strategy. Most of the sports drinks contain about 6 to 7 percent carbohydrate, so one liter will give 60 to 70 grams of carbohydrate, which adds up to about 250 to 300 calories. Drinking five liters of a sports drink can give up to 1,500 calories—this may be more than half the total daily energy needs of many riders who are not training intensively. Most popular soft drinks contain even more. An athlete drinking five liters of cola per day will get more than 2,000 calories before even beginning to eat any solid food. While the energy that these drinks provide may be helpful during periods of hard training, when it may be difficult to eat enough solid food to stay in energy balance, it will not be appropriate for everyone. For the well-fed, well-rested rider, water or low-energy drinks may be the best choice at times when there is a need to restrict energy intake.

Drinking During Exercise

Fluid intake during exercise is aimed at countering the effects of dehydration and also can provide a source of energy, usually in the form of carbohydrate. Recent results show that the benefits of providing fluid and carbohydrate are independent and additive in that fluid *and* carbohydrate together improve performance more than either fluid or carbohydrate separately (Below et al. 1995). So, sports drinks or other similar formulations are clearly best. In some situations, there are limited opportunities for fluid intake during competition because of the nature of the event or because of restrictions imposed by the rules. In most situations, however, voluntary intake is insufficient to match losses and increasing intake would likely be beneficial. Particularly in training, riders often have limited access to fluids on long rides. In warm weather, riders should stop to refill water bottles at regular intervals, using any available clean water source: gas stations, hotels, and public restrooms often are convenient for this purpose. If necessary, powder versions of the popular sports drinks can be carried and added to water picked up en route.

The rate at which fluids can be replaced is limited by the rate of gastric emptying and of intestinal absorption of water and nutrients. Therefore, in short events there may not be enough time for drinks to enter the bloodstream, while in longer events it is important that any ingested fluids be available quickly. There are large individual differences in the rate at which these processes occur, so each rider must establish his or her own best drinking pattern.

Gastric emptying of liquids is influenced by a number of factors, the most important of which are the volume of fluid in the stomach and the energy density of the drink. Replacing fluids quickly requires a high volume of fluid in the stomach. An initial large drink followed by regular drinking of small volumes is the best way to keep the stomach filled up. The feeling of a full stomach during exercise is uncomfortable in the early stages, but the body adapts in time if the athlete persists. The time to adapt is in training; it is too late on competition day. This is also the time to experiment with different drinks to establish individual taste preference. Riders who do not experiment with different strategies in training are unlikely to develop an optimum drinking strategy for competition. Training also offers an opportunity to estimate typical sweat losses in

© Nigel Farrow

Tyler Hamilton and Lance Armstrong stop for water during training. Sometimes cyclists have to find water wherever they can!

different conditions. By weighing themselves before and after training, riders can estimate sweat loss. Each kilogram of weight loss, after correction for any drinks taken during the ride, represents approximately one liter of sweat loss. The aim should be to drink sufficient fluid to limit the weight loss to less than about 1 percent of the initial body weight, and this should be possible in all but the most extreme conditions.

Water absorption occurs mainly in the upper part of the small intestine, and it depends on osmotic gradients. Hypotonic drinks give the fastest rates of water absorption, but because active absorption of glucose and sodium promotes water absorption, diluted glucose-electrolyte solutions are more effective than plain water. Strongly hypertonic solutions (such as fruit juices or cola-type drinks) cause a temporary net secretion of water into the intestine. Although this water is eventually reabsorbed in the lower part of the intestine, the delay in rehydration is not helpful when speed of fluid replacement is critical.

Men and women respond similarly to exercise in the heat, and the variation among individuals outweighs any meaningful gender difference. The sensation of thirst does not normally promote sufficient intake to match losses, and some degree of dehydration is normally observed, so cyclists should choose drinks that taste good and encourage consumption. Children are particularly susceptible to problems in the heat, and young riders must be encouraged to drink beyond the levels of intake dictated by thirst (Bar-Or and Wilk 1996).

Types of Drinks

Water is a useful drink in many situations, and many studies have shown that ingesting water during prolonged exercise can improve performance. Water has limited appeal, however, when large volumes of fluid must be consumed. It is also clear that water is less effective in promoting improvements in performance levels than a drink that also supplies substrate in the form of carbohydrate, usually as glucose, sucrose, or maltodextrin. This is the basis of the formulation of sports drinks. Drinks with a low-sugar content (about 2 to 4 percent, or 20 to 40 grams per liter) will not supply much energy, but if they are hypotonic and have a high sodium content (about 40 to 60 millimoles per liter, equivalent to about 1 to 1.5 grams per liter or one teaspoon), they will give the fastest possible water replacement (Maughan and Shirreffs 1998). The fastest rate of energy supply is achieved with high sugar concentrations (15 to 20 percent—150 to 200 grams per liter—or even more), but this limits the rate at which water is absorbed. Electrolyte replacement is not normally a high priority during exercise, but it may become important in prolonged events (four hours or more) in which sweat losses are large and when there is no opportunity to take solid food. The primary function of added electrolytes in most situations is to stimulate intestinal water absorption.

Choice of Drink

The balance among the demands for water, carbohydrate, and electrolyte replacement will influence the choice of drink. In hot conditions when sweat losses are high, a hypotonic, low-carbohydrate, electrolyte drink is best, but more concentrated carbohydrate drinks may have advantages in cold weather in which the main aim is to supply fuel for the working muscles. Most of the commercially available sports drinks are a compromise aimed at providing both water and carbohydrate in proportions that will suit most people in most situations. Athletes and teams should discuss their individual requirements with a qualified sports nutritionist or dietitian to identify the most appropriate approach.

Drinking After Exercise

Recovery after exercise requires replacement of the energy stores (especially muscle and liver glycogen) and restoration of water and electrolyte balance. A carbohydrate-electrolyte drink can therefore help to achieve all these goals. The ideal composition of the drink may depend on the circumstances. The following sections deal with these issues—how much of each of the ingredients riders should take in the hours after exercise.

What to Drink

Glycogen replacement is fastest if carbohydrate is consumed immediately after exercise, and the athlete can achieve this by eating or drinking 50 to 100 grams of carbohydrate within the first one to two hours. Taking high-carbohydrate drinks or eating high-carbohydrate foods (sweets, low-fat cookies) with water is equally effective. When sweat losses are high, athletes should consume large volumes of fluid, and some extra salt may usefully be added to the first meal. A change in the appetite for salt normally ensures an adequate intake without the rider taking salt tablets. If he takes no solid food before the next training session or the next race, some salt should be present in the fluids consumed, and sports drinks will help to provide this. If the electrolytes lost in sweat are not replaced, the cyclist does not retain the ingested fluid and a diuretic response is invoked, preventing full recovery even when he ingests large volumes of fluid (Maughan and Leiper 1995).

How Much to Drink

The sweat loss during training or racing can be estimated from the change in body weight: A loss of one kilogram of body weight means a sweat loss of one liter. Riders are often advised to replace sweat losses by drinking one liter of fluid for each kilogram of weight lost. However, this is not enough; because water continues to be lost in urine and through other routes after exercise, more than this is required to effectively replace the water lost during exercise (Shirreffs et al. 1996). As a guide, the volume of fluid ingested should be at least 1.5 times the volume of sweat lost.

Drinks with a high alcohol content (spirits, wine) are likely to have a strong diuretic effect, and the caffeine in tea and coffee can produce a similar effect. These drinks stimulate urine output and will delay the rehydration process by promoting water loss in the urine even before rehydration is complete. Low-alcohol drinks, including some beers, and tea and coffee do not have to be excluded from the postexercise diet. In those accustomed to these drinks and especially in individuals who are somewhat dehydrated, there will be little or no measurable diuretic action, and these drinks may play a useful role in helping to ensure an adequate fluid intake. It does not seem sensible for those accustomed to drinking tea, coffee, or cola drinks to suddenly cease intake of these, as there may be detrimental caffeine-withdrawal symptoms. Drinks with a high carbonation level may cause gastrointestinal problems and should form only a small part of the total fluid intake. The gas content can lead to a feeling of stomach fullness and discomfort, which in turn inhibits further intake of drinks.

Summary

High levels of physical activity are associated with high rates of metabolic heat production, and the sweating response is invoked to limit the rise in body temperature, especially when the ambient temperature is high. Basal levels of water turnover for healthy humans living in a temperate climate are about 2 to 3 liters per day, but this can be increased to something in excess of 10 to 12 liters per day during periods of hard training or racing in hot climates. A water deficit is poorly tolerated, and a deficit of as little as 1 percent of body mass may impair performance. The electrolyte content of sweat is highly variable, but losses, especially of sodium, will be large when sweat losses are high. Replacement of water and electrolyte losses is therefore vital, but the relative insensitivity of the thirst mechanism may make this difficult to achieve in practice.

Rates of water and carbohydrate replacement may be limited by the rates of gastric emptying and intestinal absorption, and ingested fluids should be formulated to take account of these factors. Taste is also important in stimulating intake. Few riders drink enough in competition or in training, but requirements vary greatly, so general prescriptions are not helpful. Riders should monitor weight loss in simulated races and aim to ensure that sufficient fluid is consumed to limit the fall in body mass to about 1 percent or less.

Drinking water is better than nothing, but the best drink will contain carbohydrate, probably at a concentration of about 2 to 8 percent, and sodium at a concentration of at least 20 mmol per liter. Fluid intake after exercise should be 1.5 times the volume lost and should ideally consist of a carbohydrate-electrolyte solution to replace both glycogen and sweat losses. Control of fluid balance is intimately linked with electrolyte (especially sodium) balance, and maintenance of hydration when sweat rates are high requires replacement of electrolyte losses as well as the volume loss.

Preparing for One-Day Races

Mark Hargreaves

One-day cycling races are characterized by a number of individual and team events that provide a range of physiological and nutritional challenges for the competitive cyclist. Individual time trials can include short (3 to 6 kilometers), moderate (40 to 60 kilometers), and longer (approximately 100 kilometers) distances that need to be completed in as short a time as possible. In these situations an individual's ability to generate maximal, sustainable power to overcome resistance plays a key role in determining success. Power outputs in the range of 300 to 450 watts have been reported in professional cyclists during individual time trials of varying distances. Team time trials are conducted over similar distances; however, the physiological demands vary according to position within the team. For example, drafting behind other riders can reduce the energy cost of cycling by 25 to 40 percent. Finally, road races involve many cyclists competing over distances ranging from 50 to 60 kilometers up to 250 to 300 kilometers, with an extreme example of 600 kilometers (Paris-Brest-Paris). On average, during road races over 200 kilometers, the power output ranges between 150 and 300 watts, with potentially higher values during intermittent hill climbs. Recently, Jeukendrup et al. (2000) published a good overview of the bioenergetics of elite cycling.

With such high power outputs sustained over shorter periods, or with relatively lower power outputs maintained for several hours, there is a heavy reliance on the oxidative metabolism of carbohydrate for energy provision. In addition, rates of fluid

© Newsport Photography

Cyclists in power and endurance events rely on adequate carbohydrate stores and pre-race hydration to fuel the requisite bursts of maximal speed.

loss are high because of the sweating rates required to dissipate the heat produced during such exercise. Muscle glycogen depletion and hypoglycemia are associated with fatigue during prolonged strenuous cycling (Coyle et al. 1986), and just a small degree of dehydration can impair endurance performance (Walsh et al. 1994). Thus, the major priorities in formulating a nutritional strategy to prepare for a one-day race are to minimize the potential fatiguing effects of carbohydrate depletion and dehydration. This can be achieved by ensuring adequate dietary carbohydrate and fluid intake and by undertaking periods of rest in the one to two days before the one-day event.

Carbohydrate Nutrition Before Exercise

The goal of carbohydrate ingestion in the one to two days and hours before a one-day event is to maximize endogenous carbohydrate stores (i.e., liver and muscle glycogen). Most attention has focused on dietary carbohydrate loading in the one to two days before an event and carbohydrate ingestion in the hours preceding exercise.

Glycogen Loading

The importance of muscle glycogen for endurance exercise performance was clearly established by the classic studies of Scandinavian researchers in the late 1960s and verified by a number of studies since that time (see Hawley et al. 1997 for review). The ergogenic effect of elevated pre-exercise muscle glycogen is most apparent during exercise to fatigue in events lasting longer than approximately 90 minutes, but there appears to be little benefit during exercise bouts lasting 60 to 90 minutes. That said, cyclists must ensure that their normal dietary carbohydrate intake is sufficient for optimal pre-exercise muscle glycogen levels. For a 70-kilogram (154-pound) man the total liver and muscle carbohydrate stores are in the order of 500 to 700 grams, so 7 to 10 grams per kilogram body mass carbohydrate should be sufficient to achieve such a goal. Although the original glycogen-loading protocol included the so-called "depletion phase," a more recent study has indicated that this is not necessary in trained athletes. It is likely that this is the consequence of training adaptations in these athletes, such as increased skeletal muscle GLUT-4 expression and glycogen synthase activity, which enhance their glycogen storage capacity.

Carbohydrate Three to Four Hours Before Exercise

Ingestion of a carbohydrate-rich meal (containing 140 to approximately 330 grams carbohydrate) three to four hours before exercise has been shown to increase muscle glycogen levels (Coyle et al. 1985) and enhance exercise performance. An increase in pre-exercise muscle glycogen is one explanation for the enhanced performance. In addition, because liver glycogen levels can be substantially reduced after an overnight fast, ingestion of carbohydrate may replenish these reserves and contribute, together with any ongoing absorption of the ingested carbohydrate, to the maintenance of blood glucose levels during the subsequent exercise bout. Despite plasma glucose and insulin returning to basal levels, ingestion of carbohydrate in the hours before exercise often results in a transient fall in glucose with the onset of exercise, increased carbohydrate oxidation, and a blunting of free fatty acid (FFA) mobilization (Coyle et al. 1985). These metabolic perturbations can persist for up to six hours after carbohydrate ingestion (Montain et al. 1991) but do not appear to be detrimental to exercise performance, with an increased carbohydrate availability compensating for the greater carbohydrate utilization. From a practical perspective, if access to carbohydrate during exercise is limited or nonexistent, ingestion of 200 to 300 grams carbohydrate three to four hours before exercise may be an effective strategy for enhancing carbohydrate availability during the subsequent exercise period.

Carbohydrate 30 to 60 Minutes Before Exercise

Ingesting carbohydrate in the hour before exercise results in a large increase in plasma glucose and insulin. With the onset of exercise, however, there is a rapid fall in blood glucose as a consequence of the combined stimulatory effects of hyperinsulinemia and contractile activity on muscle glucose uptake and inhibition of the exercise-induced rise in liver glucose output (Marmy Conus et al. 1996), despite ongoing absorption of the ingested carbohydrate. An enhanced uptake and oxidation of blood glucose by skeletal muscle may account for the increased carbohydrate oxidation often observed after pre-exercise carbohydrate ingestion (Costill et al. 1977). In addition, an increase in muscle glycogen degradation has been seen in some studies, although several investigations have observed no effect on muscle glycogenolysis. The increase in plasma FFA with exercise is attenuated after pre-exercise carbohydrate ingestion, as a consequence of insulin-mediated inhibition of lipolysis. Fat oxidation is reduced because of the lower plasma FFA availability, but also as a result of inhibition of intramuscular lipid oxidation since restoration of plasma FFA availability did not completely return fat oxidation to levels seen during exercise in the fasted state.

Because these metabolic effects of pre-exercise carbohydrate ingestion are a consequence of hyperglycemia and hyperinsulinemia, there has been interest in strategies that minimize the changes in plasma glucose and insulin before exercise. These have included ingesting fructose, or carbohydrate types other than glucose with differing glycemic indexes, varying the carbohydrate load and ingestion schedule, adding fat, or including warm-up exercise in the pre-exercise period. In general, while these various interventions do modify the metabolic response to exercise, there appears to be no great advantage for exercise performance in blunting the pre-exercise glycemic and insulinemic responses. Finally, when carbohydrate is ingested during prolonged exercise, the glycemic index (GI) of pre-exercise carbohydrate feedings has no effect on metabolism and performance (Burke et al. 1998). The glycemic responses during exercise preceded by carbohydrate ingestion are determined by a number of factors that include the combined stimulatory effects of insulin and contractile activity on muscle glucose uptake, the balance of inhibitory and stimulatory effects of insulin and catecholamines on liver glucose output, and the magnitude of ongoing intestinal absorption of glucose from the ingested carbohydrate (Kuipers et al. 1999). Furthermore, the inhibition of lipolysis and fat oxidation occurs with just small increases in plasma insulin, for example, after fructose (low GI) ingestion.

Thus, it could be argued that if pre-exercise carbohydrate ingestion is the only mechanism by which an athlete can increase carbohydrate availability *during* exercise, he or she would be well advised to ingest as much carbohydrate as possible, without undue gastrointestinal distress, so as to compensate for the reduced fat oxidation and to provide a pool of glucose that becomes available for use during the later stages of exercise.

The metabolic alterations associated with ingestion of carbohydrate in the 30 to 60 minutes before exercise have the potential to influence exercise performance. It was postulated that the increase in muscle glycogenolysis observed previously (Costill et al. 1977) would result in an earlier onset of fatigue during exercise, and this was suggested in a subsequent study. In contrast, every study since has shown either unchanged or enhanced endurance exercise performance after ingestion of carbohydrate in the hour before exercise. Thus, notwithstanding the well-documented metabolic effects of pre-exercise carbohydrate ingestion and the possibility of negative consequences in susceptible individuals, there appears to be little evidence to support the practice of avoiding carbohydrate ingestion in the hour before exercise, provided sufficient carbohydrate is ingested. Individual practice must be determined on the basis of individual experience with various pre-exercise carbohydrate ingestion protocols.

Fluid Ingestion Before Exercise

In addition to carbohydrate depletion, dehydration is a major contributor to fatigue with levels as low as 1 to 2 percent associated with impaired exercise performance (Walsh et al. 1994). Thus, while preparing for one-day races, cyclists should ingest sufficient quantities of fluid to ensure euhydration before exercise. This is best monitored by body mass. Ingesting large amounts of water may result in hyperhydration before exercise, but it also has the potential for diuresis and gastrointestinal distress. There has been some interest in adding glycerol to hydration beverages to enhance fluid retention and maintain a relative hyperhydration before and during exercise. The studies in the literature have produced conflicting results (Hitchins et al. 1999; Latzka et al. 1998), and there is the possibility that glycerol can promote intracellular dehydration with potential negative consequences such as headaches. It is perhaps premature to recommend glycerol hyperhydration at this stage.

Carbohydrate Intake During the Race

Before a race (or training) cyclists have to start thinking about taking food during the race. During the race fluid losses need to be replenished and energy has to be provided to prevent depletion of carbohydrate stores. We have discussed in detail the need for fluids in chapter 13, so it is therefore not repeated here. We discuss the need for carbohydrate in the following paragraphs.

Several studies have shown that carbohydrate ingestion during exercise longer than about 45 minutes can improve exercise performance. Early studies demonstrated that cyclists could ride 20 to 25 percent longer in rides to exhaustion at 65 to 70 percent $\dot{V}O_2max$. More recently it was also shown that simulated 40-km time trial performance improved by more than a minute with carbohydrate ingestion compared to a water placebo (Jeukendrup et al. 1997).

During exercise longer than 90 minutes the improvement in performance is likely to be the result of a better maintenance of blood glucose concentrations and high carbohydrate oxidation rates. However, during high intensity exercise such as a 40-km time trial the mechanisms are less clear.

Some carbohydrates are oxidized at higher rates than others (Jeukendrup and Jentjens 2000). Fructose and galactose especially are oxidized at lower rates. Glucose, maltodextrins, sucrose, maltose, and soluble starches can be oxidized at rates up to 1 gram per minute. Often it is assumed that more is better. However, in the case of carbohydrate ingestion this may not be true. Higher rates of intake will not necessarily result in higher oxidation rates. Ingestion of about 1 to 1.2 grams per minute (60 to 70 grams per hour) results in maximal oxidation rates (Jeukendrup and Jentjens 2000). Excess carbohydrate intake may cause reduced gastric emptying and gastrointestinal distress. The advice is therefore simple: try to ensure a carbohydrate intake of 60 to 70 grams per hour of training or competition. The amount of water comsumed with this carbohydrate depends on fluid losses (see chapter 13). If a cyclist's sweat loss is 1 liter per hour, the preferred drink would be a 6-percent carbohydrate solution (60 grams of carbohydrate in 1 liter of water). The drink should also contain sodium to enhance fluid absorption (see chapter 13).

Summary

Depletion of carbohydrate reserves and dehydration are major causes of fatigue during prolonged, strenuous cycling exercise. Pre-exercise nutritional strategies should be aimed at maximizing the availability of liver and muscle glycogen and ensuring euhydration. Such practices are associated with enhanced performance. Carbohydrate intake during exercise must be calculated beforehand, and cyclists should take 60 to 70 grams of carbohydrate per hour of training or competition.

chapter 15

Eating Strategies for Stage Races

Roy Jentjens

Recovery is extremely important both in training and after races. A faster recovery will generally enable the athlete to train more or to avoid overtraining. The recovery period is also important because training adaptations are developed in the recovery period and nutrition may influence the rate at which these adaptations occur. Finally, in stage races in which there is often less than 16 hours between the finish of one stage and the start of the next, a quick recovery is crucial for performance. Glycogen stores (in liver and muscle) play an important role in the recovery process. Cyclists who are training or competing on a daily basis should therefore be aware of the best ways to refill their glycogen stores. Before exploring how dietary carbohydrate intake can improve the recovery process during training and competition, we first discuss the importance of carbohydrate stores in the body.

Carbohydrate Stores and Use During Exercise

The importance of carbohydrates as a fuel source during prolonged, endurance exercise has been recognized since the 1930s. Carbohydrates metabolized by the body are derived from exogenous (ingested carbohydrate) and endogenous (glycogen stored in the body) sources. The vast majority of ingested carbohydrate enters the circulation as glucose and in the resting state is directed toward the sites of carbohydrate storage within the body. Approximately 75 to 100 grams of glycogen can be found in the liver in the hours after a meal (see table 12.1, page 144). During fasting (i.e., when sleeping), liver glycogen falls because of a sustained glucose output into the blood to maintain euglycemia. An additional 15 to 20 grams of glucose can be found in the blood and extracellular space, but by far the largest carbohydrate store is found in skeletal muscle.

Muscle glycogen stores are quite variable depending on training status, daily exercise, and dietary carbohydrate intake. In untrained individuals, muscle glycogen stores vary between 200 and 300 grams (Bergström et al. 1967). Trained individuals who are exercising daily and consuming a moderate carbohydrate intake (5 to 7 grams of carbohydrate per kilogram of body weight per day) typically have muscle glycogen stores between 350 and 500 grams. If trained athletes stop training for several days and consume a high-carbohydrate diet (8 to 10 grams of carbohydrate per kilogram of body weight per day), muscle glycogen concentrations may exceed 700 grams (Sherman et al. 1981). The energy stores in the form of carbohydrate in a 70-kilogram man are relatively small compared to the fat stores (2,000 versus 135,000 kilocalories; see table 12.1). Because carbohydrate stores are limited, it is important to have optimal glycogen stores before the start of exercise.

Glycogen Use During Exercise

The amount of glycogen that is used during cycling depends mainly on the intensity and duration of the exercise. As the exercise intensity increases linearly, muscle glycogen use increases exponentially. At high intensities (greater than 80 percent maximal oxygen uptake, or $\dot{V}O_2max$), glycogen is the primary energy substrate and the duration of exercise can be limited by the glycogen supply. During intense exercise (greater than 100 percent $\dot{V}O_2max$), muscle glycogen can be depleted by 50 percent in as little as 10 minutes. Muscle glycogen utilization also is affected by its availability. Studies have shown that the reliance on muscle glycogen during exercise is greater when glycogen levels are elevated at the onset of exercise (Hargreaves et al. 1995; Sherman et al. 1981).

Glycogen and Performance

Various studies have investigated the effects of increased dietary carbohydrate intake on muscle glycogen concentration and exercise performance. One of the first studies showed that the capacity to cycle at work rates between 70 and 85 percent $\dot{V}O_2max$ was related to the initial muscle glycogen stores (Bergström et al. 1967). A high-carbohydrate diet resulted in high muscle glycogen stores and increased time-to-exhaustion. Conversely, when glycogen stores become depleted, the work rate has to be reduced to about 50 to 60 percent $\dot{V}O_2max$.

It is important to note that in most studies, *endurance capacity* is assessed as the time taken to exercise to exhaustion, whereas *endurance performance* is the time taken to complete a predetermined workload on a cycle ergometer or to cycle a predetermined distance. The latter seems a more important and realistic assessment of cycling performance since the aim of most cycling events is to complete a certain distance as fast as possible. Hawley et al. (1997) recently reviewed the effect of high-carbohydrate diets and high muscle glycogen levels on exercise performance. It has been suggested that elevated muscle glycogen levels above "normal" values (300 to 400 grams) do not improve high-intensity exercise lasting less than five minutes (e.g., sprinting, track cycling, interval training). Normal glycogen levels should be adequate to supply the required energy for this type and duration of exercise.

In addition, increasing muscle glycogen levels before moderate-intensity exercise lasting 60 to 90 minutes (i.e., a 40-kilometer time trial) seems to have a minimal effect on performance. However, there is some evidence to indicate that elevated muscle glycogen contents can improve cycling performance by 2 to 3 percent in events lasting longer than 90 minutes.

From this discussion we can conclude that high-carbohydrate diets that increase pre-exercise muscle glycogen concentrations above normal levels can be beneficial for endurance cycling performance (greater than 90 minutes). While maintaining high glycogen levels is important for all cyclists, it is especially important for those athletes who are competing on consecutive days. Under these circumstances, each day of racing depletes muscle glycogen, which, if not restored, will result in underperformance.

Replenishment of Muscle Glycogen Stores

In cycling, there are competitions in which cyclists race two to seven hours per day for several consecutive days. The failure to maintain glycogen stores during stage races may even lead to premature retirement from the competition. Many cyclists train or compete repeatedly on the same day (i.e., a road race in the morning followed by a time trial in the afternoon), and hence a rapid recovery of muscle glycogen is extremely important for an optimal subsequent performance. When there is only a short recovery period (less than eight hours), it may not be possible to restore muscle glycogen completely. However, appropriate nutritional practices can help to replenish glycogen stores optimally in the limited time available.

The rate at which glycogen can be synthesized in the hours immediately after exercise is dependent on several factors. The following sections discuss these factors.

Factors Affecting Muscle Glycogen Replenishment

The replenishment of glycogen stores is dependent on the amount of carbohydrate ingested, the timing of carbohydrate intake after exercise, and the type and form of carbohydrate. More recently it has also been suggested that the coingestion of other macronutrients (protein or fat) may be of influence.

Amount of Carbohydrate

The most important factor determining the rate of muscle glycogen synthesis is the amount of carbohydrate consumed after exercise. In general, the rate of muscle glycogen storage is directly related to the quantity of carbohydrate consumed. When no carbohydrates are taken after exercise, the rate of muscle glycogen synthesis is very low. A large carbohydrate intake can increase muscle glycogen synthesis rates up to about 25 grams per hour.

More than 10 years ago, researchers claimed that a carbohydrate intake of 50 grams every two hours after exercise resulted in maximal glycogen synthesis rates (Ivy et al. 1998b). More recent studies have manipulated the amount of carbohydrate given to athletes to determine the maximal rate of glycogen synthesis after exercise. A study by van Loon et al. (2000) has shown that an increase in carbohydrate ingestion from 0.8 to 1.2 grams per kilogram body weight per hour provided at 30-minute intervals resulted in faster muscle glycogen synthesis. It seems, therefore, that maximal muscle glycogen synthesis rates are not achieved at a carbohydrate intake around 0.8 gram per kilogram body weight per hour.

Figure 15.1 illustrates maximal muscle glycogen synthesis rates found in studies after the ingestion of different rates of carbohydrate in the early hours postexercise. It can be seen that the maximal rate of muscle glycogen synthesis is reached at a carbohydrate intake of between 1.2 and 1.4 grams per minute (75 to 90 grams of carbohydrate per hour). A carbohydrate intake of more than 90 grams per hour provides no additional benefits in terms of muscle glycogen storage and may only increase the risk of gastrointestinal discomfort. The following list shows examples of foods that provide 90 grams of carbohydrate:

- 4 medium, ripe bananas
- 2 apples
- 100 grams of cornflakes
- 1–1.5 liter of a sports drink
- 260 grams of lemon sorbet
- 400 grams of boiled spaghetti
- Half bag of jelly beans
- 4 slices of white bread (medium sliced)
- 2.5 chocolate bars

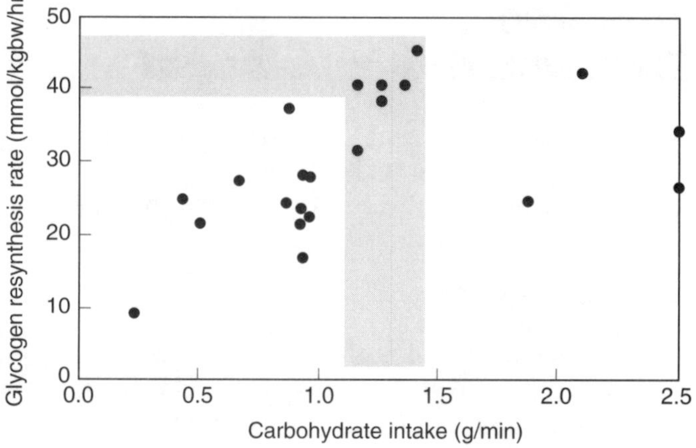

Figure 15.1 Peak muscle glycogen synthesis rates depicted against the rate of carbohydrate ingestion.

Timing of Food and Drink

The timing of carbohydrate intake is important when a fast recovery is required. Complete glycogen repletion can be accomplished within 24 hours, providing the amount and timing of carbohydrate is right. The most rapid replenishment of glycogen stores occurs in the first 60 to 90 minutes after exercise. One study found that the rate of glycogen storage is almost twice as fast if carbohydrate supplements are provided immediately after exercise compared to several hours after (Ivy et al. 1988a).

© Human Kinetics

Replenishing carbohydrates immediately after exercise boosts the rate of glycogen storage and speeds up recovery.

An important mechanism that makes possible this rapid synthesis of muscle glycogen is an exercise-induced increase in the permeability of the muscle cell membrane to glucose. Muscle contractions stimulate glucose transport directly by inducing glucose transporters (GLUT-4) to the cell membrane. Furthermore, a low muscle glycogen content after exercise is associated with an increased rate of glucose transport into the muscle. Upon entering the muscle cell, glucose is phosphorylated and can be converted into glycogen by the enzyme glycogen synthase. Glycogen synthase activity has been found to be increased after exercise. Although glycogen synthase is the rate-limiting enzyme for glycogen formation, glycogen formation can only occur when glucose is available. Therefore, glucose transport seems to be a very important factor in the process of muscle glycogen synthesis. Several studies have demonstrated that endurance training results in an increased ability to accumulate muscle glycogen after exercise because of a higher GLUT-4 content after exercise. The higher glucose transport capacity correlated with glycogen synthesis rates.

Besides an enhanced glucose transport, muscle contraction also increases the muscle's sensitivity to insulin. When carbohydrates are ingested after exercise, both glucose concentrations and insulin concentrations rise in the blood. The increase in circulating insulin not only functions to increase muscle glucose uptake but also stimulates glycogen synthase. Thus, the increase in membrane permeability to glucose, the increase in insulin sensitivity, and the activation of glycogen synthase will result in a relatively rapid glycogen synthesis after exercise. It is therefore recommended that athletes consume carbohydrate as soon as possible after exercise to enhance the restoration of muscle glycogen stores. The highest rates of muscle glycogen synthesis have been reported in studies in which carbohydrates were provided at regular intervals (every 15 to 30 minutes). This is most probably due to the maintenance of high blood glucose and insulin concentrations for a longer duration. Thus, eating frequent small meals appears to have an extra benefit over eating a few large meals. Additionally, eating small meals is likely to reduce the risk of gastrointestinal discomfort.

Type and Form of Carbohydrate

Glucose is the only type of carbohydrate that the skeletal muscle can readily metabolize for energy and that can be stored as glycogen. All other types of carbohydrate need to be broken down in the gut and/or converted into glucose by the liver before entering into muscle. Although glucose is the most common type of carbohydrate in sports drinks, it is certainly not the only type of carbohydrate present in our diet. For example, sucrose makes up 20 to 25 percent of the daily energy intake in the Western world. Examples of sucrose-containing foods are beet and cane sugar, maple syrup, and honey. Studies have shown similar rates of muscle glycogen synthesis when either glucose or sucrose was ingested. This is remarkable since sucrose consists of glucose and fructose. Fructose (a sugar found in fruits) must be converted in the liver to glucose before it is available for muscle glycogen synthesis. It might be that fructose inhibits the uptake of glucose by the liver, and because of that more glucose might be available for muscle glycogen synthesis. However, glucose and sucrose increased the muscle glycogen stores twice as rapidly as did fructose alone. This is possibly because fructose is absorbed slowly by the intestine and requires conversion to glucose by the liver before it can be metabolized in the skeletal muscle.

Although in most studies pure carbohydrate sources such as glucose or fructose were used, in daily life athletes will often eat foods that contain combinations of different nutrients. Therefore, it is useful to concentrate on the criteria for food products that result in the fastest glycogen synthesis rates. For optimal glycogen replenishment after exercise, it is important to consume easily digestible carbohydrate-rich foods. The rate at which glucose becomes available after a meal is usually reflected by the measure known as the glycemic index (GI). This is a measure of the rise in blood glucose after a certain food product is ingested compared to the rise in blood glucose after an equal amount of pure glucose is ingested. Thus, food products with a moderate to high GI enter the circulation more rapidly and result in a higher rate of glycogen storage compared to low-GI foods (Burke et al. 1998). The GI of a food product is influenced by varying factors, including the type of sugar and the content of dietary fat, protein, and fiber present in the food. Fat, protein, and fiber slow down the rate of gastric emptying and therefore you should avoid them in the postexercise diet when you want fast muscle glycogen repletion. Table 15.1 lists some food products with a high, moderate, and low GI. High- and moderate-GI foods should have priority in the postexercise period.

The effect of liquid versus solid carbohydrate foods on muscle glycogen repletion has also been investigated. There appears to be no difference in muscle glycogen synthesis when either liquid or solid forms of carbohydrate are consumed in the first few hours after exercise. However, liquid forms of carbohydrate or carbohydrate foods with a high fluid content often are recommended to athletes because they are easy to digest and less filling and therefore do not tend to adversely affect one's normal

TABLE 15.1 Glycemic Indexes of Common Foods

High (greater than 80)	Moderate (60-80)	Low (less than 60)
Bagels	Bananas, ripe	Apple
Baked potatoes	Croissant	Baked beans
Bread, white and whole wheat	Ice cream	Banana, unripe
Corn syrup	Mars bar	Chocolate
Cornflakes	Muesli	Cookies
Crackers	Muffins	Fructose
Honey	Pasta	Kidney beans
Raisins	Potato chips	Lentils
Rice cakes	Rye bread, whole grain	Mixed-grain bread
Rice, white	Soft drinks	Milk
Sports drinks	Sucrose	Porridge
	Sweet corn	Yogurt

appetite. Liquid carbohydrate supplements also provide a source of fluid that may be beneficial for rapid rehydration.

Coingestion of Other Macronutrients

As mentioned earlier, insulin is an important hormone in promoting muscle glycogen synthesis after exercise. Therefore, some studies have focused on enhancing insulin release during recovery to stimulate glycogen synthesis. Several studies have shown that coingestion of protein and/or amino acids with carbohydrate almost doubles the insulin response and increases the rate of muscle glycogen synthesis by 40 to 100 percent (van Loon et al. 2000; Zawadzki et al. 1992). However, a recent study from our own laboratory (Jentjens et al. 2001) has shown that when the total carbohydrate intake is very high (1.2 grams per kilogram body weight per hour), the presence of a protein–amino acid mixture does not further increase the rate of muscle glycogen synthesis despite a much higher insulin response. This study as well as others (van Hall et al. 2000; van Loon et al. 2000) suggests that insulin is not the limiting factor for muscle glycogen synthesis when total carbohydrate intake is high (1.2 grams per kilogram body weight per hour) and provided at regular intervals. Therefore, there is no need for proteins or amino acids in recovery drinks when total carbohydrate intake is sufficient.

The factors that determine the maximal rate of glycogen storage after exercise are largely unknown. Studies that examined gastric emptying in relation to the oxidation of ingested carbohydrate have shown that the rate of gastric emptying was not the limiting step in the oxidation of the oral-ingested carbohydrate (Jeukendrup and Jentjens 2000). Thus, gastric emptying is also unlikely to be the limiting factor in the rate of glycogen synthesis process. There is also convincing evidence that the limitation is not located at the muscular level (Price et al. 2000). Therefore, most likely the rate of muscle glycogen synthesis is limited by the rate of digestion, absorption of carbohydrate by the intestine, and subsequent transport of glucose into the circulation regulated by the liver. The relative role of gut absorption and liver retention of glucose in the glycogen synthesis process remains to be determined in future research.

Although protein intake may not always have an effect on muscle glycogen synthesis, evidence starts to accumulate that protein feeding in the hours after exercise may increase protein synthesis or reduce protein breakdown. Although at present it is unclear how important protein intake is in the recovery process, it is tempting to think that increased net protein synthesis after exercise could result in a more rapid repair of damaged muscle and a more rapid synthesis of various enzymes and mitochondria. This may mean that adaptations could develop more rapidly after training, and fatigue and muscle soreness could be decreased during stage races. However, this is all speculative and hopefully future studies will tell us whether this protein intake really has an effect and, if so, how much protein and which types of proteins (or amino acids) should be ingested.

Muscle Glycogen Replenishment Within 24 Hours

There often is less than 24 hours between the finish of one race or hard training session and the start of the next one. In those conditions it may be crucial to optimize muscle glycogen replenishment. The previous sections discussed the factors that influence glycogen synthesis in the hours after exercise. Now we shall translate that information into practical advice. What do we need to eat or drink in the first four hours after exercise, and what do we do in the remaining time until the start of the next race or training session?

First Four Hours After Exercise

For a rapid restoration of muscle glycogen, it is recommended that the athlete ingest 75 to 90 grams of carbohydrate (1.2 grams per kilogram body weight) immediately after exercise. Consuming this much every hour or as multiple small meals will maintain a maximal rate of glycogen storage for as many as four to six hours after exercise. When the athlete consumes sufficient carbohydrate (1.2 grams per kilogram body weight per hour), there is no need for protein ingestion to enhance the insulin levels. Higher insulin levels do not further increase the rate of muscle glycogen synthesis when carbohydrate intake is sufficient. Fat intake should be minimized in the first two hours after exercise because fat, like protein, decreases the rate of gastric emptying. It is important to select easily digestible carbohydrate-rich food with a moderate to high GI. Whether the carbohydrate supplement is in solid form or liquid form does not seem to affect the rate of muscle glycogen synthesis. When appetite is suppressed immediately after exercise, there is preference for drinking fluids rather than eating solid foods. Therefore, carbohydrate beverages are recommended in the first few hours after exercise since they also provide fluid for a rapid rehydration.

Remaining Hours

In the next 12 to 24 hours after exercise, the cyclist should continue to try to restore muscle glycogen contents back to pre-exercise levels. Several studies have shown that muscle glycogen levels were not maintained during daily training when carbohydrate intake was less than 8 grams per kilogram body weight per day (Kirwan et al. 1988; Sherman et al. 1993). Therefore, a diet that contains 8 to 10 grams per kilogram body weight per day of moderate- to high-GI carbohydrate sources should be consumed within 24 hours. The exact amount of carbohydrate required to restore muscle glycogen levels within 24 hours after exercise is more or less dependent on the energy requirements of the athlete (see table 15.2). When carbohydrate intake is adequate, coingestion of moderate amounts of fat and protein does not appear to have a direct effect on glycogen storage during 24 hours of recovery (Burke et al. 1995). Since sleeping hours interrupt the feeding possibilities, it is recommended that the athlete ingest approximately 250 grams of easily digestible carbohydrate-rich food (e.g., 25 grams per hour for a 10-hour sleep period) before sleeping to reach a total carbohydrate intake of 8 to 10 grams per kilogram body weight over 24 hours.

TABLE 15.2 Carbohydrate Intake Goals for Cyclists

Goal	Amount of carbohydrate intake
High glycogen stores	
5-6 hours of extremely prolonged and moderately intense exercise. Very high total energy requirements, daily muscle glycogen recovery, and continued refueling during exercise. (Tour de France cyclist)	10-12 g/kg body weight daily
Moderate glycogen stores	
To maximize daily muscle glycogen recovery to enhance prolonged daily training, or "load" the muscle with glycogen before a prolonged exercise competition longer than an hour.	8-10 g/kg body weight daily

Reprinted from Hawley and Burke 1998.

Summary

Glycogen is an important fuel for endurance exercise, and low muscle glycogen stores generally result in decreased performance. A single bout of exercise can already deplete muscle glycogen and it is important to replenish these stores. Especially when the next race or training session will take place within 24 hours, it is important to adopt eating and drinking strategies to optimize glycogen synthesis.

It is recommended that athletes ingest 1.2 grams per kilogram body weight carbohydrate as soon as possible after exercise and aim for a carbohydrate intake of 1.2 grams per kilogram body weight per hour during the first four hours postexercise.

They should consume a total carbohydrate intake of 8 to 10 grams per kilogram body weight within 24 hours. Although liquid and solid forms of carbohydrate seem to result in similar rates of muscle glycogen synthesis, a liquid supplement is highly recommended after exercise since this also provides a source of fluid for rehydration. The addition of protein to carbohydrate feedings to enhance the insulin response does not seem to be more beneficial in terms of glycogen synthesis when the total amount of carbohydrate intake is adequate.

chapter 16

Principles of Eating for Cycling

Louise Burke

The previous four chapters have summarized the science of nutrition for cycling; this chapter aims to translate it into practice. There are several challenges to the process of interpreting scientific guidelines into eating plans and food choices. The first is to integrate a variety of different nutritional goals into a single eating plan. Nutrition is a complex science involving an overlay of goals that are specific to each cyclist or the period of the cycling calendar. For example, the following list summarizes a number of nutrition goals that may be important to a cyclist during training and competition. The cyclist's nutritional plan must be able to accommodate various goals—including, on occasion, goals that seem mutually exclusive or contradictory. It can take considerable expertise to find foods or meal plans that allow the cyclist to meet several goals simultaneously or to prioritize divergent goals according to short-term or long-term needs.

Summary of sports nutrition goals for cyclists

During training, cyclists should aim to:

Meet energy and fuel needs required to support and optimize their training program.

Achieve and maintain an ideal physique for their event—that is, manipulate training and nutrition to achieve a level of body mass, body fat, and muscle mass that is consistent with long-term good health and good performance.

Refuel and rehydrate well during each training session so that they perform at their best each session.

Practice any intended race nutrition strategies so that beneficial practices can be identified and fine-tuned.

Enhance adaptation and recovery between training sessions by providing all the nutrients associated with these processes.

Maintain optimal health and function, especially by achieving the increased needs for some nutrients resulting from a heavy training program.

Reduce the risk of sickness during heavy training periods by maintaining a healthy physique and energy balance and by supplying nutrients believed to assist immune function (e.g., consume carbohydrate during prolonged exercise sessions).

Make use of supplements and specialized sports foods that have been shown to enhance training performance or meet training nutrition needs.

Eat for long-term health by paying attention to community nutrition guidelines.

Continue to enjoy food and the pleasure of sharing meals.

For races, road cyclists should:

"Fuel up" adequately before a race, consume carbohydrate, and achieve an exercise taper during the day(s) before the event according to the importance and duration of the event. Use carbohydrate-loading strategies when appropriate.

Minimize dehydration during the race by using opportunities to drink fluids before, during, and after the event.

Consume carbohydrate during events longer than one hour in duration or other events in which body carbohydrate stores become depleted.

Achieve pre-race and during-race eating and drinking strategies without causing gastrointestinal discomfort or upset.

Promote recovery after the race, particularly during stage races.

Achieve adequate energy and nutrient intake during stage races toward total nutritional goals.

Make use of supplements and specialized sports foods that have been shown to enhance race performance or meet race nutrition goals.

A second challenge is for nutritional plans to encompass practical features—such as the food likes and dislikes of each cyclist, cultural and social food practices, and the availability of foods. The cyclist often has to juggle meals and snacks with many other commitments in a busy lifestyle. Nutritional goals before, during, and after exercise often recommend an intake of food or fluid that is in contrast to the opportunities to eat and drink, or it is more than a cyclist would consume according to his appetite and gastrointestinal comfort. Only through creative menu planning and food use will the cyclist be able to achieve his nutritional needs. Luckily, the overall diversity of the food supply means that there are almost infinite combinations of foods and fluids that can achieve a required nutrient and practical profile. The bottom line is that there is no single ideal eating plan for a cyclist, rather a range of options to meet a range of situations.

This chapter reviews eating strategies that help to meet common nutritional goals in cycling, and it provides examples of meals or snack choices that these strategies might include. However, all cyclists should be aware of the potential for other creative solutions to nutritional challenges. When nutritional challenges are complex and an individual solution is required, the expertise of a sports dietitian is extremely useful.

Goal 1: Meet Carbohydrate Needs for Training, Racing, and Recovery

Body carbohydrate stores provide a critical source of fuel for training and racing, and they must continually be replaced or supplemented by dietary carbohydrate intake. Table 16.1 summarizes carbohydrate intake recommendations presented in other chapters of this book.

Because these goals are higher than the carbohydrate intakes typically provided by Western eating patterns and, in many cases, are greater than what would be achieved as a result of appetite, gastrointestinal comfort, or opportunity, special strategies are needed to ensure that the cyclist meets his carbohydrate needs. Typically, a cyclist may need to devote 50 to 70 percent of his total energy intake to carbohydrate needs to achieve the fuel requirements for training and competition. If carbohydrate-rich choices are to make up the backbone of the cyclist's diet, it is important that he consider how other nutritional needs might be met simultaneously from these foods or menu plans. For example, in the everyday diet, carbohydrate-rich foods or meals that are also good sources of protein and micronutrients have value toward meeting the cyclist's overall nutritional requirements. In addition, a cyclist can manipulate the

TABLE 16.1 Carbohydrate Intake Goals for a Cyclist

Situation	Recommended carbohydrate intake	Further information
Pre-race meal	Meal eaten 1-4 hours pre-race providing 1-4 g/kg	Chapter 14
Carbohydrate intake during races and training	1 g/min. or 60 g/hour	Chapter 14
Glycogen restoration during general training or for carbohydrate loading before events	Daily intake of 8-10 g/kg	Chapter 15
Extreme need for fuel and glycogen restoration during stage races involving 5-6 hours per day of moderate-high-intensity cycling	Daily intake of 10-12+ g/kg	Chapter 15
Rapid recovery after training session or stage in Tour, especially when there is less than 8 hours until next session	Hourly intake of 1.0-1.2 g/kg for first 4 hours or until regular meal patterns providing 8-10 g/kg daily are resumed	Chapter 15

total energy content of his diet through the choice of carbohydrate food types. For example, he can restrict energy intake by choosing low-fat, carbohydrate-rich combinations and by choosing carbohydrate-rich foods that have a high satiety effect. By contrast, compact sources of carbohydrate are preferred if a high intake of carbohydrate and energy is needed.

We propose the following eating strategies to assist in meeting carbohydrate intake goals:

- The cyclist must be prepared to be different. The typical eating patterns in most countries are not likely to achieve a high-carbohydrate diet. The cyclist may need to try new foods or change the ratio of foods at meals to promote carbohydrate-rich sources, and he may need to reduce intake of other foods.
- Meals and snacks should be based around nutrient-dense, carbohydrate-rich foods, which should take up at least half of the room on the plate:
    - Whole-grain breads and breakfast cereals
    - Rice, pasta, noodles, and other grain foods
    - Fruits
    - Starchy vegetables (e.g., potatoes, corn)
    - Legumes (e.g., lentils, beans, soy-based products)
    - Sweetened dairy products (e.g., fruit-flavored yogurt, milk shakes)
- The cyclist should be aware of the fat content of carbohydrate-rich foods and recipes. Many of the foods believed to be high in carbohydrate are actually high-fat foods. Ideas for low-fat eating will help to promote fuel foods rather than a high-fat intake.
- Sugar and sugary foods should be considered as a compact carbohydrate source. They may be particularly useful in a high-energy diet, or when carbohydrate is needed before, during, and after exercise.
- Carbohydrate-rich drinks (e.g., fruit juices, soft drinks, fruit or milk smoothies) also provide a compact fuel source for special situations or very high-carbohydrate diets. This category includes many of the supplements specially made for athletes (e.g., sports drinks, sports gels, liquid meal supplements).
- When energy and carbohydrate needs are high, cyclists should increase the number of meals and snacks they eat, rather than the size of the meals. This will mean being organized to have snacks on hand on a busy day.
- Lower-fiber choices of carbohydrate-rich foods are useful when energy needs are high, or when you are eating just before exercise.
- Carbohydrate consumed before and during prolonged races and training sessions will provide an additional muscle fuel source. As well as taking care of the acute needs of the exercise session, these foods make up part of the day's total carbohydrate intake (see also goals 5 and 6).
- Effective restoration of muscle fuel begins with the intake of a high-carbohydrate meal or snack; when recovery time between sessions is short (less than six to eight hours), this intake should occur within 30 minutes after the first session. High-glycemic index (GI) carbohydrate foods should make up the basis of recovery meals because

low-GI carbohydrate foods (e.g., oats, lentils, legumes) appear to be less effective for muscle refueling. Cyclists should achieve a carbohydrate intake of approximately 1 gram per kilogram (50 to 100 grams) each hour by snacking until they can resume their normal pattern of high-carbohydrate meals. Nutrient-rich carbohydrate choices may simultaneously provide the body with other nutrients that are important for recovery. Table 16.2 provides examples of recovery snacks.

- Information for planning or assessing carbohydrate intake can be obtained from nutrient information on food labels. Such information, as provided in table 16.3, can be useful for keeping track when carbohydrate needs are high.

Goal 2: Organize a High-Energy Intake

The workloads typically associated with periods of heavy training and stage racing produce large energy requirements. For example, dietary surveys and energy balance studies of male cyclists undertaking some of the major professional stage races report apparent energy needs of up to approximately 25 megajoules per day or 300 to 350 kilojoules per kilogram body mass per day over extended periods (van Erp-Baart et al. 1989; Saris et al. 1989; Garcia-Roves et al. 1998, 2000; see also chapter 12). Data on female cyclists undertaking heavy workloads are scarce (for a review, see Burke 2001); the only investigation of elite performers suggests energy requirements of 12 to 15 megajoules per day or greater than 200 kilojoules per kilogram body mass per day (Martin 2001). However, the racing demands of these females were considerably less than those seen in male cycling.

Unless the cyclist wants to create a deliberate energy deficit to achieve a loss of body fat, these large energy requirements must be met on a daily basis. Although many cyclists may desire weight loss at some point in their careers (see goal 3), and anecdotal reports suggest that some cyclists deliberately under-eat during major tours to achieve dramatic weight reductions (Burke 2001), it is likely that optimal racing performance is achieved when the cyclist is in energy balance and able to fully meet muscle fuel requirements. As summarized earlier, key challenges to the achievement of high energy intakes include gastrointestinal comfort, access to food, and opportunities to eat. These challenges are particularly evident during the extreme demands of professional stage races.

Because a considerable portion of the cyclist's waking hours may be spent on the bike each day, it makes sense to use this riding time as an opportunity for intake of energy-containing foods and fluids. Intake of fluid and carbohydrate during prolonged cycling is important for optimizing the performance of that session; however, it may achieve a dual role in making a substantial contribution to total daily energy requirements. Early studies of the nutritional practices of cyclists undertaking the Tour de France reported that cyclists consumed large amounts of carbohydrate-rich drinks and foods during each day's stage, providing up to half of the total day's intake of carbohydrate and energy (Saris et al. 1989). However, recent work suggests that more aggressive riding techniques in the peloton may interfere with opportunities for proactive intake of fluid and foods on the bike (Garcia-Roves et al. 1998). In this study, cyclists were able to meet their total daily energy needs with a different eating pattern—namely, a larger reliance on pre-race breakfasts and post-race recovery meals.

TABLE 16.2 Carbohydrate-Rich Food Choices for Special Situations

Postexercise carbohydrate-rich recovery snacks	Ideas for carbohydrate intake on the bike
75-g carbohydrate portions	Sports drink
1,000-1,200 ml of sports drink	Sports gels
2 sports gels plus 250-300 ml of sports drink	Sports bars
750 ml of fruit juice or soft drink	Cereal bars
300-500 ml of carbohydrate loader drink	Granola bars
80 g packet of jelly beans	Sandwiches or rolls
3 slices toast or bread with jam, or honey plus large banana	Bananas and other fruit
1 chocolate bar (65 g) plus 375 ml soft drink	Cake
3 cereal bars	Fruit bread
Cup of thick vegetable soup plus large bread roll plus 1 apple	
1.5-2 sports bars (check the label)	
100 g (1 large or 2 small) muffin, fruit bun, or scone plus 400 ml fruit juice	
375 g can creamed rice plus piece of fruit	
220 g (large) baked potato with salsa filling plus 250 ml soft drink	
150 g pancakes (3-stack) plus 50 g syrup	
Portable carbohydrate-rich foods suitable for travel	**Postexercise carbohydrate-rich recovery snacks**
Breakfast cereal (plus skim-milk powder)	***75 g carbohydrate plus valuable source of protein and micronutrients***
Cereal bars or granola bars	350-500 ml liquid meal supplement
Dried fruit	350-500 ml milk shake or fruit smoothie
Rice crackers or dry biscuits	1.5-2 sports bars (check labels for protein)
Spreads such as jam or honey	80 g (large bowl) breakfast cereal with milk plus 200 g carton fruit-flavored yogurt
Sports bars	350 g baked beans on 3 slices of toast
Liquid meal supplements—powder and ready-to-drink tetra packs	Large bread roll with cheese or meat filling, plus large banana
Sports drink	
Sports gels	

Source of food-composition data: USDA Nutrient Database for Standard Reference, Release 14 (July 2001).

TABLE 16.3 50 Gram Carbohydrate Portions from Carbohydrate-Rich Foods

Each of the following selections provides approximately 50 g of carbohydrate.

Food	Serving
Cereals	
Wheat biscuit cereal	60 g (5 biscuits)
"Light" breakfast cereal (cornflakes, Wheaties)	60 g (2 cups)
Muesli flake breakfast cereal	65 g (1-1.5 cups)
Toasted muesli	90 g (1 cup)
Porridge–made with milk	350 g (1.3 cups)
Porridge–made with water	410 g (2 cups)
Rolled oats	90 g (1 cup)
Muesli bar	2.5
Rice cakes	6 thick or 10 thin
Rice, boiled	180 g (1 cup)
Pasta or noodles, boiled	200 g (1.3 cups)
Canned spaghetti	440 g (large can)
Crisp breads or dry biscuits	6 large or 15 small
Fruit-filled biscuits	5
Plain sweet biscuits	8-10
Cream-filled or chocolate biscuits	6
Bread	110 g (4 slices white or 3 thick whole grain)
Bread rolls	110 g (1 large or 2 medium)
Pita or Lebanese bread	100 g (2 pitas)
Chapati	150 g (2.5)
English muffin	120 g (2 full muffins)
Crumpet	2.5
Cake-style muffin	115 g (1 large or 2 medium)
Pancakes	150 g (2 medium)
Scones	125 g (3 medium)
Iced fruit bun	105 g (1.5)
Croissant	140 g (1.5 large or 2 medium)
Rice cream	330 g (1.5 cups)
Fruit	
Fruit crumble	1 cup
Fruit packed in heavy syrup	240 g (1 cup)
Fruit stewed or canned in light syrup	360 g (1.5 cups)
Fresh fruit salad	500 g (2.5 cups)
Bananas	2 medium-large
Mangoes, pears, grapefruit, or other large fruit	2-3
Oranges, apples, or other medium-sized fruit	3-4
Nectarines, apricots, or other small fruit	12
Grapes	470 g (2 cups)
Melon	900 g (5 cups)
Strawberries	760 g (5 cups)
Sultanas or raisins	70 g (4 tbsp)
Dried apricots	115 g (22 halves)
Vegetables and legumes	
Potatoes	350 g (1 very large or 3 medium)
Sweet potatoes	350 g (2.5 cups)
Corn	300 g (1.2 cups creamed corn or 2 cobs)
Green beans	750 g (7 cups)
Baked beans	440 g (1 large can)
Lentils	400 g (1.5 cups)
Soy beans or kidney beans	500 g (3 cups)
Tomato puree	500 ml (2 cups)
Pumpkin or peas	800 g (4 cups)
Dairy products	
Milk	1 liter
Flavored milk	560 ml
Custard	300 g (1.3 cups)
"Diet" yogurt or natural yogurt	800 g (4-5 individual tubs)

(continued)

TABLE 16.3 (continued)

Food	Serving	Food	Serving
Dairy products (continued)		***Drinks***	
Flavored nonfat yogurt	350 g (2 individual tubs)	Fruit juice, unsweetened	600 ml
Ice cream	250 g (10 tbsp)	Fruit juice, sweetened	500 ml
Sugars and confectionery		Cordial	800 ml
Sugar	50 g	Soft drinks and flavored mineral water	500 ml
Jam	3 tbsp	Fruit smoothie	250-300 ml
Syrups	4 tbsp	***Sports foods***	
Honey	3 tbsp	Sports drink	700 ml
Chocolate	80 g	Carbohydrate loader supplement	250 ml
Chocolate bar and other 50-60 g bars	1.5 bars	Liquid meal supplement	250-300 ml
Jelly beans	60 g	Sports bar	1-1.5 bars
Mixed dishes		Sports gels	2 sachets
Pizza	200 g (medium—1/4 thick crust or 1/3 thin crust)	Glucose polymer powder	60 g
Hamburgers	1.3 Big Macs		
Lasagna	400 g serving		
Fried rice	200 g (1.3 cups)		

Source of food-composition data: USDA Nutrient Database for Standard Reference, Release 14 (July 2001).
Adapted from Hawley and Burke 1998.

We recommend the following eating strategies to help cyclists achieve high-energy intakes:

• Cyclists must be organized. They need to apply the same dedication to their eating program as they apply to training in order to increase their intake of energy-dense foods. This additional food should supply carbohydrate to fuel the training sessions and adequate protein and micronutrients for the development and support of new tissue.

• During stage races, the responsibility for feeding cyclists may be assumed by team members such as *soigneurs*. It is important that this role is treated seriously and creatively. Providing ready access to foods and energy-rich drinks during and after the race is a key strategy for ensuring adequate intake. The carer should not underestimate the value of monitoring and encouraging intake, especially when the cyclist is fatigued. Equally, individualizing food choices to suit the specific likes of each cyclist also enhances intake.

- Overall, the cyclist should increase the number of times that he or she eats rather than the size of the meals. This will enable greater intake of food with less risk of overfilling and gastrointestinal discomfort. This will require a supply of energy-dense, carbohydrate-rich snacks to be available between meals, particularly during and after exercise sessions. Table 16.2 provides examples of such snacks.
- Ensuring a ready supply of palatable and easy-to-consume foods is an important way to help a cyclist eat to his or her optimal appetite level and beyond. Providing a constantly changing variety of food forms and flavors can help to overcome *eating fatigue*.
- Because dehydration interferes with gastrointestinal function and motivation, cyclists who finish a training session or race stage with a severe fluid deficit are typically unable to eat or digest a substantial intake of food. Aggressive post-race rehydration strategies, including, in some situations, intravenous rehydration techniques, can play a key role in preparing the cyclist for a later intake of food and energy-rich supplements.
- Adding sugars or lean protein choices to high-carbohydrate foods can increase the energy content. For example, thick jams and syrups can be added to toast or pancakes, and sandwiches may have two- or three-layer fillings. This adds extra kilocalories to a nutritious meal, without adding greatly to the bulkiness of the food.
- The cyclist can make food intake more compact by avoiding excessive intake of high-fiber foods. It is often impractical to consume a diet that is solely based on whole-grain and high-fiber foods.
- High-energy fluids such as milk shakes, fruit smoothies, and commercial liquid-meal supplements are useful. These drinks provide a compact and low-bulk source of energy and nutrients, and they can be consumed with meals or as snacks—including before, during, or after a training session.
- Special sports foods such as sports bars, gels, high-carbohydrate powders, and liquid meal-replacement powders also provide a compact carbohydrate and energy boost. They may be eaten as snacks, including while riding or, in the case of powders, added to everyday foods to increase total intake.

Many cyclists do not eat as much—or more importantly, as often—as they think. It is useful to examine the actual intake of athletes who fail to maintain their ideal weight yet report "constant eating." Commitments such as training, sleep, medical/physiotherapy appointments, work, or school often get in the way of eating opportunities. A food record will identify the hours and occasions of minimal food intake. Cyclists should use this information to reorganize the day or to find creative ways to make nutritious foods and drinks part of the activity.

Goal 3: Eat to Reduce Body Weight and Body-Fat Levels

Anthropometric characteristics are important in determining the performance of a cyclist according to the type of event or its components (mass start, individual or team time trial, level terrain, or uphill and downhill riding). In particular, taller and heavier cyclists have better aerodynamic characteristics per unit body mass, favoring level-terrain cycling, whereas a low body weight is an advantage for uphill cycling and low body-fat levels are typical of all elite cyclists (see chapters 7 and 9).

Because features such as body mass, muscle mass, and body-fat levels can be manipulated via changes in energy intake and training, it is probable that the dietary practices of some cyclists will reflect these interests at some time in their season or career. Loss of body mass or body fat is typically the most desired change. Lay literature and anecdotal reports from successful cyclists document a strong focus on achieving extreme leanness by top road cyclists (for a review, see Burke 2001). The strategies that already-lean cyclists allegedly use to "cut weight" include training in a fasted state, restricting food intake after training rides, and deliberately under-eating during extremely demanding stage races (Burke 2001). These practices, especially when carried out to extremes, can interfere with immediate training and racing performance. In addition, the pursuit of excessive leanness and low body mass carries the potential risk for the development of various problems related to immediate- and long-term health, performance, body image, and psychological well-being.

We suggest the following strategies for a safe and healthy approach to weight control:

- A cyclist may need expert advice to identify an "ideal" body fat/body weight target that is consistent with long-term health and performance and allows him to eat well and enjoy food.
- If losing body fat is required, the cyclist should set a realistic rate of loss (e.g., 0.5 to 1.0 kilogram per week), including both short- and long-term goals. The best time for weight loss is during the off-season or early preseason so that energy restriction does not interfere with race nutrition and performance.
- Keeping a food record for a defined period (e.g., a week) is a useful task that may allow the cyclist to appreciate exactly what he currently is eating. Many athletes who feel that they "hardly eat anything" will be amazed at their unrecognized eating habits and food-intake opportunities.
- A moderate energy restriction of 500 to 1,000 kilocalories per day (two to four megajoules) is appropriate for producing a reasonable loss of body fat but still ensures adequate food and nutrient intake. A cyclist should not attempt severe energy restriction (i.e., an intake below 1,500 to 2,000 kilocalories, or six to eight megajoules, per day) during intensive training or racing without expert advice or supervision.
- The meal plan for weight loss should not rely on skipping meals or enduring long periods without food intake. Rather, food intake should be spread over the day, particularly to allow for efficient refueling before and after training sessions and to avoid hunger (which generally precipitates overeating).
- Reducing intake of fat and oil is an effective way to reduce energy intake. Strategies include choosing low-fat and lean versions of protein foods, minimizing added fats and oils in cooking and food preparation, and enjoying high-fat snacks and sweet foods as occasional treats rather than everyday foods.

• Portion control is also an important strategy in achieving weight loss. Many cyclists benefit by reducing their typical serving sizes at meals, or by avoiding the need to finish everything that is on their plate.

• Meals and snacks can be made more "filling" by several strategies: Low-GI carbohydrate choices (oatmeal, legumes, al dente pasta, etc.) are considered to have a higher satiety value than high-GI choices (cornflakes, potatoes, etc.). Athletes should combine protein with carbohydrate-rich meals and snacks to produce greater satiety than in carbohydrate-rich foods alone. They can add low-energy-density fruits and vegetables to meals or recipes to increase the volume of food they eat.

• The cyclist also should be prudent with alcohol and sugar intake; these energy sources are typically low in nutrients. Because alcohol intake causes a relaxed feeling, it often is associated with unwise eating. Sugar-rich foods and drinks are best consumed in exercise situations in which a compact fuel source is needed. Nevertheless, the cyclist should be aware of the potential of excessively consuming calories via energy-containing fluids (e.g., juices, sports drinks, soft drinks).

• Nutrient-rich foods are valuable to the cyclist who needs to meet nutrient needs from fewer kilojoules. The cyclist also should consider a broad-range, low-dose vitamin-mineral supplement if he will be restricting energy intake below 1,500 to 1,800 kilocalories (six to seven megajoules) per day for prolonged periods.

• Many cyclists are unaware of their inappropriate eating behavior—such as eating when bored or upset, or eating too quickly. Athletes should consider strategies to redirect stress or boredom to alternative activities.

• The expertise of a sports dietitian is valuable for individualized and supervised weight-loss programs. A cyclist needs expert advice if he is struggling with an eating disorder or disordered eating behavior.

Goal 4: Meet Special Needs for Protein and Micronutrients

Requirements for many nutrients are increased in response to a demanding exercise program or a high turnover of energy. In general, cyclists who enjoy a moderate- to high-energy intake from a varied menu of nutrient-rich foods will more than meet these increased requirements for protein and micronutrients. Although increased protein requirements often are associated with strength training, in fact, endurance athletes undertaking a strenuous daily workload have similarly elevated requirements for protein—that is, 1.2 to 1.6 grams per kilogram per day (Tarnopolsky 2000). However, dietary surveys show that these needs usually are met within the moderate to high energy intakes reported by cyclists (Burke 2001). Iron and calcium are often "at-risk" nutrients for female athletes, due to increased requirements, inadequate intake, or a combination of both factors (for reviews, see Deakin 2000, Kerr et al. 2000). See table 16.4 for good food sources of iron and calcium.

We suggest the following strategies for promoting the intake of protein and key micronutrients, in conjunction with other sports nutrition goals:

TABLE 16.4 Good Food Sources of Iron and Calcium

Food	Serving	Iron (mg)
Heme iron foods		
Liver	100 g (cooked weight)	11.0
Liver paté	40 g (2 tbsp)	2-3
Lean steak	100 g (cooked weight)	4.0
Chicken (dark meat)	100 g (cooked weight)	1.2
Fish	100 g (cooked weight)	0.6-1.4
Oysters	100 g (10)	3.9
Salmon	100 g (small tin)	1.5
Nonheme iron foods		
Eggs	100 g (2)	1.0
Breakfast cereal (fortified)	30 g (1 cup)	2-8
Whole-grain bread	60 g (2 slices)	1.4
Spinach (cooked)	145 g (1 cup)	4.4
Kidney beans or lentils (cooked)	100 g (2/3 cup)	2.5
Tofu	100 g	1.9
Sultanas	50 g	0.9
Dried apricots	50 g	2.0
Almonds	50 g	2.1

Food	Serving	Calcium (mg)
Calcium-rich foods		
Skim milk	200 ml glass	250
Calcium-fortified, low-fat milk	200 ml glass	285-350
Reduced-fat cheese slice	20 g slice	160
Cottage cheese	100 g (1/2 cup)	80
Low-fat fruit yogurt	200 g carton	350
Low-fat ice cream	60 g (2 tbsp)	90
Soft-serve yogurt/ ice cream		28
Salmon with bones	100 g (small tin)	250
Sardines	100 g (drained weight)	240
Oysters	100 g (10)	135
Soy milk	200 ml glass	10
Fortified soy milks	200 ml glass	290
Tofu	100 g	32
Tahini	20 g (1 tbsp)	120
Almonds	50 g	125
Spinach (cooked)	145 g (1 cup)	136

Note: Source of food-composition data: USDA Nutrient Database for Standard Reference, Release 14 (July 2001).
Adapted from Hawley and Burke 1998.

• Including a variety of foods in the day-to-day menu enhances micronutrient intake. The cyclist should be prepared to try new foods and new recipes to keep expanding the dietary range. It is also good to take advantage of foods that are in season to introduce new variety into menus. Explore all the varieties of foods within a group, and experiment with different food forms.

• Popular diets that advise against "food combining" are unsound. Meals are improved nutritionally and flavor-wise by the integration of a number of foods into the menu. This can be done by adding individual food items together on the plate or by cooking recipes that already involve a mixture (e.g., stir fries, casseroles, main-meal salads).

• Banishing a food or food group from the diet can lead to the loss of important nutrients, as well as dietary boredom. Most foods provide some nutrient value, even if some features are not in line with other dietary principles. There may be ways to reduce or modify the intake of the food rather than discard it totally. A sports dietitian can help the cyclist to explore and maximize food variety—especially when there are sound reasons for restricting food choices (e.g., food allergies or intolerances, moral or religious sanctions).

- Meals generally will be well chosen if they follow the principle of "mixing and matching" so that protein-rich foods and fruits or vegetables are added to a high-carbohydrate base. It is useful to spread protein intake over the day rather than concentrate intake to one meal each day. Obvious protein-rich foods include meats, eggs, and dairy foods. However, grains, nuts, and seeds also add valuable amounts of protein to mixed meals.

- Because the heme form of iron found in many animal foods (e.g., red meats, shellfish, liver) is well absorbed, cyclists should include it regularly in meals—at least three to five times per week. The cyclist can add these foods as a partner to a high-carbohydrate meal (e.g., meat sauce on a pasta dish, liver pate in a sandwich). The absorption of nonheme iron (found in whole grains, cereal foods, eggs, leafy green vegetables) can be increased by including a vitamin C food at the same meal (e.g., a glass of orange juice consumed with breakfast cereal). The absorption also is enhanced by combining with a "meat" food (e.g., legumes and meat in a chili con carne).

- Cyclists who are at risk of iron deficiency should be aware of food factors (e.g., excess bran, strongly brewed tea) that interfere with iron absorption from nonheme iron foods. They should avoid these items or separate them from meals.

- Iron supplements should be taken only on the advice of a sports dietitian or doctor. They may be useful in the supervised treatment and prevention of iron deficiency, but they do not replace a holistic assessment and treatment, including integrated dietary advice.

- The cyclist should consume at least three servings of dairy foods a day, with one serving equal to a glass of milk or a carton of yogurt. Low-fat and reduced-fat types are available. The cyclist can add dairy products to a high-carbohydrate meal (e.g., milk on breakfast cereal, cheese in a sandwich).

- Extra calcium is needed for young cyclists undergoing a growth spurt, or for females who are having a baby or breast-feeding. In these situations, the cyclist should increase dairy intake to four to five servings a day. Female cyclists who are not having regular menstrual cycles also require extra calcium and should seek expert advice from a sports doctor. Fish eaten with its bones (e.g., tinned salmon, sardines) is another useful calcium source, and it also can accompany a high-carbohydrate meal (e.g., salmon casserole with rice). Cyclists who are vegetarian or unable to eat dairy products and red meat in these amounts should seek the advice of a sports dietitian. Creative ways can be found for other foods or food uses to meet iron and calcium needs (such as fortified soy products), or to use mineral supplements correctly.

Goal 5: Fuel Up for a Race

Goals of pre-race nutrition include preparing adequate fuel stores for the demands of the race, and keeping fluid levels up to ensure that the cyclist is well hydrated (see chapter 13). The fuel needs of a race and the opportunity to fuel up before the race are dependent on the type of event the cyclist is undertaking. Single-day racing generally allows the cyclist to prepare specifically for the event, especially if the race is designated as an important event in the cyclist's calendar. However, tour racing sets the difficult challenge of recovering between each day's stage. Goal 1 includes strategies for promoting adequate carbohydrate intake for recovery and refueling between daily training sessions or racing stages.

Specialized programs to increase muscle glycogen stores before an important distance race are an extension of the cyclist's everyday high-carbohydrate eating practices. In effect, conducting an exercise taper or reduced training load while consuming high-carbohydrate intakes (7 to 12 grams per kilogram per day) allows the muscle of the well-trained cyclist to supercompensate its glycogen content (or "carbohydrate load"). For most cyclists this will mean attention to the training program, with perhaps some fine-tuning of dietary intake to ensure adequate carbohydrate intake. For cyclists who need to practice moderate energy restriction to achieve body weight/fat goals, race preparation for a long event (greater than three to four hours duration) may call for a rebalancing of priorities. That is, for an important race in which optimal performance is desired, the cyclist should increase energy intake over the day(s) prior to the event to allow the intake of carbohydrate necessary to saturate glycogen storage processes.

The pre-event meal eaten in the one to four hours prior to a race provides the final opportunity to fine-tune fluid and fuel needs. Cyclists should choose foods for this meal to meet nutrient needs, but also in concern for gastric comfort during the race. Because cycling is generally a more "gut-friendly" activity than running, most cyclists can manage to eat a substantial pre-race meal based on a variety of carbohydrate-rich foods (see table 16.5 for ideas). In fact, in stage racing when the carbohydrate and energy needs are extremely high, the pre-race breakfast will serve to provide fuel and fluid for the immediate day's stage, as well as make a substantial contribution toward the cyclist's total nutritional needs. Overall, the specific goals of the pre-race meal may differ from race to race, and each race environment may provide different food choices or pre-race rituals. Therefore, cyclists should experiment both in training and in racing to develop a variety of pre-race eating strategies that meet their individual needs and likes.

TABLE 16.5 Examples of Carbohydrate-Rich Pre-Race Meal Choices

- Steamed rice* or noodles* with low-fat sauce
- Creamed rice* made with sugar and milk
- Breakfast cereal* with milk or yogurt
- Pancakes with syrup
- Toast* or English muffins* with jam
- Crumpets* with honey
- Rice cakes or bread rolls* with sliced banana
- Fresh fruit or fruit salad
- Baked potato with low-fat sauce or filling
- Toast* with canned spaghetti or baked beans
- Fruit smoothie made with milk, yogurt, and fruit
- Commercial liquid meal supplement
- Sports bars

* For low-fiber meals, choose "white" types of cereal food.

Goal 6: Meet Carbohydrate and Fluid Needs During Training and Racing

Chapters 14 and 15 explain the importance of consuming fluid and additional carbohydrate during lengthy cycling sessions. These strategies will serve to improve performance during that specific session as well as contribute to overall nutritional goals. In general, cyclists are able to consume a range of fluids and carbohydrate-rich foods while cycling (table 16.2), although there is some evidence that more aggressive riding tactics in some road races and cycle tours have reduced the opportunities for and perhaps the culture of "during-race eating."

The following guidelines provide strategies for optimal intake of fluid and carbohydrate on the bike, and they may be adapted according to the needs and opportunities encountered in each race:

- As far as it is practical and tolerated, the cyclist should aim to drink sufficient fluid during a cycling session to keep pace with sweat losses (i.e., to replace at least 80 percent of sweat losses). It is difficult to gauge sweat losses during the session. However, monitoring changes in body mass before and after similar sessions can provide a guide to typical sweat losses and the cyclist's current success in replacing those losses. (A loss of one kilogram is approximately equal to one liter of sweat loss.) The cyclist should check this from time to time to get an estimate of expected sweat losses in different events and conditions.
- Staying well hydrated during training will mean better performance during that session and a chance to practice the fluid intake strategies intended for races. There is considerable difference in individual (gastrointestinal) tolerance to drinking large volumes of fluid; however, there is some evidence that practice can increase the tolerance of reluctant drinkers.
- The cyclist should begin all exercise sessions well hydrated. This includes strategies to recover fluid losses from previous training sessions or stages, and hydrating well before any sessions undertaken in hot conditions. Hyperhydration techniques (acute fluid overloading) may be useful for specific situations of high sweat rates and reduced opportunities to drink during the session (e.g., an individual time trial carried out in very hot weather). However, cyclists should practice these tactics in advance and they are best done under the supervision of appropriate medical or scientific support staff.
- The cyclist and support staff should be aware of the needs and opportunities for drinking during each race (and training session). Fluids may be made available from feed stations, handlers, and team support cars. Generally in team races, the *domestique* undertakes some of the responsibility to get drinks to targeted riders. Each rider should aim to keep fluid deficits as small as is practical during the race. Fluid intake should start early in the race and continue frequently at a comfortable rate, with a philosophy of preventing dehydration rather than trying to reverse a severe fluid deficit.
- The provision of cool, palatable drinks will encourage fluid intake. In stage races, it is useful to vary the flavors of drinks to continue to stimulate voluntary intake. Sports drinks are ideal for providing fluids during races, as well as contributing

to fuel needs. The replacement of electrolytes via sports drinks is probably valuable in very long races and stage racing.

• Cyclists can achieve carbohydrate intake during races via sports drinks, special sports products (e.g., gels, bars), and other everyday foods. During stage racing, this intake may contribute to total fuel and carbohydrate needs as well as the fuel needs of the immediate stage. Variety in choices may help to enhance voluntary intake. Some cyclists experiment with a race plan that concentrates on fluid intake early in the race (water, diluted sports drinks), then gradually increase carbohydrate intake (full-strength sports drinks, gels, solid foods) toward the end of the stage as muscle fuel stores become depleted.

• After each training session or race, the cyclist should enhance recovery with active rehydration and refueling strategies. Goal 1 covers carbohydrate issues. Rehydration requires an intake of greater volumes of fluid than the postexercise fluid deficit. In general, the cyclist will need to drink 150 percent of the post-race fluid deficit to ensure that fluid balance is achieved—for example, if the post-race fluid deficit is two kilograms (two liters), the cyclist should drink three liters of fluid over the next hours to rehydrate. Note that alcohol- and caffeine-containing beverages may promote urine production and are not ideal rehydration beverages. On occasions of extreme fluid loss during a tour, a cyclist may need intravenous rehydration to restore hydration status and improve appetite or gastrointestinal function to promote adequate food intake. Cyclists should undertake this practice only under the supervision of appropriate medical support staff.

Goal 7: Meet Goals While Traveling

National and international travel is a way of life for high-performing cyclists. Professional teams may spend 5 to 10 months of each year on the road, traveling from race to race. They also may travel to foreign locations to undertake specialized training in the heat or at altitude. Catering often is prearranged within the organization underpinning large stage races or at the athlete villages associated with major international competitions. Alternatively, in many cycling teams, a *soigneur* or other team support member may take responsibility for organizing meals and training/racing snacks for the cyclists. However, on many occasions a cyclist will need to take care of his own food requirements.

Regardless of the level of support, eating away from home poses challenges such as reduced access to food (or suitable food) because of reliance on menus from planes, trains, hotels, restaurants, and so forth, and the loss of usual and important foods that are either unavailable or too expensive in the new destination. Many cyclists are unskilled at handling problems with food hygiene and the lack of a safe water supply in some countries, or at responding to the sudden change in needs for fluid, fuel, or energy that accompanies a new exercise program or a change in temperature or altitude.

We offer the following strategies to cyclists (or a team support crew) to achieve their nutritional goals while on the road:

• Before leaving, the cyclist should investigate the food resources at his destination. People who have traveled previously to that country, event, or accommodation facility may be able to warn of likely problems. The cyclist should allow a plan to be prepared in advance.

- It is useful to organize special menus and meals in airplanes, hotels, or restaurants in advance.
- The cyclist should research food hygiene and water safety when traveling to new countries. He or she should be aware of locations in which fluid intake should be restricted to bottled or boiled drinks, and know how to avoid foods that are high risk for contamination (e.g., unpeeled fruits and vegetables).
- It is useful to take food supplies to locations where important items are likely to be unavailable or expensive. See table 16.2 for a list of foods that are portable and low in perishability for the traveling cyclist.
- The cyclist should be aware of special nutritional requirements in the new location—for example, to be prepared to meet increased requirements for fluid, carbohydrate, and other nutrients.

Summary

Turning the nutritional requirements for cycling into an eating plan requires sophisticated nutrition knowledge and an understanding of the practical and lifestyle challenges commonly found in this sport. The cyclist's eating plan must be able to accommodate a number of nutritional goals as well as encompass practical features such as food preferences, social eating occasions, and the availability of foods. Each cyclist has a unique set of nutritional needs that may include meeting the muscle-fuel requirements for training, racing, and recovery; manipulating body weight and body fat levels; and achieving special needs for energy, protein, and micronutrients.

Replacing carbohydrate and fluid during prolonged exercise is a key requirement for optimal competition performance, but it also must be achieved and practiced in training. Practical challenges that athletes must address include eating well while traveling and meeting requirements for energy and nutrients at times when it is not convenient or comfortable to consume large amounts of foods or fluids. Although the needs and successful practices of each cyclist are individual, the common principles by which these nutrition goals are achieved can provide a valuable starting point for designing an eating plan.

chapter 17

Cycling Supplements

Jeffrey C. Little
Stella L. Volpe

Previous chapters have stressed the importance of maintaining an adequate nutrient intake to meet the physical demands of cycling as well as proper eating strategies to achieve optimal performance during competition. All athletes are encouraged to meet these demands through a balanced diet. However, athletes may be unable to meet their energy (caloric) requirements through their normal diet, or they may feel that consuming more of a particular substance will be beneficial in improving their performance. In either case, since ancient times athletes have been turning to dietary supplements as a way of satisfying their needs or as an attempt to gain a competitive edge in their performance. In most cases, the effectiveness of many of these substances has not been substantiated. Although in the majority of cases additional research is warranted, there are situations in which athletes' physical requirements may benefit from the use of supplementation.

Collectively, these performance-enhancing substances are referred to as *nutritional ergogenic aids*. Ergogenic aids can be classified into four classes, products that

1. represent an energy source (e.g., carbohydrate supplements);
2. enhance anabolic growth (e.g., protein/amino acid supplements);

3. act as cellular components in metabolism (e.g., pyruvate, sodium bicarbonate, and carnitine); or
4. may play a role in recovery from physical exertion (e.g., antioxidants and β-hydroxy-β-methylbutyrate).

There are an enormous number of dietary supplements available for purchase today, and a complete account of those supplements would be impossible in this chapter. Therefore, we have focused on the documented ergogenic potential of several commonly used dietary supplements and have discussed which supplements are appropriate to consume, which may be potentially harmful, and which can be attained easily through the diet.

Regulation of Supplements

Prior to discussing the specific supplements, it is important to have some knowledge of the regulation of these supplements. We must first understand the difference between medicines and nutritional supplements. Medicines must undergo rigorous clinical trials prior to being approved and becoming available on the market. In addition, the purity of medicines must be established and guaranteed. This is not the case, however, for nutritional supplements. As a result, when an individual purchases vitamins, minerals, herbs, or other nutritional or non-nutritional supplements, the purity of that product cannot be guaranteed, and the actual amounts listed on the labels and the quality of substances within supplements may not be accurate. We are stating this as a general reminder, to make you aware of the inconsistencies of substance types and amounts in each supplement, even within the same company. This issue recently received a tremendous amount of attention because athletes who tested positive in drug testing claimed that this was due to supplements that had been contaminated. In fact, there is some evidence that certain supplements can result in a positive doping test for nandrolone.

Creatine

Creatine has received a tremendous amount of attention in the field of sport nutrition over recent years and presently has become one of the most widely used ergogenic aids by athletes. Creatine's popularity has continued to grow as scientific research has substantiated the claims that short-term creatine loading may increase power output during intense, intermittent exercise bouts and aid in muscle recovery (Kraemer and Volek 1999).

Creatine is an energy-producing substance that is endogenously synthesized in the liver, pancreas, and kidney from amino acids and can also be obtained exogenously from meat products in the diet. It is predominately found within the skeletal muscles of the body in both the free and phosphorylated forms. Creatine, and in particular phosphocreatine (PCr), aids in rapidly replenishing the energy source of working muscles (adenosine triphosphate, or ATP) during intense exercise bouts (e.g., 10 to 30 seconds). In high-intensity activities, the ATP in working muscles is quickly hydrolyzed (broken down) to adenosine diphosphate (ADP) plus inorganic phosphate

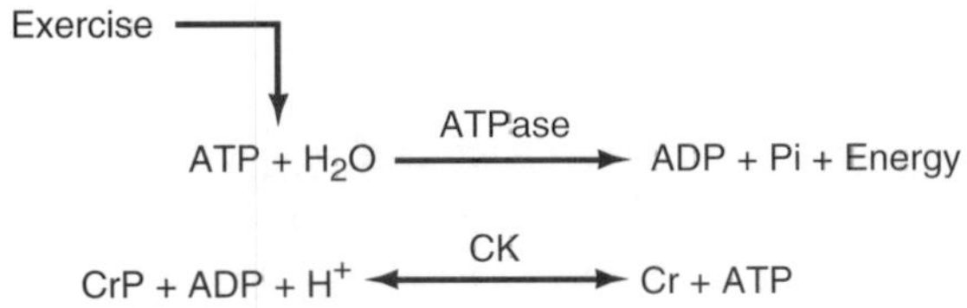

Figure 17.1 The role of creatine phosphate in energy production. ATP = adenosine triphosphate; H_2O = water; CK = creatine kinase; ADP = adenosine diphosphate; Pi = inorganic phosphate; CrP = creatine phosphate; H^+ = hydrogen ion; Cr = creatine; ATPase = adenosine triphosphatase.

via creatine phosphokinase, and in the process, energy is released. PCr donates its phosphate group to ADP to regenerate ATP that will be available for energy production again (see figure 17.1). The benefit of this process is that it is rapid and provides a high-power energy system; the negative aspect is that it is short in duration because the muscle's supply of PCr is limited.

Thus, by the athlete orally ingesting creatine, the skeletal muscles may be able to increase their storage capacity of PCr and, in turn, prolong the muscles' ability to produce this high-power energy. Research has shown that the most effective way to increase muscle creatine stores is by applying a loading phase of creatine followed by intake of a lower maintenance dose. The loading phase should consist of 0.3 gram of creatine per kilogram of body weight per day (in the form of creatine monohydrate) in four to five doses throughout the day for a period of five to seven days. After that, a dosage of 0.3 gram of creatine per kilogram of body weight per day is adequate to maintain creatine stores.

Research on the efficacy of creatine loading has produced numerous positive results on the ability to improve performance during intense, single-bout, exhaustive activities. In particular, studies on creatine supplementation in cyclists have shown a significant enhancement in the ability to maintain muscular force and power output during exhaustive bouts of cycling (Vandebuerie et al. 1998).

The role of creatine in energy production is predominantly during short, high-intensity, anaerobic activities; athletes engaging in endurance activities that rely predominately on oxidative energy metabolism may not observe a performance-enhancing effect from creatine supplementation. There are no studies that have demonstrated a positive effect of creatine supplementation on endurance performance. In fact, Williams (1998) has suggested that creatine loading may even have a detrimental effect on endurance athletes because of the accumulation of water within the muscles that often accompanies creatine supplementation.

As with many supplements, the safety of creatine has become a concern. To date, the short-term oral supplementation of creatine (20 grams per day for five days) has not produced any documented adverse effects on such measures as renal function; however, mild side effects such as muscle cramping, nausea, and gastrointestinal distress have been reported in some cases (Kraemer and Volek 1999). The evidence of the long-term effects of creatine supplementation has yet to be established and it warrants further investigation.

It is also interesting to note that many sports organizations, such as the National Collegiate Athletic Association, have placed creatine on their banned substance lists.

Protein

Protein and its amino-acid subunits are essential for synthesis of muscle, hormones, enzymes, and connective tissue within the body. In addition, amino acids can serve as an available energy source when carbohydrate stores (glycogen) and fat are low, during prolonged physical activity. Like creatine, amino acids can be obtained exogenously from the diet—for example, muscle and organ tissue and plant proteins (soy)—as well as endogenously from carbohydrates, fats, and ammonia. However, there is a select group of amino acids that the body cannot synthesize and must be obtained through the diet. These amino acids are referred to as *essential amino acids*. Amino acids that can be synthesized by the body are called *nonessential amino acids*. Table 17.1 provides a listing of the essential and nonessential amino acids needed by the body. A complete protein source (e.g., eggs) contains both essential and nonessential amino acids that are required for optimum growth and recovery. The Recommended Dietary Allowance for protein is 0.8 grams per kilogram of body weight (0.36 grams per pound of body weight) per day for the average adult. Therefore, a 75-kilogram person (165 pounds) would have a protein requirement of 60 grams per day.

Cyclists engaged in strenuous training have increased protein needs because of increased amino-acid oxidation and possibly increased protein synthesis. The research on exactly how much an athlete should increase protein intake is still not fully defined; however, most researchers agree that athletes may need to increase their daily protein intake to 1.0 to 1.5 grams per kilogram of body weight (about 0.5 to 0.7 gram per pound of body weight) per day. If we use the 75-kilogram adult as an example again, an athlete may need to consume between 75 and 113 grams of protein per day. It has even been suggested in extreme events, such as the Tour de France, that protein requirements may increase up to 2.0 grams per kilogram of body weight per day.

TABLE 17.1 Essential and Nonessential Amino Acids in the Human Body

Essential	Nonessential
Phenylalanine	Alanine
Valine	Arginine
Threonine	Aspartic acid
Tryptophan	Asparagine
Histidine+	Cysteine*
Isoleucine	Glutamine
Leucine	Glutamic acid
Lysine	Glycine
Methionine	Proline
	Serine
	Tyrosine*

+ Histidine has only been shown to be essential in infants although small amounts are required in adults.

* These nonessential (conditionally essential) amino acids can be made from essential amino acids within the body.

However, when athletes increase their energy expenditure, they usually increase their energy intake in order to maintain energy balance. In doing so, protein intake is typically increased. Even in extreme races such as the Tour de France, the protein intake of the riders seems sufficient to maintain nitrogen balance without their taking additional protein supplements.

In light of this, athletes still continue to supplement their diets with protein by consuming manufactured products, and they often attribute success in their respective sport to the supplements. Protein supplementation includes consuming protein powders, amino-acid supplements, free-form amino-acid supplements, and branched-chain amino-acid supplements. As with all manufactured supplements, the efficacy of these substances requires additional research. There are concerns about the quality of protein found in many of these products because there are no standards for protein composition—the Food and Drug Administration does not regulate dietary supplements. In addition, the economical burden of purchasing these often-expensive products is another concern. If you wish to supplement your diet with additional protein, first do so with natural food products in which you can be assured of receiving high-quality protein sources in addition to naturally containing vitamins and minerals.

Glycerol

Glycerol is an ergogenic aid that is believed to have a performance-enhancing effect on aerobic power during endurance events by preserving vital fluid reserves within the body. Continuous exercise, particularly in warm environments, places a considerable stress on the body's thermoregulatory system, which attempts to maintain a homeostatic environment. In the event of prolonged activity, the exercising muscles release a tremendous amount of energy in the form of heat. This increase in heat production stimulates the thermal regulatory center of the brain (hypothalamus), which, in turn, initiates different mechanisms that increase external heat loss to return the body to its normal temperature (37 degrees Celsius). The most important of these mechanisms is the vasodilatation of peripheral blood vessels combined with stimulation of sweat glands, leading to an increase in heat transport from the body's core to the skin via blood (fluid) and ultimately evaporation into the air. When high sweat rates are coupled with insufficient fluid intakes, a condition of hypohydration may occur. Hypohydration can result in a decreased sweat rate, which may lead to an increase in core body temperature, increased heart rate, and a decrease in cutaneous blood flow; the end result of which is impaired exercise performance.

The rationale of glycerol supplementation is due to its water-binding properties. When consumed in conjunction with an optimal fluid intake, glycerol may provide a reservoir of available water (hyperhydration), which may delay dehydration and, in turn, prolong endurance capacity, theoretically improving performance. The research on glycerol supplementation, however, has been inconclusive. Lyons et al. (1990) induced hyperhydration in their six subjects by asking them to ingest one gram of glycerol per kilogram of body weight, with orange juice and water, 2.5 hours prior to a 1.5-hour exercise bout on a treadmill. Subjects exercised at 60 percent of their maximal oxygen consumption ($\dot{V}O_2max$) in a warm environment (42 degrees Celsius). Glycerol supplementation resulted in a smaller increase in core body temperature and therefore lower sweat losses.

Conversely, Lamb et al. (1997) observed no difference in plasma volume changes, heart rate, core body temperature, and sweat rate in 13 trained cyclists consuming a glycerol-supplemented carbohydrate solution compared to those same cyclists consuming just a carbohydrate solution. Subjects were performing cycling exercise bouts to exhaustion at 75 percent of their $\dot{V}O_2max$; but unlike the previously mentioned study, these procedures were not conducted in a warm environment. It appears that additional research on glycerol supplementation is needed, with standardized protocols to assess the efficacy of increasing fluid volume and subsequent improvements in endurance performance in differing climates.

Glycerol is a naturally occurring metabolite in the body and has not presently been found to pose any adverse effects. Athletes wishing to experiment with glycerol supplementation should be aware of the potential discomfort that may be associated with increased fluid volume within the body at the onset of exercise. In addition, experimentation should be conducted prior to competition as a result of the unfamiliarity of the stiffness (water accumulation) that accompanies glycerol supplementation. The sidebar below presents a procedure for glycerol supplementation by Williams (1998).

Possible Procedure for Glycerol Hyperhydration

1. Determine your body weight in kilograms (multiply your weight in pounds by 0.454).
2. Consume one gram of glycerol per kilogram body weight. If you weigh 70 kilograms (154 pounds), you would consume 70 grams of glycerol.
3. Glycerol as glycerin or Glycerate should not be consumed full strength but must be diluted in other fluids before drinking.
4. With Glycerate or similar commercial products, follow the instructions on the packet. With glycerin, make a 5 percent solution with water. Add 50 grams of glycerin to a liter (1,000 milliliters) of water, or about 1.5 ounces of glycerin in a quart of water. Each 100 milliliters of fluid contains 5 grams of glycerol, so to obtain 70 grams, our 70-kilogram athlete must drink about 1,400 milliliters of the glycerin-water mixture (100 milliliters/5 × 70 kilograms = 1,400 milliliters).
5. Consume the fluid from 2.5 to 1.5 hours before exercise.

Adapted from Williams 1998.

Vitamin and Mineral Supplements

Vitamins and minerals are essential in the body for a variety of processes such as energy production, hemoglobin synthesis (e.g., iron), maintaining a healthy immune system (e.g., vitamin A, zinc), prevention and repair of tissue from oxidative damage (e.g., antioxidants), maintaining healthy bones (e.g., calcium, vitamin D), and the synthesis and maintenance of muscle tissue during exercise. Athletes can obtain the daily requirements of vitamins and minerals by adhering to the Dietary Reference Intakes (DRI, see table 17.2) established by the Food and Nutrition Board, Institute of

TABLE 17.2 Dietary Reference Intakes: Recommended Intakes and Tolerable Upper-Intake[1] Levels of Vitamins and Minerals

	Vitamin A (μg/d)[3]		Vitamin C (mg/d)		Vitamin D (μg/d)[4,5]		Vitamin E (mg/d)[6]		Vitamin K (μg/d)		Thiamin (mg/d)		Riboflavin (mg/d)		Niacin (mg/d)[7,9]		Vitamin B_6 (mg/d)		Folate (μg/d)[8]	
Life Stage	RDA	UL	RDA	UL	AI	UL	RDA	UL	AI	UL	RDA	UL	RDA	UL	AI	UL	RDA	UL	RDA	UL
Children																				
1-3 years	**300**	600	**15**	400	5*	50	**6**	200	30*	ND[2]	**0.5**	ND[2]	**0.5**	ND	6	10	**0.5**	30	150*	300
4-8 years	**400**	900	**25**	650	5*	50	**7**	300	55*	ND	**0.6**	ND	**0.6**	ND	8	15	**0.6**	40	200*	400
Males																				
9-13 years	**600**	1,700	**45**	1,200	5*	50	**11**	600	60*	ND	**0.9**	ND	**0.9**	ND	12	20	**1.0**	60	300*	600
14-18 years	**900**	2,800	**75**	1,800	5*	50	**15**	800	75*	ND	**1.2**	ND	**1.3**	ND	16	30	**1.3**	80	400*	800
19-30 years	**900**	3,000	**90**	2,000	5*	50	**15**	1,000	120*	ND	**1.2**	ND	**1.3**	ND	16	35	**1.3**	100	400*	1,000
31-50 years	**900**	3,000	**90**	2,000	5*	50	**15**	1,000	120*	ND	**1.2**	ND	**1.3**	ND	16	35	**1.3**	100	400*	1,000
51-70 years	**900**	3,000	**90**	2,000	10*	50	**15**	1,000	120*	ND	**1.2**	ND	**1.3**	ND	16	35	**1.7**	100	400*	1,000
> 70 years	**900**	3,000	**90**	2,000	15*	50	**15**	1,000	120*	ND	**1.2**	ND	**1.3**	ND	16	35	**1.7**	100	400*	1,000
Females																				
9-13 years	**600**	1,700	**45**	1,200	5*	50	**11**	600	60*	ND	**0.9**	ND	**0.9**	ND	12	20	**1.0**	60	300*	600
14-18 years	**700**	2,800	**65**	1,800	5*	50	**15**	800	75*	ND	**1.0**	ND	**1.0**	ND	14	30	**1.3**	80	400*	800
19-30 years	**700**	3,000	**75**	2,000	5*	50	**15**	1,000	90*	ND	**1.1**	ND	**1.1**	ND	14	35	**1.3**	100	400*	1,000
31-50 years	**700**	3,000	**75**	2,000	5*	50	**15**	1,000	90*	ND	**1.1**	ND	**1.1**	ND	14	35	**1.3**	100	400*	1,000
51-70 years	**700**	3,000	**75**	2,000	10*	50	**15**	1,000	90*	ND	**1.1**	ND	**1.1**	ND	14	35	**1.5**	100	400*	1,000
> 70 years	**700**	3,000	**75**	2,000	15*	50	**15**	1,000	90*	ND	**1.1**	ND	**1.1**	ND	14	35	**1.5**	100	400*	1,000

Note: This table presents Recommended Dietary Allowance (RDA) in bold type and Adequate Intakes (AI) in ordinary type followed by an asterisk (*). RDAs are set to meet the needs of almost all (97 to 98 percent) individuals in a group. The AI is the mean intake.

[1]UL = The maximum level of daily nutrient intake that is likely to pose no risk of adverse effects. Unless otherwise specified, the UL represents the total intake from food, water, and supplements. Due to lack of suitable data, ULs could not be established for vitamin K. In the absence of ULs, extra caution may be warranted in consuming levels above recommended intakes.

[2]ND = Not determined due to lack of adverse effects in this age group and concern with regard to lack of ability to handle excess amounts. Source of intake should be from food only to prevent high levels of intake.

[3]As retinol equivalents (RAEs). 1 RAE = 1 μg retinol, 12 μg β-carotene, 24 μg α-carotene, or 24 μg β-cryptoxanthin in foods. To calculate RAEs from REs of provitamin A carotenoids in foods, divide the REs by 2. For preformed vitamin A in foods or supplements and for provitamin A in supplements, 1 RE = 1 RAE.

[4]Cholecalciferol. 1 μg cholecalciferol = 40 IU vitamin D.

[5]In the absence of adequate exposure to sunlight.

[6]As α-tocopherol includes RRR -α-tocopherol, the only form of α-tocopherol that occurs naturally in foods and the 2R-stereoisomeric forms of α-tocopherol that occur in fortified foods and supplements.

[7]As niacin equivalents (NE). 1 mg of niacin = 60 mg of tryptophan.

[8]As dietary folate equivalents (DFE). 1 DFE = 1 μg of folic acid from fortified food or as a supplement consumed with food = 0.5 μg of a supplement taken on an empty stomach.

[9]The ULs for niacin apply to synthetic forms obtained from supplements, fortified foods, or a combination of the two.

(continued)

Source: Food and Nutrition Board, Institute of Medicine, 1997, 1998, 2000, 2001.

TABLE 17.2 (continued)

	Vitamin B_{12} (µg/d)		Pantothenic acid (mg/d)		Biotin (µg/d)		Choline[10] (mg/d) (g/d)		Calcium (mg/d) (g/d)		Chromium (µg/d)		Copper (µg/d)		Fluoride (mg/d)		Magnesium (mg/d)		Manganese (mg/d)	
Life stage	AI	UL	AI	UL	AI	UL	AI	UL	AI	UL	AI	UL	RDA	UL	AI	UL	RDA	UL	AI	UL
Children																				
1-3 years	0.9*	ND[2]	2*	ND	8*	ND	200*	1.0	500*	2.5	11*	ND[2]	**340**	1,000	0.7*	1.3	**80**	65	1.2*	2
4-8 years	1.2*	ND	3*	ND	12*	ND	500*	1.0	800*	2.5	15*	ND	**440**	3,000	1.0*	2.2	**130**	110	1.5*	3
Males																				
9-13 years	1.8*	ND	4*	ND	20*	ND	375*	2.0	1,300*	2.5	25*	ND	**700**	5,000	2*	10	**240**	350	1.9*	6
14-18 years	2.4*	ND	5*	ND	25*	ND	550*	3.0	1,300*	2.5	35*	ND	**890**	8,000	3*	10	**410**	350	2.2*	9
19-30 years	2.4*	ND	5*	ND	30*	ND	550*	3.5	1,000*	2.5	35*	ND	**900**	10,000	4*	10	**400**	350	2.3*	11
31-50 years	2.4*	ND	5*	ND	30*	ND	550*	3.5	1,000*	2.5	35*	ND	**900**	10,000	4*	10	**420**	350	2.3*	11
51-70 years	2.4[11]*	ND	5*	ND	30*	ND	550*	3.5	1,200*	2.5	30*	ND	**900**	10,000	4*	10	**420**	350	2.3*	11
> 70 years	2.4[11]*	ND	5*	ND	30*	ND	550*	3.5	1,200*	2.5	30*	ND	**900**	10,000	4*	10	**420**	350	2.3*	11
Females																				
9-13 years	1.8*	ND	4*	ND	20*	ND	375*	2.0	1,300*	2.5	21*	ND	**700**	5,000	2*	10	**240**	350	1.6*	6
14-18 years	2.4*	ND	5*	ND	25*	ND	400*	3.0	1,300*	2.5	24*	ND	**890**	8,000	3*	10	**360**	350	1.6*	9
19-30 years	2.4*	ND	5*	ND	30*	ND	425*	3.5	1,000*	2.5	25*	ND	**900**	10,000	3*	10	**310**	350	1.8*	11
31-50 years	2.4*	ND	5*	ND	30*	ND	425*	3.5	1,000*	2.5	25*	ND	**900**	10,000	3*	10	**320**	350	1.8*	11
51-70 years	2.4[11]*	ND	5*	ND	30*	ND	425*	3.5	1,200*	2.5	20*	ND	**900**	10,000	3*	10	**320**	350	1.8*	11
> 70 years	2.4[11]*	ND	5*	ND	30*	ND	425*	3.5	1,200*	2.5	20*	ND	**900**	10,000	3*	10	**320**	350	1.8*	11

[10]Although AIs have been set for choline, there are few data sets to assess whether a dietary supply of choline is needed at all stages of the life cycle, and it may be that the choline requirement can be met by endogenous synthesis at some of these stages.

[11]Because 10 to 30 percent of older people may malabsorb food-bound B_{12}, it is advisable for those older than 50 years to meet their RDA mainly from consuming foods fortified with B_{12} or a supplement.

Source: Food and Nutrition Board, Institute of Medicine, 1997, 1998, 2000, 2001.

TABLE 17.2 (continued)

	Molybdenum (μg/d)		Phosphorus (mg/d)/(g/d)		Iodine (μg/d)		Iron (mg/d)		Selenium (μg/d)		Zinc (mg/d)		Arsenic[12]	Boron (mg/d)	Nickel (mg/d)	Silicon	Vanadium (mg/d)[13]
Life stage	RDA	UL	AI	UL	RDA	UL	RDA	UL	RDA	UL	RDA	UL	UL	UL	UL	UL	UL
Children																	
1-3 years	**17**	300	460*	3	**90**	200	**7**	40	**20**	90	**3**	7	ND	3	0.2	ND	ND
4-8 years	**22**	600	500*	3	**90**	300	**10**	40	**30**	150	**5**	12	ND	6	0.3	ND	ND
Males																	
9-13 years	**34**	1,100	1,250*	4	**120**	600	**8**	40	**40**	280	**8**	23	ND	11	0.6	ND	ND
14-18 years	**43**	1,700	1,250*	4	**150**	900	**11**	45	**55**	400	**11**	34	ND	17	1.0	ND	ND
19-30 years	**45**	2,000	700*	4	**150**	1,100	**8**	45	**55**	400	**11**	40	ND	20	1.0	ND	1.8
31-50 years	**45**	2,000	700*	4	**150**	1,100	**8**	45	**55**	400	**11**	40	ND	20	1.0	ND	1.8
51-70 years	**45**	2,000	700*	4	**150**	1,100	**8**	45	**55**	400	**11**	40	ND	20	1.0	ND	1.8
> 70 years	**45**	2,000	700*	3	**150**	1,100	**8**	45	**55**	400	**11**	40	ND	20	1.0	ND	1.8
Females																	
9-13 years	**34**	1,100	1,250*	4	**120**	600	**8**	40	**40**	280	**8**	23	ND	11	0.6	ND	ND
14-18 years	**43**	1,700	1,250*	4	**150**	900	**15**	45	**55**	400	**9**	34	ND	17	1.0	ND	ND
19-30 years	**45**	2,000	700*	4	**150**	1,100	**18**	45	**55**	400	**8**	40	ND	20	1.0	ND	1.8
31-50 years	**45**	2,000	700*	4	**150**	1,100	**18**	45	**55**	400	**8**	40	ND	20	1.0	ND	1.8
51-70 years	**45**	2,000	700*	4	**150**	1,100	**8**	45	**55**	400	**8**	40	ND	20	1.0	ND	1.8
> 70 years	**45**	2,000	700*	3	**150**	1,100	**8**	45	**55**	400	**8**	40	ND	20	1.0	ND	1.8

[12]Although the UL was not determined for arsenic, there is no justification for adding arsenic to food or supplements.

[13]Although vanadium in food has not been shown to cause adverse effects in humans, there is no justification for adding vanadium to food, and vanadium supplements should be used with caution. The UL is based on adverse effects in laboratory animals and this data could be used to set a UL for adults but not children and adolescents.

Source: Food and Nutrition Board, Institute of Medicine, 1997, 1998, 2000, 2001.

Medicine. If an individual obtains an insufficient amount of vitamins and minerals through malnutrition, by restricting energy intake (e.g., for weight loss), or from disease, nutrition imbalance can occur and potentially lead to serious health ailments. Cyclists who are trying to lose body weight and who rely on low-energy intakes will place themselves at risk for not meeting the DRI for vitamins and minerals. This will quickly lead to impaired cycling performance.

The food guide pyramid has been developed to provide the general population with a tool for making food choices that will satisfy daily vitamin and mineral requirements (see figure 17.2). Following the food guide pyramid should sufficiently supply 100 percent of the DRI and not require additional supplementation. There is, however, an issue of whether the requirements established for the general population are adequate for the energy requirements of cyclists who are engaged in strenuous training programs or competition.

It does not appear that this issue will be resolved in the near future. In addition, vitamin and mineral supplementation is as popular as ever, both in the general population as well as among athletes, which means that recommendations for their use are necessary. In most cases, these supplements are providing vitamins or minerals well above the DRI, which potentially could be harmful.

In theory, an increase in requirements can result from a decreased absorption in the gastrointestinal tract, increased losses through excretion in sweat and urine, and biochemical adaptations to training. In general, the effectiveness of vitamin-mineral supplementation on exercise performance has been negligible. Singh et al. (1992) observed no significant improvements in maximal aerobic capacity, endurance capacity, and isokinetic measurements in a group of healthy, physically active males consuming a multivitamin-mineral supplement for 90 days versus a placebo group. In addition,

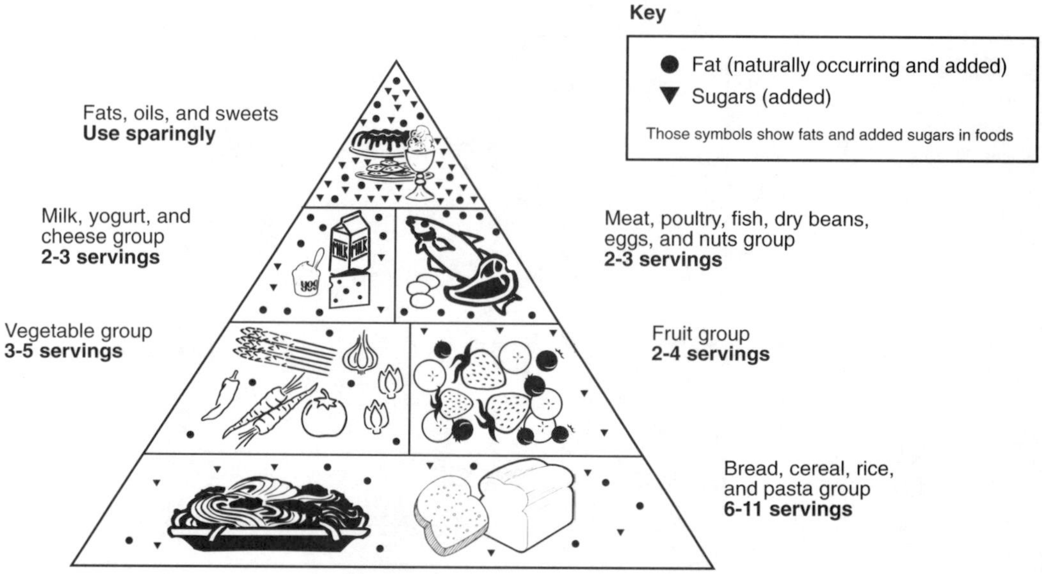

Figure 17.2 The food guide pyramid. (Source: U.S. Department of Agriculture and U.S. Department of Health and Human Services)

seven to eight months of vitamin-mineral supplementation in athletes consuming the dietary requirements showed no improvements in athletic performance (Telford et al. 1992).

The majority of vitamins (those that are water soluble) and most minerals are safe to supplement in the diet because in most cases the excess nutrients that the body does not require are typically excreted in the urine. Nonetheless, tolerable upper-intake levels have been established to minimize any negative consequences of high intakes (table 17.2). However, there are certain nutrients that, if supplemented on a regular basis, should be taken with caution. Specifically, the fat-soluble vitamins A, D, E, and K, when taken in excess, can potentially be toxic to the body. They are stored in the adipocytes (fat cells) of the body, which means they can build up in the body, and achieving toxic levels of these through supplementation can ultimately result in serious health ailments. In addition, consuming regular doses of mineral supplements (e.g., iron, copper, zinc), in conjunction with a person's regular diet, can impose absorption problems of those minerals because many minerals compete with one another at the same absorption sites. This may result in a deficiency of one mineral, while at the same time resulting in an excess of another.

If you feel that you are lacking in specific nutrients and that vitamin-mineral supplementation is the answer, it is important to first assess your dietary intake. Vitamins and minerals that are missing from a diet are by far the easiest supplement to replace naturally and economically, simply by increasing or improving your dietary intake with high-quality, nutrient-dense foods (e.g., fruits, vegetables, whole grains, lean meats, low-fat milk products). In some instances, supplements may be medically essential (e.g., iron supplementation in athletes with iron deficiency anemia); however, in general, it does not appear that vitamin-mineral supplements consumed in addition to a healthy diet are effective as ergogenic aids. Nonetheless, supplementation above the recommended values does not appear to be detrimental to health and performance, and it may be needed for some athletes, especially if they are traveling a lot and are not consuming their normal diets. However, ingesting megadoses can be dangerous and should be discouraged.

B-Complex Vitamins

A group of vitamins called B-complex vitamins have become a popular form of supplementation as an ergogenic aid, particularly in endurance activities, because of their co-enzyme function within the major metabolic pathways of the body that are involved in energy production. Specifically, these water-soluble vitamins are thiamin (B_1), riboflavin (B_2), niacin (B_3), pantothenic acid (B_5), pyridoxine (B_6), and cyanocobalamin (B_{12}). Together, these vitamins play an integral role in the metabolism of carbohydrates, fats, and proteins—and thus, energy production. The theory behind B-complex supplementation is a purported enhancement of these metabolic pathways and a subsequent improvement in energy production that will result in improved performance. As previously mentioned, these vitamins are found readily in commonly consumed foods and an athlete can replace them easily by consuming a healthy diet. Table 17.3 presents some of the common dietary sources of the B-complex vitamins. With B-vitamins in virtually every type of food we consume, supplementation of these vitamins does not appear to be necessary even for athletes, assuming these individuals are consuming a varied diet with the proper amount of energy. If you

TABLE 17.3 Common Dietary Sources of Water-Soluble B-Complex Vitamins

Vitamin	Food source
Thiamin (B_1)	Fruits and vegetables, nuts, legumes, whole-grain products, and pork products
Riboflavin (B_2)	Milk, whole-grain and enriched breads and cereals, dark-green leafy vegetables, and eggs
Niacin (B_3)	Meat, fish, poultry, legumes, whole grains, and enriched breads and cereals
Pantothenic acid (B_5)	Meat, fish, poultry, whole grains, legumes, fruits, and vegetables
Pyridoxine (B_6)	Meat, fish, poultry, legumes, whole-grain products, and brown rice
Cyanocobalamin (B_{12})	Meat, fish, poultry, eggs, milk, and cheese

become deficient in any of the B-vitamins, supplementation may be warranted; however, supplementing well-nourished, healthy athletes has proven ineffective in improving physical performance (Benardot 2000). Refer to table 17.2 for the DRIs of the B-complex vitamins.

Antioxidant Vitamins (Vitamins E and C)

Vitamins E and C, in conjunction with the mineral selenium, co-enzyme Q10, and beta-carotene (precursor of vitamin A), make up the body's natural defense mechanism against oxidative damage to lipid membranes of all cells within the body. The production of free radicals is a natural occurrence within the body and often is accentuated during periods of intense aerobic endurance activities, such as long-distance cycling. Under normal circumstances, the body relies on the dietary constituents previously mentioned to inactivate these free radicals and harmlessly eliminate them from the body. However, in the event that the antioxidant capacity of the body is challenged as a result of long periods of muscular damage, altitude training, or a lack of dietary essential antioxidant vitamins, oxidative damage to the cell membranes of the muscle cells can occur. Specifically, this damage involves the lipid peroxidation of the cellular membrane of cells that have a phospholipid component, ultimately leading to disruption of the normal functioning of that cell. Once free radical formation begins and the subsequent peroxidation of cell membranes occurs, the cycle accelerates and continues to cause damage to the cells, which could negatively affect cycling performance.

Vitamin E

Vitamin E is the body's first defense in halting the further peroxidation of cellular membranes, particularly during periods of increased physical activity (Dekkers et al. 1996). The link between vitamin E, its prevention of oxidative damage to cellular membranes, and its potential ergogenic capacity has been studied in humans. The results agree with prior literature indicating that vitamin E supplementation does reduce the exercise-induced oxidative damage to skeletal muscle cells; however, the results are inconclusive as to vitamin E's ability to improve athletic performance as a result of its antioxidant capabilities (Tiidus and Houston 1995). Therefore, until conclusive evidence is established of the effectiveness of vitamin E supplementation in improving athletic performance through its antioxidant capabilities, the controversy will continue over whether athletes need more than the established recommendations.

Vitamin C

Vitamin C is a water-soluble vitamin that also has been touted as a potential ergogenic aid through its interaction with vitamin E in resisting oxidative damage in cells. However, the results of vitamin C supplementation are equivocal, and the majority of studies performed have not observed improvements in endurance and strength performance in individuals with adequate vitamin C stores (Clarkson and Thompson 2000).

Thus, although increases in vitamins E and C may be required to prevent the oxidative damage that occurs with long-distance cycling, using these supplements to improve performance is not warranted. Refer to table 17.2 for the DRIs of vitamins E and C.

L-Carnitine

L-carnitine supplementation has been marketed as a performance-enhancing aid for improving endurance exercise as well as delaying the depletion of muscle glycogen stores within the muscle. L-carnitine is a naturally occurring cofactor within the body that can be endogenously produced through the conversion of two amino acids, methionine and lysine, as well as through a healthy diet—in particular, via consumption of meat, fish, poultry, and some dairy products. L-carnitine is predominantly found in the skeletal and cardiac muscles of the body where long-chain fatty acids (greater than 16 carbons) are oxidized (via a process called β-oxidation) as the predominant energy source during low to moderate exercise intensities. Specifically, L-carnitine is responsible for transporting an intermediate of fatty-acid metabolism (Acyl-CoA) from the outer mitochondrial membrane into the inner-mitochondrial membrane via the carnitine acyltransferase enzyme. Then, Acyl-CoA undergoes further β-oxidation, ultimately producing the energy-rich compound Acetyl-CoA.

The theory behind L-carnitine supplementation is that, by increasing the amount of available L-carnitine in the skeletal muscle mitochondria, athletes will enhance fatty-acid oxidation and obtain greater aerobic power. In addition, it has been suggested that, through the use of more fatty acids, the skeletal muscles will then rely less on their muscle glycogen reserves, potentially delaying muscle fatigue. Finally, L-carnitine has been theorized to improve anaerobic power by decreasing the amount of lactic-acid accumulation, but these claims have not been substantiated.

Direct measurements in muscle after 14 days on four to six grams of L-carnitine per day failed to show increases in the muscle carnitine concentration (Barnett et al. 1994; Vukovich et al. 1994). This implies that L-carnitine supplementation cannot increase fat oxidation during exercise and improve athletic performance by the proposed mechanism. It indeed has been confirmed in many original investigations and is summarized by numerous reviews that carnitine supplementation does not increase fat oxidation nor reduce glycogen breakdown and does not improve performance during prolonged cycling and running exercise in humans.

In addition, Villani et al. (2000) found that five out of eight subjects receiving two grams of L-carnitine per day experienced nausea and/or diarrhea. Thus, the lack of research and possible side effects of L-carnitine seem to indicate greater risks than benefits.

Summary

Dietary supplements have always been very popular and are continually gaining popularity as they propose an easy way to improve performance. The dietary supplement industry plays an important role through its marketing and often confuses the consumer with many unsubstantiated claims and promises. It is important to note that, in some instances, supplementing the diet may be medically essential. However, in the majority of cases, supplements are used in an attempt to boost performance, and there is little evidence that most supplements will have this effect. Nevertheless, athletes in all sports, not just cycling, will continue to practice supplementation regardless of what the research has shown.

Athletes should consult the appropriate professionals (e.g., physicians, registered dietitians, or sport nutritionists) to ensure that they have the most up-to-date information on the efficacy and potential harmful side effects of supplement use. We do not recommend basing supplementation decisions on peer influence or misinformed sources (e.g., magazines, television commercials); this potentially could be detrimental to cycling performance and overall health. Finally, many substances are banned by sports-governing bodies, or they could be contaminated with illegal substances and result in a positive drug test. Therefore, athletes need to think twice and think critically before buying and using nutrition supplements.

part V

Conditioning and Recovery

In addition to training, nutrition, and equipment, there are other factors that we need to consider when optimizing performance. There has been considerable debate, for instance, about the role of strength training. Injury prevention is another important aspect, and if injuries occur they must be treated effectively.

Most cyclists know from experience that hard training often is associated with the development of colds and minor illnesses. This is likely to be related to a suppression of the immune system in response to chronic hard training or even to one single hard-training session. There are several preventive measures that you can take to minimize the risk of catching a cold, and chapter 20 discusses these in detail.

Unfortunately, cycling often is associated with drug abuse and in particular the use of erythropoietin (EPO). Especially after the 1998 Tour de France, there was much suspicion regarding EPO use among the professional cyclists. Unfortunately, any cyclist who wins a major event today is automatically suspected of using drugs. This is a tragedy for those talented, hard-working cyclists who have been able to excel without doping. However, the Union Cycliste Internationale and other organizations are working hard to develop tests that eventually will eliminate EPO use.

At the end of part V, chapter 22 summarizes the conclusions of all the chapters in this book. Most chapters discuss methods for improving performance, but it is often difficult to compare the improvements obtained from nutritional interventions or training and those obtained from changes in body position. Therefore, we express these changes in performance in a common unit: 40-kilometer time-trial performance. By comparing 40-kilometer times, it becomes possible to compare, for instance, the effects of carbohydrate feeding with the effect of choosing a three-kilogram-lighter bicycle.

chapter 18

Strength and Flexibility

Adrie van Diemen
Jabik Jan Bastiaans

During racing, generating the power to close a gap or the power to break away from the bunch over a hill is critical to performance. Cyclists who are concerned about having sufficient endurance to finish a race strongly often overlook the development of this kind of explosive, short-term power, and the preparation of road cyclists for the competition season generally consists of high-volume endurance training at a relatively slow pace. This type of training is thought to decrease your short-term, explosive performance (Bastiaans et al. 2001; Widrick et al. 1996), which is consistent with the often-heard complaint of road cyclists who, after a period of high-volume endurance ("base") training, are lacking "speed." This lack of speed could be seriously limiting in competition because deciding moves usually require speed.

Stretching is thought to increase the flexibility of the muscle-tendon unit, which is believed to prevent injuries. However, stretching is only hesitantly incorporated into the rather conservative cycling community. The last section of this chapter explains whether these nonstretching cyclists are right.

Strength

To improve your short, high-intensity exercise performance, you need to increase the maximal power output you can produce during a relatively short period of time—for instance, 30 seconds. Power output (in watts) is the resultant of cadence (revolutions per minute, or rpm) and force. For instance, imagine you are cycling on a flat road with a cadence of 90 rpm. Your power output is 200 watts. If you keep cycling at the exact same speed but at a lower gear, the cadence will be higher. The resistance (force) on the pedals will be lower, although the power output remains the same. It is easy to imagine that when you are cycling at a cadence of 20 rpm, the resistance is higher than when you're cycling at a much higher power output but at a cadence of 100 rpm. The strength to overcome the resistance is therefore less important than the ability to produce a high power output. Thus, strength training to improve cycling performance should aim primarily at improving power, not strength. Maybe *power training* is a better term than *strength training*.

Bastiaans et al. (2001) recently investigated whether replacing a portion of endurance training with strength training improves cycling performance. The strength training in this investigation aimed at an improvement of power rather than strength. This means that the training consisted of high-speed movements with a relatively low resistance. The research population was divided into two groups. The first group (E) performed combined strength and endurance training (total training time of nine hours per week) for nine weeks, whereas the second group (C) performed only endurance training (intensity up to maximal lactate steady state). The short-term performance was measured by assessing the mean power output of the subjects during a 30-second all-out test.

The results showed that the power output of the C group decreased, whereas the power output in the E group increased. The researchers also investigated whether the low volume of endurance training in the E group (5.5 hours per week versus 9 hours per week in the C group) would be detrimental to endurance capacity. They assessed this by a simulated one-hour time trial. After nine weeks, both groups improved but progression was not significantly different between the groups. Despite the fact that the E group had a much lower endurance-training volume, both groups increased their endurance capacity at the same rate. The investigators hypothesized that the strength training, apart from improving maximal power output, also could improve endurance performance by changing the muscle-fiber recruitment pattern. After strength training, the power output of slow-twitch muscle fibers increases. Then, for a given power output, fewer fast-twitch fibers have to be recruited to produce this power.

This may enhance the efficiency of cycling because slow-twitch muscles are more efficient than fast-twitch (Horowitz et al. 1994). In practical terms, this suggests that strength training has the potential to improve performance at, for example, one-hour climbs or time trials. The strength training program of the aforementioned investigation was designed according to this hypothesis. The number of repetitions was set at 30, to ensure a recruitment pattern of fast twitch to slow twitch (Jacobs et al. 1981). However, it should be noted that this investigation could not determine the supposed increase of power output of the slow-twitch muscle fibers, and therefore it remains hypothetical that the strength training increased the subjects' endurance capacity (Bastiaans et al. 2001).

Scheduling Strength Training

Strength training is most important during the period when most of your endurance (base) work is done. Before you can do this, however, a good level of "base" strength is required that you have to develop in the off-season. For most professional road cyclists, this is during the months of October, November, and December. During this period you can boost your strength to a high level, which can be maintained throughout the season with only one or two strength sessions a week.

So in this way you may benefit an entire year from the acquired training effects in the winter. Figure 18.1 makes a suggestion for alternating the frequency of your strength training sessions and the volume of endurance training.

After this initial development of strength, it is highly advisable that you continue strength training throughout the season. This is especially true during the base or foundation period when you perform high-volume endurance training (Hawley 1995; chapter 1). In this period, you should alternate endurance and strength training (see figure 18.2). An example would be performing high-volume endurance training for three weeks with only one strength workout a week, followed by a week with low-volume endurance training and two or three strength workouts (figure 18.2).

In this manner, you increase your strength in only one week, then keep it at this level with a minimum of strength training. Additionally, if you do strength training regularly, a week of frequent strength training as an alternation of high-volume training can be considered a recovery week because it enhances recovery due to short-term hormonal changes. Sometimes it can be difficult to perform strength training during the racing season because of a busy racing schedule or stage races. However, the gains obtained from strength training, like endurance training, may disappear quickly. After one or two weeks without strength training, your short, high-intensity exercise

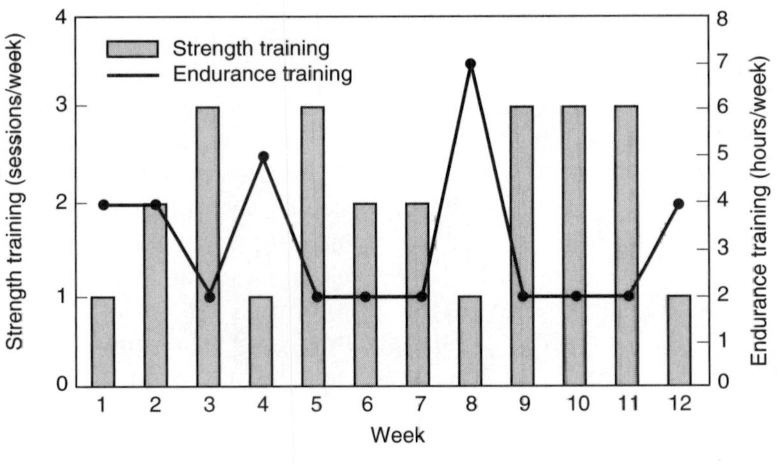

Figure 18.1 A suggestion for the combination of strength and endurance training in the period in which training volume is relatively low (typically October to December).

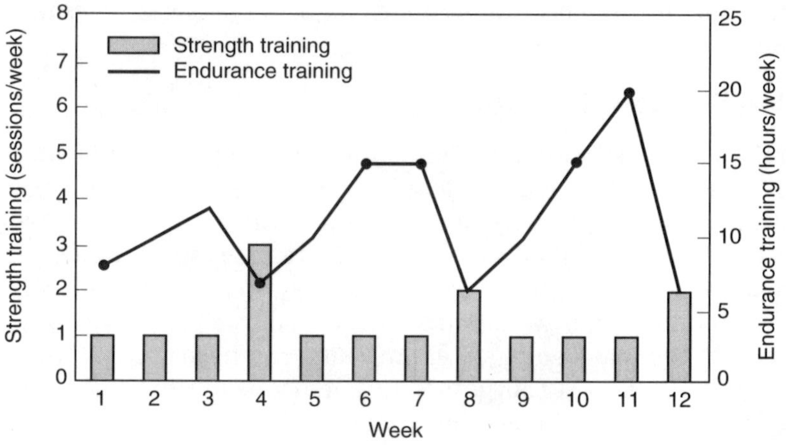

Figure 18.2 A suggestion for the combination of strength and endurance training in the base/foundation training period, typically around January to March.

performance may decrease noticeably. Thus, you should try to pick a week every month in which you can do at least two strength workouts. If you can continue your strength training throughout the season, the effect of one week of more frequent strength training may well result in increased performance.

Strength Training Key Points

Strength training needs to be done according to rather strict guidelines. This section explains which key points you need to consider when you are thinking of incorporating strength training into your training schedule.

Use Exercises That Resemble Cycling Movements

The first important point with strength training is that much of the effect is via the establishment of improved neural pathways. These are the connections between the brain and the muscle. It has been shown that much of the initial effects of strength training occur before the muscle has a chance to grow (hypertrophy) and therefore must be due to improved communication between the brain and each muscle fiber. Therefore, the movements that you incorporate into a strength training program should resemble the coordination of the pedaling motion. This is because it is thought that these neural pathways develop in a highly specific way, individual to the movement that created them. For example, hill running may improve your running strength but not your cycling strength. The seated leg extension, for instance, trains the quadriceps muscle and therefore seems a good strength training exercise for cycling. However, the coordination of this exercise is different from the cycling movement and thus it has no potential of improving cycling performance (Rutherford et al. 1986).

Make Sure Strength Training Is Explosive

The effect of strength training is also velocity specific. This means that the effect of strength training on cycling performance is restricted to movements that are executed at the same movement velocity as during cycling (Behm and Sale 1993; Kraemer et al. 1998). The angle velocity at the knee when you are cycling at 80 and 110 rpm is 190 and 260 degrees per second, respectively, which may be difficult to reach during strength training. However, there is also evidence that the intent to make a high-speed contraction may be more important than the actual movement velocity (Behm and Sale 1993); that is, the rate of force application may be more important in training than the actual movement speed (Morrissey et al. 1995). Therefore, you need to try to initiate each movement as explosively as possible.

Use Specific Joint Angles

During normal seated riding, the highest force on the pedal is applied when the crank is at an angle of approximately 90 degrees, that is, straight forward on the downstroke (Coyle et al. 1991). With the crank in that position, the knee angle is approximately (depending on saddle height) 100 degrees. Because strength gains are greatest at the specific joint angles used during the training (Morrissey et al. 1995), the knee angle should never be smaller than 100 degrees (or 90 degrees as a rule of thumb). Once the knee angle falls below this critical point, the weight that can be safely lifted falls and the training effect at the most important knee angle of 100 degrees is reduced.

The angle of the hip joint is less important. However, it is recommended that you try to keep the hip angle quite small—that is, with a leg press try to sit in a slightly upright position.

Focus on Concentric Movements

Eccentric contractions (in which the muscle lengthens under load, that is, the "down" phase on the squat) during strength training need to be avoided. The reasons for this are twofold: First, the cycling movement has no eccentric contraction and thus eccentric training would not be specific enough. Second, eccentric contractions result in a higher rate of muscle damage and thus the recovery period from eccentric contractions is longer (Costill et al. 1990). Finally, eccentric contractions result in greater muscle hypertrophy (growth) (Sale and MacDougall 1981), which needs to be avoided because body mass in cycling is a key factor. Thus, in exercises that have an unavoidable eccentric phase (e.g., the squat), you need to do the eccentric movement at an easy and steady pace.

Use Exercises, Repetitions, and Resistance

Bearing in mind the rules mentioned, which exercises are useful to the cyclist? Well, the leg press, the squat, the step-up, the leg pull, and, of course, strength training on the bicycle all fulfill the criteria and can be combined in a strength training program. You should do the leg press single legged because evidence shows that the force in the bilateral (i.e., two-legged) maximal contraction is less than the sum of the force produced in unilateral muscle contractions (Howard and Enoka 1991). It is possible to reduce the strain of the eccentric phase by using both legs during flexion. With each leg, do 30 repetitions while trying to initiate the movement as explosively as possible—that is, apply your maximal force as quickly as possible. Do not extend your leg fully, because the maximal knee angle should be approximately the same as the maximal knee angle when you're cycling. You should set the resistance so that during the first 20 repetitions your effort results in a high-speed movement but during the last 10 reps the velocity of the movement decreases. If you can finish the series without a decrease in velocity, you need to increase the resistance.

The squat is a technical exercise that requires practice. Once you master the exercise, you should do 30 repetitions in a similar manner to those you've done with the leg press. Again the eccentric phase is done at a slow, constant pace, and when a knee angle of 90 degrees is reached try to extend as explosively as possible. The maximal knee angle should be approximately the same as the maximal knee angle when you're cycling.

For the step-up, you need a small bench. The bench should be high enough so that when you're stepping up on it, the knee angle is slightly larger than 90 degrees. Place the bench in front of you, and step on it with one leg. Extend this leg, until the approximate maximal knee angle when you're cycling is reached (i.e., do not extend completely). The force should be delivered by the stepping leg, not the pushing leg! Again, perform 30 repetitions, followed by a change of leg. You can use dumbbells or a barbell to increase the resistance, with the barbell having the advantage of enhancing balance.

The leg pull is the opposite of the previously mentioned exercises. It doesn't train the extension of the knee and hip, but the flexion. As mentioned earlier, the highest force is applied on the pedal when the crank is at an angle of 90 degrees, pointing straight forward. But, when you're accelerating or sprinting (out of the saddle), the pedal also is pulled upward and forward. This movement can be trained by the leg pull. To do this, you need a fitness machine with a pulley located close to the ground. Stand with your back toward the pulley, preferably on a small bench. Lean forward, place your hands on a supporting bench or bar, and pull the pulley up and forward by moving your knee toward your chest. It is important that the movement is diagonal, that is, up as well as forward. If you find that the movement is only forward, then the pulley is too high. If this is the case, then use a (higher) bench on which to stand. Again, try to do the eccentric movement (in this case, extension) at a constant and easy pace, whereas you should initiate the concentric phase as explosively as possible. You can do 15 or 20 repetitions for each leg.

Strength Training Program

To build these exercises into a strength training program, start with a warm-up of at least 10 minutes of cycling. Once you're fully warmed up, start with two sets of squats. The recovery (around three minutes) should be complete so that your performance does not decrease during consecutive sets. If performance does decrease during the second set, lengthen the recovery period. After the squats, do two sets (on each leg) of leg pulls. There is no need for recovery here because the legs are alternated. Next, you can do two sets (each leg two sets) of single-legged leg presses. After the first set of both legs, have a recovery period of three minutes, in which you can do some easy cycling. We advise you to include some exercises that enhance the back and abdominal muscles, partially for the purpose of active rest and partially for core stability while on the bike. After that, you finish your strength training with the step-up—again two sets for each leg with no rest in between.

The last phase of the training is a cycle workout of at least 15 minutes at an endurance pace (around 75 percent of maximal heart rate) and a high cadence (greater than 110 rpm). This training demands a high level of concentration. Always stay focused on initiating every movement explosively. Try to put as much effort into the exercises as possible. The quality of the training effect depends on this!

Strength Training on the Bicycle

Strength training on your bicycle actually should be approached the same way as strength training in the gym, only you are now using your bike as the strength training instrument. The optimum way to do strength training on the bicycle is as follows: Find a steep hill, preferably one that abruptly goes from flat to steeply uphill. Cycle on a big gear at a cadence of about 60 rpm to the foot of the hill. Once you are on the hill, simply try to maintain your cadence, and as soon as your cadence drops below 50 rpm, stop. Your choice of gear is important—you need to be able to do 30 to 40 pedal revolutions (i.e., 20 left and 20 right) before you drop below 50 rpm. If you drop below 50 rpm before 30 pedal revolutions, then you have to choose a lighter gear. You can do this exercise both out of the saddle as well as sitting down, but it is best to do most of the series sitting down because the neuromuscular pathways generated then will be applicable to general riding as well as climbing and sprinting.

You can incorporate these on-the-bike strength training exercises into the first half of a normal road endurance session. To do this, perform, for example, four sets of 30 to 40 pedal revolutions, followed by a complete recovery of three minutes or longer. Each set should feel equally difficult—if you feel like it's becoming harder, you need a longer recovery period. During the recovery period the intensity is very low, equal to recovery training. After completing the four sets, you can continue your endurance training or do another four series after 20 minutes at endurance pace.

Flexibility

Flexibility generally is associated with both a healthy and physically fit muscle. The main argument for increasing an athlete's flexibility is that a more flexible or compliant muscle-tendon unit is less likely to be injured (Magnusson et al. 1998; Shrier 1999). It is commonly believed that stretching and warming up can improve flexibility. Therefore, stretching and warming-up exercises are a widespread practice among athletes (Magnusson et al. 1998). Whether these exercises can indeed improve flexibility is clarified in the following sections.

Flexibility and Stretching

The ability of stretching exercises to increase muscle flexibility recently has received criticism. To understand this, the difference between range of motion (ROM) and muscle stiffness needs to be understood. This is best explained by the so-called straight leg raise: A subject is lying on his or her back while a physician or special instrument raises the straight leg. When the leg is raised higher and higher, a point will arise when the subject can no longer tolerate the stretch. This angle is called the ROM of the concerned joint (the hip in this case). The force the physician has to apply to raise the leg to a certain angle is the resistance to stretch, and the graph of the resistance to stretch and the angle represents the muscle stiffness. Figure 18.3 shows an example of a stretching-tension curve.

Thus, the curve of a less-stiff muscle is located to the right of a more-stiff muscle with less force required to achieve a specific angle. The general belief is that stretching will cause the muscle stiffness curve to move to the right. This means that at a given

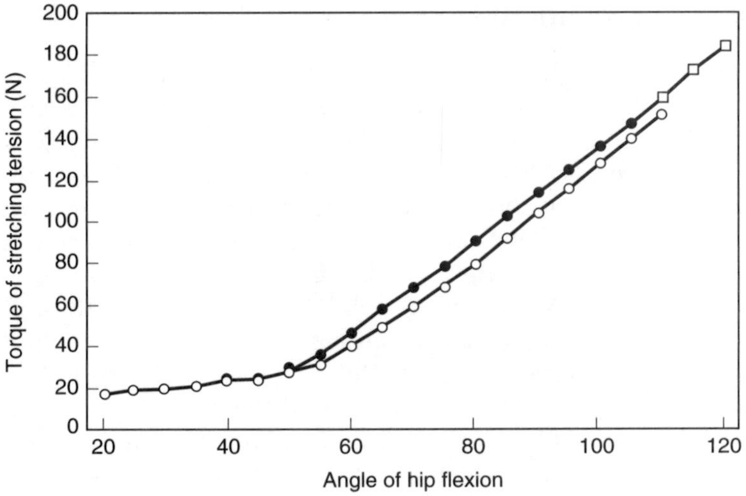

Figure 18.3 A theoretical example of a hip-angle stretching tension curve, before (filled circles) and after (open circles) a 10-minute warm-up. After the warm-up, the torque at a given hip angle is lower: The flexibility has increased. The empty squares indicate the effect of a stretching maneuver. The torque at a given angle remains the same, that is, the flexibility doesn't change. The range of motion increases but the corresponding torque increases concomitantly.

angle the resistance of the muscle to the stretch will diminish: This more compliant muscle-tendon unit is less likely to be injured.

However, recent research has revealed that although structural stretching does increase the ROM of a joint, it does not alter the muscle stiffness curve (Halbertsma et al. 1999; Magnusson et al. 1998, 2000). The increase in ROM is instead caused by an increase of the so-called stretch tolerance of the subject. Figure 18.3 illustrates the effect of a stretching maneuver. The filled circles represent the hip-angle stretching-tension curve before stretching. The empty squares indicate the effect after stretching. The torque at a given angle is the same—only the subject can tolerate a higher stretching tension! You only can attain an acute effect on muscle stiffness by doing several long-standing stretching maneuvers (three times 90 seconds), but this effect disappears within 30 minutes (Magnusson et al. 2000). How far this can be applied in practice is questionable. There is, in any case, no structural effect of stretching on muscle stiffness.

Flexibility and Warming Up

In contrast to stretching exercises, warming up can alter the muscle stiffness. A 15-minute cycling warm-up has been shown to lower muscle stiffness (Wiemann and Hahn 1997). This may be caused by an improved liquid content of the muscle that reduces the muscle stiffness due to an enlargement of the viscous compliance (imagine adding water to a paste to make it more "runny"). It should be noted, however, that this effect is dependent on the exercise that is performed during the warm-up. Running for example, does not lower muscle stiffness (Magnusson et al. 2000). Figure 18.3 shows the effect of a 10-minute warming up (cycling) on muscle stiffness.

How to Improve Flexibility

© Human Kinetics

Maintaining an aerodynamic position for long periods of time requires greater flexibility than the normal position because of the high range of hip motion.

Flexibility to reduce the risk of injuries cannot be improved by stretching. In contrast, a 10-minute warm-up is sufficient to increase flexibility. For most cyclists this is enough as far as flexibility is concerned. However, sometimes more flexibility is needed: when cycling in an aerodynamic position, for instance, in a flat time trial. A good aerodynamic position requires a high range of motion of the hip joint. It is an often-heard complaint that cyclists are unable to maintain the aerodynamic position during a long time trial because of soreness and pain that is not related to the actual pedaling action. Of course, this is a great drawback because a change in position could ruin the outcome of a time trial. In this case, a 10-minute warm-up will not be sufficient. It is highly advisable that the cyclist regularly train in the aerodynamic position, not only during the days preceding a time trial, but once a week throughout the racing season. It is important that this training be a mixture of intensive and endurance work so that performance in the aerodynamic position will be improved without any extra training time.

Summary

Strength training should be an important part of any cyclist's schedule. The exercises you do should use similar movements to those used in cycling (squats, leg presses, step-ups, leg pulls, strength training on the bicycle). You should perform two sets of 30 repetitions. Set the resistance so that only the last 10 repetitions of each set are slower because of fatigue. Initiate each movement as explosively as possible. Do not exceed the range of motion of the knee that you normally use on the bike. Use the bike to warm up and down before and after the strength session. You need to include strength sessions in every week of training and you can use them in the "off" week to promote recovery.

Increased flexibility reduces the risk of injuries. Warming up increases flexibility; stretching does not. Flexibility for maintaining a good aerodynamic position is achieved by regular training in this position.

chapter 19

Injury Prevention and Management

Grahame Brown

Most cyclists will have experienced an injury of one form or another in their lives. These injuries can vary in their cause, severity, duration, and location, and many have the potential to reduce both performance and enjoyment of cycling. As a result, having some knowledge of the causes and treatments of many common cycling injuries certainly has the potential to increase your cycling performance.

Injuries to cyclists can be classified into two groups: *extrinsic* (trauma) or *intrinsic* (overuse). The majority of trauma injuries arise from crashes and result in only minor injuries such as abrasions, contusions, and lacerations. These superficial wounds accounted for 60 to 70 percent of injuries in most studies of off-road riders (Kronisch and Rubin 1994). (Most trauma data are available for off-road riding; there is unlikely to be any major difference in the site of injury for road and track riding.) Fractures and concussions are less common (20 to 30 percent and 3 to 12 percent of injuries, respectively). The majority of fractures and dislocations occur to the arms and most commonly involve the fingers, metacarpals, wrists, and radial heads. The shoulder is particularly vulnerable to injury with clavicle (collarbone) fractures and acromioclavicular separations commonly occurring when a cyclist lands on his shoulder. In a study of 84 off-road riders presenting to an accident-and-emergency department during the course of one year, 36 percent had injuries to the upper limb; six patients had life-threatening injuries (Jeys et al. 2001). Prevention of these acute types of traumatic injuries is limited to good cycle maintenance, bike-handling skills, helmet use, obeying the rules of racing, and common sense.

This chapter deals mainly with the recognition, management, and, where possible, strategies for prevention of overuse injuries that cyclists encounter. Highlighted in the text are factors unique to cycling that are important to consider when managing these injuries. If you wish to study details of clinical injury treatment and rehabilitation, we recommend the many excellent texts on sports injuries and trauma. There is a remarkable lack of data on the prevalence and incidence of overuse injury syndromes in cyclists. Studies of road cyclists indicate that overuse syndromes of the knee are common: In one series of 354 cyclists from recreational to elite level, 60 to 70 percent reported having had knee problems at one time or another (Holmes et al. 1994). A study of 265 off-road riders reported that 30 percent recently had experienced knee pain associated with riding, 37 percent reported low back pain while riding, and 19 percent reported wrist and hand numbness (Kronisch and Rubin 1994).

Injury Prevention

We can view prevention in three ways: preventing a problem from occurring at all (primary), preventing the problem from becoming a chronic one once it has occurred (secondary), and preventing the problem from recurring once it has been resolved (tertiary). Primary prevention is, of course, the preferred option. Unfortunately, however, there is little research to help us identify the measures that could accomplish this type of prevention. Even the issue of whether helmets reduce the incidence of head injury is controversial: Methodological flaws are inherent in the research studies and there are equally valid arguments for and against (Cook and Sheikh 2000; Jacobsen 2001). Countries and regions that have introduced compulsory helmet use in cyclists have recorded a decrease in head injuries in cyclists, but at the expense of greatly decreased cycle use—arguably to the detriment of the environment and public health. Regular utility cycling offers one of the most effective and sustainable forms of physical activity for promoting and maintaining good health and preventing obesity from developing.

Risk Factors for Injury

Compared with most other sports, cycling has a very low rate of injury per hour spent doing the activity. This is partly related to the fact that the activity is not weight bearing. In running, for instance, the body has to carry its own weight and absorb the shocks with every step whereas in cycling the weight is mainly supported by the saddle. However, there are a number of risk factors unique to cycling.

First of all, there is the repetitive action of the cycling movement: Cyclists average 5,000 revolutions per hour, and although a slight biomechanical flaw through one revolution is insignificant, once multiplied by 5,000, the smallest point of weakness or malalignment (e.g., wrong position of cleats) can lead to dysfunction, impaired performance, and pain.

Another risk factor is the limited range of movement of the hips, knee, and ankle. The hip never moves into extension and uses less than 50 percent of its available range during a full pedal revolution.

Finally, a prolonged static fixed posture with the spine in flexion also increases the risk of injuries.

Overuse Injuries

Overuse injuries are chronic overload, microtraumatic problems. They occur over a period of time when the forces applied to a structure (e.g., a knee tendon) are increased faster than the structure can adapt. Table 19.1 lists the usual causes. Overuse injuries can affect tendons, muscles, fasciae, bursas, and nerves.

TABLE 19.1 Main Causes of Overuse Injuries in Cyclists

Cause	Example
Training error	The most common causes are too many miles too soon, excessive hill or speed work, and too-big gears.
Position on the bicycle	Knee pain is the most common problem in cycling; this may be due to the saddle too high or too low, too far forward or backward, cranks too long, too close together or too far apart, pedal axle bent, cleat position, or degree of cleat float.
Body type	Examples of these types of problems include leg-length discrepancies of as little as five millimeters; a wide pelvis placing the knees further apart and stressing the outside of the knee; excessive foot pronation (flat foot) associated with medial (inside) knee pain; an internal twist of the shinbone (tibia) twisting the foot inward; and unbalanced muscles leading to maltracking of the kneecap.
Off-the-bike activities	For example, running, especially on hills; deep squats and leg presses in weight training. These activities can precipitate knee and shin pain.

Tendons

The early stage of overuse injuries to tendons is known as *tendinitis* and much of the pain is caused by inflammation. In addition, a crackling (*crepitus*) due to fluid accumulation can sometimes be detected. In the more long-standing (chronic) tendon problems, degenerative changes occur within the tendon and begin to contribute more and more to the pain. At this point the condition is known as *tendinosis*. Because of the complex tissue breakdown, these conditions are properly called *tendinopathies* (Khan et al. 2000a,b). Tendinopathies are known to be associated with the use of performance-enhancing drugs, especially anabolic steroids. The explanation is that muscle strength develops more rapidly and the tendon has insufficient time to adapt to the increased loading.

Muscles and Fasciae

Muscle and fascia problems are usually conditions of neuromuscular dysfunction. The effect on the muscle is for it to shorten and to fatigue easily, and become painful, sometimes with cramps and sensory disturbances. The affected muscles have painful trigger points that can refer pain some distance away (Travell and Simons 1992). Causes of muscle and fascia problems in cyclists include muscle overloads due to biomechanical imbalances and they often affect the spine. If the spine is affected, it is commonly referred to as *spinal segmental dysfunction*. A reduction in the range of motion of a spine segment occurs usually slowly and is clinically silent until it potentially presents itself with a whole variety of symptoms. An example of a problem frequently seen in cyclists is spinal segmental dysfunction at the lumbar 2/3 or 3/4 vertebral segments. This can give backache alone or present itself with thigh pain referring to the knee, or both. In this case, physical signs of tendinopathy or other knee disorders are absent and both the thigh muscle and the spine need treatment. Myofascial pain is a common cause of chronic (i.e., long-standing) pain.

Bursas

Bursas are structures that form between surfaces that move over each other—either tendon, bone, or muscle. They are the body's "grease ports" and act to reduce friction between the moving parts. Bursitis is irritation or inflammation of the bursa, and inflamed bursas adjacent to tendons will present with symptoms and signs similar to tendinitis, for example, iliotibial band syndrome and Achilles tendinitis.

Nerves

Compression neuropathy is a disorder of peripheral nerve function. In cyclists the most common problems of this nature are with the ulnar nerve in the hand because of pressure on the inside of the wrist (from the handlebar) and in men the pressure on the pudendal nerve from the saddle resulting in a numb penis.

Treatment of Overuse Injuries

The treatment of overuse injuries—which includes secondary and tertiary prevention—follows four fundamental principles of management: adjusting the activity, reducing inflammation, strengthening the musculo-tendon tissue involved, and correcting any biomechanical stresses or training errors.

Adjusting the activity is usually preferable to complete rest. The typical healing time for skin is 1 to 2 weeks; for muscle injury, 2 to 3 weeks; for ligaments, 4 to 6 weeks; and for tendon and bone, 6 to 12 weeks. However, chronic tendon problems may require much longer.

The advice is to reduce any inflammation and swelling by using ice applications for up to 20 minutes periodically; oral nonsteroidal anti-inflammatory drugs (NSAIDs, e.g., acetaminophen, ibuprofen); physical therapy modalities such as ultrasound; and cortisone injections. Ice is especially useful in the first 48 hours of symptom development.

Stretch and strengthen the musculo-tendon tissue involved and its antagonist muscle with progressive resistance exercise; correct any muscle imbalances through training; restore balance and coordination reflexes; and gradually rehabilitate to sport-specific activities. We strongly recommend that a state-registered physiotherapist trained in sports rehabilitation supervise this process.

Correcting biomechanical stresses or training errors includes checking and modifying bicycle fit and cleat placement as necessary. The bicycle fit must be specific to the individual rider; for example, when the problem is the distance between the feet, you may make correction by adjusting the cleat position, using a different length bottom bracket axle, using cranks with a different offset, or using a shim between the crank and pedal.

Knee Pain

Knee pain is the most common reason that a cyclist seeks medical attention. Major problems such as fractures, dislocations, and ligament ruptures will only occur in cyclists after major trauma, and these need prompt medical attention and are not discussed here. Overuse type injuries, however, are much more common in cyclists. We examine the most common sites of knee pain, with suggestions of the possible causes and treatments.

Anterior Knee Pain

Anterior (front) knee pain is the most common cyclist complaint and is also known as the *patello-femoral pain syndrome*. It is thought to be due to maltracking of the kneecap (patellar) in the thigh-bone (femur) groove (femoral condyles). In advanced cases there is damage to the cartilage surface of the patellar *(chondromalacia patellae)*, which only can be diagnosed by knee surgery. See figure 19.1.

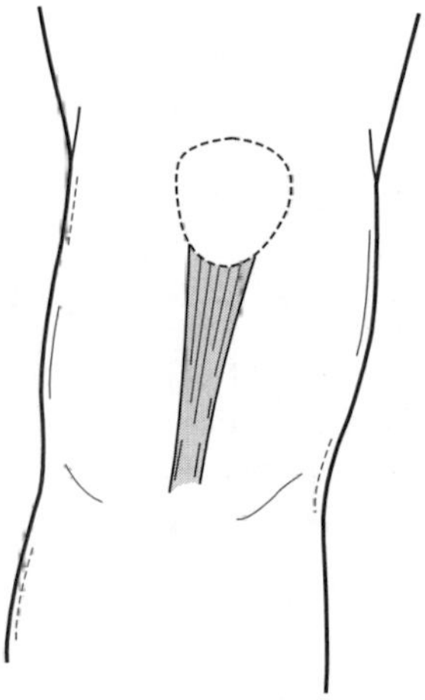

Figure 19.1 Tenderness at the front of the knee is usually due to patellar tendinopathy. Pain from patellofemoral pain syndrom is typically felt around the whole of the front of the knee.

Causes

Anterior knee pain may develop when excessive forces push the patellar on the surface of the femur creating stress and shearing forces. Causes include the saddle being too low, excessive hill climbing, and too-high gears. Muscle imbalance creating a relative weakness of the inside thigh muscle (*vastus medialis*) is also known to be a cause. A wide pelvis and "knock knees"(*valgus knee*) will make this condition more likely. If the problem is only on one side, then it is important to check for any leg-length discrepancy. Off the bicycle, weight training and running are implicated. The disorder often occurs in early season when training loads are increased rapidly.

Management

On the bicycle. A relatively high-in-the-saddle position helps. With the shoe in the cleat and at bottom dead center, the knee should not be flexed more than 25 degrees. Additional things that may help include gearing down to spin more (at least 85 revolutions per minute), avoiding hills until the condition settles, avoiding long cranks, checking your cleat position, using cleats with more float, using a spacer between the pedal and crank, and using cranks with more offset or a wider bottom bracket axle. Also, if you detect a leg-length discrepancy, set the saddle height to the longer leg and place a shim under the cleat of the shorter leg.

Another potential treatment is to encourage quadriceps strengthening with terminal (i.e., end of the range of motion) extension and isometric exercises. Limit the knee to 20 degrees of flexion; for example, place a pillow under the knee and with a weight on the ankle straighten the knee and hold for a few seconds, and lower slowly. Working at about 20 repetitions maximum, do three to five sets daily and increase the resistance gradually, stretching the quadriceps, hamstring, and iliotibial band in between sets. In addition, avoid running, deep squats, and weight training activities as these put a high load on the patella-femoral joint. Progress to weight-bearing knee dips (closed chain exercises) to improve strength and function of the stabilizing muscles.

Medical. Icing for periods up to 20 minutes, followed by stretching the quadriceps, may help. Look for and release painful muscle trigger points in the quadriceps, especially the vastus medialis (acupuncture needles are extremely effective). Look for and treat lumbar dysfunction at lumbar 3/4. The cause of the problem may lie at the hip, and so ruling this out will help identify the problem. In addition, a short course of NSAIDs may be helpful. Taping and knee supports may help some people but are not very useful for cyclists. Cortisone injections are not used in this disorder and surgery is an absolute last resort.

Patellar Tendinopathy

Patellar tendinopathy also manifests itself through anterior knee pain. Tenderness, often exquisite, is well localized at the lower end of the patella. Early recognition of this condition is vital for effective treatment because a prolonged period of recovery may be required if the disorder becomes chronic.

Causes

The onset often is related to a sudden increase in mileage or hill work. Excess angular pulling on the tendon while you are pedaling may be responsible, as may all of the causes for anterior knee pain previously discussed.

Management

The same recommendations apply as for anterior knee pain. If active foot pronation is present during pedaling, then you can use orthotics (inserts inside the shoe). Orthoses for cyclists are rigid compared with the semi-rigid type prescribed for runners. There is evidence to support the use of eccentric loading of the quadriceps during strength training in which the emphasis is on lowering the ankle slowly under load, following the same repetition maximum and progression principles as are normally employed in weight training. The rehabilitation of chronic tendinopathies (more than three months' duration) may require up to 12 months and riders need to be aware that recovery can be slow. The use of cortisone injection in this condition is the subject of much debate. It can be used effectively as a one-off treatment placed beneath the lower end of the patella in the fat pad to assist pain control. This then may allow rehabilitation to progress. However, injections are not a substitute for the hard work required in rehabilitation.

Medial Knee Pain

Medial (inside) knee pain often is caused by anserine tendinitis and/or bursitis (see figure 19.2). The anserine tendon attaches to the upper medial aspect of the shinbone (tibia). It is the junction of three muscles: the semitendinosus, gracilis, and sartorius. In the case of anserine tendinitis and/or bursitis, the tendon and/or its bursa is inflamed. At worst, medial joint line pain may be early degenerative osteoarthritis in the knee.

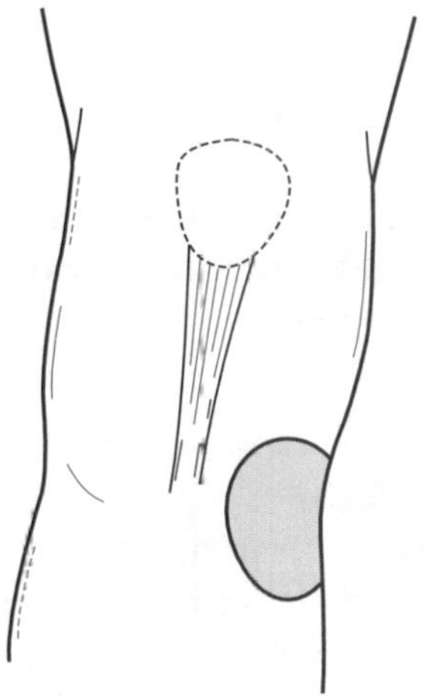

Figure 19.2 Medial knee tenderness is often due to anserine tendinitis but can also result from internal knee injuries.

Causes

Increased pressure on the inside of the knee may cause this kind of pain. This may be because the cyclist has the toes pointed outward or the knees too far apart when cycling. Exiting clipless pedals that have too much tension stresses the medial knee. Those with a turned-in shin tibia, foot pronation, and "bowlegs" (*varus knee*) are more vulnerable.

Management

On the bicycle. If you are using fixed cleats, adjusting them so that the toes point more inward will help to reduce the load on the tendon. If you are using floating cleats, limit the float to 5 degrees and reduce the tension of the pedal release mechanism. Consider reducing the bottom bracket axle width or using cranks with less offset. Check the saddle position in the same way that you would for anterior knee pain. Reduce mileage and spin a lower gear. Sometimes a wedge between the cleat and shoe, which acts to tip the foot outward, is necessary if there is significant biomechanical misalignment. Avoid running and skiing, but unfortunately there are no specific remedial strengthening exercises.

Medical. The common treatments of icing and stretching should be followed and it is possible that NSAIDs may help. Cortisone injections are useful in this area. Orthotics also may help. Look for and treat muscle trigger points in adductor muscles and any lumbar segmental dysfunction at lumbar 2/3. Internal knee disorders—for example, meniscus cartilage tears and cysts—can cause medial knee pain. These conditions may require surgery.

Lateral Knee Pain

Lateral (outside) knee pain usually is characterized by the abrupt onset of well-localized pain with pedaling. It's also often known as *iliotibial band syndrome* and is due to irritation from repetitive friction of the iliotibial band over a protuberance of the thighbone known as the *lateral femoral condyle*; this causes inflammation of the tendon and/or bursa. Contact of the iliotibial band with the condyle is most pronounced at approximately 30 degrees of knee flexion. See figure 19.3.

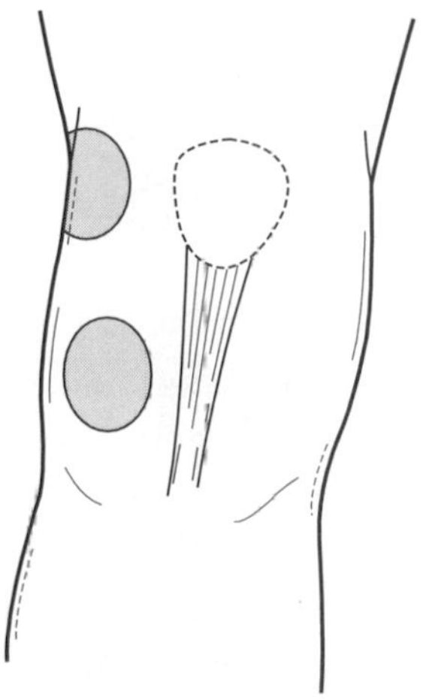

Figure 19.3 Lateral knee tenderness is often due to iliotibial band tendinitis.

Causes

Too much pull on the outside of the knee may cause this kind of pain. Badly adjusted cleats with the toe pointing in is the most common cause in cyclists. Using a narrow bottom bracket, a low saddle, high gearing, and excessive hill work also may precipitate the condition. This is also an area commonly affected in a fall: Trauma may be a cause. A wide pelvis, bowlegs, and tight glutei muscles may be contributing factors.

Management

Adjust cleats to allow the toe out a little. Switch from fixed to float cleats, but limit to 5 degrees. Increase the distance between the feet by using a wider bottom bracket axle; offset the cranks or use a spacer between the crank and the pedal. Elevating the saddle height and checking for leg-length discrepancy also may be important. Avoid hills and reduce mileage. Stretch the iliotibial band and avoid running and weight training. NSAIDs may help in the early stages. Cortisone injections are useful in this condition. Surgery is used as a last resort.

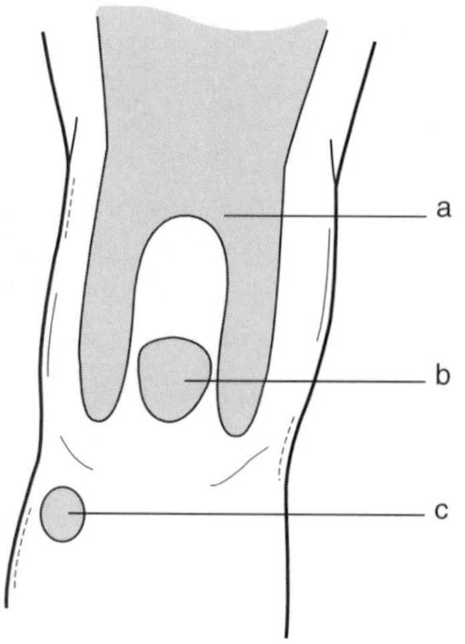

Figure 19.4 Back of the knee pain: (a) pain here is usually due to hamstring problems; (b) tenderness here is usually caused by a Baker's cyst; (c) pain here results from biceps femoris tendinitis or bursitis.

Posterior Knee Pain

The most likely disorder causing pain at the back of the knee (posterior knee pain) is biceps tendinitis. This is inflammation of the tendon of biceps femoris, one of the hamstring muscles where it attaches to the head of the shinbone (fibular). See figure 19.4. Low back disorders commonly refer pain into the back of the thigh and therefore also must be considered.

Causes

High saddle position, sitting too far back, poor hamstring flexibility, dropping the heel when pedaling, and too-high gears may be factors. Excessive cleat float is sometimes related because the hamstrings help to stabilize the leg while the cyclist is pedaling. Muscle imbalance between quadriceps and hamstrings also has been implicated.

Management

On the bicycle. Sit further forward and lower the saddle. Avoid dropping the heel when pushing big gears or during hill work. Limit cleat float to 5 degrees. Stretch the hamstring regularly on the bicycle. Check for leg-length discrepancy. Stretching the hamstrings and lumbar spine is most important.

Medical. Once again, ice and stretch. Strengthen the hamstrings. Look for and release trigger points in biceps femoris (acupuncture needling). Neither orthotics nor cortisone injections are useful in this disorder. Look for and treat lumbar spine segmental dysfunction at the lumbar-sacral joint and sciatic nerve root irritation. Sacroiliac joint dysfunction can project pain to the posterior thigh.

Swollen Knee

In cyclists a swollen knee is most likely to occur after trauma and consequently must be medically examined. A swelling on the posterior of the knee, known as a *Baker's cyst*, can occur spontaneously. It may give pain, or it may rupture to give a swelling in the calf. It is a benign condition that occasionally will need surgery. In some circumstances, an inflamed patellofemoral joint will give rise to a small effusion (water on the knee). It is important that swelling of the knee in the absence of any trauma be examined by a medical practitioner.

Neck and Back Pain

Neck pain and back pain are complaints that affect every human at some time in their life. The vast majority of episodes of back and neck ache will settle down spontaneously without treatment within a few weeks. However, a significant number of cyclists of all abilities will experience chronic or recurring problems and consequently will need to learn how to manage the problem.

Causes of Neck Pain

Most neck pain in cyclists is caused by the extra tension developed in the muscles of the shoulder, neck, and upper spine to keep the neck in the hyperextended position for long periods of time. The jarring caused by rough road surfaces or riding off road aggravates the problem. Myofascial (muscle) pain is by far the most common clinical disorder accounting for this type of neck pain. Trigger points become active as a result of prolonged isometric contraction of muscles in sometimes awkward postures aggravated by fatigue, cold, or mental tension. Another, but uncommon, problem is the thoracic outlet syndrome in which the nerve-vessel bundle is under tension (but not trapped) near the base of the neck. The cause is usually poor posture, but in rare cases it can be due to an extra rib on the lowest cervical spine. The condition gives postural-related aching into the arm with a variety of disordered sensations including coldness in the affected arm. These symptoms may only manifest themselves during or after cycling. Aching felt between the shoulder blades usually is due to stiffness and dysfunction in the upper thoracic spine.

Management of Neck Pain

On the bicycle. Consider raising the bars, changing the bars to those with a shallow drop, or getting a shorter bar extension to release some pressure of the musculature. A frame with a shorter top tube may be necessary. While riding, consciously relax the upper body. Look around and take opportunities to stretch the neck. Ride with the hands on the hoods and tops and not on the drops all the time. Bar extensions (tri-bars or aerobars) can be relaxing for the upper body (but are not allowed in road races). These bars, however, also can increase tension in the muscles of the shoulder and neck if the bars are too low or too close together.

Off the bicycle. To decrease the tension of the muscles of the neck and shoulders, it is important to learn and regularly practice spinal stretching exercises that include not just the neck but also the thoracic and lumbar spine. Neck pain usually is associated with mid and upper thoracic spine stiffness and dysfunction. The whole spinal posture needs to be improved. Ice and stretch painful muscles or release with manual treatment or acupuncture needles. Thoracic and cervical spine mobilization and manipulation can be helpful. Special medical investigations are rarely helpful. For some people, learning relaxation exercises can be helpful. Yoga, the Alexander Technique, and Pilates (Robinson and Thomson 1999) are examples of the type of exercise programs that are useful for these problems. Nerve root irritation due to disc disruption in the cervical spine usually will manifest itself with pain spreading down the arm to the hand. "Pins and needles" sensations and numbness also may be present. Surgery is considered urgently for the (uncommon) nerve root pain with associated muscle weakness, or for nerve root pain that has persisted beyond the time that natural recovery normally would occur (approximately six to eight weeks).

Causes of Low Back Pain

The problem for the human spine is that it is constantly being compressed while upright and sitting, with maximum pressure at the base of the spine. Most of what we do in modern lifestyles involves sitting and slumping forward, which of course includes cycling. The vital stabilizing muscles for the lumbar spine, notably *transverses abdominus* and *multifidus*, are allowed to weaken in these postures. This, combined with inadequate spinal movement, causes the spinal joints (segments) to slowly stiffen and the discs to dry out. The joint then stops working effectively and the spine develops stiff links just like a bicycle chain might do. The most common stiff links (segmental dysfunction) are the lowest lumbar (lumbar 5/sacral 1) and upper lumbar vertebra (thoracic 12/lumbar 1/lumbar 2).

Sooner or later, these stiff links will cause trouble by aching or, in serious cases, cause incapacitating pain. The end result of disc dehydration is a failure of the disc which may protrude or rupture and irritate the adjacent sciatic nerve (*sciatica*). Despite what many people have believed for more than 60 years, most low back pain, however, is not the direct result of disc rupture. Given correct and active management, low back pain need not affect performance on the bicycle nor the enjoyment of cycling or any other activity, except in rare cases.

Management of Low Back Pain

On the bicycle. Adjust saddle height (usually down slightly), reach, and bar height. Adjusting the saddle so that it is nose down slightly, approximately 10 degrees from the horizontal, can be helpful. Check carefully for leg-length discrepancy and adjust the fit to the longer leg. Stretch and change position on the bicycle frequently. Use lower gears, especially on long climbs.

Off the bicycle. Learn and practice spinal stretching exercises. This practice needs to continue—even after the pain has subsided. Practice exercises indefinitely to activate, coordinate, and strengthen the core stability muscles such as the deeper abdominals and the *multifidus* and *erector spinae complex*. Pilates is an excellent example of this type of exercise program, which many elite and professional sports and performing arts people are practicing to manage and prevent lumbar spine disorders. We recommend that you study some of the excellent texts on these types of exercises (Robinson and Thomson 1999; Summers and Davies 2000; Norris 2001).

Mellion (1994) gives a good account of a stabilization exercise program designed for cyclists.

Medical. NSAIDs and muscle relaxants are helpful during an acute episode to control pain and allow early active management. Prescribed bed rest of more than a day or two must never be allowed for these conditions. Manual treatment, especially manipulations, is effective, especially in the first few months. Physiotherapists and doctors trained in manipulative techniques, osteopaths, and chiropractors are able to provide these treatments. Trigger-point acupuncture can be effective at relieving stubborn muscle tension that is preventing recovery (provided by some doctors, physiotherapists, and osteopaths who are trained in the techniques). Injections have an important role to play in some cases in which pain is persistent and preventing active treatment—for example, epidural steroid for sciatica, trigger-point injections, and sclerosant ligament injections (prolotherapy)—but these treatments must only be provided by doctors trained in the techniques.

Special investigations are sometimes needed but will rarely indicate the source of the pain if the symptoms are felt only in the back. Surgery is an absolute last resort for back pain in the absence of serious disease. However, surgery plays an important role in cases of sciatica that are not responding to nonsurgical management beyond the time anticipated for natural recovery of this condition (approximately 12 weeks). It is important to note that the onset of back pain with difficulty holding urine or controlling bowel function—or with numbness in the crotch, or with pain to the foot and inability to walk on heels or toes—is a potential surgical emergency and must be examined urgently by a specialist spinal surgeon.

Hand Problems

Handlebar problems affecting the hand can be divided simply into compression syndromes and overuse conditions. Of the compression syndromes, ulnar nerve lesions are by far the most reported, with median nerve lesions a distant second. The most common overuse problem is de Quervain's tenosynovitis, which affects the thumb tendons (see figure 19.5).

Ulnar nerve compression producing sensory symptoms or muscular weakness has been recognized in cyclists for more than 100 years with the first case reported in a cyclist in 1896. Over the years it has come to be known as *cyclist's palsy*.

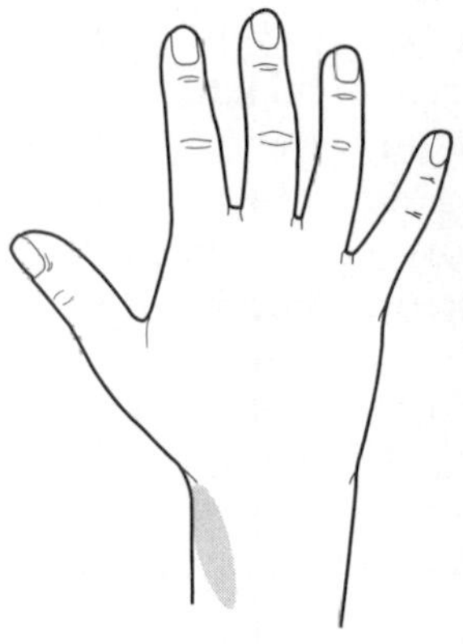

Figure 19.5 Pain, tenderness, or swelling here results from de Quervain's tenosynovitis.

Causes

The common cause is a compression of the fibers of the ulnar nerve as it enters the hand through the canal of Guyon, which is situated on the medial (little finger) side of the wrist. Vibration increases the risk of the condition developing. Median nerve compression arises in the carpal tunnel of the wrist. See figure 19.6.

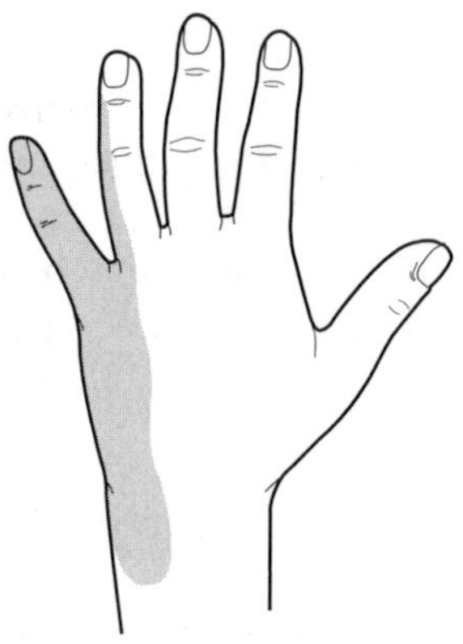

Figure 19.6 Pain and sensory disturbance here is often due to irritation or compression of the ulnar nerve.

Management

On the bicycle. Take pressure off the medial side of the hand: Adjusting bar position or height, changing the bars to a different style, and using thicker bar tape or padded mitts all can help. Suspension forks may help road riders but might be essential for off-road riders. Also helpful is using a bicycle with a shorter top tube, moving the saddle back a little, and making sure it is not tilted nose down. Tenosynovitis of the thumb tendons is most likely due to gear shifting, especially some designed for off-road bicycles. Changing the shifter solves the problem. The main treatment is to take the pressure off the hand.

Medical. NSAIDs or cortisone injection may be necessary in resistant cases. Again, surgery is a last resort.

Saddle Sores and Crotch Problems

Of all the nontraumatic pain syndromes experienced by cyclists, symptoms related to the saddle are the most common. Probably every cyclist will have encountered these problems at some time. This is not surprising given that a cyclist's entire weight is supported by a small area of the saddle. Seat-related problems frequently cause discomfort and may cause the rider to limit cycling activities.

Much of the medical literature on saddle and crotch problems is anecdotal. Most recommendations regarding prevention and treatment are empirical with little attempt at any scientific research to support them.

Most research conducted to determine the frequency of crotch/seat symptoms has involved riders participating in ultra long-distance rides. On the 1976 4,500-mile ride across America, Kulund and Brubaker (1978) interviewed a sample of 89 (out of 1,200) cyclists who completed the ride. Mild saddle soreness was experienced by all riders. Marked saddle soreness was reported by 9 percent and crotch numbness by 7 percent. In a 500-mile weeklong tour, Weiss (1985) reported that 33 percent of riders experienced crotch/groin pain and 64 percent experienced pain in their buttocks. One-third of those with crotch/groin pain and 52 percent of those with buttock pain had problems severe enough to require a change in riding style or a temporary cessation of riding. These were amateur riders and therefore their preparation for the event would likely vary.

When discussing bicycle-related seat problems, it is helpful to classify the problems into three broad categories:

- Skin problems
- Neuropathic problems
- Urological problems

Skin Problems

Infection, pressure, and friction are the three main causes of skin saddle sores. These develop as a result of bacteria entering blocked sweat or sebaceous glands, or diminished circulation to the skin impairing nutrition and repair processes, or both. Riders who always have sores on one side may have a shorter leg on that side, which should be corrected if identified. From the clinical point of view, sores can be classified in five ways: chafing, furuncles and folliculitis, skin ulceration, ischial tuberosity pain, and subcutaneous nodules.

- **Chafing** Chafing appears on the medial side of the thigh. It is due to friction caused by the inner thigh rubbing against the saddle during the up-and-down motion. Typically, chafing takes the form of mild inflammation in the skin, including redness, dryness, and mild pain. With severe and prolonged irritation, the rider may develop extreme inflammation, maceration, ulceration, or secondary infection. Low-dose topical steroid creams may be necessary to treat established cases.
- **Furuncles and folliculitis** Furuncles and folliculitis are blocked or infected glands and lumps caused by chronic sweating, irritation, chafing, and pressure. When severe they may cause the rider to withdraw from an event, as has happened to many world-class riders. The bacteria *staph-aureus* and *strep-pyogenes* would commonly inhabit these lesions. In established cases, antibiotic therapy or surgical incision is necessary.
- **Skin ulceration** Skin ulceration is when the top layer of skin, the epidermis, has completely broken down, and this can cause severe pain. The mechanism of injury is a combination of shearing forces and pressure necrosis. Cessation of riding and antibiotic therapy may be necessary treatment. Keeping the skin clean and dry helps prevent chafing, furuncles, and ulceration. Cycling shorts should have an absorbent lining and not have a seam or stitching on the medial thigh. They should be washed daily. Petroleum jelly has been favored for many years as a prevention when rubbed onto the skin before riding.
- **Ischial tuberosity pain** Typically, the rider experiences pain, redness, and tenderness of the skin overlying the ischial tuberosity bones. Cyclists who are not used to riding regularly usually experience the problem worse. The design of the saddle may be a contributing factor. Well-padded cycling shorts are the most effective prevention strategy.
- **Subcutaneous nodules** Unlike saddle sores that are more common in novice and amateur cyclists, subcutaneous nodules are unique to elite and professional male cyclists. They typically form on each side of the midline, just posterior to the scrotum. Because of their appearance and position, cyclists sometimes refer to them as a "third testis." The lesions are pseudocysts that contain little cellular material. They develop in areas of aseptic pressure necrosis in the superficial peroneal fascia and are due to chronic microtrauma of the perineum related to pressure from the saddle. Surgery may be required to treat them if they become a serious handicap.

Neuropathic Problems

Neuropathic processes are responsible for two cycle seat-related problems. The first is pressure neuropathy, the symptoms of which are tingling and numbness of the pudendal nerve. The second is erectile dysfunction (impotence).

• **Pudendal neuropathy** Neuropathic symptoms in the distribution of the pudendal and genitofemoral nerves are common in male cyclists. Fifty percent of riders in long-distance and multiple-day events may experience these symptoms at some time, and up to 7 percent of riders may have to change their riding style because of them. Cold weather may increase the likelihood of developing symptoms. The most common symptoms reported include anesthesia of the scrotum and numbness of the penile shaft.

The cause is compression of the dorsal branch of the pudendal, or the genital branch of the genitofemoral nerve, between the symphasis pubis and the saddle, resulting in temporary ischaemic insult to the nerve.

Treatment involves changing the saddle position, usually to slightly nose down, or changing the saddle. Well-padded shorts are also important.

• **Impotence** The medical literature contains case reports of impotence (presumably) due to cycling. Definitive information concerning its prevalence, prevention, and treatment is unavailable. Desai and Gingell (1989) reported on a 27-year-old whose impotence persisted for eight months. Electrophysiological studies showed that the individual had reversible ischaemic neuropathy of the dorsal (sensory) and cavernous (vasomotor) nerves of the penis induced by compression between the saddle and the pubic bone.

Urological Problems

There have been several reports of urological problems in cyclists. These include testicular torsion, urethritis, scrotal swellings, prostatitis, and hematuria.

• **Testicular torsion** As with impotence, the literature contains only case reports of testicular torsion. In these reports the riders were using long, narrow saddles, and in some cases the pain of the torsion developed while they were riding. Speculation as to the cause includes mechanical trauma of the testicle between the saddle and the thigh and exposure to cold, which induces a contraction of the cremaster muscle.

• **Urethritis** Again, there are only case reports of urethritis. The symptoms are frequent and painful micturition in the absence of bacteria in the urine. The cause is probably direct pressure of the urethra on the saddle.

• **Scrotal swellings** A study by Frauscher and colleagues (2000) produced some startling findings; they used ultrasound scanning of the scrotum of 45 mountain-bicycle riders, riding off-road at least two hours a day, six days a week. Ninety-six percent had detectable pathological abnormalities in the scrotum, compared with 16 percent of a control group. The disorders were all benign and were calcified masses resulting from hematomas (serious bruises) and inflammations inside the scrotum but not in the substance of the testis. Microtrauma was the presumed cause.

• **Prostatitis** Prostatitis presents with symptoms of urinary outflow obstruction, such as frequency, dribbling, nocturia (urinating in the night), and incomplete bladder emptying. The prostate is not enlarged on examination, as would be the case in "traditional" prostatitis. Pressure on the perineum is the cause. Anecdotal evidence indicates that this is particularly common in riders participating in six-day races. These are winter indoor track races on steeply banked tracks where riders circle the track for many hours at speed; the pressure on the perineum due to the high "g-force" on the banking is thought to be the cause.

- **Hematuria** The hematuria that can occur in road runners does not happen in cyclists. Cyclists report instances of blood in the urine after riding. This is thought to be due to urethritis. Vaginal infections, hemorrhoids ("piles"), and other common complaints can, of course, occur in cyclists, but cycling is unlikely to be the cause.

External Iliac Stenosis

There are increasing numbers of case reports in the literature of external iliac stenosis affecting elite and professional riders (Taylor et al. 1997). This provokes a unilateral exercise-induced leg pain that cannot be accounted for by the more common conditions. One explanation for the condition is that it arises after trauma when a rider lands heavily on the buttock. It can be difficult to diagnose and requires special investigations. Surgery is curative.

First Aid and Basic Life Support Skills

Any coach, manager, or other person regularly attending riders at races is strongly advised to learn and maintain first aid and basic life support skills. This is now a stipulation for coaches affiliated to the governing bodies of most sports. Team managers and race organizers must be aware that when there is a risk of injury occurring, they must carry out a suitable risk assessment. This probably will include having first-aid providers and ensuring that their qualifications are up to date. Case law now dictates this practice to be prudent.

Summary

Compared with most other sports, cycling has a very low rate of injury per hour spent doing the activity. Falls from the bicycle result, in the majority of cases, in cuts, abrasions, or fractures of upper limb bones. Overuse injuries in cyclists must be diagnosed accurately and managed with the knowledge of the rider's style and bicycle fit in addition to clinical treatment protocols. Treatment of overuse injuries can be very specific to the type of injury.

chapter 20

Immune System Response

Michael Gleeson

The immune system is involved in tissue repair after injury and in the protection of the body against potentially damaging (pathogenic) microorganisms such as bacteria, viruses, and fungi. We can divide the immune system into two broad functions (see tables 20.1, 20.2, and 20.3): innate immunity (natural or nonspecific) and adaptive immunity (acquired or specific), which work together synergistically. An infectious agent (pathogen) attempting to enter the body immediately activates the innate system. This first line of defense contains three general mechanisms with the common goal of restricting microorganism entry into the body. Those mechanisms are physical or structural barriers (skin, epithelial linings, mucosal secretions); chemical barriers (pH of bodily fluids and soluble factors); and phagocytic cells (e.g., neutrophils, monocytes, or macrophages) and other nonspecific killer cells (e.g., natural killer lymphocytes).

The failure of the innate system and the resulting infection activate the adaptive system, which aids recovery from infection. The adaptive immune system responds with a proliferation of cells that either attack the invader directly or produce specific defensive proteins, antibodies (also known as *immunoglobulins*), which help to counter the pathogen in a variety of ways. This is helped greatly by receptors on the cell surface of T and B lymphocytes that recognize the antigen (foreign substance—usually the proteins located on the surface of the bacteria or virus), engendering specificity and "memory" that enable the immune system to mount an augmented response

TABLE 20.1 Main Elements of Immune System

Innate components	Adaptive components
Cellular	
Natural killer cells (CD16+, CD56+)	T-cells (CD3+, CD4+, CD8+)
Phagocytes (neutrophils, eosinophils, basophils, monocytes, macrophages)	B-cells (CD19+, CD20+, CD22+)
Soluble	
Acute-phase proteins	Immunoglobulins: IgA, IgD, IgE, IgG, IgM
Complement	
Lysozymes	
Cytokines (interleukins, interferons, colony-stimulating factor, tumor necrosis factors)	

CD = Clusters of differentiation or cluster designators.
Reprinted from Maughan.

when the host is reinfected by the same pathogen. The components of the immune system include both cellular and soluble elements. Soluble factors of the immune system act to activate leukocytes (white blood cells), work as neutralizers (killers) of foreign agents, and act as regulators of the immune system. Such factors include the cytokines, polypeptide messenger substances that stimulate the growth, differentiation, and functional development of specific clones of lymphocytes that are able to recognize and respond to the antigen. Other soluble factors are complement, lysozyme, and the specific antibodies secreted from B lymphocytes.

In some circumstances, the immune system can become functionally depressed (known as *immunosuppression*), and this may result in an increased susceptibility to infection. Although there is little information regarding cyclists, other athletes engaged in heavy training programs, particularly those involved in endurance events, appear to be more susceptible than normal to infection (Gleeson and Bishop 1999). For example, sore throats and flu-like symptoms are more common in endurance athletes than in the general population.

There is some convincing evidence that this increased susceptibility to upper respiratory tract infection (URTI) arises because of a depression of immune system function, and there is plenty of evidence that immunosuppression is present after prolonged cycling (Nieman et al. 1994; Robson et al. 1999). Chronic immunosuppression resulting from heavy training is undoubtedly multifactorial in origin (see figure 20.1). Training and competitive surroundings may increase the cyclist's exposure to pathogens and provide optimal conditions for pathogen transmission.

Prolonged strenuous cycling is associated with numerous hormonal and biochemical changes, many of which potentially can have detrimental effects on immune function. Furthermore, other stressors, including extreme environmental conditions, psychological stress, and improper nutrition (Gleeson and Bishop 1999), can compound the negative influence of heavy exertion on immune function. An accumulation of stress

TABLE 20.2 Characteristics and Functions of Different Leukocytes

Leukocytes (or white blood cells) have diverse functions despite their common origin: the hemipoietic stem cell of the bone marrow.

Leukocyte	Main characteristics
Granulocytes	60-70% of leukocytes
Neutrophils	>90% of granulocytes Phagocytose (ingest and digest) foreign substances Have a receptor for antibody; phagocytose antigen-antibody complexes Display little or no capacity to recharge their killing mechanisms once activated
Eosinophils	2-5% of granulocytes Phagocytose parasites Triggered by IgG to release toxic lysosomal products
Basophils	0-2% of granulocytes Produce chemotactic factors Tissue equivalent = the mast cell, which releases histamine and an eosinophil chemotactic factor
Monocytes/macrophages	10-15% of leukocytes Enter tissues (e.g., liver, spleen) and differentiate into the mature form: the macrophage Phagocytose foreign material enabling antigen presentation to lymphocytes Secrete immunomodulatory cytokines Coordinate adaptive (acquired) immune response Retain their capacity to divide after leaving the bone marrow
Lymphocytes	20-25% of leukocytes Activate other lymphocyte subsets Produce cytokines Recognize antigens Produce antibodies Exhibit memory Exhibit cytotoxicity

Reprinted from Maughan.

may lead to chronic immunosuppression and, hence, increased susceptibility to URTI in a competitive cyclist. For the competitive cyclist it is important to realize that even medically harmless infections may significantly affect exercise performance. Hence, cyclists, their coaches, and their medical support personnel are seeking guidelines on the ways to reduce the risk of illness, which when it occurs is likely to compromise training and competition performance. The strategies that need to be considered include the management of the training load, the ways to minimize the impact of environmental

TABLE 20.3 Characteristics and Functions of Different Lymphocyte Subsets

Lymphocyte subset	Main function and characteristic
T-cells (CD3+)	60-75% of lymphocytes
TH (CD4+)	60-70% of T-cells "Helper" cells Recognize antigen to coordinate the acquired response Secrete cytokines that stimulate T- and B-cell proliferation and differentiation
TC/TS (CD8+)	30-40% of T cells TS ("suppressor") involved in the regulation of B- and T-cell proliferation by suppressing certain functions TS may be important in "switching off" the immune response TC (cytotoxic) kill a variety of targets, including some tumor cells
B cells (CD19+ CD20+, CD22+)	5-15% of lymphocytes Produce and secrete antibody specific to the antigen Exhibit memory
Natural killer cells (CD16+, CD56+)	10-20% of lymphocytes Large, granular lymphocytes Express spontaneous cytolytic activity against a variety of virus-infected cells and tumor cells Activity is not dependent on previous exposure to antigen Do not express the CD3 cell-surface antigen Triggered by IgG Control foreign materials until the antigen-specific immune system responds

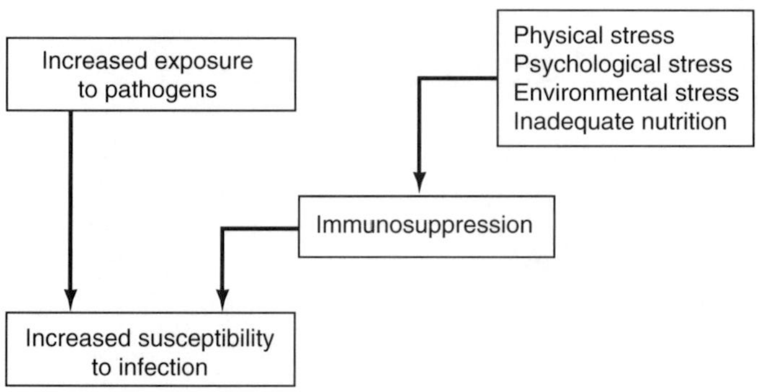

Figure 20.1 Factors contributing to infection incidence in cyclists.

stress, the development of psychological coping skills, the provision of adequate nutrition, and appropriate sport science and medical support.

Exercise and Training

Both acute bouts of exercise and long-term exercise training have effects on immune function. In general, exercise of low-moderate intensity lasting less than one hour has minimal effects on immune function (if anything, the effects actually may be beneficial compared to a sedentary lifestyle). In contrast, both acute prolonged strenuous bouts of exercise and periods of heavy training have immunosuppressive effects. We describe these here.

Acute Effects of Exercise

During cycling the athlete's exposure to airborne pathogens is increased because of the higher rate and depth of breathing. An increase in gut permeability also may allow increased entry of gut bacterial toxins into the circulation, particularly during prolonged exercise in the heat. An acute bout of exercise is accompanied by responses that are remarkably similar in many respects to those induced by infection. For instance, there is a substantial increase in the number of circulating leukocytes, the magnitude of which is related to both the intensity and duration of exercise. There are also increases in the plasma concentrations of various substances that are known to influence immune function.

Hormonal changes also occur in response to cycling, including rises in the plasma concentration of several hormones (e.g., adrenaline, cortisol, growth hormone, and prolactin) that are known to have immunomodulatory effects. In some cases, the activity of a particular component of the immune system can be temporarily increased, but its capacity to respond to pathogens is decreased. For example, phagocytic neutrophils—whose function is to ingest and destroy bacteria and damaged tissue—appear to be temporarily activated by an acute bout of exercise, but they show a diminished responsiveness to stimulation by bacteria and reduced killing capacity after exercise lasting for many hours (Robson et al. 1999).

After a single bout of prolonged cycling, the plasma concentration of glutamine has been reported to fall by about 20 percent and may remain depressed for some time (Robson et al. 1999). Glutamine is required for the optimal function of various leukocytes, and falls in the plasma concentration of glutamine have been implicated in causing the immunosuppression associated with prolonged exercise and heavy training. Furthermore, after prolonged strenuous exercise there is a marked reduction in the production of cytokines, which function as the activating chemical messengers of the immune system. Because cytokines are important regulators of several immune functions, this may be one of the main mechanisms by which acute exercise stress temporarily suppresses immune function.

Thus, these changes during early recovery from exercise would appear to weaken the potential immune response to pathogens and have been suggested to provide an "open window" for infection, representing the most vulnerable time period for athletes in terms of their susceptibility to coming down with an infection. Certainly, at this time, there does seem to be a temporary reduction in several aspects of immune function, and athletes should be encouraged to adopt practices such as the following that minimize the risk of contracting an infection:

- Avoid contact with people with symptoms of infection and those just "coming down with a cold."
- Minimize contact with children of school age and avoid large crowds.
- Wash hands regularly, particularly after touching surfaces that are frequently handled by the public such as doorknobs, handrails, and telephone receivers.
- Avoid hand-to-eye and hand-to-mouth contact to prevent transferring microbes to sensitive mucosal tissues.
- Maintain good oral hygiene.
- Avoid getting a dry mouth, both during competition and at rest; this can be done by drinking at regular intervals and maintaining hydration status.
- Never share drink bottles or cutlery.
- Use properly treated water for consumption and swimming.
- Avoid shared saunas, showers, and Jacuzzis.
- Be aware that you may be particularly vulnerable after training or competition.
- Remember that good personal hygiene and thoughtfulness are the best defenses against respiratory infection.

For exercise lasting less than one hour, exercise intensity is the most critical factor in determining the degree of exercise-induced immunosuppression. When subjects cycled for a fixed duration of 45 minutes, immune system changes were greater at an intensity of 80 percent $\dot{V}O_2max$ compared with 50 percent $\dot{V}O_2max$ (Nieman et al. 1994). However, very prolonged exercise sessions seem to be the most potent depressor of immune function for cyclists. A recent study (Robson et al. 1999) showed that exercising for three hours at 55 percent $\dot{V}O_2max$ produced greater changes in circulating leukocyte numbers, plasma glutamine concentration, plasma cortisol concentration, and neutrophil function than exercising to fatigue in less than an hour at 80 percent $\dot{V}O_2max$ (see figure 20.2). Furthermore, 24 hours after exercise, neutrophil function had recovered to pre-exercise levels after the shorter, higher-intensity bout, but not after the longer bout.

Chronic Effects of Exercise

Chronic exercise also both enhances and suppresses different aspects of immune function; however, the balance suggests there is an overall decrease in immune system function, particularly when training loads are high. Circulating numbers of leukocytes are generally 20 to 40 percent lower in well-trained cyclists at rest compared with sedentary people (see table 20.4). A low blood-leukocyte count may arise from the hemodilution (expansion of the plasma volume) associated with training, or it may represent altered leukocyte movement or distribution including a diminished release from the bone marrow. Indeed, the large release of neutrophils that accompanies a bout of prolonged exercise could, over periods of months or years of heavy training, deplete the bone marrow reserve of these important cells. Certainly, the blood

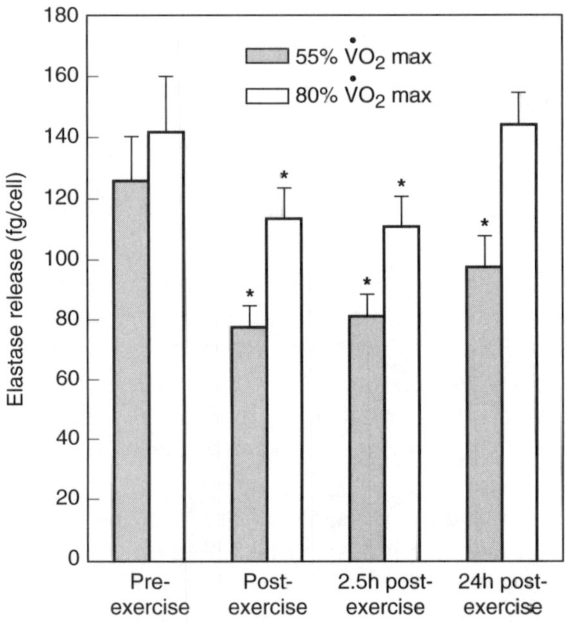

Figure 20.2 Changes in the in vitro LPS-stimulated neutrophil degranulation response (elastase release per cell) after three hours of cycling at 55 percent $\dot{V}O_2$max and after cycling to fatigue at 80 percent $\dot{V}O_2$max (mean exercise duration: 38 minutes) in 10 well-trained cyclists. Data are means and SEM. * $P < 0.05$ compared with pre-exercise. Main effect of treatment $P < 0.05$: 55 percent $\dot{V}O_2$max versus 80 percent $\dot{V}O_2$max.

Reprinted from Robson et al. 1999.

TABLE 20.4 **Numbers of Circulating Leukocytes in Well-Trained, Middle-Aged Male Cyclists and Sedentary Males**

Blood cell count ($x \times 10^9$/l)	Sedentary (n = 8)	Trained cyclists (n = 8)
Leukocytes	6.62 (0.87)	4.36 (1.15)*
Neutrophils	3.83 (0.86)	2.46 (0.87)*
Lymphocytes	2.02 (0.27)	1.36 (0.20)*

Note: * $P < 0.01$ trained versus sedentary subjects. Subjects were matched for age and body mass.
Reprinted from Blannin, Chatwin, Cave, and Gleeson 1996.

population of these cells seems to be less mature in elite cyclists than in sedentary individuals and the effectiveness of blood neutrophils has been reported to be markedly lower in well-trained cyclists compared with age- and weight-matched sedentary controls (Blannin et al. 1996). Levels of secretory immunoglobulins such as immunoglobulin A (IgA) in saliva are lower in well-trained subjects, and the ability of lymphocytes to respond to foreign material is impaired (Gleeson and Bishop 1999). Furthermore, even in well-trained individuals, sudden increases in the training load are accompanied by signs of more severe immunosuppression.

Management of the Training Load

Given that many reports have linked heavy training with impaired immune function, any training program should be appropriate to the individual cyclist's physical condition. The cyclist's responses to the training stress, including performance, mood, fatigue, muscle soreness, and perception of effort, should be monitored closely (see also chapter 2). Training strategies for minimizing the risk of immunosuppression need to consider the management of training volume and intensity, training variety to overcome monotony and strain, a periodized and graded approach to increasing training loads, spreading the training over the course of the day, and providing adequate rest and recovery periods. This implies the use of some means to measure the training load in terms of intensity as well as duration or distance covered. The availability of heart rate monitors makes this possible; it should be a relatively simple task for the coach to record in a daily log the time spent by the cyclist in specified heart rate zones (see chapter 1).

Many factors can increase the stress hormone response to exercise, and hence the degree and duration of exercise-induced immunosuppression. Some of these factors are fasting, low glycogen stores, dehydration, hypoglycemia, heat or cold, altitude (hypoxia), psychological stress, sleep deprivation, or jet lag and travel across time zones. It is important that the impact of these factors be kept to a minimum. Training has to be hard if cyclists are going to compete successfully, but the training should be managed such that hard training days are followed by much lighter training days to allow recovery. On days where the training load is high, training should be split into two or more sessions. Prolonged immunosuppression is more likely to develop if all the exercise on a hard training day is done in a single session. When a cyclist plans an increase in the weekly training load, it is probably advisable that he limit the increase to no more than 10 percent above the previous week's load.

Environmental Stress

Cyclists often are required to compete in environmental extremes that can range from hot and dry to cold and wet. For many top cyclists, periods of training at altitude may be required. Exercising in these environmental extremes is associated with an increased stress hormone response and perception of effort. The general consensus is that exhaustive physical activity and severe environmental stress generally have at least an additive effect on stress responses, including immunosuppression. For cold and altitude, there is relatively little information available on their impact on immune function and susceptibility to infection in humans. In contrast, there has been substantial interest on the effects of heat exposure on immune function for many years.

It is well known that the growth and replication rates of certain bacteria, viruses, and fungi are impaired by high temperatures. Of course, our own body reacts to infections by increasing body core temperature. This is achieved by increasing the production of certain cytokines that raise the temperature set-point in the brain by a few degrees, initiating what we call a fever. This increase in body temperature appears to enhance the individual's resistance to infection. Body temperature increases a few degrees during strenuous exercise, and Brenner et al. (1996) evaluated the combined

Exercising in extreme environmental conditions has an effect on the body's immune system response. High temperatures result in higher stress hormone responses that can suppress immune function.

effects of exercising in a hot environment on immune function. However, the general conclusion from these studies has been that exercise performed in the heat (approximately 30 degrees Celsius) causes greater immunosuppression than when the same exercise is performed in temperate conditions (approximately 18 degrees Celsius). This is not unexpected given that adrenaline and cortisol responses are greater when an athlete is exercising in hot compared with cool conditions.

Severe cold stress generally reduces immune responses, apparently with some increase in the risk of infection. Inhaling cold, dry air may impair mucosal defenses by drying out the mucous membranes and reducing the secretion of IgA. These effects will slow the clearance of invading microorganisms. In addition, increased ventilation during exercise and the onset of mouth breathing (bypassing the warming, humidifying, and filtering action of the nasal passages) exposes the tracheal mucosa to colder and drier air and increased quantities of airborne pathogens and air pollutants.

On ascent to altitude there is a generalized stress response with increased plasma cortisol levels. There is some evidence of impaired immune function at high altitude and this may contribute to an increased incidence of illness. However, in human studies it is difficult to ascribe this directly to the effects of hypoxia (low oxygen availability), since other factors including acute mountain sickness, air travel, cold climate, and unfamiliar and cramped living conditions may have contributed to the reported observations of increased incidence of illness.

Limiting initial exposure when training or competing in adverse environmental conditions (heat, humidity, cold, altitude, or polluted air), and acclimating or acclimatizing where appropriate will reduce the effects of environmental stress on the stress hormone response to exercise and, hence, would be expected to be beneficial for maintaining immune function. However, research-based evidence currently is lacking in this area, and we should remember that a period of acclimatization may be associated with a temporary deterioration of physical condition as normal training schedules are likely to be disrupted.

With frequent international competition now being the norm for elite cyclists, competitors are faced with regular air travel, with the associated problems of sleeplessness, jet lag, and limited food choices. Traveling for many hours in a confined space with a few hundred other individuals (a certain proportion of which are bound to have infections) and rebreathing the same dry air in hypobaric conditions is highly conducive to the spread of infection. Recommended precautions include the wearing of a filter mask, maintaining hydration, avoiding alcohol, and trying to get some sleep.

Psychological Stress

As discussed in chapter 2, overtraining may result in mood disturbances, with low scores on psychological questionnaires for vigor and rising scores for negative moods such as depression, tension, anger, fatigue, and confusion. These disturbances may increase when training progresses. The mood changes may reflect underlying biochemical or immunological changes that are communicated to the brain via hormones and cytokines. Stress is a nonspecific response to any demand—physical, physiological, or psychological—and it is likely that in many situations these effects are additive and extreme stress can result in breakdown.

Although acute psychological stressors can evoke a temporary increase in some aspects of immune function, various forms of chronic psychological stress very clearly have the opposite effect. Traumatic life events such as bereavement, divorce, or prolonged care of an aged or disabled relative are perceived as stressful and generally result in depressed immune function and increased incidence of infection. For example, subjects who were assigned to a high-stress group on the basis of their responses to a life-events history questionnaire (the Daily Hassles Scale) and the General Health Questionnaire showed more frequent URTIs than a low-stress group (2.5 versus 1.75 episodes over a six-month prospective study) (Graham et al. 1986). Furthermore, in the high-stress group, the duration of each episode was longer than for the low-stress group (28 versus 17 symptom-days).

However, human reactions to psychological stress depend not only on the perceived severity and duration of the stress, but also on the coping skills and strategy adopted to deal with the stress. In a study in which participants were inoculated with nasal drops containing one of five respiratory viruses, rates of URTIs and clinical colds were related to inter-individual differences in psychological stress as assessed from a life-events scale, coping ability, and current attitudes. In other words, as the measured stress levels increased, so did the amount of infections, showing how important stress levels are.

Elite cyclists have to train hard to compete successfully, so some degree of physical training stress is unavoidable. In addition, there is the added psychological stress of competition, team and commercial pressures, international travel, selection pressures, funding pressures, and other major life events. The aim of the coach, working with a sport psychologist, should be to anticipate these additional stressors and, through appropriate evaluation and planning, eliminate or minimize as far as possible their impact upon the athlete. Appropriate strategies may include realistic evaluation and internal attribution, thorough performance preparation, imagery use, distraction control, the development of the athlete's own coping skills, and access to social support.

Competing in international high-profile events, especially in a foreign country, imposes many psychological stresses on elite cyclists. Allowing contact with family members and friends (if only by phone calls) and providing familiar music, videos, and food may help to distract from and minimize the impact of stress. Relaxation therapies including sauna, massage, Jacuzzi, and gentle swimming also may help reduce the level of overall stress, though facilities should be checked out in advance to evaluate any possible inadequacies in hygiene. Realistically evaluating the chances of success may help the athlete to deal with the depression of inevitable competitive failures. Psychological stress in competition may be heightened by disputes with officials, opposition, or even members of the same team. Anxiety and anger may be provoked by the presence of a hostile crowd or the unsporting or aggressive tactics of an opponent. Discussion and counseling may be able to help control these problems, put them into perspective, and better prepare the athlete for similar future experiences.

During training, athletes may undertake psychological profiling to some effect using self-scored profiles of mood states (POMS); some scientists believe that the best gauge of excessive training stress is how the athlete feels. The abbreviated POMS scale is just one example of a simple questionnaire that can be used on a daily basis to assess the impact of training on the cyclist's psyche; another one is the Daily Analysis of Life Demands in Athletes questionnaire described in chapter 2. When rising scores for negative moods such as depression, tension, anger, and confusion occur, this may an indication that it is time to reduce the training load and/or allow some days of recovery. We also recommend gauging sensations of muscle soreness and fatigue during and after each training session; this may be an effective way of monitoring the recovery from deliberate overreaching and identifying early development of overtraining syndrome.

Nutrition

Nutrient availability has the potential to affect almost all aspects of the immune system because many nutrients are involved in energy metabolism and protein synthesis. Most immune responses involve cell replication and the production of proteins with specific functions (e.g., antibodies). Inadequate dietary intakes of carbohydrate, protein, vitamins, and some trace elements are detrimental to immune function.

The extent of the impact of a certain nutrient deficiency on the functioning of the immune system depends upon the duration of the deficiency as well as the cyclist's nutritional status as a whole. The severity of the deficiency is a further influencing factor, though even a mild deficiency of a single nutrient can result in an altered immune response. Excessive amounts of specific nutrients (e.g., omega-3 polyunsaturated fatty acids, vitamin E, iron, and zinc) also have the potential to cause detrimental effects to immune function. Hence, cyclists must consider all aspects of their diet in order to optimize immune function.

Carbohydrate

The diet in the days preceding an acute bout of exercise has been shown to have the potential to alter the immune system's response. Exercise after several days on a low-carbohydrate diet is associated with a larger stress hormone response and greater suppression of the immune system at two hours' postexercise compared with the same exercise performed after two to three days on a high-carbohydrate diet (Gleeson and Bishop 2000). There are also benefits to consuming carbohydrate during prolonged exercise. Consuming a carbohydrate-based energy drink has been shown to reduce many of the negative immune changes that occur during and after an acute exercise bout (Gleeson and Bishop 2000).

Consuming carbohydrate in beverages during prolonged cycling also may have an additional benefit in helping to prevent dehydration and maintain saliva flow rate during exercise. Saliva contains several proteins with antimicrobial properties, including IgA, lysozyme, and α-amylase. During periods of heavy training, endurance athletes have been found to have lower levels of IgA in their saliva, and there is some evidence that this may contribute to their increased incidence of URTIs (Gleeson and Bishop 1999). Saliva secretion is under nervous control, and as dehydration develops during prolonged exercise, nervous stimulation causes constriction of the blood vessels to the salivary glands and results in a reduction in saliva secretion. Regular fluid intake during exercise is reported to prevent this effect, and a recent study has confirmed that regular consumption of carbohydrate-containing drinks during prolonged cycling helps to maintain saliva flow rate compared with a restricted fluid-intake regimen (Bishop et al. 2000). Taken together, these results suggest that carbohydrate intake before and during prolonged cycling may help to offset some of the detrimental effects of exercise on immune function.

Protein

The daily protein requirement is approximately doubled in endurance athletes compared with the sedentary population. An intake of less than 1.6 grams protein per kilogram body mass per day (i.e., 112 grams of protein per day for a 70-kilogram cyclist) is likely to be associated with a negative nitrogen balance in cyclists who are training hard, particularly endurance riders. However, there is no need for commercial supplements. Provided that cyclists consume a well-balanced diet that meets their requirement for energy, the increased requirement for protein will be met.

In view of this, those individuals at most risk from protein deficiency would be cyclists undertaking a program of food restriction in order to lose weight, vegetarians, and cyclists consuming unbalanced diets (e.g., with an excessive amount of carbohydrate at the expense of protein). It is well accepted that a prolonged inadequate intake of protein impairs host immunity, resulting in increased incidence of infections. Essentially all aspects of immune function have been shown to be affected by protein-energy malnutrition in humans, depending on the severity of the protein deficiency relative to energy intake. Although it is unlikely that athletes would ever reach a state of such extreme malnutrition unless dieting very severely, it is worth noting that some impairment of immune function is observed even in moderate protein deficiency. For guidelines on how to achieve sufficient protein intake, see chapter 16.

Trace Elements and Vitamins

Cross-sectional studies of athletes and nonathletes indicate that long-term physical training may lead to a chronic depression of plasma iron and zinc (Gleeson 2000). Zinc deficiency results in decreased macrophage ingestion and killing capacity, whereas iron is needed by natural killer cells, neutrophils, and lymphocytes for optimal function. Studies concerning the relationship among immune function, exercise, and zinc status in athletes are lacking. However, the overadministration of zinc (150 milligrams twice a day) to 11 healthy males for a six-week period was associated with *reduced* immune function. Hence, we do not recommend megadoses of zinc. Athletes should be encouraged to emphasize zinc-rich foods in the diet (e.g., poultry, meat, fish, and dairy products). Vegetarians have been recommended to take a 10- to 20-milligram supplement of zinc daily (the recommended daily allowance is 10 milligrams for males and 12 milligrams for females), but in view of the potential immune depression that can be caused by overdosing on zinc, supplements at the lower end of this range may be more suitable for vegetarian athletes.

The immune system itself appears to be particularly sensitive to the availability of iron. Iron deficiency has neither completely harmful nor enhancing effects on immune function (Gleeson 2000). On the one hand, free iron is necessary for bacterial growth: Removal of iron from the body fluids reduces bacterial multiplication. Iron deficiency actually may protect an individual from infection, whereas supplementation may predispose the individual to infectious disease, particularly because iron catalyzes the production of hydroxyl free radicals and a high intake of iron can impair gastrointestinal zinc absorption. On the other hand, iron deficiency depresses various aspects of immune function (Gleeson 2000).

The general consensus is that all athletes should be aware of heme-iron-rich foods such as lean red meat, poultry, and fish and include them in the daily diet. Endurance cyclists are recommended to have daily iron intakes of 17.5 milligrams per day for men and around 23 milligrams per day for normally menstruating women. You can meet these requirements through the diet. Vegetarian athletes should ensure that plant food choices are iron dense—for example, green leafy vegetables. Breakfast cereals usually are fortified with iron and provide a good source of this mineral. We do not advise megadoses of iron, and athletes should not take routine oral iron supplements without medical advice. The body responds to acute infection by reducing free iron availability, probably to help restrict bacterial growth. Thus, it would appear counterproductive and inadvisable to take iron supplements during periods of infection. Other trace elements including copper, selenium, and manganese also are required for normal immune function. However, deficiency of these minerals is extremely rare in humans.

There are no indications in the literature to suggest that vitamin intake among athletes in general is insufficient. Cyclists tend to ingest above-average quantities of these micronutrients and it may be that, as with dietary protein requirements, any increase in need is countered by increased dietary intake. However, vitamins with antioxidant properties (including vitamins C, E, and beta-carotene) may be required in increased quantities in athletes to balance the increased free-radical production that is associated with exercise (Gleeson and Bishop 2000). The oxygen free-radical formation that accompanies the dramatic increase in oxidative metabolism during exercise could potentially inhibit immune responses.

Some recent studies suggest that the incidence of URTIs in endurance athletes may be reduced by vitamin C supplementation of around 1,000 milligrams per day. For example, Peters et al. (1993) determined that a daily supplementation of 600 milligrams of vitamin C reduced the incidence of URTI symptoms (68 percent compared with 33 percent in age- and sex-matched control runners) after participation in a 90-kilometer ultramarathon. In a follow-up study, the same group found that increasing the vitamin C intake to 1,000 milligrams per day was even more effective than an intake of approximately 500 milligrams per day in reducing URTI incidence in the weeks following an ultramarathon race.

Other vitamins essential for immunocompetence include vitamins A, E, and B_6. Decreases in the ability of lymphocytes to proliferate and produce antibodies result from vitamin A and E deficiency, and although isolated vitamin B_6 deficiency is rare in humans, profound effects on immune function are seen in animals. Vitamin B_{12} and folic acid are essential for the normal production of red and white blood cells in the bone marrow.

It has been shown that the poor nutritional status of some athletes may predispose them to immunosuppression. A well-balanced diet and appropriate supplementation of minerals and vitamins appear to reduce this risk. Nevertheless, we should understand the dangers of oversupplementation; many micronutrients given in quantities beyond a certain threshold will, in fact, reduce immune responses.

Dietary Immunostimulants

Several herbal preparations are reputed to have immunostimulatory effects, and consumption of products containing *echinacea purpurea* is widespread among athletes. However, few controlled studies have examined the effects of dietary immunostimulants on exercise-induced changes in immune function. In one recent double-blinded and placebo-controlled study, Berg et al. (1998) investigated the effect of a daily oral pretreatment with pressed juice of echinacea purpurea for 28 days in 42 triathletes before and after a sprint triathlon. A subgroup of athletes also was treated with magnesium as a reference for supplementation with a micronutrient important for optimal muscular function. The most important finding was that during the 28-day pretreatment period, none of the athletes in the echinacea group fell ill, compared with three subjects in the magnesium group and four subjects in the placebo group who became ill.

The mechanism of action of echinacea treatment may be mediated by an increased cytokine-synthesizing capacity of human monocytes. The increase in immune cell chemical messengers allows the immune system to communicate the presence of infection to all responding "units" more effectively. Therefore, treating acute URTI episodes with echinacea purpurea could be effective in reducing the severity of symptoms and the number of training days lost because of infections. Nevertheless, the hypothesis that echinacea counteracts the immunosuppressive effects of exhaustive exercise has to be verified and confirmed in larger, controlled trials.

Glutamine is the most abundant free amino acid in human muscle and plasma and is used at very high rates by leukocytes. Prolonged cycling is associated with a fall in the plasma concentration of glutamine, and it has been hypothesized that such a decrease could impair immune function. Heavy training schedules are associated with a chronic reduction in plasma glutamine levels, and this could be partly responsible for the immunosuppression apparent in many endurance athletes.

It has been suggested that providing oral glutamine supplements may be beneficial by preventing the impairment of immune function after prolonged exercise. However, several recent studies that have investigated the effect of glutamine supplementation during exercise on various indexes of immune function have not found any beneficial effect. A glutamine solution (0.1 gram per kilogram body mass) given at 0, 30, 60, and 90 minutes after a marathon race prevented the fall in the plasma glutamine concentration but did not prevent the fall in lymphocyte function (Rohde et al. 1998). Similarly, maintaining the plasma glutamine concentration by consuming glutamine in drinks taken both during and after two hours of cycling at 60 percent $\dot{V}O_2max$ did not affect leukocyte redistribution or prevent the exercise-induced fall in neutrophil function (Walsh et al. 2000). Furthermore, neither glutamine nor milk protein (casein) supplements taken during and after exercise in amounts sufficient to prevent the postexercise fall in the plasma glutamine concentration could prevent the exercise-induced decrease in lymphocyte function and salivary IgA secretion rate (Krzykowski et al. 2000).

Unlike the feeding of carbohydrate during exercise, it seems that glutamine supplements do not affect the immune-function responses that have been examined to date. Because about 20 to 30 grams of glutamine have to be taken to prevent postexercise falls in the plasma glutamine concentration, and this will prove costly, we cannot recommend it.

Good Hygiene Practice and Medical Support

Other behavioral lifestyle changes, such as good hygiene practice, may limit the transmission of contagious illnesses by reducing exposure to common sources of infection, including airborne pathogens and physical contact with infected individuals. Medical support including regular checkups, appropriate immunization, and pharmacological intervention may be particularly important for athletes who are at high risk of succumbing to recurrent infection.

Although impairment of immune function sometimes leads to reactivation of a latent Epstein-Barr virus, which is widely prevalent in the young population, the development of clinical infection generally involves exposure to an external pathogen. The latter may be passed from one individual to another by skin contact or breathing the air exhaled from an infected person. Coughing and sneezing can propel airborne pathogens very effectively in a confined space, so the best advice to cyclists is to avoid contact with sick people, avoid rubbing the sensitive mucosa of the nose and eyes, avoid sharing drink bottles, and wash hands thoroughly before eating food.

Cyclists should ensure that their immunization schedule is updated regularly. They need to consider which viruses are prevalent at international competition venues and have the necessary inoculations at the appropriate time. This will require close liaison with the coach and team doctor.

When a cyclist is suffering from an infection, some deterioration in performance is to be expected. It is important for the team doctor to determine if there is a systemic viral infection present. A simple URTI requires no more than some reduction in training load, with the use of a decongestant by day and an antihistamine or nonsteroidal anti-inflammatory drug at night. Of course, athletes must take care to ensure that any prescribed medication does not breach the anti-doping rules. If the individual has developed a systemic viral illness (e.g., with symptoms below the neck, including swollen glands, aching joints and muscles, vomiting, diarrhea, fatigue, and a chesty cough), he or she should stop exercise for several days. Heavy training can increase the severity and duration of such disease. Although rare, enteroviral infections of skeletal muscle and the heart have been known to result, with incapacitating and life-threatening consequences.

Summary

The immune system protects the body against potentially damaging microorganisms. Athletes engaged in heavy endurance training programs often are reported to have depressed immune function and suffer from an increased incidence of upper respiratory tract infections. Excessive training with insufficient recovery can lead to recurrent infections and a debilitating syndrome in which performance and well-being can be affected for months.

A cyclist exercising in a carbohydrate-depleted state experiences larger increases in circulating stress hormones and a greater degree of immunosuppression. Consuming carbohydrate (but not glutamine) during prolonged cycling attenuates rises in stress hormones such as cortisol and appears to limit the degree of exercise-induced immunosuppression. The poor nutritional status of some athletes may predispose them to immunosuppression. For example, dietary deficiencies of protein and specific micronutrients have long been associated with depressed immune function. An adequate intake of iron, zinc, and B vitamins is particularly important, but we also should emphasize the dangers of oversupplementation: Many micronutrients taken in quantities beyond a certain threshold will in fact reduce immune responses and may have other toxic effects that are detrimental to health.

Sustained endurance training appears to be associated with an adaptive up-regulation of the antioxidant defense system. However, such adaptations may be insufficient for protecting cyclists who train extensively, and these individuals should consider increasing their intakes of nutritional antioxidants such as vitamin C, vitamin E, and beta-carotene to reduce free-radical damage. There is some evidence that vitamin C in doses of 1,000 milligrams per day can reduce the risk of URTIs in endurance athletes, but direct evidence that this works by preventing exercise-induced immunosuppression is lacking. In general, we do not recommend supplementation of individual micronutrients or consumption of large doses of simple antioxidant mixtures. Cyclists should obtain complex mixtures of antioxidant compounds from an increased consumption of fruits and vegetables. Consuming megadoses of individual vitamins (not uncommon in cyclists) is likely to do more harm than good.

Although it is impossible to counter the effects of all of the factors that contribute to exercise-induced immunosuppression, it has been shown that minimizing the effects of many factors is possible (summarized in the sidebar on the next page). Cyclists can help themselves by eating a well-balanced diet that includes adequate protein and carbohydrate, sufficient to meet their energy requirements. This will ensure a more than adequate intake of trace elements without the need for special supplements. By reducing other life stresses, maintaining good hygiene, obtaining adequate rest, and spacing prolonged training sessions and competition as far apart as possible, cyclists can reduce their risk of infection.

Strategies to Minimize Risk of Immunosuppression

- Allow sufficient time between training sessions for recovery. Include one or two days of resting recovery in the weekly training program; more training is not always better.
- Avoid extremely long training sessions. Restrict continuous activity to less than two hours per session. For example, a three-hour session might be better performed as two 1.5-hour sessions, one in the morning and one in the evening.
- Periodization of training will help to avoid becoming stale.
- Avoid training monotony by ensuring variation in the day-to-day training load: Ensure that a hard training day is followed by a day of light training.
- When increasing the training load, do this by increasing the load on the hard days. Do not eliminate the recovery days.
- When recovering from overtraining or illness, begin with very light training and build gradually.
- Monitor and record your mood, feelings of fatigue, and muscle soreness during training; decrease the training load if the normal session feels harder than usual.
- Keep other life/social/psychological stresses to a minimum.
- Get regular and adequate sleep (at least six hours per night).
- More rest may be needed after travel across time zones to allow circadian rhythms to adjust.
- Diet is important and many vitamins and minerals are associated with the ability to fight infection, particularly vitamin C, vitamin A, and zinc. A good, well-balanced diet should provide all the necessary vitamins and minerals, but if fresh fruit and vegetables are not readily available, multivitamin supplements should be considered.
- Ensure adequate total dietary energy, carbohydrate, and protein intake. Be aware that periods of carbohydrate depletion are associated with immunosuppression.
- Drinking carbohydrate sports drinks before, during, and after prolonged workouts appears to reduce some of the adverse effects of exercise on immune function.
- You might consider discussing vaccination with your coach or doctor. Influenza vaccines take five to seven weeks to take effect, and intramuscular vaccines may have a few small side effects, so it is advisable to vaccinate out of season. Don't vaccinate pre-competition or if symptoms of illness are present.

EPO

David T. Martin
Christopher J. Gore
Allan G. Hahn

Before boarding an airplane for domestic travel, all your carry-on bags are scanned by an X-ray machine, you walk through a metal detector, and security staff might search your luggage. What about personal rights? What about privacy? In today's high-risk world, passengers give up certain personal rights when they decide to fly. Society accepts increased security as the price they must pay for improved safety.

Similarly, there may come a day when all cyclists competing in a prestigious race such as the Tour de France will be required to have their blood and urine tested the night before, and immediately after, each stage of the race. Authorities in charge of major cycling races are suspicious about the use of performance-enhancing drugs. And this suspicion is warranted, as there is now substantial evidence documenting that some professional cyclists have used illegal drugs to improve performance in races. If tests indicate suspicious supplement practices, the cyclist would be disqualified and prevented from accepting prize money. This way, the race organizers, sponsors, and cyclists would be more confident that the cyclists and not the sports doctors were responsible for winning the race. Unfortunately, today any cyclist who wins a major event is automatically suspected of using drugs (Wieting 2000). This is a tragedy for those talented, hard-working cyclists who have been able to excel without doping.

Recombinant Human Erythropoietin

Erythropoietin (EPO) is a hormone naturally produced by the kidneys when oxygen supply is low. Thus, EPO concentrations in the blood increase when a cyclist is anemic, at altitude, or exposed to carbon monoxide due to inhaling cigarette smoke or other pollution (carbon monoxide binds competitively to hemoglobin, thereby decreasing oxygen transport). EPO acts as a signal for the bone marrow to increase the rate at which red blood cells are released into circulation. The resultant increase in red blood cells improves oxygen supply to tissues throughout the body, including the kidneys. This enriched oxygen supply suppresses the low oxygen signal to the kidneys and thus returns the production of EPO toward normal. The low oxygen–EPO–red blood cell relationship illustrates a classic endocrine negative feedback loop enabling a cyclist to resist the stress of a hypoxic environment.

Production of r-HuEPO

Synthetic human EPO is produced by inserting the human gene responsible for EPO into a mammalian cell (e.g., a hamster ovary) and then stimulating this gene to produce the hormone EPO. When produced in this manner, the hormone is known as recombinant EPO (r-HuEPO). Clinical trials using r-HuEPO began in 1985 (Winearls 1998) by medical researchers interested in an alternative treatment for patients with conditions requiring blood transfusions (i.e., chronic anemias often related to kidney failure). Recombinant EPO has proven immensely effective and is now a preferred alternative to blood transfusions (Winearls 1998).

Physiological Effects of r-HuEPO

Early trials showed that 200 international units (IU) per kilogram per week of r-HuEPO increased the hematocrit of hemodialysis patients by approximately 3 to 4 percent over a period of three weeks. Since then, the administration of r-HuEPO has progressed from intravenous to subcutaneous injections and lower doses have been shown to be equally effective (Winearls 1998). More recently, researchers in Australia have observed that injecting r-HuEPO at a dose of 150 IU per kilogram per week over three weeks can promote an increase in resting hematocrit from 45 to 50 percent in recreational endurance athletes (Parisotto et al. 2000). Birkeland et al. (2000) reported a similar finding; they found that the injection of 181 to 232 IU per kilogram per week increased the hematocrit of well-trained male athletes from 43 to 51 percent over four weeks.

In addition to increasing hematocrit, the prolonged use (one to three weeks) of r-HuEPO can cause an increase in reticulocytes (young red blood cells), macrocytes (large red blood cells), soluble transferrin receptor (a marker of accelerated red cell production and high iron demand within the bone marrow), and serum erythropoietin (Parisotto et al. 2000). Additionally, even when r-HuEPO treatments are given in conjunction with iron, the accelerated rate of red blood cell production can cause iron stores (as indicated by serum ferritin) to decrease (Parisotto et al. 2000; Birkeland et al. 2000). As this chapter later discusses, many of these hematological and biochemical changes form the basis for developing methods aimed at detecting r-HuEPO abuse by athletes.

Effects of r-HuEPO on Performance

It is now well documented that endurance performance is improved in athletes after an increase in red blood cell mass. This improvement in performance appears to occur regardless of whether red blood cell volume is increased by infusing red blood cells or stimulating the bone marrow to produce more red blood cells by injecting r-HuEPO (Ekblom 2000). $\dot{V}O_2max$ is commonly used to reflect aerobic fitness, and in some cases improvements in $\dot{V}O_2max$ are synonymous with improvements in endurance performance. $\dot{V}O_2max$ increased from 63.3 to 68.1 milliliters per kilogram per minute following four weeks of r-HuEPO injections in a group of well-trained endurance athletes (Birkeland et al. 2000). This 7.6 percent improvement in maximal aerobic capacity was not observed in control subjects and could not be explained based on a change in body mass. Subjects treated with r-HuEPO also showed a 9.4 percent increase in exercise time during a maximal incremental intensity cycling test. Improvements in $\dot{V}O_2max$ and performance time were greatest immediately after the four weeks of r-HuEPO injections but also were noticeable up to three weeks after the last injection (Birkeland et al. 2000).

Dangers of r-HuEPO

Many cyclists have heard stories about r-HuEPO use killing cyclists (Ramotar 1990). Although it is important to point out that no direct links have been made between r-HuEPO and unexplained cycling deaths, the possibility does exist that some cyclists have died from excessive use of this drug. The physiological explanation of these deaths would center on the fact that too much r-HuEPO can increase hematocrit and significantly increase blood viscosity. This "thick" blood would cause the heart to work excessively hard, a condition that could lead to a heart attack. Although this scenario is intuitively appealing, there are other health concerns regarding r-HuEPO use that are less frequently addressed.

Dr. Mario Cazzola (2000) from the University of Pavia School of Medicine in Italy has reviewed many of the potential health complications associated with r-HuEPO treatment. Unfortunately, many of the athletes who use this drug are either unaware of these dangers or have decided that the illegal performance benefits outweigh the risks. Of most concern is the fact that r-HuEPO increases the risk of thromboembolic complications because of an increased endothelial activation and platelet reactivity. Athletes who experience these complications may die or become seriously handicapped. Increases in hematocrit generally come with increases in blood pressure, which result in a greater cardiovascular strain during submaximal exercise.

Also of concern is the iron overload that will occur when large amounts of iron are administered to facilitate the effectiveness of the r-HuEPO. Iron overload can ". . . produce organ damage comparable to that occurring in genetic hemochromatosis, including the risk of developing hepatic carcinoma" (Cazzola 2000). Ironically, once prolonged r-HuEPO treatment stops there is the possibility that suppressed endogenous production of EPO will lead to anemia. Finally, preliminary evidence from animals suggests that long-term use of r-HuEPO could lead to myeloproliferative disorders. In summary, although relatively safe when under clinical supervision, some health risks are associated with r-HuEPO use.

Attempts to Test for r-HuEPO

Researchers have developed methods in an attempt to test for r-HuEPO use, but only recently have techniques become suitable for routinely screening athletes. Testing strategies generally can be categorized as direct or indirect. Some researchers have been able to make a direct distinction between natural EPO and r-HuEPO in the urine and blood, but because of the rapid clearance times of r-HuEPO (approximately 4 to 11 hours) (Flaharty et al. 1990), this type of testing must take place within days of the last r-HuEPO injection if an athlete is to be detected. Indirect tests are based on the observation that many hematological and biochemical changes occur during and following r-HuEPO treatment. The advantages of indirect tests are that they tend to be less expensive and can be used to identify r-HuEPO users for up to three weeks after the last injection. Both direct and indirect detection strategies have advanced and the r-HuEPO test recently adopted at the Sydney 2000 Olympics used a combination of these approaches.

Gel Electrophoresis

Wide et al. (1995) have established that r-HuEPO can be distinguished from endogenous EPO in both urine and serum samples using gel electrophoresis. The method is based on the observation that endogenous EPO generally has a greater negative charge than r-HuEPO. Although the technique apparently produces no false-positive results, it can detect the use of r-HuEPO for only three days after the last injection. Its success would therefore depend upon random "out-of-competition" sample collections. It is currently very laborious and expensive, making wide-scale testing of athletes impractical, although rapid refinements now are occurring.

Macrocytic Hypochromic Cells

Using sophisticated scattering laser technology, Bayer has introduced a series of hematology analyzers that allow for red blood cell volume and hemoglobin content to be evaluated on a cell-by-cell basis. Casoni and colleagues (1993) observed changes in red blood cell size and hemoglobin content after treatment with r-HuEPO. Unfortunately, these differences were only apparent in r-HuEPO-treated subjects toward the end of and for 10 days after the 45-day treatment period. Also, approximately 60 percent of r-HuEPO-treated subjects tested negative, indicating that this method could produce false-negative results.

Soluble Transferrin-Ferritin Ratio

Birkeland and colleagues (2000) from Norway performed a double-blind, placebo-controlled study examining the effects of r-HuEPO (181 to 232 IU per kilogram per week) on hematological and biochemical parameters in well-trained male athletes. During the four-week r-HuEPO treatment period, which included high doses of an oral iron supplement, serum ferritin rapidly decreased to 50 percent of initial values and the soluble transferrin receptor (sTfR) concentration nearly doubled. This supported the concept of using an sTfR-ferritin ratio to indirectly detect r-HuEPO use. The changes in sTfR took approximately one week to become significant, and the unique response persisted for one week following the last r-HuEPO injection.

Unfortunately for those interested in drug testing, neither sTfR, ferritin, nor the sTfR-ferritin ratio was significantly different from baseline measures three to four weeks after the last r-HuEPO injection, whereas noticeable improvements in cycling performance continued to be observed.

French Urine Test

Researchers in France refined the gel-electrophoresis technique of Wide and colleagues, allowing them to directly distinguish between natural EPO and exogenous r-HuEPO (Lasne and Ceaurriz 2000). When the protein EPO is produced within a cell it is chemically modified before release into circulation. One of these modifications is known as *post-translational glycosylation*—a term that refers to the process of carbohydrates binding to a newly formed protein. The EPO post-translational modifications are unique in different animals. For this reason, r-HuEPO produced from a hamster ovary cell line has a slightly different chemical composition than EPO normally produced by a human kidney. The French analytical chemists were able to use a sophisticated technique to distinguish natural EPO from r-HuEPO in the urine based on the differences between these forms of EPO (Lasne and Ceaurriz 2000).

As indicated earlier, because the average halftime for clearance of r-HuEPO is approximately 4 to 11 hours (Flaharty et al. 1990), direct detection techniques can only identify r-HuEPO use within one to two days after the last injection. In addition, the urine test is limited to r-HuEPO and does not detect any other r-HuEPO-like drugs (e.g., mimetic peptides). However, for random out-of-competition testing, this method is likely to be highly effective because it provides strong and direct evidence of two types of EPO in the urine of an individual—a phenomenon that is not legally defensible.

Australian Blood Test

Sport scientists from the Australian Institute of Sport teamed with colleagues at the Australian Sports Drug Testing Laboratory to perform an EPO treatment trial on 30 healthy volunteers (Parisotto et al. 2000). Unlike previous research that focused on one or two blood parameters to indirectly detect the use of r-HuEPO (Birkeland et al. 2000; Gareau et al. 1994), the Australian researchers used multiple indirect markers of this hormone and a multivariate statistical approach. Additionally, they used this novel approach not only to detect subjects currently using r-HuEPO ("ON" model) but also to detect subjects who recently had stopped using r-HuEPO ("OFF" model). Similar to previous research, the following variables were shown to be uniquely influenced by r-HuEPO:

- Serum EPO
- Soluble transferrin receptor
- Hematocrit
- Percent macrocytes
- The number and mean cell volume of reticulocytes (which together could be used to calculate reticulocyte hematocrit)

Although both of the variables required to calculate reticulocyte hematocrit previously had been shown to change with EPO administration, the Australian researchers were the first to introduce this variable. The ON model could identify 94 to 100 percent of r-HuEPO use during the final two weeks of the four-week r-HuEPO treatment phase. Furthermore, researchers observed that two-thirds of the subjects on r-HuEPO could be detected 12 to 21 days after treatment had stopped, based on a severe depression of normal red blood cell production. The depression appears to be species independent (Piron et al. 2001). These data are important as they indicate for the first time that the residual effects of r-HuEPO treatment can be used to enhance r-HuEPO testing capabilities.

As a follow-up, researchers evaluated both the ON and OFF models using 556 blood samples collected from male and female athletes who had completed normal training, a six-day cycling stage race, or exposure to natural or simulated altitude. For the ON model, no false positives were identified in either the athletes engaged in various types of training or the subjects who were administered the placebo. However, of particular concern was the fact that the OFF model produced two false positives—one in the placebo group and one in an athlete who recently was exposed to altitude.

Testing Adopted by the UCI

At their annual meeting in Geneva (January 1997), Union Cycliste Internationale (UCI) delegates, in consultation with medical professionals, decided to implement blood testing to deter the alleged use of r-HuEPO. They imposed a 50 percent upper limit on hematocrit. UCI president Hein Verbruggen has repeatedly indicated that this testing is a "health check" and that a positive result does not imply r-HuEPO use. The UCI established the testing primarily to ensure that professional cyclists do not begin a major road race with a "dangerously high" hematocrit. In contrast to a positive drug test, which can result in prolonged suspension from competition, riders with a hematocrit greater than 50 percent were suspended only until values decreased to an acceptable level. As of April 1, 2001, the UCI has refined its blood testing policy so that any cyclist with a hematocrit greater than 50 percent or a reticulocyte count greater than 2.4 percent is subjected to the French r-HuEPO urine test. Also, the French r-HuEPO urine test is administered to podium finishers and randomly to any other cyclist finishing the race. In contrast to the light penalty for having a hematocrit greater than 50 percent, failing the French r-HuEPO urine test will constitute a doping infraction.

Normal Hematocrit

Given that the UCI places strong reliance on hematocrit as a health check, it is salient to carefully evaluate the normal resting hematocrit levels of professional cyclists. Saris and co-workers (1998) collected 353 blood samples from 34 professional road cyclists and reported an average hematocrit of 43 percent with a range of 39 to 48 percent. Robinson et al. (2000) observed a slightly higher average hematocrit and range (46 percent; 40 to 52 percent) in 146 male professional road cyclists in the morning before the third day of the 1999 Tour de Suisse. Similarly, Schumacher et al. (2000) showed that elite German cyclists have an average hematocrit of 46 percent.

Because of the new UCI hematocrit rule, scientists also have been interested in determining the number of cyclists with hematocrits greater than 50 percent. They observed such hematocrits in 4.1 percent of the professional cyclists competing in the

1999 Tour de Suisse (Robinson et al. 2000), in approximately 7 percent of elite German cyclists during the competitive season (Schumacher et al. 2000), and in 0 percent of samples collected from 34 Dutch professional cyclists tested between 1980 and 1986 (Saris et al. 1998). A retrospective analysis of 360 blood samples collected from top Australian road cyclists between 1987 and 1996 resulted in 10 hematocrit values that exceeded 50 percent. Thus, 2.8 percent of blood samples from the Australian road cyclists exceeded the 50 percent hematocrit limit set by the UCI (unpublished observations).

Effects of Racing on Hematocrit

Interestingly, Saris and colleagues (1998) observed that resting hematocrit decreased from 45 to 42 percent after 21 days of racing in the 1984 Tour de France. This observation is significant because it demonstrates that successive days of cycle racing (before the availability of r-HuEPO) did not typically produce an increase in resting hematocrit due to dehydration. Thus, the early-morning resting hematocrit in male professional road cyclists can average between 43 and 46 percent and typically decreases in response to heavy training loads and racing, and up to 7 percent of professional cyclists normally present values greater than 50 percent during the competitive season. The latter issue is a limitation of this screening test if those cyclists with a naturally high hematocrit are discriminated against unfairly. However, this problem should be surmountable with repeated testing to demonstrate the normal hematocrit range for an individual, in conjunction with random urine tests for r-HuEPO to verify that endogenous sources are not contributing to the high hematocrit.

Professional Road Cycling and r-HuEPO

Under Article 2 of the UCI anti-doping regulations, the following practices are specifically prohibited: (a) blood doping; (b) administration of artificial oxygen carriers or plasma volume expanders; and (c) pharmacological, chemical, or physical manipulation. Additionally, similar to other peptide hormones, the UCI specifically bans the use of r-HuEPO and analogues. However, because r-HuEPO abuse cannot be detected easily and because the effects of r-HuEPO on cycling performance are substantial, the use of r-HuEPO by professional cyclists has been suspected for several years.

Festina Affair

In regard to r-HuEPO and professional road cycling, testimonials and rumors are prolific. Probably one of the most famous confessions occurred during the 1998 Tour de France when Bruno Roussel, the Festina team director, admitted that illegal products were administered to his cyclists by members of his support team with the intention of improving performance. Roussel said that the team purchased the drugs and gave them to the cyclists under strict medical control in attempts to protect the riders' health (Wieting 2000). With the exception of confessions, the truth about the use of r-HuEPO by top cyclists is difficult to ascertain. Recently, however, peer-reviewed scientific journals have published two reports that indirectly address the supplement practices of elite male cyclists.

1999 Tour de Suisse

Robinson and colleagues (2000) from Lausanne, Switzerland, working in conjunction with the UCI were able to obtain resting blood samples from all 146 professional cyclists competing in the 1999 Tour de Suisse. They collected the samples early in the morning after two days of racing. The average hematocrit was 46 percent with a range from 40.0 to 52.2 percent. Five cyclists from four different teams had hematocrits above 51 percent, and 32 cyclists (approximately one-fifth of the peloton) presented with hematocrits above 48 percent. Of particular interest was the observation that in one team, "... all [hematocrit] values were contained between 46.9 and 48.8 percent" (Robinson et al. 2000). The authors commented that this unique hematocrit distribution demonstrated much lower variability and a higher average than that observed for the majority of the other teams.

Robinson et al. (2000) also presented ferritin data (indicative of cellular iron stores) in this study. Seven cyclists had values greater than 1,000 nanograms per milliliter, which is more than three times the upper limit of the normal clinical reference range (300 nanograms per milliliter). Fifty-eight percent of the cyclists exceeded the normal upper limit. Five cyclists had serum EPO concentrations greater than the normal clinical range and eight cyclists had reticulocyte (young red blood cells) counts that were above normal. These clinically unusual data do not provide direct evidence that any cyclists were using, or had been using, r-HuEPO. However, it is possible that the disturbed blood characteristics of some cyclists were a result of injecting both iron and r-HuEPO and then using intravenous fluid-replacement techniques to lower resting hematocrit. It is noteworthy that for r-HuEPO injections to be fully effective in increasing red blood cell production, concurrent administration of iron is necessary.

1998 Tour de France

After the 1998 Tour de France, there was much suspicion regarding r-HuEPO use among the professional cyclists, particularly in view of the "Festina Affair" in which vials of r-HuEPO were found in one of the Festina team cars. The UCI followed up on a new policy in which urine samples collected for routine drug tests could be preserved and subjected to novel drug tests at a later date. The French researchers who developed the new r-HuEPO test examined the urine EPO concentrations of 102 urine samples collected during the 1998 Tour de France and established that 28 samples had EPO concentrations higher than normal (Lasne and Ceaurriz 2000). The 14 samples with the highest EPO concentrations were analyzed using the new r-HuEPO urine test. The researchers report that all of these samples ". . . gave rise to a banding pattern typical of r-HuEPO," suggesting that the cyclists who produced these samples were using a banned drug (Lasne and Ceaurriz 2000).

Surprisingly, all of the urine samples that did not have EPO concentrations above normal had concentrations *below* the detectable limit of the EPO assay (less than .6 IU per liter). This is particularly interesting in light of research documenting that the natural production of EPO is suppressed following cessation of prolonged r-HuEPO use (Piron et al. 2001). More specifically, when athletes stop using this hormone, serum EPO concentrations drop to very low levels for two to three weeks until the natural production of EPO returns to normal (Parisotto et al. 2000).

© Newsport Photography

Suspicions concerning r-HuEPO use that arose after the 1998 Tour de France resulted in the development of a new r-HuEPO test.

In summary, data obtained during the 1998 Tour de France cannot discount the possibility that all of the 102 urine samples collected came from cyclists who were using or recently had stopped using r-HuEPO. However, much more information is needed about the normal distribution of urinary EPO concentration and EPO isoforms before these findings can be interpreted definitively. This probably explains the lack of punitive action taken by the UCI. However, the affirmative recognition of the French test on April 1, 2001, suggests that doubts no longer exist.

The Future of Doping: If Not r-HuEPO, What Next?

It is important to note that emergency medicine and not sports medicine research is responsible for the many novel techniques recently being developed to improve oxygen transport. Whereas r-HuEPO was the first drug produced to stimulate the production of red blood cells, there are now other drugs available that are basically fragments of the EPO protein with the ability to bind to the EPO receptor.

Additionally, some cyclists may turn to the rapidly expanding list of blood substitutes such as perfluorocarbon emulsions, stabilized hemoglobin, and recombinant hemoglobin (Chang 2000). These solutions, injected the night before or on the morning of a race, would improve oxygen delivery without causing the failure of current drug tests. Of particular interest are the free-hemoglobin solutions using small oxygen-carrying proteins that could easily pass through narrow capillaries, partially occluded by the swelling associated with inflamed tissue—a condition that may occur during strenuous racing.

In the future there certainly will be more out-of-competition testing for drugs such as steroids, growth hormone, and r-HuEPO. The effectiveness of testing before and after major races will be enhanced by the availability of rapid automated analyzers with improved sensitivity. The speed of the analysis will mean that all competitors can be tested. Because financial rewards are high for cyclists who win and some drugs are proven to provide athletes with a performance benefit, supplement practices of professional cyclists will always need to be monitored. Even today some professional cyclists apparently believe that if no tests are available for a supplement, then its use is acceptable regardless of ethical and health implications.

Today's cycling fans probably will never really know the truth behind the doping issues surrounding the sport. Some stories allege that all cyclists in the peloton during big races such as the Tour de France are using illegal drugs, whereas others assure us that there are only a few "bad apples" among the bunch. Regardless, there has been an alarming number of deaths, and more recently there have been many reported incidents of cyclists failing drug tests. The future of cycling now depends upon systematic drug-testing efforts aimed at all the major classes of drugs that professional cyclists could use (e.g., stimulants, anti-inflammatory, blood substitutes, blood stimulants, steroids).

Whereas the approach in the past has been to catch the cheats by surprise, a more suitable approach may be one in which scientists and cycling federations work together with the athletes to develop and implement wide-scale testing. With this approach it would become much more difficult to use drugs to "beat the system." Some have described the drug-taking athletes as victims, albeit very wealthy ones. And to some extent this is perhaps true. The cyclists in the professional peloton all started as young athletes with a desire to perform well in the big races. However, somewhere along the way, a number of them may have begun to participate in an unspoken professional practice involving the use of banned drugs. In their own minds, they may have been able to rationalize this practice on the grounds that "everyone is doing it" and also that the drugs are required to survive the incredible physical demands of competition.

Truck-Driving Analogy

Consider this analogy: Assume you are a truck driver and you have been employed by a company to drive products from Town A to Town B. The speed limit on this particular road is 50 kilometers per hour and you are paid based on how many trips you complete each week. After driving the route for two weeks, you make some observations: (a) There are other truck drivers driving at close to 100 kilometers per hour; (b) truck drivers who speed make more money than those who stay within the speed limit; (c) truck drivers who don't speed don't get contracts with the good trucking companies; (d) truck drivers who speed don't necessarily crash or have more accidents than those driving at 50 kilometers per hour; and (e) the police don't enforce the speed limit and even if they do catch someone speeding, the fines are minimal.

What would you do if you want to excel at your profession? More than likely you would at some point in time be tempted to push the speed limit, especially if you come under financial pressures. This analogy highlights the pressures that some professional cyclists may feel as they strive to succeed in a very competitive environment. This analogy is not perfect, and unlike the truck drivers who are only successful if they break the law (i.e., speed limit), there are likely professional cyclists who are successful without taking drugs. Unfortunately, many of these extremely talented cyclists currently are considered guilty by some competitors and fans—until proven innocent.

We can continue with the truck-driving analogy and explore methods for cleaning up the alleged drug problem. Assume that the police decide that the speeding trucks are a risk and the speeding must be stopped. There are two possible approaches: (1) Organize a large and well-equipped army of police to monitor speeding in an unannounced manner and arrest and cancel the license of everyone who is speeding, or (2) implement the same approach but in a very open and transparent manner. Option 1 would likely result in a tremendous number of arrests and seriously damage the trucking industry, whereas option 2 may reform driving practices without treating the majority of drivers as criminals. It is likely that truck drivers currently speeding would even assist the police so that speed cameras and speeding detection methods could be used in the most effective manner possible.

Similarly, it is important to recognize that the cyclists who apparently use performance-enhancing drugs are generally not "bad" people. They are more likely athletes who love their sport and desire success. Most professional cyclists probably would welcome a sophisticated universal testing program that minimized the use of illegal drugs. The implementation of such testing programs will have the most desired effects if they are openly developed and instigated. With the increased funding now available for drug testing research and the formation of the World Anti-Doping Agency, it seems that the dream of a drug-free professional peloton may someday become a reality.

Acknowledgments

The authors gratefully acknowledge Robin Parisotto from the Australian Institute of Sport who edited this chapter, making many noticeable improvements. We also thank Robin for the many stimulating discussions we have had over the past four years with regard to r-HuEPO testing in professional cyclists, as these conversations formed the basis for the major concepts that this chapter presents.

chapter 22

Effective Training

Asker Jeukendrup
Luke Moseley

The chapters that make up this book are all based on the latest scientific research and ideas. We have presented the most up-to-date knowledge in a format that makes it accessible to all cyclists, coaches, and sport scientists. The final result, this book, is filled with advice and guidance that give you the opportunity to use the latest sport science to optimize your performance. However, the number of variables that affect cycling performance is large and they cannot all be changed at the same time. Athletes and coaches have to make decisions about which factor is worth investing time and money in. What approach will give the optimal effect for a certain financial investment and time investment? This chapter, therefore, aims to compare and weigh the advice given so far to guide you in maximizing the efficiency of your training. The chapter is based on a previous publication (Jeukendrup and Martin 2001).

It is obvious that the relative importance of the factors discussed in this book, such as interval training, carbohydrate feeding, and aerodynamic bicycle components, is difficult to directly compare. Therefore, some common measure is required that allows the comparison of the relative importance of each of these factors. To do this, we used the mathematical model developed by Jim Martin and colleagues (1998; see chapter 9 for details). This model combines all the factors involved in cycling velocity into one equation, which then allows us to change one variable (bicycle weight, for instance) and see the effect on overall bike speed. In this final chapter, we use this approach to compare the physiological, mechanical, and environmental factors that affect cycling performance. Keep in mind, however, that every model is a simplification that helps us to understand how things work. Although we believe that this model is very good and closely reflects reality, there are, of course, factors of cycling performance such as tactics or bike handling that we cannot incorporate in this model.

Introducing the Model Riders

To compare the effects discussed in this book, we have enlisted three imaginary riders: a novice cyclist (rider A), a trained cyclist (rider B), and a well-trained and talented cyclist (rider C). Our riders have agreed to help us by testing each different variable on their local 40-kilometer time-trial circuit. Fortunately for us, each of our volunteers is very consistent in his performances and the weather on our course never changes, so we know that any change in performance is only due to the factor in which we are interested.

Rider A is a novice cyclist with a relatively short history of cycling training. The $\dot{V}O_2$max of this rider is 48 milliliters per kilogram per minute and his lactate threshold is determined at 65 percent $\dot{V}O_2$max. Rider A goes out on his bicycle every Sunday and sometimes does a shorter ride during the week or on Saturday. Sunday rides are with the slower group of a local club, and our rider is thinking of entering a novice's race in a couple of months.

Rider B is a trained, serious cyclist who is preparing for an important big race. This rider went in to a laboratory and had his $\dot{V}O_2$max and lactate threshold determined. His $\dot{V}O_2$max was 66 milliliters per kilogram per minute with a lactate threshold at 75 percent $\dot{V}O_2$max. This cyclist trains on average three to four times a week including a long four-hour ride. Rider B is a keen racer and tries to race most weekends; his main aim this season is getting his first category license and he's planning his training to peak for a local 130-kilometer road race.

Rider C is an elite road cyclist ($\dot{V}O_2$max is 80 milliliters per kilogram per minute with a lactate threshold at 80 percent $\dot{V}O_2$max). This rider started riding at a young age and is competing in 60 to 100 races a year. Rider C is a semiprofessional rider for a second-division team and is team leader for some smaller races this season. He is hoping to be "spotted" by a first-division team and is peaking for a weeklong stage race in which he hopes to finish in the top 10. Table 22.1 gives a summary of all the riders' characteristics.

TABLE 22.1 Selected Anthropometric and Physiological Variables of Our Imaginary Testers

Variable	Rider A	Rider B	Rider C
Age (years)	25	25	25
Height (cm)	180	180	180
Weight (kg)	70	70	70
Body fat (%)	15	10	5
$\dot{V}O_2$max (ml/kg/min.)	55	66	80
Lactate threshold (% $\dot{V}O_2$max)	65	75	80
Peak power (watts)	300	400	500

Introducing the Time-Trial Course

The time-trial course that our imaginary cyclists are going to ride is exactly 40 kilometers and is an out-and-back course (see figure 22.1). The out stretch has a constant tailwind of 2 meters per second and one hill with a 5-kilometer-long constant 1 percent gradient, followed by a 5-kilometer 1 percent downhill. The hill is followed by a 10-kilometer flat section to the turnaround. The riders do not have to brake or accelerate to make it around the turn before returning along the flat and over the hill with a 2-meters-per-second head wind. The riders do not sprint or fatigue and they cycle with a constant power output for the entire duration. In the baseline condition, riders have 10-kilogram bikes and a standard aero position; they use aero wheels and only drink water. In these conditions we would record times of 1:12:56 (hour, minutes, seconds), 58:35, and 52:02 for riders A, B, and C, respectively. This relates to average speeds of 32.91 kilometers per hour for rider A, 40.97 kilometers per hour for rider B, and 46.12 kilometers per hour for rider C. All comparisons are reported as the change in average speed as a result of changing a single factor from the control position or setup. Figures 22.2, 22.3, and 22.4 present, in bar-graph format, the effects of the different variables on simulated 40-kilometer time-trial performance.

Internal Factors

Both internal and external factors affect cycling performance. The internal factors deal with the production of power. Improving these factors will result in an increased power output and subsequently improved performance. One of the most obvious ways of improving this power output is training (see chapter 1). On the other hand, we also can improve performance by changing the external factors. External factors will affect the resistance that a cyclist has to overcome. The most important resistance is usually air resistance, and chapters 9 and 10 discuss various ways to reduce aerodynamic drag. In the following sections, we summarize the effects of these different factors and express improvements in a common unit—namely, improvements in average velocity over 40 kilometers.

Training

Chapter 1 discusses that, apart from genetic endowment, no factor plays a more important role in determining cycling performance than the physiological adaptations

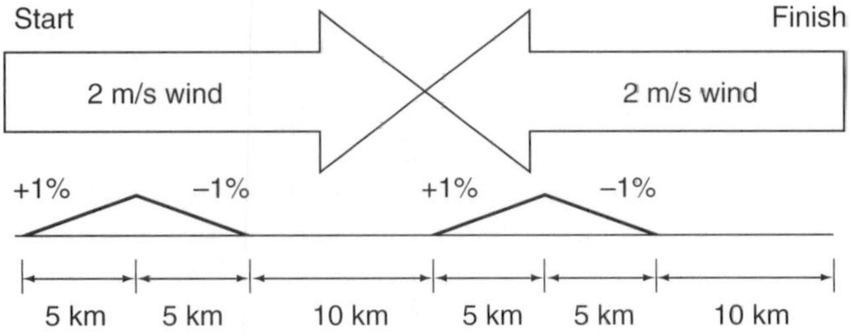

Figure 22.1 Overview and profile schematic of the virtual time-trial course upon which equipment changes are tested.

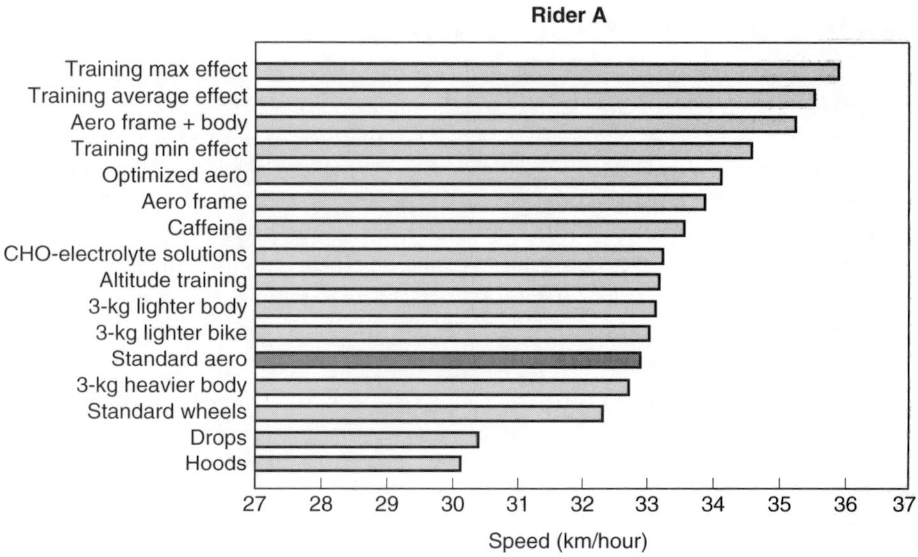

Figure 22.2 Comparison of the effect of optimizing different variables on speed (in kilometers per hour) over a 40-kilometer time trial for rider A. The baseline is a 10-kilogram bike, aerodynamic wheels, and a 70-kilogram rider with a standard aero position (red bar). Bars show average speed for the 40-kilometer rolling time trial.

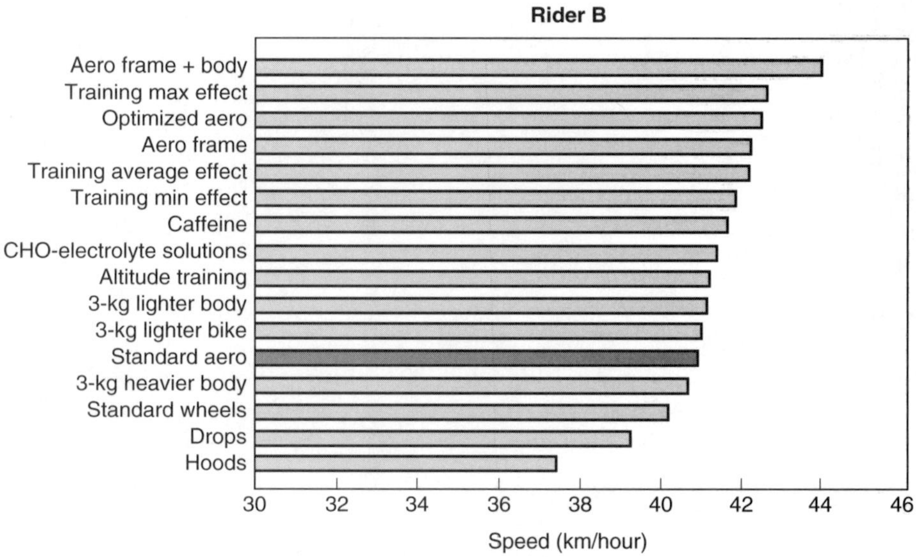

Figure 22.3 Comparison of the effect of optimizing different variables on speed (in kilometers per hour) over a 40-kilometer time trial for rider B. The baseline is a 10-kilogram bike, aerodynamic wheels, and a 70-kilogram rider with a standard aero position (red bar). Bars show average speed for the 40-kilometer rolling time trial.

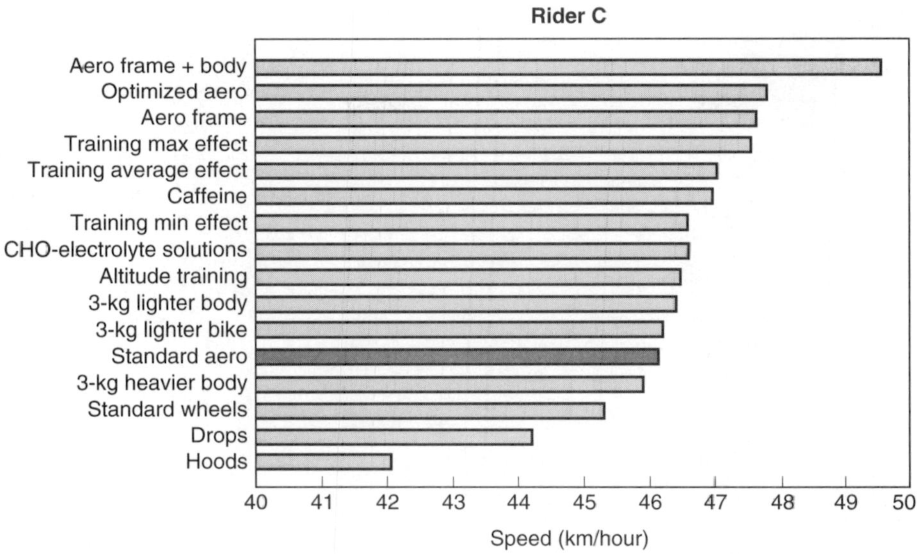

Figure 22.4 Comparison of the effect of optimizing different variables on speed (in kilometers per hour) over a 40-kilometer time trial for rider C. The baseline is a 10-kilogram bike, aerodynamic wheels, and a 70-kilogram rider with a standard aero position (red bar). Bars show average speed for the 40-kilometer rolling time trial.

induced by training. Improvements in cycling performance require applying the training principles that chapter 1 describes. Although there is quite a bit of information about the effects of planned exercise training on performance or indirect markers of overtraining in relatively untrained individuals, there is a lack of scientific information concerning the effects of training on athletes who are already well trained (chapter 1).

Early reports show that untrained subjects can increase their $\dot{V}O_2max$ by 20 to 38 percent by training for 9 to 10 weeks. These large increases in $\dot{V}O_2max$ were observed in elderly individuals, whereas younger subjects showed somewhat smaller improvements. A consistent finding among training studies is that having a low initial $\dot{V}O_2max$ at the beginning of a training period results in a greater improvement compared with someone with a higher $\dot{V}O_2max$. Unfortunately, $\dot{V}O_2max$ is not always a good indicator of exercise performance. Cyclists with a high $\dot{V}O_2max$ are not necessarily the best cyclists and some cyclists with a relatively low $\dot{V}O_2max$ can perform very well. In some studies, groups of athletes with a very similar $\dot{V}O_2max$ showed that their performances were actually vastly different.

Therefore, it is difficult to predict performance improvements from studies in which only $\dot{V}O_2max$ was measured. However, it is likely that the majority of these training programs resulted not only in an increased $\dot{V}O_2max$ but also in a significant change in the lactate threshold. On the basis of these studies and experiences with elite cyclists, Jeukendrup and Martin (2001) estimated some changes in 40-kilometer time-trial performance that would occur after training.

For novice cyclists, a training program that includes high-intensity intervals and sustained endurance efforts can increase performance by as much as 5 to 10 percent. The effects of intensified training on 40-kilometer time-trial performance in already

© Nigel Farrow

Giro d'Italia 2000 winner Stefano Garzelli in training—an important factor for success.

well-trained individuals are less (2 to 4 percent), and the margins for improvement are likely to be even smaller in elite cyclists (1 to 2 percent). Using the model, we see that these changes result in a new average speed of 34.6 to 35.9 kilometers per hour for rider A, 41.8 to 42.7 kilometers per hour for rider B, and 46.6 to 47.5 kilometers per hour for rider C. (Throughout this chapter, refer to figures 22.2, 22.3, and 22.4 for results.)

Altitude Training

In chapter 3, Dave Martin extensively discusses the effects of altitude training. As he covers in that chapter, there is some evidence that living high and training low or living low and training high might have positive effects on some athletic events.

Most of the studies of the effects of altitude exposure on athletic performance have been performed on runners and there is little direct information relating to cycling performance. In addition, these studies' performance measurements typically have been of short duration (less than 20 minutes), which make it difficult to extrapolate these findings to cycling. In general, if performance improvements do occur as a result of altitude training, they appear to be small (0 to 2 percent). We have used these data to optimistically estimate a value for the performance enhancements that altitude training might elicit and predicted a 2 percent increase in performance power for all our riders. With such an improvement, the model predicts an increase in 40-kilometer time-trial speed to 33.2, 41.3, and 46.5 kilometers per hour for riders A, B, and C, respectively.

Nutrition

Chapters 12 through 17 deal with all aspects of nutrition and there is no doubt that nutrition can enhance athletic performance. For this comparison, we examined the scientific evidence relating to the effects of energy drinks (carbohydrate-electrolyte solutions) and a popular, but also controversial, supplement (caffeine).

Carbohydrate-Electrolyte Solutions

Chapters 12 through 17 discuss the effects of nutrition on endurance performance. The performance-enhancing effects of consuming a carbohydrate-electrolyte solution have been specifically investigated and suggest that the ingestion of water and carbohydrate can result in an improvement in 40-kilometer time-trial performance of between 1 and 3 percent (Below et al. 1995; el-Sayed et al. 1997; Jeukendrup et al. 1997). For example, Jeukendrup et al. (1997) reported that power output during a simulated 40-kilometer time trial was increased by 2.3 percent by the ingestion of a carbohydrate beverage compared with a placebo in well-trained athletes. Interestingly, Below et al. (1995) found that carbohydrate feedings improved performance by 12 percent during a 10-minute maximal effort that followed 50 minutes of steady cycling. This result is particularly relevant to cycling because it mimics what may occur in many races—a maximal breakaway after a steady period.

Taken together, these and other results indicate that performance during a 40-kilometer time trial could be increased by approximately 2 to 3 percent with the use of carbohydrate ingestion. Using these data in the model, it predicts that performance would improve by 0.3 kilometer per hour for rider A, 0.4 kilometer per hour for rider B, and 0.5 kilometer per hour for rider C. This equates to improvements of 42 seconds for rider A, 36 seconds for rider B, and 32 seconds for rider C.

Caffeine

Several investigators have reported that ingesting caffeine improves exercise capacity (time-to-exhaustion) or performance (time to complete a certain amount of work) (Kovacs et al. 1998; Spriet et al. 1992). To our knowledge, however, there is only one study of the effects of caffeine ingestion on 40-kilometer cycling time-trial performance. Kovacs et al. (1998) investigated the effects of ingesting different levels of caffeine in combination with a carbohydrate-electrolyte drink on performance in 15 trained cyclists (with a $\dot{V}O_2$max of approximately 67 milliliters per kilogram per minute). They observed the best performances (an improvement of 5 percent) when cyclists ingested the highest caffeine dosages (225 and 320 milligrams). It is important to note that the dosage of caffeine used in this study was small and did not result in high caffeine levels in urine (less than five milligrams per liter). Pasman et al. (1995) also showed large improvements in time-to-exhaustion at 80 percent $\dot{V}O_2$max with a relatively high dosage of caffeine (five milligrams per kilogram).

These studies observed large effects on endurance capacity over a fairly large range of aerobic fitness levels, suggesting that caffeine has similar effects in relatively untrained cyclists and elite cyclists. Therefore, we assumed that ingesting caffeine would increase power output by 5 percent for all three of the modeled subjects. This 5 percent increase in power resulted in our imaginary riders (A, B, and C) increasing their average speed by 0.6, 0.7, and 0.8 kilometers per hour, respectively. This equates to a time savings of 84 seconds for the novice cyclist, 63 seconds for the trained cyclist, and 55 seconds for the elite cyclist.

Body Cooling

In chapter 4, Matthew Bridge and Mark Febbraio describe how hyperthermia can induce fatigue and decrease performance. They suggest that using cooling jackets to prevent the buildup of heat during a warm-up could increase performance in a subsequent time trial. Studies have shown that improvements in both anaerobic power and aerobic endurance are possible with precooling. However, it must be realized that these studies used extreme ways to cool the body, compared with cooling jackets, and exercise was performed in hot conditions. During cycling, especially at high speeds, there is always significant wind cooling. Because no studies have directly investigated the effects of cooling jackets on time-trial performance, we think that at present it is impossible to predict performance changes.

External Factors

Much of the cycling media are devoted to changing external factors—new bikes, new wheels, and new components. Chapters 9 and 10 examine the effects of different body positions, bicycles, wheels, and tires on performance and use the model to make some comparisons. In this chapter we again model the effects of these changes to make comprehensive comparisons. The possibility of spending large sums of money on these external factors makes examination of their effect important for the consumer.

Bicycle Mass

The baseline bicycle used in the model has a mass of 10 kilograms. Of course, most amateur racers will use bikes weighing less than 10 kilograms. Therefore, we have used the model to predict the effect of using a 7-kilogram bicycle—which is just above the limit set by the Union Cycliste Internationale for bikes in competition—on 40-kilometer time-trial performance. It is interesting that, compared with the 10-kilogram bicycle used in the baseline calculations, the lighter bicycle would increase average speed by only 0.1 kilometer per hour for all our riders. This is despite the simulated course involving 10 kilometers of climbing up a 1 percent gradient. If we compare these improvements with those achieved with aerodynamic wheels, then we can put into perspective the importance of bicycle weight on performance over a relatively flat course.

Body Mass

Of course, it is much cheaper to lose body mass than it is to reduce the weight of your bicycle. In fact, a given decrease in body mass has a greater improvement on performance than the same decrease in bike mass. This is due to the reduction in body size improving aerodynamics. To accurately assess the effects of increases or decreases to body mass on cycling performance, we must account for both the mass and the resulting change in body surface area in the model parameters. Scientific research has resulted in formulas that predict drag area from body mass, and we used these in the model to predict the performance changes.

Using these new numbers, we predicted a *decrease* of 3 kilograms in body mass to improve 40-kilometer velocity by 0.2 kilometer per hour for riders A and B and by 0.3 kilometer per hour for rider C. Conversely, a 3-kilogram *increase* in body mass results in decreases of a similar magnitude in predicted 40-kilometer time-trial velocity. It is an important observation that increases in performance are two to three times greater when mass is lost from the body compared with when mass is lost from the bike.

1 kilometer = 0.62 miles

1 kilogram = 2.2 pounds

The predicted effects of changes in bicycle and body mass on 40-kilometer time-trial performance seem low (less than 25 seconds). This small effect is due, in part, to the low gradient of the climbs on the modeled course profile, but also to the fact that any extra weight provides additional propulsive force on the descent portions of the course. In certain situations, however, the advantage of additional weight during the descent will be balanced by other factors. For example, if the descent is technical and the cyclist must brake to get around the corners, then the advantage of increased weight is reduced.

Aerodynamics

The importance of good aerodynamics cannot be understated. At speeds over approximately 20 kilometers per hour, a cyclist uses most of his energy to displace the air in front of him. This amount of energy increases with the square of the speed and therefore aerodynamics is even more important at higher speeds. Our riders can reduce their drag factor in one of two ways: by reducing the drag of their bodies (see chapter 9) or reducing the drag of their bicycles (see chapter 10).

Body Position

The effects of body position on time-trial performance were analyzed in four typical positions: a rider with his hands on the brake hoods (drag area of 0.358 meter squared), a rider with his hands on the drops of road handlebars (0.307 meter squared), a rider with his elbows on time-trial handlebars (0.269 meter squared; baseline condition), and a rider with a wind-tunnel-optimized position (0.240 meter squared). John E. Cobb at the Texas A&M University Aerodynamics Laboratory recorded the drag areas used to represent these positions. Figures 22.2, 22.3, and 22.4 incorporate the effects of these three alternative positions.

Compared with the standard aero position, riding with the hands on the handlebar drops would decrease speed by 1.5 to 2.5 kilometers per hour, whereas riding with the hands on the brake hoods would decrease performance by a huge 4 kilometers per hour (leading to a five- to seven-minute slower time trial). However, having an optimized aero position, as can be achieved with wind-tunnel testing or by trial and error at home (see chapter 9), can improve speed by 1.2 to 1.7 kilometers per hour. It is clear that the amount of time that a rider can save by improving body position is dramatic and is effectively "free." Cyclists can gain minutes with little financial outlay.

Bicycle

In our imaginary time trial, each of our riders rode both a regular round tubed bike and an aerodynamic frame while maintaining the same body position. With the aerodynamic frame, the model predicted an increase in velocity of 1.0 kilometer per hour (equivalent to 2 minutes, 8 seconds faster), 1.3 kilometers per hour (1:47 minutes), and 1.5 kilometers per hour (1:36) for riders A, B, and C, respectively.

Frame and Body Position Combined

In the next scenario, our cyclists used the aerodynamic frames while adjusting them to optimize their aero position. If we assume that the aerodynamic savings are additive, then total drag area will be dramatically decreased. Based on this combined effect, the model predicts speed increases of 3.0 to 3.4 kilometers per hour, leading to performance times being decreased by a dramatic 4:52 minutes for rider A, 6:02 minutes for rider B, and 3:37 minutes for rider C.

Wheels

The baseline parameters of the model assumed that our riders are using aerodynamic wheels. However, many people race on regular spoked wheels and it is clear that this will affect performance. Our riders therefore rode the imaginary time-trial course again with regular 36-spoke wheels. This resulted in decreased performance for all riders (0.6 to 0.8 kilometer per hour, a decrease that was greater than the effect of increasing bicycle weight by three kilograms.

Climbing: Weight and Aerodynamics

In chapter 10, John Cobb and Jim Martin discuss climbing performance and the complex interaction among power output, road grade, mass, and aerodynamics. They note that the advantages of a particular bicycle setup are dependent on this relationship and use the model to give some indications of the effects of aerodynamic or lightweight equipment on climbing performance. In this final chapter we use a similar comparison with our three riders in which they ride a mountain time trial, once with aerodynamic wheels and once with lightweight climbing wheels (assumed to be 500 grams lighter than the aero wheels but to have 0.165-meter-squared greater drag area).

Our virtual mountain time-trial course was 10 kilometers in length and had a constant gradient of either 3, 6, or 12 percent. In this case, wind speed was assumed to be zero. As Cobb and Martin show (chapter 10), the aerodynamic wheels resulted in increased speed on the 3 percent road grade for all three modeled riders. For the 6 percent grade, the lightweight wheel set was faster for riders A and B, but the aerodynamic wheel was slightly better for rider C. Finally, at 12 percent, the lightweight wheels provided an advantage for all three riders (see figure 22.5). Thus, the optimal wheel depends on the fitness or power output of the rider and on the grade of the climb. However, although different wheels are better in different situations, a lighter bike always offers a performance advantage when the rider is climbing.

We discuss earlier how a 3-kilogram weight reduction resulted in only a small increase in performance over the simulated time-trial course. However, the effects of reduced mass are much greater on long mountain time trials or mountaintop finishes in which the additional effect of the weight on the downhill is not important. To illustrate this, our imaginary riders used a 7-kilogram bike instead of their baseline 10-kilogram bike on the three mountain time trials (3, 6, and 12 percent). Figure 22.5 illustrates the results, and the importance of a lighter bike is clear. The model predicts that the use of a 7-kilogram bicycle by rider A on the 12 percent climb increases his speed from 5.9 to 6.1 kilometers per hour—a seemingly small increase but one that results in an overall gain of seven minutes (figure 22.5). Indeed, such a time savings would have a significant effect on the outcome of a road or stage race.

Road Races

The model we describe in this chapter may be applicable to time-trial racing, but predicting road-race performance with such a model may be inaccurate. This is largely because of the other factors that determine performance in road racing: It is not always the rider who produces the most power, the best power-to-weight ratio, or the best aerodynamics who wins a race. Skill, the position of other riders, and tactics all play important roles in determining final placings in road races.

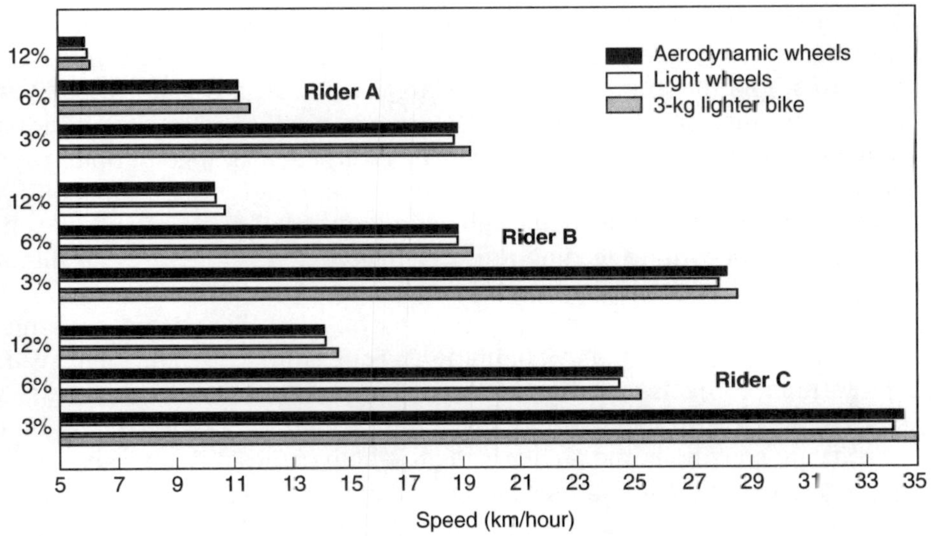

Figure 22.5 Comparison of the effect of reducing bicycle mass and the effects of aero or lightweight wheels on a 20-kilometer climb with either a 3, 6, or 12 percent constant gradient. Bars show average speed (in kilometers per hour) for the 20-kilometer mountain time trial.

As chapter 6 discusses, during the Tour de France it was observed that one of the riders managed to reduce his average power output to just 98 watts (Jeukendrup et al. 2000) on a stage that averaged 40 kilometers for six hours. In optimal conditions with no wind and level roads and with a good aerodynamic position, riding at that speed normally would require approximately 275 watts (Martin et al. 1998). It is therefore important to realize that cyclists often may enter the final stages of a road race (at a time when many races are won or lost) having performed very different amounts of work, and subsequently they'll be at very different levels of fatigue.

Overview and Conclusions

This chapter analyzes the potential effects of several of the variables that can influence exercise performance, using a model developed by Jim Martin and colleagues (Martin et al. 1998). The factors we examine are, according to the current scientific literature, the most important factors for performance enhancement. Support for the performance-enhancing effects of other supposed (legal) ergogenic aids is less scientifically sound, and therefore we have not included those factors in this analysis.

This chapter aims to compare and weigh the advice given in earlier chapters to allow you to make an informed decision as to how to improve your performance. In doing this, we have highlighted some interesting results. First, it won't surprise anyone to see that training is the most important factor influencing performance for our novice cyclist, rider C. However, when the level of fitness rises, the amount that can be gained from training decreases, and thus training is not the most effective performance-enhancing variable for our trained and elite riders (B and C).

Throughout this chapter we can see that rider A has significantly more scope for improvement than the well-trained rider C. Although increases in speed may be similar, the novice rider is on the course for a longer time and therefore benefits from the increased speed to a greater degree. This effect is visible both in the internal and external factors, and the improvements are larger for novice cyclists when they are expressed in absolute or relative terms. However, we must note that performance improvements may not always be additive. For example, a change in body position may result in a reduction in aerodynamic drag but may cause discomfort or a poor biomechanical position that may reduce power output. On the other hand, the effects of training and carbohydrate feeding are very likely to be additive to all the other variables.

We must mention again that the data and analysis that this chapter presents are based on a model and, as such, have limitations. For example, no data were available on the performance effects of eating a nutritious, healthy diet for many years, and thus we were not able to include that factor in our model. Additionally, the model assumes constant conditions and no rider fatigue—both of these are unlikely scenarios. However, regardless of the limitations of the model, it provides an important base for comparing and contrasting the effects of different modifications of equipment and training on performance.

It generally can be seen that someone with a suboptimal position easily can gain significant amounts of time. Also, financial investments may result in improved time-trial performances. However, we also have to keep in mind that the model we use does not take into account factors such as bike handling and bike behavior. A very aerodynamic bike is not necessarily the best bike for all conditions. Everyone knows the disadvantages of disc wheels in windy conditions. Another important observation is that training can result in large performance improvements, but the effect becomes smaller the more trained a person becomes. At the elite level, enormous efforts may result in relatively small improvements of power output.

Whether the changes resulting from the different factors discussed in this book and summarized in this concluding chapter are additive is not known. We hope, however, that this book forms a stimulus for you to think carefully about all these factors and that critical and analytical thinking will help to improve your performance. Most of all, we hope that this book demonstrates that sport science can add to the passion for this fantastic sport and that it does not replace it.

references

Chapter 1

Bannister, E.W. 1991. Modeling elite athletic performance. In *Physiological testing of elite athletes*, edited by H.J. Green, J.D. McDougall, and H. Wenger. Champaign, IL: Human Kinetics, pp. 403–24.

Bannister, E.W., J.B. Carter, and P.C. Zarkadas. 1999. Training theory and taper: Validation in triathlon athletes. *Eur J Appl Physiol* 79:182–91.

Bouchard, C., F.T. Dionne, J.A. Simoneau, and M.R. Boulay. 1992. Genetics of aerobic and anaerobic performances. *Exerc Sports Sci Rev* 20:27-58.

Coyle, E.F., W.H. Martin, D.R. Sinacore, M.J. Joyner et al. 1984. Time course of loss of adaptations after stopping prolonged intense endurance training. *J Appl Physiol* 57:1857-1864.

Hawley, J.A. 2000. Training techniques for successful running performance. In *Running*, edited by J.A. Hawley. Oxford: Blackwell Science, pp. 44–57.

Hawley, J.A., and L.M. Burke. 1998. *Peak performance: Training and nutritional strategies for sport*. Sydney: Allen & Unwin.

Hawley, J.A., K.H. Myburgh, T.D. Noakes, and S.C. Dennis. 1997. Training techniques to improve fatigue resistance and enhance endurance performance. *J Sports Sci* 15:325–33.

Hopkins, W.G. 1998. Measurement of training in competitive sports. *Sportscience* 2(4). Available: sportsci.org/jour/9804/wgh.html.

Jeukendrup, A.E., N.P. Craig, and J.A. Hawley. 2000. Bioenergetics of world class cycling. *J Sci Med Sport* 3(4):414–433.

Jeukendrup, A.E., and A. van Diemen. 1998. Heart rate monitoring during training and competition in cyclists. *J Sports Sci* 16:S91–99.

Lindsay, F.H., J.A. Hawley, K.H. Myburgh, H.H. Schomer, and T.D. Noakes. 1996. Improved athletic performance in highly-trained cyclists after interval training. *Med Sci Sports Exerc* 28:1427–34.

Padilla, S., I. Mujika, J. Orbañanos, and F. Angulo. 2000. Exercise intensity during competition time trials in professional road cycling. *Med Sci Sports Exerc* 32:850–56.

Palmer, G.S., S.C. Dennis, T.D. Noakes, and J.A. Hawley. 1994. Heart-rate responses during a 4-d cycle stage race. *Med Sci Sports Exerc* 26:1278–83.

Shepley, B., J.D. MacDougall, N. Cipriano, J.R. Sutton, M.A. Tarnopolsky, and G. Coates. 1992. Physiological effects of tapering in highly trained athletes. *J Appl Physiol* 72:706–11.

Stepto, N.K., J.A. Hawley, S.C. Dennis, and W.G. Hopkins. 1999. Effects of different interval-training programs on cycling time-trial performance. *Med Sci Sports Exerc* 31:736–41.

Wells, C.L., and R.R. Pate. 1988. Training for performance of prolonged exercise. In *Perspectives in exercise science and sports medicine*, Vol. 1, edited by D.R. Lamb and R. Murray. Indianapolis: Benchmark Press, pp. 357–91.

Westgarth-Taylor, C., J.A. Hawley, S. Rickard, K.H. Myburgh, T.D. Noakes, and S.C. Dennis. 1997. Metabolic and performance adaptations to interval training in endurance-trained cyclists. *Eur J Appl Physiol* 75:298–304.

Chapter 2

Bakheit, A.M.O., P.O. Behan, T.G. Dinan, C.E. Gray, and V. O'Keane. 1992. Possible upregulation of hypothalamic 5-hydroxytryptamine receptors in patients with postviral fatigue syndrome. *British Medical Journal* 304:1010–12.

Barron, J.L., T.D. Noakes, W. Levy, C. Smith, and R.P. Millar. 1985. Hypothalamic dysfunction in overtrained athletes. *Journal of Clinical Endocrinology & Metabolism* 60:803–06.

Budgett, R. 1998. Fatigue and underperformance in athletes: The overtraining syndrome. *Br J Sports Med* 32:107–10.

Budgett, R., E. Newsholme, M. Lehmann, C. Sharp, D. Jones, T. Peto, D. Collins, R. Nerurkar, and P. White. 2000. Redefining the overtraining syndrome as the unexplained underperformance syndrome. *Br J Sports Med* 34:67–68.

Foster, C. 1998. Monitoring training in athletes with reference to overtraining syndrome. *Med Sci Sports Exerc* 30:1164–68.

Fry, R.W., A.R. Morton, P. Garcia-Webb, G.P. Crawford, and D. Keast. 1992. Biological responses to overload training in endurance sports. *Eur J Appl Physiol & Occup Physiol* 64:335–44.

Hooper, S.L., L.T. MacKinnon, R.D. Gordon, and A.W. Bachmann. 1993. Hormonal responses of elite swimmers to overtraining. *Med Sci Sports Exerc* 25:741–47.

Jeukendrup, A. 1999. Possible links between nutrition and overtraining. *Vlaams Tijdschrift Sportgeneeskunde & Wetenschappen* 80:37–44.

Jeukendrup, A.E., M.K. Hesselink, A.C. Snyder, H. Kuipers, and H.A. Keizer. 1992. Physiological changes in male competitive cyclists after two weeks of intensified training. *Int J Sports Med* 13:534–41.

Keizer, H. 1998. Neuroendocrine aspects of overtraining. In *Overtraining in sport*, edited by R. Kreider, A. Fry, and M. O'Toole. Champaign, IL: Human Kinetics, pp. 145–67.

Kreider, R.B., A.C. Fry, and M.L. O'Toole. 1998. *Overtraining in sport*. Champaign, IL: Human Kinetics, pp. xi.

Kuipers, H., and H.A. Keizer. 1988. Overtraining in elite athletes: Review and directions for the future. *Sports Med* 6:79–92.

Lehmann, M.J., W. Lormes, A. Opitz-Gress, J.M. Steinacker, N. Netzer, C. Foster, and U. Gastmann. 1997. Training and overtraining: An overview and experimental results in endurance sports. *Journal of Sports Medicine & Physical Fitness* 37:7–17.

O'Toole, M.L. 1998. Overreaching and overtraining in endurance athletes. In *Overtraining in sport*, edited by R. Kreider, A. Fry, and M. O'Toole. Champaign, IL: Human Kinetics, pp. 3–17.

Rushall, B.S. 1990. A tool for measuring stress tolerance in elite athletes. *J Appl Sport Psych* 2:51–66.

Snyder, A.C., H. Kuipers, B. Cheng, R. Servais, and E. Fransen. 1995. Overtraining following intensified training with normal muscle glycogen. *Med Sci Sports Exerc* 27:1063–70.

Urhausen, A., H.H. Gabriel, and W. Kindermann. 1998. Impaired pituitary hormonal response to exhaustive exercise in overtrained endurance athletes. *Med Sci Sports Exerc* 30:407–14.

Urhausen, A., H.H. Gabriel, B. Weiler, and W. Kindermann. 1998. Ergometric and psychological findings during overtraining: A long-term follow-up study in endurance athletes. *Int J Sports Med* 19:114–20.

Chapter 3

Baker, A., and W.G. Hopkins. 1998. Altitude training for sea-level competition. *Sport Science Training and Technology, Internet Society for Sport Science*. Available: http://www.sportsci.org/traintech/altitude/wgh.html.

Brosnan, M.J., D.T. Martin, A.G. Hahn, C.J. Gore, and J.A. Hawley. 2000. Impaired interval exercise responses in elite female cyclists at moderate simulated altitude. *J Appl Physiol* 89(5):1819–24.

Burke, E.R. 1995. *Serious cycling*. Champaign, IL: Human Kinetics.

Dick, F.W. 1992. Training at altitude in practice. *Int J Sports Med* 13:S203–06.

Gore, C.J., A. Hahn, A. Rice, P. Bourdon, S. Lawrence, C. Walsh, T. Stanef, P. Barnes, R. Parisotto, D. Martin, D. Pyne, and C. Gore. 1998. Altitude training at 2690m does not increase total haemoglobin mass or sea level $\dot{V}O_2$max in world champion track cyclists. *J Sci Med Sport* 1(3): 156–70.

Gore, C.J., S.C. Little, A.G. Hahn, G.C. Scroop, K.I. Norton, P.C. Bourdon, S.M. Woolford, J.D. Buckley, T. Stanef, D.P. Campbell, D.B. Watson, and D.L. Emonson. 1997. Reduced performance of male and female athletes at 580 m altitude. *Eur J Appl Physiol Occup Physiol* 75(2): 136–43.

Hahn, A.G., and C.J. Gore. 2001. The effect of altitude on cycling performance: A challenge to traditional concepts. *Sports Med* 31(7):533–57.

Hahn, A.G., C.J. Gore, D.T. Martin, M.J. Ashenden, A.D. Roberts, and P.A. Logan. 2001. An evaluation of the concept of living at moderate altitude and training at sea level. *Comp Biochem Physiol A Mol Integr Physiol* 128(4):777–89.

Levine, B.D., and J. Stray-Gundersen. 1992. A practical approach to altitude training: Where to live and train for optimal performance enhancement. *Int J Sports Med* 13:S209–12.

Lucia, A., J. Hoyos, and J.L. Chicharro. 2001. Physiology of professional road cycling. *Sports Med* 31(5):325–37.

Morris, D.M., J.T. Kearney, and E.R. Burke. 2000. The effects of breathing supplemental oxygen during altitude training on cycling performance. *J Sci Med Sport* 3(2):165–75.

Stray-Gundersen, J., R.F. Chapman, and B.D. Levine. 2001. "Living high–training low" altitude training improves sea level performance in male and female elite runners. *J Appl Physiol* 91(3): 1113–20.

Terrados, N., J. Melichna, C. Sylven, E. Jansson, and L. Kaijser. 1988. Effects of training at simulated altitude on performance and muscle metabolic capacity in competitive road cyclists. *Eur J Appl Physiol Occup Physiol* 57(2):203–09.

Vogt, M., A. Puntschart, J. Geiser, C. Zuleger, R. Billeter, and H. Hoppeler. 2001. Molecular adaptations in human skeletal muscle to endurance training under simulated hypoxic conditions. *J Appl Physiol* 91(1):173–82.

West, J.B. 2001. Safe upper limits for oxygen enrichment of room air at high altitude. *High Alt Med Biol* 2(1):47–51.

Wilber, R.L. 2001. Current trends in altitude training. *Sports Med* 31(4):249–65.

Chapter 4

Crowley, G.C., A. Garg, M.S. Lohn, N. Van Someren, and A.J. Wade. 1991. Effects of cooling the legs on performance in a standard Wingate anaerobic power test. *Br J Sports Med* 25:200–03.

Ellis, A. 2001. Cool helmets. *Bicycling Australia* 12:56–68.

Galloway, S.D.R., and R.J. Maughan. 1997. Effects of ambient temperature on the capacity to perform prolonged cycle exercise in man. *Med Sci Sports Exerc* 29:1240–49.

Gonzalez-Alonso, J. 1998. Separate and combined influences of dehydration and hyperthermia on cardiovascular responses to exercise. *Int J Sports Med* 19, Suppl. 2:S111–14.

Gonzalez-Alonso, J., C. Teller, S.L. Andersen, F.B. Jensen, T. Hyldig, and B. Nielsen. 1999. Influence of body temperature on the development of fatigue during prolonged exercise in the heat. *J Appl Physiol* 86:1032–39.

Haymes, E.M., and C.L. Wells. 1986. *Environment and human performance*. Champaign, IL: Human Kinetics.

Horswill, C. 1991. Does rapid weight loss by dehydration adversely affect high-power performance? *Gatorade Sports Science Exchange* 4:1–4.

Kay, D., D.R. Taaffe, and F.E. Marino. 1999. Whole-body pre-cooling and heat storage during self-paced cycling performance in warm humid conditions. *J Sports Sci* 17:937–44.

Marvin, G., L. Nobbs, A. Sharma, and D.A. Jones. 1998. Hypothalamic thermoreceptors and central fatigue. In *Third Annual Congress of the European College of Sports Science*. Manchester, U.K., p. 154.

Nielsen, B., J.R.S. Hales, S. Strange, N.J. Christensen, J. Warberg, and B. Saltin. 1993. Human circulatory and thermoregulatory adaptations with heat acclimation and exercise in a hot, dry environment. *J Physiol* 460:467–85.

Nielsen, B., S. Strange, N.J. Christensen, J. Warberg, and B. Saltin. 1997. Acute and adaptive responses in humans to exercise in a warm, humid environment. *Pflugers Arch – Eur J Physiol* 434:49–56.

Parkin, J.M., M.F. Carey, S. Zhao, and M.A. Febbraio. 1999. Effect of ambient temperature on human skeletal muscle metabolism during fatiguing submaximal exercise. *J Appl Physiol* 86:902–08.

Rennie, D.W., Y. Park, A. Veicsteinas, and D. Pendergast. 1980. Metabolic and circulatory adaptation to cold water stress. In *Exercise bioenergetics and gas exchange*, edited by P. Cerretelli and B.J. Whipp. Amsterdam, Holland: Elsevier/North Holland Biomedical Press, pp. 315–21.

Sargeant, A.J. 1987. Effect of muscle temperature on leg extension force and short-term power output in humans. *Eur J Appl Physiol* 56:693–98.

Sawka, M.N., and C.B. Wenger. 1988. Physiological responses to acute exercise-heat stress. In *Human performance physiology and environmental medicine at terrestrial extremes*, edited by K.B. Pandolf, M.N. Sawka, and R.R. Gonzalez. Indianapolis: Benchmark Press.

Takahashi, H., M. Tanaka, Y. Morita, S. Igawa, and H. Kita. 1992. Warming-up under cold environment. *Ann Physiol Anthropol* 11:507–16.

Tatterson, A.J., A.G. Hahn, D.T. Martin, and M.A. Febbraio. 2000. Effects of heat stress on physiological responses and exercise performance in elite cyclists. *J Sci Med Sport* 3:186–93.

Vallerand, A.L., and I. Jacobs. 1992. Energy metabolism during cold exposure. *Int J Sports Med* 13, Suppl. 1:S191–93.

Chapter 5

Billat, V.L., B. Flechet, B. Petit, G. Muriaux, and J.P. Koralsztein. 1999. Interval training at $\dot{V}O_2$max: Effects on aerobic performance and overtraining markers. *Med Sci Sports Exerc* 31:156–63.

Costill, D.L., M.G. Flynn, J.P. Kirwan, J.A. Houmard, J.B. Mitchell, R. Thomas, and S.H. Park. 1988. Effects of repeated days of intensified training on muscle glycogen and swimming performance. *Med Sci Sports Exerc* 20:249–54.

Gnehm, P., S. Reichenbach, E. Alteter, H. Widmer, and H. Hoppeler. 1997. Influence of different racing positions on metabolic cost in elite cyclists. *Med Sci Sports Sci* 29:818–23.

Goldsmith, R.L., J.T. Bigger, D.M. Bloomfield, and R.C. Steinman. 1997. Physical fitness as a determinant of vagal modulation. *Med Sci Sports Exerc* 29:812–17.

Gonzalez-Alonso, J., R. Mora-Rodriguez, P.R. Below, and E.F. Coyle. 1997. Dehydration markedly impairs cardiovascular function in hyperthermic endurance athletes during exercise. *J Appl Physiol* 82:1229–36.

Gonzalez-Alonso, J., C. Teller, S.L. Andersen, F.B. Jensen, T. Hyldig, and B. Nielsen. 1999. Influence of body temperature in the development of fatigue during prolonged exercise in the heat. *J Appl Physiol* 86:1032–39.

Gonzalez-Alonso, J., R. Mora-Rodriguez, and E.F. Coyle. 2000. Stroke volume during exercise: Interaction of environment and hydration. *Am J Physiol* 278:H321–30.

Hedelin, R., G. Kentta, U. Wiklund, P. Bjerle, and K. Henriksson-Larsen. 2000a. Short-term overtraining: Effects on performance, circulatory responses, and heart rate variability. *Med Sci Sports Exerc* 32:1480–4.

Hedelin, R., U. Wiklund, P. Bjerle, and K. Henriksson-Larsen. 2000b. Cardiac autonomic imbalance in an overtrained athlete. *Med Sci Sports Exerc* 32:1531–33.

Heil, D.P., A.R. Wilcox, and C.M. Quinn. 1995. Cardiorespiratory responses to seat-tube angle variation during steady-state cycling. *Med Sci Sports Exerc* 27:730–35.

Jeukendrup, A., and A. van Diemen. 1998. Heart rate monitoring during training and competition in cyclists. *J Sports Sci* 16:1–9.

Jeukendrup, A.E., M.K.C. Hesselink, H. Kuipers, and H.A. Keizer. Physiological changes in male competitive cyclists after two weeks of intensified training. 1992. *Int J Sports Med* 13:534–41.

Lucia, L., J. Hoyos, and A. Carvajal. 1999. Heart rate response to professional road cycling: The Tour de France. *Int J Sports Med* 20:167–72.

Padilla, S., I. Mujika, and J. Orbañanos. In press. Exercise intensity and load during mass-start stage races in professional road cycling. *Med Sci Sport Exerc.*

Padilla, S., I. Mujika, J. Orbañanos, and F. Angulo. 2000. Exercise intensity during competition time trials in professional road cycling. *Med Sci Sport Exerc* 32:850–56.

Palmer, G.S., J.A. Hawley, S.C. Dennis, and T.D. Noakes. 1994. Heart rate responses during a 4-d cycle stage race. *Med Sci Sports Exerc* 26:1278–83.

Pichot, V., F. Roche, J.-M. Gaspoz, F. Enjolras, A. Antoniadis, P. Minimi, F. Costes, T. Busso, J.-R. Lacour, and J.C. Barthelemy. 2000. Relation between heart rate variability and training load in middle distance runners. *Med Sci Sport Exerc* 32:1729–36.

Sheel, A.W., I. Lama, P. Potvin, K.D. Coutts, and D.C. McKenzie. 1996. Comparison of aero-bars versus traditional cycling postures on physiological parameters during submaximal cycling. *Can J Appl Physiol* 21:16–22.

Shin, K., H. Minamitani, S. Onishi, H. Yamazaki, and M. Lee. 1997. Autonomic differences between athletes and nonathletes: Spectral analysis approach. *Med Sci Sports Med* 29:1482–90.

Stray-Gundersen, J., T. Videman, and P.G. Snell. 1986. Changes in selected parameters during overtraining. *Med Sci Sports Exerc* 18:S54–55.

Urhausen, A., H.H. Gabriel, B. Weiler, and W. Kindermann. 1998. Ergometric and psychological findings during overtraining: A long-term follow-up study in endurance athletes. *Int J Sports Med* 19:114–20.

Uusitalo, A.L., A.J. Uusitalo, and H.K. Rusko. 2000. Heart rate and blood pressure variability during heavy training and overtraining in the female athlete. *Int J Sports Med* 21:45–53.

Chapter 6

Broker, J.P., C.R. Kyle, and E.R. Burke. 1999. Racing cyclist power requirements in the 4000-m individual and team pursuit. *Med Sci Sports Exerc* 31:1677–85.
Grazzi, G., N. Alfieri, C. Borsetto, I. Casoni, F. Manfredini, G. Mazzoni, and F. Conconi. 1999. The power output/heart rate relationship in cycling: Test standardization and repeatability. *Med Sci Sports Exerc* 31:1478–83.
Hawley, J.A., and T.D. Noakes. 1992. Peak power output predicts maximal oxygen uptake and performance time in trained cyclists. *Eur J Appl Physiol* 65:79–83.
Jeukendrup, A.E., and A. van Diemen. 1998. Heart rate monitoring during training and competition in cycling. *J Sport Sci* 16:S91–99.
Jeukendrup, A.E., N. Craig, and J.A.H. Hawley. 2000. Bioenergetics of world class cycling. *J Sci Med Sport* 3(4):414–433.
Keen, P. 1997. A measured life. *Odyssee* 3:58–64.
Kyle, C.R. 1979. Reduction of wind resistance and power output of racing cyclists and runners travelling in groups. *Ergonomics* 22:387–97.
Lucia, A., J. Hoyos, A. Carvajal, and J.L. Chicharro. 1999. Heart rate response to professional road cycling: The Tour de France. *Int J Sports Med* 20:167–72.
Martin, J.C., D.L. Milliken, J.E. Cobb, K.L. McFadden, and A.R. Coggan. 1998. Validation of a mathematical model for road cycling power. *J Appl Biomech* 14:276–91.
McCole, S., K. Claney, J.-C. Conte, R. Anderson, and J.M. Hagberg. 1990. Energy expenditure during bicycling. *J Appl Physiol* 68:748–53.
Padilla, S., I. Mujika, F. Angulo, and J.J. Goiriena. 2000a. Scientific approach to the 1-h cycling world record: A case study. *J Appl Physiol* 89:1522–27.
Padilla, S., I. Mujika, J. Orbañanos, and F. Angulo. 2000b. Exercise intensity during competition time trials in professional road cycling. *Med Sci Sports Exerc* 32:850–56.

Chapter 7

Åstrand, P.O. 1970. *Work tests with the bicycle ergometer*. Varberg, Sweden: Monark-Crescent AB.
Banister, E.W. 1991. Modeling elite athletic performance. In *Physiological testing of elite athletes*, edited by H.J. Green, J.D. McDougal, and H. Wenger. Champaign, IL: Human Kinetics, pp. 403–24.
Craig, N., C. Walsh, D.T. Martin, S. Woolford, P. Bourdon, T. Stanef, P. Barnes, and B. Savage. 2000. Protocols for the physiological assessment of high-performance track, road, and mountain cyclists. In *Physiological tests for elite athletes*, edited by C.J. Gore. Champaign, IL: Human Kinetics, pp. 258–77.
Di Prampero, P.E., G. Cortili, P. Mognoni, and F. Saibene. 1979. Equation of motion of a cyclist. *J Appl Physiol* 47:201–06.
Du Bois, D., and E.F. Du Bois. 1916. Clinical calorimeter: A formula to estimate the approximate surface area if height and weight be known. *Arch Intern Med* 17:863–71.
Hagberg, J.M., and E.C. Coyle. 1983. Physiological determinants of endurance performance as studied in competitive racewalkers. *Med Sci Sports Exerc* 15:287–89.
Hawley, J.A., and T.D. Noakes. 1992. Peak power output predicts maximal oxygen uptake and performance time in trained cyclists. *Eur J Appl Physiol* 65:79–83.
Jeukendrup, A., and A. van Diemen. 1998. Heart rate monitoring during training and competition in cyclists. *J Sports Sci* 16:S91–99.
Jeukendrup, A.E., N.P. Craig, and J.A. Hawley. 2000. The bioenergetics of world class cycling. *J Sci Med Sport* 3(4): 414–33.
Kuipers, H., F.T.J. Verstappen, H.A. Keizer, and P. Geurten. 1985. Variability of aerobic performance in the laboratory and its physiological correlates. *Int J Sports Med* 6:197–201.
Lucía, A., J. Hoyos, A. Carvajal, and J.L. Chicharro. 1999. Heart rate response to professional road cycling: The Tour de France. *Int J Sports Med* 20:167–72.
Lucía, A., J. Hoyos, M. Pérez, and J.L. Chicharro. 2000. Heart rate and performance parameters in elite cyclists: A longitudinal study. *Med Sci Sports Exerc* 32:1777–82.
Lucía, A., J. Pardo, A. Durántez, J. Hoyos, and J.L. Chicharro. 1998. Physiological differences between professional and elite road cyclists. *Int J Sports Med* 19:342–48.
Padilla, S., I. Mujika, G. Cuesta, and J.J. Goiriena. 1999. Level ground and uphill cycling ability in professional road cycling. *Med Sci Sports Exerc* 31:878–85.

Padilla, S., I. Mujika, F. Angulo, and J.J. Goiriena. 2000a. Scientific approach to the 1-h cycling world record: A case study. *J Appl Physiol* 89:1522–27.
Padilla, S., I. Mujika, J. Orbañanos, J. Santisteban, F. Angulo, and J.J. Goiriena. 2001. Exercise intensity and load during mass-start stage races in professional road cycling. *Med Sci Sports Exerc* 33:796–802.
Padilla, S., I. Mujika, J. Orbañanos, and F. Angulo. 2000b. Exercise intensity during competition time trials in professional road cycling. *Med Sci Sports Exerc* 32:850–56.
Padilla, S., I. Mujika, G. Cuesta, J.M. Polo, and J.-C. Chatard. 1996. Validity of a velodrome test for competitive road cyclists. *Eur J Appl Physiol* 73:446–51.
Palmer, G.S., J.A. Hawley, S.C. Dennis, and T.D. Noakes. 1994. Heart rate responses during a 4-d cycle stage race. *Med Sci Sports Exerc* 26:1278–83.
Sjödin, B., and I. Jacobs. 1981. Onset of blood lactate accumulation and marathon running performance. *Int J Sports Med* 2:23–26.
Swain, D.P., J.R. Coast, P.S. Clifford, M.C. Milliken, and J. Stray-Gundersen. 1987. Influence of body size on oxygen consumption during bicycling. *J Appl Physiol* 62:668–72.

Chapter 8

Australian Sports Commission. 2000. *Physiological tests for elite athletes*. Champaign, IL: Human Kinetics.
Coyle, E.F. 1995. Integration of the physiological factors determining endurance performance ability. In *Perspectives in exercise science and sports medicine*, edited by C.V. Gisolfi and D.R. Lamb. Indianapolis: Benchmark Press, pp. 25–63.
Coyle, E.F., A.R. Coggan, M.K. Hopper, and T.J. Walters. 1988. Determinants of endurance in well trained cyclists. *J Appl Physiol* 64:2622–30.
Coyle, E.F., M.E. Feltner, S.A. Kautz, M.T. Hamilton, S.J. Montain, A.M. Baylor, L.D. Abraham, and G.W. Petrek. 1991. Physiological and biomechanical factors associated with elite endurance cycling performance. *Med Sci Sports Exerc* 23:93–107.
Di Prampero, P.E., G. Cortili, P. Mognoni, and F. Saibene. 1979. Equation of motion of a cyclist. *J Appl Physiol* 47(1):201–06.
Faria, I.E., E.W. Faria, S. Roberts, and D. Yoshimura. 1989. Comparison of physical and physiological characteristics in elite young and mature cyclists. *Research Quarterly for Exercise and Sport* 60:388–95.
Hawley, J.A., and N.K. Stepto. 2001. Adaptations to training in endurance cyclists: Implications for performance. *Sports Med* 31(7):511–20.
Hopkins, W.G., E.J. Schabort, and J.A. Hawley. 2001. Reliability of power in physical performance tests. *Sports Med* 31(3):211–34.
MacDougall, J.D., H.A. Wenger, and H.J. Green, eds. 1991. *Physiological testing of the high-performance athlete*. Champaign, IL: Human Kinetics.
Martin, D.T., B. McLean, C. Trewin, H. Lee, J. Victor, and A.G. Hahn. 2001. Physiological characteristics of nationally competitive female road cyclists and demands of competition. *Sports Med* 31(7):469–77.
Maud, P.J., and C. Foster, eds. 1995. *Physiological assessment of human fitness*. Champaign, IL: Human Kinetics.
Padilla, S., I. Mujika, G. Cuesta, J.M. Polo, and J.C. Chatard. 1996. Validity of a velodrome test for competitive road cyclists. *Eur J Appl Physiol Occup Physiol* 73(5):446–51.
Palmer, G.S., S.C. Dennis, T.D. Noakes, and J.A. Hawley. 1996. Assessment of the reproducibility of performance testing on an air-braked cycle ergometer. *Int J Sports Med* 17(4):293–98.

Chapter 9

Heil, D.P., T.R. Derrick, and S. Whittlesey. 1997. The relationship between preferred and optimal positioning during submaximal cycle ergometry. *Eur J Appl Physiol Occup Physiol* 75:160–65.
Heil, D.P., A.R. Wilcox, and C.M. Quinn. 1995. Cardiorespiratory responses to seat-tube angle variation during steady-state cycling. *Med Sci Sports Exerc* 27:730–35.
Lemond, G., and K. Gordis. 1987. *Greg Lemond's complete book of bicycling*. New York: Putnam.
Martin, J.C., D.L. Milliken, J.E. Cobb, K.L. McFadden, and A.R. Coggan. 1998. Validation of a mathematical model for road cycling power. *J Appl Biomech* 14:276–91.

Price, D., and B. Donne. 1997. Effect of variation in seat tube angle at different seat heights on submaximal cycling performance in man. *J Sports Sci* 15:395–402.

Ryschon, T.W., and J. Stray-Gundersen. 1991. The effect of body position on the energy cost of cycling. *Med Sci Sports Exerc* 23:949–53.

Chapter 10

Greenwell, D.I., N.J. Wood, E.K.L. Bridge, and R.J. Addy. 1995. Aerodynamic characteristics of low-drag bicycle wheels. *Aeronautical Journal* 99:109-120.

Jeukendrup, A.E., N. Craig, and J.A.H. Hawley. 2000. Bioenergetics of world class cycling. *J Sci Med Sport* 3(4):414–433.

Kyle, C. 1986. Mechanical factors affecting the speed of a cycle. In *Science of Cycling*, edited by Edmund R. Burke. Champaign, IL: Human Kinetics.

Martin, J.C., D.L. Milliken, J.E. Cobb, K.L. McFadden, and A.R. Coggan. 1998. Validation of a mathematical model for road cycling power. *J Appl Biomech* 14:276–91.

Chapter 12

Achten, J., M. Gleeson, and A.E. Jeukendrup. In press, 2002. Determination of the exercise intensity that elicits maximal fat oxidation. *Med Sci Sports Exerc* 34:1.

Brouns, F., W.H.M. Saris, J. Stroecken, E. Beckers, R. Thijssen, N.J. Rehrer, and F. ten Hoor. 1989. Eating, drinking, and cycling. A controlled Tour de France simulation study, part I. *Int J Sports Med* 10: S32–S40.

Garcia-Roves, P., N. Terrados, S. Fernandez, and A. Patterson. 1997. Macronutrients intake of top level cyclists during continuous competition change in the feeding pattern. *Int J Sports Med* 19:61–67.

Jensen, C.D., E.S. Zaltas, J.H. Whittam. 1992. Dietary intakes of male endurance cyclists during training and racing. *J Am Diet Assoc* 92:986–87.

Jeukendrup, A., N. Craig, and J.A. Hawley. 2000. The bioenergetics of world class cycling. *J Sci Med Sport* 3:400–19.

Jeukendrup, A.E., W.H.M. Saris, and A.J.M. Wagenmakers. 1998. Fat metabolism during exercise: A review. Part I: Fatty acid mobilization and muscle metabolism. *Int J Sports Med* 19:231–44.

Johnson, A., P. Collins, I. Higgings et al. 1985. Psychological, nutritional and physical status of Olympic road cyclists. *Br J Sports Med* 19:11–14.

Saris, W.H.M., M.A. van Erp-Baart, F. Brouns, K.R. Westerterp, and F. ten Hoor. 1989. Study on food intake and energy expenditure during extreme sustained exercise: The Tour de France. *Int J Sports Med* 10:S26–31.

van Erp-Baart, A.M.J., W.H.M. Saris, R. Binkhorst, and F. ten Hoor. 1989. Nationwide survey on nutritional habits in elite athletes. *Int J Sports Med* 10:S3–10.

Chapter 13

Armstrong, L.E., C.M. Maresh, J.W. Castellani, M.F. Bergeron, R.W. Kenefick, K.E. LaGasse, and D. Riebe. 1994. Urinary indices of hydration status. *Int J Sports Nutr* 4:265–79.

Bar-Or, O., and B. Wilk. 1996. Water and electrolyte replenishment in the exercising child. *Int J Sport Nutr* 6:93–99.

Below, P., R. Mora-Rodriguez, J. Gonzalez-Alonso, and E.F. Coyle. 1995. Fluid and carbohydrate ingestion independently improve performance during 1 h of intense cycling. *Med Sci Sports Exerc* 27:200–10.

Craig, N.P., and K.J. Norton. 2001. Characteristics of track cycling. *Sports Med* 31:457–68.

Gonzalez-Alonso J., J.A.L. Calbet, and B. Nielsen. 1998. Muscle blood flow is reduced with dehydration during prolonged exercise in humans. *J Physiol* 513:895–905.

Leiper, J.B., A. Carnie, and R.J. Maughan. 1996. Water turnover rates in sedentary and exercising middle-aged men. *Br J Sports Med* 30:24–26.

Maughan, R.J. 1985. Thermoregulation and fluid balance in marathon competition at low ambient temperature. *Int J Sports Med* 6:15–19.

Maughan, R.J., and J.B. Leiper. 1995. Effects of sodium content of ingested fluids on post-exercise rehydration in man. *Eur J Appl Physiol* 71:311–19.

Maughan, R.J., and S.M. Shirreffs. 1998. Fluid and electrolyte loss and replacement in exercise. In *Oxford textbook of sports medicine*, 2nd ed., edited by M. Harries, C. Williams, W.D. Stanish, and L.L. Micheli. New York: Oxford University Press, pp. 97–113.

Montain, S.J., and E.F. Coyle. 1992a. Fluid ingestion during exercise increases skin blood flow independent of increases in blood volume. *J Appl Physiol* 73:903–10.

Montain, S.J., and E.F. Coyle. 1992b. Influence of graded dehydration on hyperthermia and cardiovascular drift during exercise. *J Appl Physiol* 73:1340–50.

Nielsen B, J.R.S. Hales, S. Strange, N.J. Christensen, J. Warberg, and B. Saltin. 1993. Human circulatory and thermoregulatory adaptations with heat acclimation and exercise in a hot, dry environment. *J Physiol* 460:467–86.

Nielsen, B., R. Kubica, A. Bonnesen, I.B. Rasmussen, J. Stoklosa, and B. Wilk. 1982. Physical work capacity after dehydration and hyperthermia. *Scandinavian Journal of Sports Sciences* 3:2–10.

Shirreffs, S.M., and R.J. Maughan. 2000. Water turnover and regulation of fluid balance. In *Sports drinks*, edited by R.J. Maughan and R. Murray. Boca Raton, FL: CRC Press, pp. 29–44.

Shirreffs, S.M., A.J. Taylor, J.B. Leiper, and R.J. Maughan. 1996. Post-exercise rehydration in man: Effects of volume consumed and sodium content of ingested fluids. *Med Sci Sports Ex* 28:1260–71.

Chapter 14

Burke, L.M., A. Claasen, J.A. Hawley, and T.D. Noakes. 1998. Carbohydrate intake during prolonged cycling minimizes effect of glycemic index of preexercise meal. *J Appl Physiol* 85:2220–26.

Costill, D.L., E. Coyle, G. Dalsky, W. Evans, W. Fink, and D. Hoopes. 1977. Effects of elevated plasma FFA and insulin on muscle glycogen usage during exercise. *J Appl Physiol* 43:695–99.

Coyle, E.F., A.R. Coggan, M.K. Hemmert, and J.L. Ivy. 1986. Muscle glycogen utilization during prolonged strenuous exercise when fed carbohydrate. *J Appl Physiol* 61:165–72.

Coyle, E.F., A.R. Coggan, M.K. Hemmert, R.C. Lowe, and T.J. Walters. 1985. Substrate usage during prolonged exercise following a preexercise meal. *J Appl Physiol* 59:429–33.

Hawley, J.A., E.J. Schabort, T.D. Noakes, and S.C. Dennis. 1997. Carbohydrate-loading and exercise performance: An update. *Sports Med* 24:73–81.

Hitchins, S., D.T. Martin, L. Burke, K. Yates, K. Fallon, A. Hahn, and G.P. Dobson. 1999. Glycerol hyperhydration improves cycle time trial performance in hot humid conditions. *Eur J Appl Physiol* 80:494–501.

Jeukendrup, A.E., F. Brouns, A.J. Wagenmakers, and W.H. Saris. 1997. Carbohydrate-electrolyte feedings improve 1-h time trial cycling performance. *Int J Sports Med* 18:125–29.

Jeukendrup, A.E., N.P. Craig, and J.A. Hawley. 2000. The bioenergetics of world class cycling. *J Sci Med Sport* 3:414–33.

Jeukendrup, A.E. and L.P.G. Jentjens. 2000. Efficacy of carbohydrate feedings during prolonged exercise: Current thoughts, guidelines and directions for future research. *Sports Med* 29(6):407–24.

Kuipers, H., E.J. Fransen, and H.A. Keizer. 1999. Pre-exercise ingestion of carbohydrate and transient hypoglycemia during exercise. *Int J Sports Med* 20:227–31.

Latzka, W.A., M.N. Sawka, S.J. Montain, G.S. Skrinar, R.A. Fielding, R.A. Matott, and K.B. Pandolf. 1998. Hyperhydration: Tolerance and cardiovascular effects during uncompensable exercise-heat stress. *J Appl Physiol* 84:1858–64.

Marmy Conus, N., S. Fabris, J. Proietto, and M. Hargreaves. 1996. Pre-exercise glucose ingestion and glucose kinetics during exercise. *J Appl Physiol* 81:853–57.

Montain, S.J., M.K. Hopper, A.R. Coggan, and E.F. Coyle. 1991. Exercise metabolism at different time intervals after a meal. *J Appl Physiol* 70:882–88.

Walsh, R.M., T.D. Noakes, J.A. Hawley, and S.C. Dennis. 1994. Impaired high-intensity cycling performance time at low levels of dehydration. *Int J Sports Med* 15:392–98.

Chapter 15

Bergström J., L. Hermansen, E. Hultman, and B. Saltin. 1967. Diet, muscle glycogen and physical performance. *Acta Physiol Scand* 71:140–50.

Burke L., G.R. Collier, S.K. Beasley, P.G. Davis, P.A. Fricker, P. Heeley, K. Walder, and M. Hargreaves. 1995. Effect of coingestion of fat and protein with carbohydrate feedings on muscle glycogen storage. *J Appl Physiol* 78:2187–92.

Burke, L.M., G.R. Collier, and M. Hargreaves. 1998. Glycemic index: A new tool in sport nutrition? *Int J Sport Nutr* 8:401–15.
Hargreaves, M., G. McConnell, and J. Proietto. 1995. Influence of muscle glycogen on glycogenolysis and glucose uptake during exercise in humans. *J Appl Physiol* 78:288–92.
Hawley, J.A., and L.M. Burke. 1998. *Peak performance: Training and nutritional strategies for sport.* St. Leonards: Allen and Unwin.
Hawley, J.A., E.J. Schabort, T.D. Noakes, and S.C. Dennis. 1997. Carbohydrate-loading and exercise performance. *Sports Med* 24:72–81.
Ivy, J.L., A.L. Katz, C.L. Cutler, W.M. Sherman, and E.F. Coyle. 1988. Muscle glycogen synthesis after exercise: Effect of time of carbohydrate ingestion. *J Appl Physiol* 64:1480–85.
Ivy, J.L., M.C. Lee, J.T. Brozinick, and M.J. Reed. 1988. Muscle glycogen storage after different amounts of carbohydrate ingestion. *J Appl Physiol* 65:2018–23.
Jentjens, R.L.P.G., L.J.C. van Loon, C.H. Mann, A.J.M. Wagenmakers, and A.E. Jeukendrup. 2001. Addition of protein and amino acids to carbohydrates does not enhance post-exercise muscle glycogen synthesis. *J Appl Physiol* 91:839–46.
Jeukendrup, A.E., and R. Jentjens. 2000. Oxidation of carbohydrate feedings during prolonged exercise: Current thoughts, guidelines and directions for future research. *Sports Med* 29:407–24.
Kirwan, J.P., D.L. Costill, J.B. Mitchell, J.A. Houmard, M.G. Flynn, W.J. Fink, and J.D. Beltz. 1988. Carbohydrate balance in competitive runners during successive days of exercise. *J Appl Physiol* 65:2601–06.
Price, T.B., D. Laurent, K.F. Petersen, D.L. Rothman, and G.I. Shulman. 2000. Glycogen loading alters muscle glycogen resynthesis after exercise. *J Appl Physiol* 88:698–704.
Sherman, W.M., D.L. Costill, W.J. Fink, and J.M. Miller. 1981. Effect of exercise-diet manipulation on muscle glycogen and its subsequent utilisation during performance. *Int J Sports Med* 2:114–18.
Sherman, W.M., M.A. Doyle, D.R. Lamb, and R.H. Strauss. 1993. Dietary carbohydrate, muscle glycogen and exercise performance during 7 d of training. *Am J Clin Nutr* 57:27–31.
Van Hall, G., S.M. Shirreffs, and J.A. Calbet. 2000. Muscle glycogen resynthesis during recovery from cycle exercise: No effect of additional protein ingestion. *J Appl Physiol* 88:1631–36.
Van Loon, L.J.C., W.H.M. Saris, M. Kruijshoop, and A.J.M. Wagenmakers. 2000. Maximizing post-exercise muscle glycogen synthesis: Carbohydrate supplementation and the application of amino acid or protein hydrolysate mixtures. *Am J Clin Nutr* 72:106–11.
Zawadzki, K.M., B.B. Yaspelkis III, and J.L. Ivy. 1992. Carbohydrate-protein complex increased the rate of muscle glycogen storage after exercise. *J Appl Physiol* 72:1854–59.

Chapter 16

Burke, L.M. 2001. Nutritional practices of road cyclists. *Sports Med* 31:521–32.
Deakin, V. 2000. Iron depletion in athletes. In *Clinical sports nutrition*, 2d ed., edited by L.M. Burke and V. Deakin. Sydney: McGraw-Hill, pp. 273–311.
Garcia-Roves, P.M, N. Terrados, S.F. Fernandez, and A.M. Patterson. 1998. Macronutrients intake of top level cyclists during continuous competition–change in the feeding pattern. *Int J Sports Med* 19:61–7.
Garcia-Roves, P.M., N. Terrados, S.F. Fernandez, and A.M. Patterson. 2000. Comparison of dietary intake and eating behavior of professional road cyclists during training and competition. *Int J Sport Nutr Exerc Metab* 10:82–98.
Hawley, J., and L. Burke. 1998. *Peak performance: Training and nutritional strategies for sport.* Sydney: Allen and Unwin.
Kerr, D., K. Khan, and K. Bennell. 2000. Bone, exercise, nutrition and menstrual disturbances. In *Clinical sports nutrition*, 2d ed., edited by L.M. Burke and V. Deakin. Sydney: McGraw Hill, pp. 241–72.
Martin, M.K. 2001. Voluntary food intake in female endurance athletes. Master's thesis, Deakin University, Melbourne, Australia.
Saris, W.H.M., M.A. van Erp-Baart, F. Brouns, K.R. Westerterp, and F. ten Hoor. 1989. Studies on food intake and energy expenditure during extreme sustained exercise: The Tour de France. *Int J Sports Med* 10:S26–31.
Tarnopolsky, M. 2000. Protein and amino acid needs for training and bulking up. In *Clinical sports nutrition*, 2d ed., edited by L.M. Burke and V. Deakin. Sydney: McGraw-Hill, pp. 90–123.

Van Erp-Baart, A.M.J., W.H.M. Saris, R.A. Binkhorst, J.A. Vos, and J.W.L. Elvers. 1989. Nationwide survey on nutritional habits in elite athletes. Part I: Energy, carbohydrate, protein, and fat intake. *Int J Sports Med* 10:S3–10.

Chapter 17

American Dietetic Association, Dietitians of Canada, and the American College of Sports Medicine. 2000. Nutrition and athletic performance. *J Am Diet Assoc* 100(12):1543–56.

Barnett, C., D.L. Costill, M.D. Vukovich, K.J. Cole, B.H. Goodpaster, S.W. Trappe, and W.J. Fink. 1994. Effect of L-carnitine supplementation on muscle and blood carnitine content and lactate accumulation during high-intensity sprint cycling. *Int J Sports Nutr* 4:280–88.

Benardot, D. 2000. *Nutrition for serious athletes: An advanced guide to foods, fluids, and supplements for training and performance*. Champaign, IL: Human Kinetics.

Clarkson, P.M., and H.S. Thompson. 2000. Antioxidants: What role do they play in physical activity and health? *Am J Clin Nutr* 72:S637–46.

Dekkers, J.C., L.J.P. van Doornen, and H.C.G. Kemper. 1996. The role of antioxidant vitamins and enzymes in the prevention of exercise-induced muscle damage. *Sports Med* 21(3):213–38.

Food and Nutrition Board, Institute of Medicine. 1997. *Dietary reference intakes for calcium, phosphorus, magnesium, vitamin D, and fluoride*. Washington, D.C.: National Academy Press.

Food and Nutrition Board, Institute of Medicine. 1998. *Dietary reference intakes for thiamin, riboflavin, niacin, vitamin B6, folate, vitamin B12, pantothenic acid, biotin, and choline*. Washington, D.C.: National Academy Press.

Food and Nutrition Board, Institute of Medicine. 2000. *Dietary reference intakes for vitamin C, vitamin E, selenium, and carotenoids*. Washington, D.C.: National Academy Press.

Food and Nutrition Board, Institute of Medicine. 2001. *Dietary reference intakes for vitamin A, vitamin K, arsenic, boron, chromium, copper, iodine, iron, manganese, molybdenum, nickel, silicon, vanadium, and zinc*. Washington, D.C.: National Academy Press.

Kraemer, W.J., and J.S. Volek. 1999. Creatine supplementation: Its role in human performance. *Clinics in Sports Medicine* 18(3):651–66.

Lamb, D.R., W.S. Lightfoot, and M. Mayhal. 1997. Prehydration with glycerol does not improve cycling performance vs 6% CHO-electrolyte drink. *Med Sci Sports Exerc* 29:S249.

Lyons, T.P., M.L. Riedesel, L.E. Meuli, and T.W. Chick. 1990. Effects of glycerol-induced hyperhydration prior to exercise in the heat on sweating and core temperature. *Med Sci Sports Exerc* 22(4):477–83.

Singh, A., F.M. Moses, and P.A. Deuster. 1992. Chronic multivitamin-mineral supplementation does not enhance physical performance. *Med Sci Sports Exerc* 24(6):726–32.

Telford, R.D., E.A. Catchpole, V. Deakin, A.G. Hahn, and A.W. Plank. 1992. The effect of 7 to 8 months of vitamin/mineral supplementation on athletic performance. *Int J Sports Nutr* 2(2): 135–53.

Tiidus, P.M., and M.E. Houston. 1995. Vitamin E status and response to exercise training. *Sports Med* 20:12–23.

Vandebuerie, F., B. Vanden Eynde, K. Vandenberghe, and P. Hespel. 1998. Effect of creatine loading on endurance capacity and sprint power in cyclists. *Int J Sports Med* 19:490–95.

Villani, R.G., J. Gannon, M. Self, and P.A. Rich. 2000. L-Carnitine supplementation combined with aerobic training does not promote weight loss in moderately obese women. *Int J Sports Nutr* 10:199–207.

Vukovich, M.D., D.L. Costill, and W.J. Fink. 1994. Carnitine supplementation: Effect on muscle carnitine and glycogen content during exercise. *J Appl Physiol* 26:1122–29.

Williams, M.H. 1995. Nutritional ergogenics in athletics. *J Sports Med* 13:S63–74.

Williams, M.H. 1998. *The ergogenics edge*. Champaign, IL: Human Kinetics.

Chapter 18

Bastiaans, J.J., A.B.J.P. van Diemen, T. Veneberg, and A.E. Jeukendrup. 2001. The effects of replacing a portion of endurance training by strength training in trained cyclists. *Eur J Appl Physiol* 86:79–84.

Behm, D.G., and D.G. Sale. 1993. Velocity specificity of resistance training. *Sports Med* 15:374–88.

Costill, D.L., D.D. Pascoe, W.J. Fink, R.A. Robergs, S.I. Barr, and D. Pearson. 1990. Impaired muscle glycogen resynthesis after eccentric exercise. *J Appl Physiol* 69:46–50.

Coyle, E.F., M.E. Feltner, S.A. Kautz, M.T. Hamilton, S.J. Montain, A.M. Baylor, L.D. Abraham, and G.W. Petrek. 1991. Physiological and biomechanical factors associated with elite endurance cycling performance. *Med Sci Sports Exerc* 23:93–107.

Halbertsma, J.P., I. Mulder, L.N. Goeken, and W.H. Eisma. 1999. Repeated passive stretching: Acute effect on the passive muscle moment and extensibility of short hamstrings. *Arch Phys Med Rehabil* 80(4):407–14.

Hawley, J.A. 1995. State of the art training guidelines for endurance performance. *South African J of Sports Med* 2 (November):7–12.

Hickson, R.C., B.A. Dvorak, E.M. Gorostiaga, T.T. Kurowski, and C. Foster. 1988. Potential for strength and endurance training to amplify endurance performance. *J Appl Physiol* 65:2285–90.

Horowitz, J.F., L.S. Sidossis, and E.F. Coyle. 1994. High efficiency of type I muscle fibers improves performance. *Int J Sports Med* 15:152–57.

Howard, J.D., and R.M. Enoka. 1991. Maximal bilateral contractions are modified by neurally mediated interlimb effects. *J Appl Physiol* 70:306–16.

Jacobs, I., P. Kaiser, and P. Tesch. 1981. Muscle strength and fatigue after selective glycogen depletion in human skeletal muscle fibers. *Eur J Appl Physiol* 46:47–53.

Kraemer, W.J., N.D. Duncan, and J.S. Volek. 1998. Resistance training and elite athletes: Adaptations and program considerations. *J Orthop Sports Phys Ther* 28:110–19.

Magnusson, S.P., P. Aagaard, E. Simonsen, and F. Bojsen-Moller. 1998. A biomechanical evaluation of cyclic and static stretch in human skeletal muscle. *Int J Sports Med* 19(5):310–16.

Magnusson, S.P., P. Aagaard, B. Larsson, and M. Kjaer. 2000. Passive energy absorption by human muscle tendon unit is unaffected by increase in intramuscular temperature. *J Appl Physiol* 88:1215–20.

Morrissey, M.C., E.A. Harman, and M.J. Johnson. 1995. Resistance training modes: Specificity and effectiveness. *Med Sci Sports Exerc* 27 (May):648–60.

Rutherford, O.M., C.A. Greig, A.J. Sargeant, and D.A. Jones. 1986. Strength training and power output: Transference effects in the human quadriceps muscle. *Journal of Sports Sciences* 4:101–07.

Sale, D., and D. MacDougall. 1981. Specificity in strength training: A review for the coach and athlete. *Canadian Journal of Applied Sport Sciences* 6:87–92.

Shrier, I. 1999. Stretching before exercise does not reduce the risk of local muscle injury: A critical review of the clinical and basic science literature. *Clin J Sport Med* 9(4):221–27.

Widrick, J.J., S.W. Trappe, D.L. Costill, and R.H. Fitts. 1996. Force-velocity and force-power properties of single muscle fibers from elite master runners and sedentary men. *Am J Physiol* 271(2, pt. 1):C676–83.

Wiemann, K., and K. Hahn. 1997. Influences of strength, stretching and circulatory exercises on flexibility parameters of the human hamstrings. *Int J Sports Med* 18:340–46.

Chapter 19

Brukner, P., and K. Khan. 1993. *Clinical sports medicine*. New York: McGraw-Hill.

Cook, A., and A. Sheikh. 2000. Trends in serious head injuries among cyclists in England: Analysis of routinely collected data. *British Medical Journal* 321:1055.

Desai, K.M., and J.C. Gingell. 1989. Hazards of long distance cycling. *British Medical Journal* 298:1072–73.

Frauscher, F., A. Klauser, A. Hobisch, L. Pallwein, and A. Stenzi. 2000. Subclinical microtraumatisation of the scrotal contents in extreme mountain biking. *Lancet* 356:1414.

Holmes, J.C., A.L. Pruitt, N.J. Whalen. 1994. Lower extremity overuse in bicycling. *Clin Sports Med* 13(1):187–203.

Jacobsen, P. 2001. Using bicycle helmets alone will not prevent serious bicycle injuries. *British Medical Journal* 322:1064.

Jeys, L., G. Cribb, A. Toms, and S. Hay. 2001. Mountain bike injuries in rural England. *Brit J Sports Med*. 35:197–99.

Key, S. 2000. *The back sufferers' bible*. London: Vermilion.

Khan, K.M., J.L. Cook, N. Maffulli, and P. Kannus. 2000a. Where is the pain coming from in tendinopathy? It may be biochemical, not only structural in origin. *Brit J Sports Med* 34(2):81–83.

Khan, K.M., J.L. Cook, J.E. Taunton, and F. Bonar. 2000b. Overuse tendinosis, not tendinitis: A new paradigm for a difficult clinical problem. *Physician Sports Med* 28(5):38–48.

Kronisch, R.L., and A.L. Rubin. 1994. Traumatic injuries in off-road bicycling. *Clin J Sport Med* 4(4):240–44.

Kulund, D.N., and C.E. Brubaker. 1978. Injuries in the bikecentennial tour. *Phys Sports Med* 6:74–78.

Mellion, M.B. 1994. Neck and back pain in bicycling. *Clin Sports Med* 13(1):137–64.

Norris, C. 2001. *Back stability*. Champaign, IL: Human Kinetics.

Richmond, D.R. 1994. Handlebar problems in bicycling. *Clin Sports Med* 13(1):165–73.

Robinson, L., and G. Thomson. 1999. *Pilates: The way forward*. London: Pan Books.

Simons, D.G., J.G. Travell, L.S. Simons. 1999. *Myofascial pain and dysfunction the trigger point manual: Volume 1. The upper half of the body*. Baltimore: Williams & Wilkins.

Summers, N., and S. Davies. 2000. *The art of backstretching*. London: Enafel Press.

Taylor, A.J., W.G. Tennant, M.E. Batt, and W.A. Wallace. 1997. Traumatic occlusion of the external iliac artery in a racing cyclist: A cause of ill defined leg pain. *Brit J Sports Med* 31(2):155–56.

Travell, J.G., and D.G. Simons. 1992. *Myofascial pain and dysfunction the trigger point manual: the lower extremities*. Baltimore: Williams & Wilkins.

Weiss, B.D. 1985. Nontraumatic injuries in amateur long distance bicyclists. *Am J Sports Med* 13:187–92.

Chapter 20

Berg, A., H. Northoff, and D. Konig. 1998. Influence of Echinacin (E31) treatment on the exercise-induced immune response in athletes. *J Clin Res* 1:367–80.

Bishop, N.C., A.K. Blannin, and M. Gleeson. 2000. Effect of carbohydrate and fluid intake during prolonged exercise on saliva flow and IgA secretion. *Med Sci Sports Exerc* 32:2046–51.

Blannin, A.K., L.J. Chatwin, R. Cave, and M. Gleeson. 1996. Effects of submaximal cycling and long term endurance training on neutrophil phagocytic activity in middle aged men. *Br J Sports Med* 30:125–29.

Brenner, I.K.M., Y.D. Severs, P.N. Shek, and R.J. Shephard. 1996. Impact of heat exposure and moderate, intermittent exercise on cytolytic cells. *Eur J Appl Physiol* 74:162–71.

Gleeson, M. 2000. Minerals and exercise immunology. In *Nutrition and exercise immunology*, edited by D.C. Nieman and B.K. Pedersen. Boca Raton, FL: CRC Press, pp. 137–54.

Gleeson, M., and N.C. Bishop. 1999. Immunology. In *Basic and applied sciences for sports medicine*, edited by R.J. Maughan. Oxford: Butterworth Heinemann, pp. 199–236.

Gleeson, M., and N.C. Bishop. 2000. Modification of immune responses to exercise by carbohydrate, glutamine and antioxidant supplements. *Immunol Cell Biol* 78(5):554–61.

Graham, N.M.H., R.M. Douglas, and P. Ryan. 1986. Stress and acute respiratory infection. *Am J Epidemiol* 124:389–401.

Krzykowski, K., W. Wolsk Petersen, K. Ostrowski, H. Link, J. Boza, J. Halkjaer-Kristensen, and B.K. Pedersen. 2000. Effects of glutamine and protein supplementation on exercise-induced decrease in lymphocyte function and salivary IgA. *Int J Sports Med* 21:S73.

Nieman, D.C., A.R. Miller, D.A. Henson, B.J. Warren, S.L. Gusewitch, R.L. Johnson, J.M. Davis, J.E. Butterworth, J.L. Herring, and S.L. Nehlsen-Cannarella. 1994. Effect of high- versus moderate-intensity exercise on lymphocyte subpopulations and proliferative response. *Int J Sports Med* 15:199–206.

Peters, E.M., J.M. Goetzsche, B. Grobbelaar, and T.D. Noakes. 1993. Vitamin C supplementation reduces the incidence of post-race symptoms of upper respiratory tract in ultramarathon runners. *Am J Clin Nutr* 57:170–74.

Robson, P.J., A.K. Blannin, N.P. Walsh, L.M. Castell, and M. Gleeson. 1999. Effects of exercise intensity, duration and recovery on in vitro neutrophil function in male athletes. *Int J Sports Med* 20:128–35.

Rohde, T., S. Asp, D. Maclean, and B.K. Pedersen. 1998. Competitive sustained exercise in humans, and lymphokine activated killer cell activity—an intervention study. *Eur J Appl Physiol* 78:448–53.

Walsh, N.P., A.K. Blannin, N.C. Bishop, P.J. Robson, and M. Gleeson. 2000. Oral glutamine supplementation does not attenuate the fall in human neutrophil lipopolysaccharide-stimulated degranulation following prolonged exercise. *Int J Sport Nutr* 10:39–50.

Chapter 21

Birkeland, K.I., J. Stray-Gundersen, P. Hemmersbach et al. 2000. Effect of rhEPO administration on serum levels of sTfR and cycling performance. *Med Sci Sports Exerc* 32(7):1238–43.

Casoni, I., G. Ricci, E. Ballarin et al. 1993. Hematological indices of erythropoietin administration in athletes. *Int J Sports Med* 14(6):307–11.

Cazzola, M. 2000. A global strategy for prevention and detection of blood doping with erythropoietin and related drugs. *Haematologica* 85:561–63.

Chang, T.M. 2000. Red blood cell substitutes. *Baillieres Best Pract Res Clin Haematol* 13(4):651–67.

Ekblom, B.T. 2000. Blood boosting and sport. *Baillieres Best Pract Res Clin Endocrinol Metab* 14(1):89–98.

Flaharty, K.K., J. Caro, A. Erslev et al. 1990. Pharmacokinetics and erythropoietic response to human recombinant erythropoietin in healthy men. *Clin Pharmacol Ther* 47(5):557–64.

Gareau, R., M.G. Gangnon, and C. Thellen. 1994. Transferrin soluble receptor: A possible probe for detection of erythropoietin abuse by athletes. *Horm Metab Res* 26:311–12.

Lasne, F., and J. Ceaurriz. 2000. Recombinant erythropoietin in urine. *Nature* 405(8):635.

Parisotto, R., C.J. Gore, K.R. Emslie et al. 2000. A novel method utilising markers of altered erythropoiesis for the detection of recombinant human erythropoietin abuse in athletes. *Haematologica* 85(6):564–72.

Piron, M., M. Loo, A. Gothot et al. 2001. Cessation of intensive treatment with recombinant human erythropoietin is followed by secondary anemia. *Blood* 97(2):442–48.

Ramotar, J. 1990. Cyclist's death linked to erythropoietin. *The Physician and Sportsmedicine* 18:48–49.

Robinson, N., C. Schweizer, C. Cardis et al. 2000. Haematological and biochemical parameters from all professional cyclists during the Tour de Suisse 1999. *Schweizerishce Zeitschrift fur Sportmedizin und Sporttraumatologie* 48(3):104–10.

Saris, W.H., J.M. Senden, and F. Brouns. 1998. What is a normal red-blood cell mass for professional cyclists? *Lancet* 352(9142):1758.

Schumacher, Y.O., D. Grathwohl, J.M. Barturen et al. 2000. Haemoglobin, haematocrit and red blood cell indices in elite cyclists: Are the control values for blood testing valid? *Int J Sports Med* 21(5):380–85.

Wide, L., C. Bengtsson, B. Berglund et al. 1995. Detection in blood and urine of recombinant erythropoietin administered to healthy men. *Med Sci Sports Exerc* 27(11):1569–76.

Wieting, S.G. 2000. Twilight of the hero in the Tour de France. *International Review for the Sociology of Sport* 35(3):348–63.

Winearls, C.G. 1998. Recombinant human erythropoietin: 10 years of clinical experience. *Nephrol Dial Transplant* 13, Suppl. 2 (5):3–8.

Chapter 22

Below, P.R., R. Mora-Rodríguez, J. Gonzáles Alonso, and E.F. Coyle. 1995. Fluid and carbohydrate ingestion independently improve performance during 1 h of intense exercise. *Med Sci Sports Exerc* 27:200–10.

El-Sayed, M.S., J. Balmer, and A.J. Rattu. 1997. Carbohydrate ingestion improves endurance performance during a 1 h simulated time trial. *J Sports Sci* 15:223–30.

Jeukendrup, A.E., and J. Martin. 2001. Improving cycling performance: How should we spend our time and money? *Sports Med* 31:559–69.

Jeukendrup, A.E., N. Craig, and J.A.H. Hawley. 2000. Bioenergetics of world class cycling. *J Sci Med Sport* 3(4):414–433.

Jeukendrup, A.E., F. Brouns, A.J.M. Wagenmakers, and W.H.M. Saris. 1997. Carbohydrate feedings improve 1 h time trial cycling performance. *Int J Sports Med* 18:125–29.

Kovacs, E.M.R., J.H.C.H. Stegen, and F. Brouns. 1998. Effect of caffeinated drinks on substrate metabolism, caffeine excretion, and performance. *J Appl Physiol* 85:709–15.

Martin, J.C., D.L. Milliken, J.E. Cobb, K.L. McFadden, and A.R. Coggan. 1998. Validation of a mathematical model for road cycling power. *J Appl Biomech* 14:276–91.

Pasman, W.J., M.A. van Baak, A.E. Jeukendrup, and A. deHaan. 1995. The effect of varied dosages of caffeine on endurance performance time. *Int J Sports Med* 16:225–30.

Spriet, L.L., D.A. McLean, D.J. Dyck, E. Hultman, G. Cederblad, and T.E. Graham. 1992. Caffeine ingestion and muscle metabolism during prolonged exercise in humans. *Am J Physiol* 262:E891–98.

index

Note: The italicized *f* and *t* following page numbers refer to figures and tables, respectively.

about the editor

Asker E. Jeukendrup is a recognized authority on biochemistry and exercise physiology for cyclists. He has served as scientific adviser to the Rabobank professional cycling team—one of the top cycling teams in the world—and as nutrition consultant to U.K. Athletics and numerous Olympic athletes. More than 50 of his articles have been published in peer-reviewed journals.

Jeukendrup received his PhD in health sciences in 1997 in Maastricht, Netherlands, and is currently a lecturer in the school of sport and exercise sciences at the University of Birmingham in the United Kingdom. He was already an avid cyclist when he first entered the fields of exercise physiology and sport nutrition. In his work, he endeavors not only to perform cutting-edge research but also to translate his findings into terms that will be directly useful for athletes.

In his free time, Jeukendrup enjoys cycling, traveling, and competing in triathlons. He and his wife, Antoinette, live in Birmingham, England.

about the contributors

Juul Achten received her MS degree in biological health sciences from Maastricht University in the Netherlands. A doctoral student at the University of Birmingham, she received the fifth-place award in the Mars Young Investigators Award competition from the European College of Sport Science and the International Student Award from the American College of Sports Medicine in 2001. Achten's main areas of interest are fat metabolism and heart rate monitoring. She has coauthored papers and abstracts in several journals, including the *European Journal of Sports Science* and *Medicine and Science in Sports and Exercise*. She is a recreational runner.

Jabik Jan Bastiaans holds an MS in exercise physiology. He is mainly involved in scientific research in the field of sports, in particular road cycling. Recently he and his coauthors published a report about the effect of replacing a portion of endurance training with strength training in trained cyclists. Bastiaans is also involved in training endurance athletes, mainly road cyclists. As an ultimate tool for testing training methods, he is competing in road races at the regional level in the Netherlands.

Matthew Bridge received his undergraduate degree in sport and exercise sciences from the University of Birmingham and has recently completed his PhD in the area of fatigue during exercise in the heat. He is currently a research fellow in the Human Performance Lab of the school of sport and exercise sciences at the University of Birmingham. His areas of interest include the causes of fatigue during exercise in the heat, changes in neuroendocrine function with overtraining, and central fatigue during prolonged exercise. Bridge played semi-professional rugby union in the English national leagues and is now an avid cyclist and runner regularly competing in races.

Grahame Brown is a medical doctor specializing in musculoskeletal, sport and exercise medicine. Dr. Brown practices an integrated approach to medicine—the practice of orthodox medicine alongside selected complementary medicine to provide patients with a comprehensive management for their problems. He has been involved with cycling as a participant for 36 years—he continues to ride regularly for recreation, utility, and sport.

Louise Burke has over 20 years of experience as a sports dietitian, including the last 12 years as head of the department of sports nutrition at the Australian Institute of Sport. Dr. Burke's activities include clinical counseling, nutrition education, and preparation of education resources. She has written a number of books on sports nutrition, as well as numerous peer-reviewed publications, book chapters, and magazine articles. Her research interests include carbohydrate metabolism and performance, fat adaptation strategies, supplements and nutritional ergogenic aids in sport, and postexercise recovery. She is a visiting professor at Deakin University in Melbourne, Australia, where she is involved in the development and delivery of undergraduate and postgraduate units in sports nutrition. A board member of Sports Dietitians Australia, she has competed internationally in triathlon including four Hawaiian Ironman World Championship races.

John Cobb is the owner of Bicycle Sports, a cycling shop in Shreveport, Louisiana. A cyclist since 1972 and a triathlete since the beginnings of the sport, Cobb began using a wind tunnel to study cars and motorcycles in 1984. He began to use the wind tunnels to research the aerodynamics and positioning of cyclists a few years later. Among other projects, he has worked on the development of aero bars for the U.S. Postal Service professional cycling team. Cobb holds a BFA in commercial art. He enjoys working on cars and motorcycles as a hobby.

Jos de Koning is a biomechanist at the Free University of Amsterdam in the Netherlands. He was involved in the development of the clap skate which brought success to the Dutch speedskaters in many major championships. His research interests also include cycling.

Mark Febbraio is currently a member of the faculty in the department of physiology at the University of Melbourne in Australia. He received his PhD from Victoria University of Technology (Australia) in 1994, completing his thesis on the effect of environmental temperature on muscle metabolism during exercise. At the University of Melbourne he also serves as the director of the Exercise Physiology and Metabolism Laboratory. In 2000 Febbraio was honored with the New Investigator Award from International Biochemistry of Exercise. He was awarded the A.K. McIntyre Prize from the Australian Physiological and Pharmacological Society in 1999. Febbraio is a member of the American College of Sports Medicine, the Australian Physiological and Pharmacological Society, the International Society for Exercise Immunology, and the Gatorade Sports Science International Speakers Bureau. He has published his research in numerous scientific journals, including the *Journal of Applied Physiology*, *Medicine and Science in Sport and Exercise*, and the *International Journal of Sports Medicine*. Febbraio has competed in triathlon for 15 years, including at the elite level in the late 1980s and early 1990s. He has completed 5 ironman races, including the Hawaii Ironman in 9 hours and 30 minutes.

Michael Gleeson, BS, PhD, is professor of exercise biochemistry in the school of sport and exercise sciences at the University of Birmingham. Over the past 20 years he has published over 150 papers on exercise physiology, biochemistry, immunology, and sports nutrition. He is coauthor (with Ron Maughan and Paul Greenhaff) of a textbook for undergraduates entitled *Biochemistry of Exercise and Training*. He is a member of the Physiological Society, Nutrition Society, British Association of Sport and Exercise Sciences, American College of Sports Medicine, and the International Society for Exercise and Immunology. He is also an elected fellow of the European College of Sport Science. Until recently he was the physiology section editor for the *Journal of Sports Sciences*. He is now an associate editor of *Exercise Immunology Review*. His current research concerns the effects of exercise and overtraining on immune function. He is also interested in the modifying influence of diet on immune responses to exercise, particularly prolonged cycling.

Christopher J Gore, PhD, has worked for the Australian Institute of Sport for over 10 years. He has more than 50 publications in peer-reviewed journals and is the editor of another Human Kinetics book, *Physiological Tests for Elite Athletes*. Gore became a fellow of the American College of Sports Medicine in 2000. In the same year he was awarded a Sport Australia Medal for his contribution to the team that developed a blood-based test for EPO.

Allan G. Hahn is the head of physiology at the Australian Institute of Sport. He played a very important role in developing the EPO test used at the 2000 Sydney Olympic Games.

Currently pursuing her PhD at Queensland University of Technology, **Shona Halson** will complete her studies in June of 2002 after doing much of her research with Dr. Jeukendrup at the University of Birmingham. Halson completed her bachelor of applied science degree in the school of movement sciences at Queensland University of Technology in Australia and was awarded the First Class Honours Degree. She served as an Athlete Services Officer for the Australian Paralympic Committee from 1999-2000. Her main research focus is overtraining, particularly examining central nervous system fatigue and substate utilization following intense training. A member of the American College of Sports Medicine and the Australian Association for Exercise and Sport Science, Halson has been published in the *American Journal of Medicine and Sports*. She is a recreational runner.

Mark Hargreaves is the chair of the school of sports sciences and a professor of exercise physiology at Deakin University in Burwood, Australia. Before coming to Deakin, Hargreaves taught and researched exercise physiology and metabolism at Victoria University of Technology and the University of Melbourne. He received his BS and PhD degrees from the University of Melbourne, and his MA from Ball State University. He is a fellow in the American College of Sports Medicine and a member of the Australian Physiological and Pharmacological Society, the Australian Association of Exercise and Sports Science, Sports Medicine Australia, and the

American Physiological Society. Hargreaves' recent research includes examination of the physiological and metabolic responses to acute and chronic exercise, with an emphasis on the regulation of carbohydrate metabolism. His recent publications include papers in the *American Journal of Physiology* and the *Journal of Applied Physiology*.

John A. Hawley is currently director of the Exercise Metabolism Group and professor of exercise metabolism in the school of medical sciences at RMIT University, Melbourne, Australia. He obtained his PhD from the University of Cape Town where he was awarded a Medical Research Council Scholarship for outstanding foreign researcher. He received his master's degree from Ball State University and his BS degree from Loughborough University in England. He was recently awarded RMIT University Research Supervisor of the Year (2001). He has published many peer-reviewed scientific papers and articles for technical journals and has authored numerous book chapters for sports medicine/exercise biochemistry texts. A member of the American Physiological Society, the Australian Sports Medicine Association and the New Zealand Association for Sports Medicine, he became the first New Zealand researcher to be elected as a fellow of the American College of Sports Medicine in 1994.

Currently a post-doctoral research fellow, **Roy Jentjens** received his PhD from the University of Birmingham in 2002. He received his MS degree in movement sciences from Maastricht University in the Netherlands. Jentjens received the third-place award in the Mars Young Investigators Award competition from the European College of Sport Science in 2001. He has published several papers and abstracts in scholarly journals, including the *Journal of Applied Physiology*, *Medicine and Science in Sport and Exercise*, and *Sports Medicine*. Jentjens served as the nutritional advisor for the Dutch amateur cycling team in 1998 and currently advises several athletes competing at the national level on sports nutrition and training. An avid cyclist, he has participated in several national events as a member of the University of Birmingham cycling/triathlon team. Before getting involved in cycling, he competed in judo where he won several tournaments at the national level.

David Jones graduated from University of Birmingham with a degree in medical biochemistry before moving to London where he gained his PhD at the Institute of Psychiatry. His first professional contact with muscle and exercise came at the Postgraduate Medical Centre at Hammersmith, working on the biochemistry and physiology of fatigue in animal muscle preparations, normal human subjects, and patients with muscle disorders. This interest continued with a move to University College London where he was a senior lecturer in the department of medicine and the department of physiology. He returned to Birmingham in 1993 as a professor of sport and exercise sciences. The major research interests of his group are muscle physiology mechanisms of fatigue, training for strength and power, muscle damage, growth and development, and central fatigue.

Jeffrey C. Little is currently enrolled in an American Dietetic Association approved dietetic internship affiliated with St. Luke's Hospital in New Bedford, Massachusetts. He has a BS in exercise science and an MS in nutrition science from the University of Massachusetts, Amherst. He has presented his research at both regional and national conferences associated with the American College of Sports Medicine. His academic area of interest is sports nutrition with an emphasis on nutritional supplements. He is a member of the American College of Sports Medicine, the American Dietetic Association, the American Physiological Society, Sigma Xi: The Scientific Research Society, and the National Strength and Conditioning Association (NSCA). He is also a certified personal trainer through the NSCA. He was a four-year member and captain of the swimming team at the University of Massachusetts. During this time he was a recipient of the Atlantic 10 Conference Academic Honor Roll Award and led his team to its first-ever conference championship. He continues to remain physically active through the United States Masters Swimming organization, and also enjoys ocean swimming, surfing, running, weight training, tennis, and golf.

David T. Martin is currently one of five senior sport physiologists working within the department of physiology and applied nutrition at the Australian Institute of Sport in Canberra. For the last seven years, Dr. Martin has primarily been responsible for providing sport science support to AIS cross country skiers, mountain cyclists, and road cyclists. His research findings from projects in thermoregulation, quantification of training loads, competition analysis, sport specificity of laboratory testing, tapering, peaking, and altitude training have been presented at International Scientific Meetings as well as local coaching seminars. He received his BS degree in zoology from the College of Idaho, his MS degree in exercise physiology from Northern Michigan University, and his PhD in physiology from the University of Wyoming. Prior to beginning his doctoral studies, Martin worked as a research assistant at the United States Olympic Training Center in Colorado Springs.

Jim Martin is currently an assistant professor in the department of exercise and sport science at the University of Utah. His primary research interest is the mechanics of cyclic muscle contraction. Martin received his MA and PhD in kinesiology from the University of Texas at Austin. He has been published in several scholarly journals, including *Medicine and Science in Sports and Exercise*, the *Journal of Applied Biomechanics*, the *Journal of Applied Physiology*, and the *International Journal of Sports Medicine*. He also authored a monthly column in *Bicycling Magazine* from 1996 through 1998. He is a member of the American College of Sports Medicine, the American Physiological Society, and the American Society of Biomechanics. He served as the director of sports science for the Team EDS cycling team from 1989 to 1999. After receiving his BS in mechanical engineering from the University of Texas, he worked as an engineer for the Texas Department of Health and Texas Water Commission from 1984-1992.

Ronald Maughan is currently professor of human physiology at the University Medical School, Aberdeen, Scotland. He obtained his BS (physiology) and PhD from the University of Aberdeen, and held a lecturing position in Liverpool before returning to Aberdeen where he is now based in the department of biomedical sciences. His research interests are in the physiology, biochemistry, and nutrition of exercise performance, with an interest in both the basic science of exercise and the applied aspects that relate to health and sport performance.

Luke Moseley currently works at the school of sport and exercise sciences at the University of Birmingham in England. He received his BS degree with honors from the University of Birmingham. Moseley was also awarded the Munrow Prize from the university. He has been published in *Medicine and Science in Sport and Exercise*, and presented an abstract at the annual meeting of the American College of Sports Medicine in 2001. Moseley is also a reviewer for the *European Journal of Sports Science*. While in school, he served as the captain of the university triathlon team and the secretary of the surf club. He was also a member of the university cycling team.

Iñigo Mujika received his PhD in physical education and sports sciences from the University of the Basque Country in Spain in 1999, receiving the Extraordinary Doctorate Award with this degree. Mujika also received a PhD in biology of muscular exercise from the University Jean Monnet-Saint-Etienne in France in 1995. He is currently employed in the department of research and development for the Athletic Club of Bilbao (a professional soccer team). He has had 35 publications in journals, including *Medicine and Science in Sport and Exercise, International Journal of Sports Medicine, Journal of Applied Physiology*, and the *European Journal of Applied Physiology*. Mujika has also lectured at numerous international conferences. He has conducted research as a post-doctoral fellow at the Australian Institute of Sport, Royal Melbourne Institute of Technology University, Sports Science Institute of South Africa, and the University Jean Monnet-Saint-Etienne.

Sabino Padilla is currently the head doctor for Medical Services for the Athletic Club of Bilbao (professional soccer) and associate professor in the department of physiology at the University of the Basque Country. Prior to working with the Athletic Club of Bilbao, he was the head doctor for the Banesto cycling team from 1990-1996 and also worked with the professional basketball team Saski Baskonia from 1993-1994. Padilla received his MD from the University of País Vasco in 1990. He also completed graduate work in the biology of muscular exercise and sports medicine and biology at the University Jean Monnet-Saint-Etienne in France. He has had scientific papers published in numerous journals, including *Medicine and Science* *in Sports and Exercise, European Journal of Applied Physiology, Sports Medicine*, and the *International Journal of Sports Medicine*.

Garry S. Palmer is a staff member in the school of sports, performing arts and leisure at the University of Wolverhampton in South Africa, where he teaches exercise physiology and nutrition. He also serves as an exercise physiology consultant to elite athletes and teams. Palmer received his PhD in physiology from the University of Cape Town in 1999. He is a member of the American College of Sports Medicine, the British Association of Sports and Exercise Sciences, and the South African Physiological Society. Palmer's main research interests include sports performance and exercise performance in the heat, and the relationships between nutrition, exercise, and health. He has been published in many scholarly journals, including the *International Journal of Sports Medicine*, the *European Journal of Applied Physiology*, and *Medicine and Science in Sports and Exercise*.

Adrie van Diemen has worked with the junior and amateur teams of Team Rabobank since 1996 and has also trained Greg LeMond (in 1993 and 1994), 3K pursuit World Champion Marion Clignet, and Amateur World Champion Danny Nelissen. He is currently coaching Alessandro Cappelotto, Tania Belverderesi, and Vera Koedooder in addition to his Team Rabobank duties. The author of Polar Finland's *Training with Power*, van Diemen received his BA in physical education from the Dutch University of Professional Education in the Hague and his MS in human movement sciences at Amsterdam University.

Knoek van Soest, PhD, is a staff member in the faculty of human movement sciences, Free University, Amsterdam, and a member of the Institute of Fundamental and Clinical Human Movement Sciences. His research interests include biomechanics, control theory, modeling and simulation, and optimization. He has authored several papers in leading scientific journals on the biomechanics and control of vertical jumping, cycling, and rowing. He is currently a board member of the I.S.B. Technical Group on Computer Simulation in Biomechanics.

Stella L. Volpe, PhD, RD, LD/N, is an associate professor in the department of nutrition, director of the Center for Nutrition in Sport and Human Performance, and an adjunct faculty member in the department of exercise science at the University of Massachusetts, Amherst. Dr. Volpe completed a two-year National Institutes of Health post-doctoral fellowship at the University of California at Berkeley, department of nutritional sciences. She has a BS in exercise science from the University of Pittsburgh, and an MS in exercise physiology/cardiac rehabilitation and a PhD in human nutrition from Virginia Tech. In 1998-1999, Dr. Volpe was the recipient of the University Distinguished Teaching Award, the highest honor given for teaching on the UMASS campus. Dr. Volpe also was the recipient of the Outstanding College Teaching Award that same year. In 1997-1998, she was selected as a Lilly Teaching Fellow. Dr. Volpe is certified by the American College of Sports Medicine as a Preventive and Rehabilitative Exercise Specialist and is a Registered Dietitian. She primarily conducts human clinical research in the areas of mineral metabolism in exercise, obesity and weight loss, and body composition. She is a fellow of the American College of Sports Medicine and a member of the American Society for Nutritional Sciences, the American Society of Clinical Nutrition, the American Dietetic Association and its dietetic practice group, SCAN (Sports, Cardiovascular, and Wellness Nutritionists), the New York Academy of Sciences, the International Society of Exercise and Immunology, Sigma Xi: The Scientific Research Society, the Women's Sports Foundation, and United States Field Hockey Association. Dr. Volpe has completed numerous road races, triathlons, and a marathon. She plays on a masters women's field hockey team and rows with a masters women's crew team.